ACCESS AND CARTEL CASES

This book examines the legislative patchwork surrounding access to the European Commission's cartel case files.

Recent legislative changes have increased the value of the files and have also highlighted the inherent tension between a number of competing interests affecting their accessibility. The Commission is undoubtedly caught between a rock and a hard place, charged with the task of ensuring due process, transparency and effectiveness, while at the same time promoting both public and private enforcement of the EU competition rules. The author considers how best to ensure a proper balance between the legitimate but often diverging interests of parties, third parties and national competition authorities in these cases.

The book provides a unique and comprehensive presentation of the EU legislation and case law surrounding access to the Commission's cartel case files. The author examines the question of accessibility from three different perspectives: that of the parties under investigation, cartel victims and national competition authorities. The author also considers the EU leniency system and whether any legislative changes could make the attractiveness of the system less dependent on the possibilities for cartel victims to access the evidence contained in the Commission's case files.

Volume 28 in the series Hart Studies in Competition Law

Hart Studies in Competition Law

Anti-Cartel Enforcement in a Contemporary Age: Leniency Religion
Edited by Caron Beaton-Wells and Christopher Tran

Public Procurement and the EU Competition Rules
Albert Sánchez Graells

The Concept of Abuse in EU Competition Law: Law and Economic Approaches
Pınar Akman

The Competitive Effects of Minority Shareholdings: Legal and Economic Issues
Panagiotis Fotis and Nikolaos Zevgolis

The More Economic Approach to EU Antitrust Law
Anne C Witt

Private Power, Online Information Flows and EU Law
Angela Daly

The Role of Competitors in the Enforcement of State Aid Law
Fernando Pastor-Merchante

The Legality of Bailouts and Buy Nationals: International Trade Law in a Crisis
Kamala Dawar

A Critical Account of Article 106(2) TFEU: Government Failure in Public Service Provision
Jarleth Burke

Dawn Raids Under Challenge
Helene Andersson

A Framework for European Competition Law: Co-ordinated Diversity
Christopher Townley

Evidence Standards in EU Competition Enforcement: The EU Approach
Andriani Kalintiri

The Metaphysics of Market Power: The Zero-sum Competition and Market Manipulation Model
George Raitt

Competition Law's Innovation Factor: The Relevant Market in Dynamic Contexts in the EU and US
Viktoria H.S.E. Robertson

Competition, Effects and Predictability: Rule of Law and the Economic Approach to Competition
Bruce Wardhaugh

Fighting Cross-Border Cartels: The Perspective of the Young and Small Competition Authorities
Pierre Horna

Conceptualising Procedural Fairness in EU Competition Law
Haukur Logi Karlsson

Experimentalist Competition Law and the Regulation of Markets
Yane Svetiev

Access and Cartel Cases: Ensuring Effective Competition Law Enforcement
Helene Andersson

Access and Cartel Cases

Ensuring Effective Competition Law Enforcement

Helene Andersson

•HART•
OXFORD • LONDON • NEW YORK • NEW DELHI • SYDNEY

HART PUBLISHING
Bloomsbury Publishing Plc
Kemp House, Chawley Park, Cumnor Hill, Oxford, OX2 9PH, UK
1385 Broadway, New York, NY 10018, USA

HART PUBLISHING, the Hart/Stag logo, BLOOMSBURY and the Diana logo are trademarks of Bloomsbury Publishing Plc

First published in Great Britain 2020

A catalogue record for this book is available from the British Library.

Library of Congress Cataloging-in-Publication data

Names: Andersson, Helene, 1971- author.

Title: Access and cartel cases : ensuring effective competition law enforcement / Helene Andersson.

Description: Oxford, UK ; New York, NY : Hart Publishing, an imprint of Bloomsbury Publishing, 2020. | Series: Hart studies in competition law ; volume 28 | Includes bibliographical references and index.

Identifiers: LCCN 2020038786 (print) | LCCN 2020038787 (ebook) | ISBN 9781509942480 (hardback) | ISBN 9781509942527 (paperback) | ISBN 9781509942497 (Epub) | ISBN 9781509942503 (pdf)

Subjects: LCSH: Antitrust law—European Union countries. | Cartels—Law and legislation—European Union countries. | Civil rights—European Union countries. | Competition, Unfair—European Union countries.

Classification: LCC KJE6471 .A93 2020 (print) | LCC KJE6471 (ebook) | DDC 343.2407/21—dc23

LC record available at https://lccn.loc.gov/2020038786

LC ebook record available at https://lccn.loc.gov/2020038787

ISBN: HB: 978-1-50994-248-0
ePDF: 978-1-50994-250-3
ePub: 978-1-50994-249-7

Typeset by Compuscript Ltd, Shannon

CONTENTS

PART II
NATIONAL COMPETITION AUTHORITIES

PART III
PARTIES AND COMPLAINANTS

PART V
SUMMING UP

TABLE OF CASES

CJEU (in alphabetical order)

CJEU (in chronological order)

Advocate General Opinions (in alphabetical order)

Advocate General Opinions (in chronological order)

The General Court (in alphabetical order)

The General Court (in chronological order)

European Court of Human Rights

National Court Rulings

Commission Decisions

Reports of the European Commission on Human Rights

TABLE OF LEGISLATION

Regulations

Directives

Proposals

Preparatory Works

ABBREVIATIONS

Access Notice	Commission Notice on the rules for access to the Commission file in cases pursuant to Articles 81 and 82 of the EC Treaty, Articles 53, 54 and 57 of the EEA Agreement and Council Regulation (EC) No 139/2004
AG	Advocate General
Antitrust Regulations	Council Regulation (EC) No 1/2003 of 16 December 2002 on the implementation of the rules on competition laid down in Articles 81 and 82 of the Treaty and Commission Regulation (EC) No 773/2004 of 7 April 2004 relating to the conduct of proceedings by the Commission pursuant to Articles 81 and 82 of the EC Treaty
Art(s)	Article(s)
Charter	European Charter of Fundamental Rights
Conduct of Proceedings	Commission Notice on Best Practices for the Conduct of Proceedings Concerning Articles 101 and 102 TFEU
Damages Directive	Directive 2014/104/EU of the European Parliament and of the Council of 26 November 2014 on certain rules governing actions for damages under national law for infringements of the competition law provisions of the Member States and of the European Union
DG COMP	Directorate-General for Competition
ECA	European Court of Auditors
ECHR	European Convention on Human Rights
ECJ	Court of Justice of the European Union
ECN	European Competition Network
ECtHR	European Court of Human Rights

EEA	European Economic Area
EU	European Union
Hearing Officer's Mandate	Decision 2011/695 of the President of the European Commission on the function and the terms of the Hearing Officer [also 'the Mandate'].
ICN	International Competition Network
NCA	national competition authority
OECD	Organisation for Economic Cooperation and Development
para(s)	paragraph(s)
Procedural Regulation	Commission Regulation (EC) No 773/2004 of 7 April 2004 relating to the conduct of proceedings by the Commission pursuant to Articles 81 and 82 of the EC Treaty
TEC	Treaty establishing the European Community
TEU	Treaty on the European Union
TFEU	Treaty on the Functioning of the European Union
Transparency Regulation	Regulation (EC) No 1049/2001 of the European Parliament and of the Council of 30 May 2001 regarding public access to European Parliament, Council and Commission documents

Introduction

I. Aim and Scope of this Book

If the European Commission's cartel case files were to be auctioned, the bids would no doubt keep reaching record levels. As will be further explored in this work, recent legislative changes have not only increased the value of these files, they have also highlighted the inherent tension between a number of competing interests that are all firmly rooted in the European Union (EU) Treaties. More specifically, the aim to ensure an effective competition law enforcement may sometimes be difficult to reconcile with the equally important interest in ensuring an administrative system that is transparent and which guarantees both good administration and adequate fundamental rights protection. Furthermore, through the adoption of the directive on antitrust damages actions,[1] it has become equally apparent that the recent emphasis on private enforcement of the EU competition rules may undermine the European Commission's own enforcement activities, especially the application of its leniency programme. These tensions have surfaced during the last couple of decades and are fuelled by rapid, but not necessarily consistent developments in three different but to some extent overlapping areas within the EU legal system: the rules on (i) competition law enforcement, (ii) openness and transparency, and (iii) fundamental rights protection.

The problem can briefly be described as follows. After decades of dealing mainly with notifications of agreements, the European Commission ('the Commission') eventually decided that the time was ripe for it to reshape its enforcement policy and step up the fight against hard-core restrictions of the EU competition rules. By introducing a leniency programme designed to make cartel offenders come forward and admit their guilt in exchange for immunity from fines, and by abolishing the notification system applied under Regulation 17/62,[2] the Commission could now focus its resources on cartels and abuse of market power. Since then, reports on record fines make the news on a regular basis, and the Commission is viewed as a tough and diligent enforcer of the EU competition rules. This new and

[1] Directive 2014/104/EU of the European Parliament and of the Council of 26 November 2014 on certain rules governing actions for damages under national law for infringements of the competition law provisions of the Member States and of the European Union [2014] OJ L349/1 ('the Damages Directive').

[2] EEC Council Regulation No 17, First Regulation implementing Articles 85 and 86 of the Treaty [1962] OJ L13/204.

more aggressive enforcement policy reflects the widespread understanding that cartels and market abuse are harmful to the economy and should be punished. In recent years, there has been increased focus on achieving corrective justice, ensuring that those who have suffered loss from competition law infringements are duly compensated. Nowadays, the Commission is prone to stress that cartel activity is not a victimless infringement of a set of administrative rules but that the gains are made at the expense of customers or consumers, and should be transferred back to them.[3] While EU competition law enforcement has traditionally mainly been handled by the Commission and the national competition authorities, recent legislative changes aimed at achieving both corrective justice and enhanced deterrence have led to a shift in the enforcement structure. Today, the EU cartel enforcement system is resting on two separate pillars – one public and one private.

A more aggressive public enforcement, combined with invigorated private enforcement of the EU competition rules, has not only affected the risks involved with engaging in cartel activity, it has also increased the value of the evidence held in the Commission's case files. The parties under investigation need to access the file in order to be able to safeguard their defence rights, but will at the same time seek to protect the evidence from being disclosed to third parties. On the other hand, both cartel victims and national competition authorities may have an obvious and legitimate interest in accessing the file and the documents contained therein. The recent developments in the areas of transparency and fundamental rights protection, which have gained in importance and are now firmly established at the top of the EU norm hierarchy, will impact the outcome of any attempts to access the evidence held by the Commission. However, as the rules are now framed and applied by the EU institutions, they are not necessarily ensuring either coherence or consistency. This book examines the legislative patchwork surrounding access to the Commission's cartel case files, and seeks to establish how to best ensure a proper balance between the often diverging – but legitimate – interests of the parties, of third parties and of national competition authorities. The following section will provide a more detailed background to the problems tackled throughout the book.

II. Setting the Scene

The EU legal system is undoubtedly in constant motion, but the speed at which it develops may vary. After decades of relatively slow development, the first steps to transform the three areas of EU competition law enforcement, transparency

[3] A Renda, 'Private Antitrust Damages Actions in the EU: Chronicle of an Attempted Golpe' in HW Micklitz and A Wechsler (eds), *The Transformation of Enforcement – European Economic Law in Global Perspective* (Oxford, Hart Publishing, 2016) 273, 275.

and fundamental rights protection were all taken in the 1990s. Since then, we have witnessed a rapid and drastic development in these areas. Coincidentally, the year 2001 bears particular significance both for the development in the competition law enforcement area and in the area of openness and transparency. This was the year when the Court of Justice of the European Union ('the Court' or 'the ECJ') delivered its ruling in *Courage v Crehan*, establishing a right for victims of competition law infringements to seek compensation for any damage sustained. The Court thereby drew attention to a part of the EU competition law enforcement system that, up until then, had received scant attention.[4] It was also the year when Regulation 1049/2001 ('the Transparency Regulation') was adopted and took effect.[5] The Transparency Regulation has the explicit aim to guarantee openness and to give the fullest possible effect to the right of public access to documents held by the EU institutions.

While the Court's ruling in *Courage* was considered seminal already in 2001, few could imagine what would come in its wake. Not only was *Courage* soon to be followed by *Manfredi*,[6] but the ruling did also prompt the Commission to launch a survey on the possibilities of being compensated for loss suffered due to competition law infringements. The report from the survey was a gloomy read, revealing a state of 'astonishing diversity and total underdevelopment' throughout the EU.[7] Few victims obtained any compensation at all.[8] As a response, the Commission later presented a proposal for a directive on antitrust damages actions. Following certain modifications, the European Parliament and the Council adopted the Damages Directive in November 2014.[9] The Damages Directive introduces a framework designed to ensure an effective private enforcement system throughout the Union, spreading a second layer of remedies over the EU public enforcement system.[10]

All Member States have now transposed the Damages Directive into their legal systems and the rules are in full swing throughout the Union. The impact

[4] Case C-453/99, *Courage Ltd v Bernard Crehan and Bernard Crehan v Courage Ltd and Others*, EU:C:2001:465.

[5] Regulation (EC) No 1049/2001 of the European Parliament and of the Council of 30 May 2001 regarding public access to European Parliament, Council and Commission documents [2001] OJ 145/43, entered into force on 3 December 2001.

[6] Case C-295/04, *Vincenzo Manfredi v Lloyd Adriatico Assicurazioni SpA*, EU:C:2006:461. Here, the Court established that anyone who has suffered loss due to a competition law infringement should be entitled to compensation not only for the actual loss, but also for the loss of profit plus interest, that is compensation in full.

[7] Ashurst, *Study on the Conditions of Claims for Damages in Case of Infringement of EC Competition Rules*, Comparative Report, August 2004, prepared by D Waelbroeck, D Slater and G Even-Shoshan for the Commission ('the Ashurst Report'). See also the Commission's Green Paper, *Damages actions for breach of the EC antitrust rules*, COM(2005) 672 final.

[8] Green Paper on damages actions for breach of the EC antitrust rules, COM (2005) 672 final.

[9] Directive 2014/104/EU (n 1).

[10] J Drexl, 'The interaction Between Private and Public Enforcement in European Competition Law' in Micklitz and Wechsler (eds), *The Transformation of Enforcement* (n 3) 136.

of the Damages Directive is endorsed and further reinforced by the ECJ, which is establishing a broad and comprehensive EU-wide basis for these damages, acknowledging, inter alia, liability for umbrella pricing,[11] liability of the parent for breaches by subsidiaries,[12] and alternative jurisdictions.[13] As a consequence, the number of damages claims is picking up by the minute, and the value of the evidence held in the Commission's files is increasing at the same pace. Cartel cases are not only complex and fact intensive, they are also characterised by information asymmetry, and cartel victims may often experience great difficulties in accessing the evidence required. The question of when and in what circumstances third parties should gain access to the evidence held in the Commission's case files is thus of more practical importance than ever. It goes without saying that no private enforcement system will become truly effective unless those who have suffered damages are able to access the evidence necessary for them to prove their loss. Access is thus key to ensuring effective private enforcement. At the same time, companies targeted by the Commission's cartel investigations now have an obvious and urgent interest in keeping the case file out of reach of third parties. However, any efforts to this effect should, at least in theory, be harder to accomplish given the development of new rules in another area of EU law, namely, those on public access and good administration.

Indeed, the year 2001 was also the year when the EU introduced a legal framework governing its adherence to the principles of openness and transparency. The first steps towards a more transparent EU administration were taken in the wake of the Danish rejection of further EU integration in 1992. The Danish referendum on the Maastricht Treaty had spurred a heated debate on questions of 'democratic deficiency' and 'institutional autism', and calls were made for a closer contact between the EU institutions and the citizens of the Union. The Council and the Commission responded by producing codes of conduct governing access to their own internal documents.[14] Further steps to enhance transparency soon followed. When the Treaty of Amsterdam entered into force in 1999, it included a right of access to the documents of the Parliament, the Council and the Commission.[15] Following the resignation of the Santer Commission in 1999, prompted by allegations of corruption and maladministration, the need to adopt detailed rules on access to documents became even more urgent, and the Transparency Regulation was finally adopted in May 2001. As from this date, there are detailed provisions governing the European administration's adherence to the principles of openness

[11] Case C-557/12, *Kone AG and Others v ÖBB-Infrastruktur AG*, EU:C:2014:1317.

[12] Case C-724/17, *Vantaan kaupunki v Skanska Industrial Solutions Oy and Others*, EU:C:2019:204.

[13] Case C-451/18, *Tibor-Trans Fuvarozó és Kereskedelmi Kft v DAF Trucks NV*, EU:C:2019:635.

[14] L Rossi and P Vinagre e Silva, *Public Access to Documents in the EU* (Oxford, Hart Publishing, 2017) 1.

[15] Art 255 of the Treaty Establishing the European Community [2002] OJ C325/1 (TEC), now Art 15 of the Treaty on the Functioning of the European Union [2012] OJ C326/47 (TFEU).

and transparency, and the purpose of the Transparency Regulation is to ensure the fullest possible effect to the right of public access to documents.[16]

The Damages Directive and the Transparency Regulation are not the only legal acts of relevance to this study. In recent years, there has been rapid development in a number of other areas, which may also impact the Commission's obligation or incentives to disclose the documents held in its case files. The Commission's Leniency Notice[17] and the European Charter of Fundamental Rights[18] ('the Charter') are two legal instruments of relevance. While one is a soft law instrument and the other forms part of EU primary legislation, they may both have a significant impact on the Commission's incentives or possibilities to share the documents or information in its case files with parties or third parties.

One of the first steps taken by the Commission when reshaping the EU cartel enforcement system was the introduction of a Leniency Notice. Having witnessed the results from the introduction of leniency programmes and sentencing guidelines in the United States, the Commission decided to change its enforcement strategy. In 1996, it adopted a Leniency Notice designed to divide cartel infringers and to help uncover cartels. The adoption of the Notice proved to be a success, leading to a sharp increase in the number of uncovered cartels.[19] Following a review of the Notice, the Commission decided to adopt a new Leniency Notice in 2002, where a lower evidence standard was applied and the scope of immunity was extended to undertakings already under investigation. As a result, leniency applications now serve as the direct cause for most cartel investigations, and there has also been a significant increase in the number of uncovered cartels.[20] Relevant to this study is the fact that the effectiveness of the leniency system is dependent on companies' willingness to voluntarily admit their guilt and submit incriminating evidence to the Commission. If companies fear that such measures will make them more vulnerable to private actions, thereby potentially putting them in a worse situation than should they refrain from reporting the cartel, the leniency programme may soon be on the brink of disuse.[21] As will be further explored in this work, to the extent that the Commission has any margin of discretion, it must carefully assess these issues when deciding what information to share with the public.

[16] For a more detailed exposition of the EU's road toward an open and transparent administration, see eg Rossi and Vinagre e Silva, *Public Access to Documents in the EU* (n 14) 1–41; and F Bignami, 'Three Generations of Participation Rights Before the European Commission' [2004] 68(1) *Law and Contemporary Problems* 61.

[17] Commission Notice on immunity from fines and reduction of fines in cartel cases [2006] OJ C298/17.

[18] Charter of Fundamental Rights of the European Union [2012] OJ C326/391 (consolidated version).

[19] J Ratliff, *EC Cartel Leniency Programme*, available at www.wilmerhale.com/files/Publication/515f785c-9663-44d7-bf82-45c19f099fd9/Presentation/PublicationAttachment/465fc5e4-addb-4a49-8bd7-4c4c179962cb/ECLENIENCY_Ratliff_Nov2004.pdf.

[20] See B Van Barlingen and M Barennes, 'The European Commission's 2002 Leniency Notice in Practice', *EC Competition Policy Newsletter*, no 3 2005, 6.

[21] As is discussed in ch 9, there are indications that companies are becoming less inclined to apply for leniency.

Another area that has undergone transformation in recent years is the area of EU fundamental rights protection. In the early days of European integration, fundamental rights were not considered part of the EU legal order. Over the years, the ECJ has acknowledged that these rights do form part of EU law, and they have slowly been woven into the EU legal system through the hands of the Court. In 2000, the Charter was adopted. It is the first formal EU document that in a single text combines the whole range of civil, political, economic and social rights, as well as certain 'third generation' rights such as the right to good administration.[22] The Charter's prime objective was not to create new rights but to make existing rights more visible. When the Charter was adopted it was not given any legal force, and for a number of years it played a rather insignificant role. This changed with the Lisbon Treaty. In December 2009, the Charter was not only made legally binding, it was also given the status of primary EU law.[23] Since then, it has gained an important role within the EU legal order, and is now the primary source of EU fundamental rights protection. The Charter contains a number of provisions relevant to this study. It provides EU citizens and companies with a right to good administration and a right of access to documents – thereby ensuring that transparency is not only a way of dealing with the democratic deficit but also a right that belongs to the individuals and which is enforceable in court.[24] It also protects the right of the defence, the principle of equality of arms, the right to privacy and the right to protection of personal data. Companies targeted by the Commission's investigations have a right to access the evidence in the Commission's case file, and they should be assured that the Commission does not disclose business secrets or other confidential information. Thus, whereas some of the Charter provisions may be invoked to ensure public access to the file and to promote further openness and transparency, others can be invoked to protect the evidence held in the Commission's file from disclosure. The Charter can thereby serve both as a sword and a shield in the quest for or protection of evidence held by the Commission.

It is not only the legal framework surrounding the Commission's enforcement activities that has transformed in recent years. In its report on challenges to international cooperation, the Organisation for Economic Cooperation and Development (OECD) notes that international trade has increased dramatically since 1990. This may be one of the reasons why an ever-growing number of uncovered cartels have an international dimension. Furthermore, the report shows that competition law has gone global in the last 30 years. According to the report, since 1990 there has been more than a 600 per cent increase in the number of jurisdictions with competition law enforcement, from fewer than 20

[22] G Di Federico, 'Fundamental Rights in the EU: Legal Pluralism and Multi-Level Protection After the Lisbon Treaty' in G Di Federico (ed), *The EU Charter of Fundamental Rights: From Declaration to Binding Instrument* (Dordrecht, Springer, 2011) 15, 40.

[23] Art 6 of the Treaty of the European Union [2016] OJ C202/1 (TEU).

[24] Arts 41 and 42 respectively.

in 1990 to about 120 in 2014.[25] As a consequence, there is a greater focus on and interest in cooperation between competition authorities, be it through international networks such as the International Competition Network (ICN) or the European Competition Network (ECN) or through bilateral cooperation agreements. Information exchange is often key to meaningful cooperation between competition authorities.

These developments have all affected the Commission's obligations and incentives to grant access to the documents held in its files. Add to that the fact that the Commission's case files are becoming more and more voluminous, containing thousands of documents, and that the granting of public access is therefore not necessarily a straightforward task. Today, there is a patchwork of legislative pieces, soft law instruments and court cases governing the Commission's actions, which the Commission will have to consider when deciding whether or not to disclose a document from its case file, be it to a party, a third party or a national competition authority. As has been illustrated in this section, these rules are not necessarily promoting the same interests, and are sometimes even pulling in different directions. As a result, we now have an order where the rules on disclosure of documents or information appear unable to ensure either optimal cartel enforcement or a sufficiently transparent administrative system.

This book maps the rules in place and examines how they are currently applied by the Commission. It is clear from the study that the Commission has been handed a delicate task of balancing the various interests against each other, and that its concern for the leniency system lies at the heart of any such balancing exercise. The survival of the leniency system, which has served the Commission for more than two decades, is threatened by the developments in areas such as private enforcement and international cooperation, and it appears that the current attempts to maintain its attractiveness are not adequate. Unless the Commission decides to sacrifice its leniency programme, the tension between the various interests may best be eased by an extension of the leniency programme into the area of private enforcement. However, this cannot be achieved by the Commission alone, and it also requires that the right enjoyed by cartel victims to receive full compensation for their loss is not endangered.

III. Outline

The book examines the question of accessibility from three different perspectives: that of (i) the parties under investigation, (ii) third parties, and (iii) national competition authorities.

[25] *Challenges of International Cooperation in Competition Law Enforcement* (OECD, 2014).

Chapter 1 provides an overview of the rules governing access to the Commission's cartel case files. The more obvious legislative pieces are the Treaties,[26] the Charter and the Transparency Regulation. However, Regulations 1/2003 and 773/2004 (jointly referred to as 'the Antitrust Regulations') are also of relevance to this study.[27] Not only do they ensure access to the file and regulate the exchange of information between competition authorities, they also contain provisions that may limit third party access. Another legislative piece of particular relevance to this study is the Damages Directive, which contains rules on disclosure and limits the possibilities of national courts to seek access to the Commission's case files. Finally, there are a number of soft law instruments relevant to the present study, such as the Commission's Notice on the rules for access to the Commission's file in cases pursuant to Articles 101 and 102 TFEU ('the Access Notice')[28] and its Notice on cooperation within the Network of Competition Authorities ('the Network Notice').[29]

Chapter 2 introduces the reader to the rules governing EU fundamental rights protection. It opens with a presentation of the historic background, followed by a discussion of the role of the European Convention on Human Rights (ECHR) within the EU legal system.[30] The chapter also examines the nature of competition law proceedings and the sanctions imposed by the Commission, and it concludes that these proceedings are to be considered criminal in nature – under both the Charter and the ECHR. This conclusion is of relevance as it affects the standard of protection to be afforded to companies targeted by the Commission's cartel investigations. The chapter closes with a brief description of the various rights that may come into play when a party, third party or national competition authority is seeking access to the file of the Commission.

The words 'no man is an island' can also be applied to competition authorities. In today's global economy cartels often cross the boundaries of jurisdictions, and these international cartels tend to be even more complex, broader in scope, larger in terms of affected volumes of commerce and more harmful to consumers than their domestic counterparts.[31] This development towards 'sophisticated

[26] The TEU and the TFEU.

[27] Council Regulation (EC) No 1/2003 of 16 December 2002 on the implementation of the rules on competition laid down in Articles 81 and 82 of the Treaty [2003] OJ L1/1 and Commission Regulation (EC) No 773/2004 of 7 April 2004 relating to the conduct of proceedings by the Commission pursuant to Articles 81 and 82 of the EC Treaty [2004] OJ L123/18.

[28] Commission Notice on the rules for access to the Commission's file in cases pursuant to Articles 81 and 82 of the EC Treaty, Articles 53, 54 and 57 of the EEA Agreement and Council Regulation (EC) No 139/2004 [2005] OJ C325/07.

[29] Commission Notice on cooperation within the Network of Competition Authorities [2004] OJ C101/03.

[30] The Convention for the Protection of Human Rights and Fundamental Freedoms, as amended by Protocols nos 11 and 14, supplemented by Protocols nos 1, 4, 6, 7, 12, 13 and 16.

[31] www.justice.gov/atr/speech/international-cartels-intersection-between-fcpa-violations-and-antitrust-violations. An OECD report of 2014 shows that in recent years, more than 90% of fines against cartels by the US authorities have been international. The number of cartel cases investigated in the EU involving a participant from outside the Union had increased by over 450% since 1990. See OECD, *Challenges* (n 25).

multinational' cartels has made competition authorities more dependent on each other. Today, proving a competition law infringement often requires cooperation with other competition authorities. An often crucial component of the cooperation between competition authorities is information exchange. The Commission considers that the power of the competition authorities within the ECN to exchange and use information is a key element of the functioning of the network.[32] On a similar note, the OECD encourages its member countries to support information exchange between competition authorities, and the ICN has manuals for the management of information exchange.[33] However, such information exchange requires careful manoeuvring. Not only is there a risk that the fundamental rights of targeted undertakings and their employees are not adequately protected when information is transmitted from one authority to another, there is also a risk that leniency systems are negatively affected if information that has been submitted within the frame of a leniency programme is later exchanged with other authorities pursuing parallel proceedings under their domestic laws. Chapter 3 discusses the need for and risks associated with information exchange between competition authorities, and examines two bilateral cooperation agreements in more detail: the one between the EU and the United States Government, and the one between the EU and Switzerland. While the first is a 'first generation agreement', which does not allow for the exchange of confidential information, the agreement with Switzerland is a 'second generation agreement', which allows for exchange of confidential information. The two agreements are examined from a fundamental rights perspective.

Chapter 3 also examines the cooperation that takes place within the EU, as this offers an additional dimension to the notion of agency cooperation. Ever since the enforcement system was revised and decentralised through Regulation 1/2003, competition authorities throughout the EU work closely together, and information gathered during the course of investigations is frequently exchanged between competition authorities within the ECN. Article 12 of Regulation 1/2003 empowers the Commission and the national competition authorities (NCAs) to exchange information and to use such information in evidence.[34] According to Article 26 of the Network Notice, a key element of the functioning of the network is the power of all authorities, including the Commission, to exchange and use information that has been collected by them for the purpose of applying Articles 101 or 102 TFEU. From a competition law enforcement perspective, this is of course a welcome development that renders the system more effective. However, it is not

[32] The Network Notice (n 29) 43–53.

[33] *Cooperation between Competition Agencies in Cartel Investigations*, Report to ICN Annual Conference 2007. See also www.internationalcompetitionnetwork.org/wp-content/uploads/2018/05/CWGInfoSharingEU.pdf.

[34] The obligation in Art 28 of Regulation 1/2003 not to use any information gathered for purposes other than those of the investigation does not apply to the exchange of information carried out under Art 12 of the Regulation.

equally evident that the system now in place is able to guarantee adequate fundamental rights protection or to safeguard the interests of the companies targeted by the Commission's investigations. Chapter 3 addresses this issue, laying out the rules and principles governing information exchange between the Commission and Member State authorities, and discussing their application from both due process and efficiency perspectives.

Chapter 4 is dedicated to the companies targeted by the Commission's cartel investigations and their possibilities to access the Commission's case files. Parties under investigation have a clear and legitimate interest in accessing the file. Not only is this right firmly established in the Charter,[35] it is also governed by the Antitrust Regulations. However, as will be further discussed in Chapter 4, the Commission's application of these rules does not always ensure full access to the file, and the Court's case law suggests that the possibilities to remedy any such failure are limited. This is due to the fact that access to the file is not considered an end in itself but is intended to protect the rights of the defence. Thus, while the EU Courts will strike evidence relied on by the Commission to which the parties have not previously been granted access, annulment of the Commission's infringement decisions requires that the parties' defence rights have been violated.

Chapters 5–8 are dedicated to third party access. While there are a number of situations where third parties may seek access to the Commission's case files, this book will mainly focus on one, and that is where Article 101 TFEU forms the basis for a cartel damages claim. Private actions may be brought concerning alleged infringements that neither are nor have been the object of public enforcement proceedings (stand-alone actions).[36] However, they may also run in parallel with or follow upon public enforcement proceedings concerning the same alleged infringement (follow-on actions). Relevant to this study are follow-on actions where the alleged cartel victim seeks access to the Commission's case file in order to prove its case in national proceedings. These requests can be made either directly to the Commission or through the national courts.

Third parties seeking access to the file of the Commission will in most cases have to rely on the Transparency Regulation. However, there are certain circumstances when third parties may also have a right to access documents from the Commission's case file under Regulation 1/2003. That is where they have a right to be heard, either because they are complainants, or because the Commission considers that they have a sufficient interest in or can contribute to the investigation. If you manage to get through the needle's eye and qualify as a complainant,

[35] Art 41(2) of the Charter.

[36] WPJ Wils, 'Private Enforcement of EU Antitrust Law and its Relationship with Public Enforcement: Past, Present and the Future' (2017) 40(1) *World Competition* 3, 3. It is usually harder for the cartel victim to substantiate its claim in this type of action where there is no finding of a competition authority to rely on. A study carried out by Laborde in 2017 identified 23 cases where damages had been awarded. Out of these 23 cases, only one was a stand-alone action. See JF Laborde, 'Cartel Damages Claims in Europe: How Courts Have Assessed Overcharges' (2017) 1 *Concurrences* 36, 38.

this does not mean that you are automatically given full access to the case file, only that you will be associated closely with the proceedings. Recently, third parties have also sought leave to intervene in annulment actions before the General Court with a view to accessing the evidence relied on by the Commission.[37] As will be discussed further in Chapter 5, it may be hard for a cartel victim to meet the criteria and be allowed to intervene, especially since the General Court has declared that, as for the right to intervene, the purpose of the appeal proceedings is not to make possible or facilitate private damages actions before national courts but to review the legality of the contested Commission decision. Chapter 5 presents the regulatory framework surrounding complainants and interveners, followed by an overview and discussion of existing case law.

Chapter 6 addresses the situation where a cartel victim relies on the Transparency Regulation and the rules on public access in order to gather the evidence necessary to prove its claim against the cartel participants. It is concluded that the Commission is consistently refusing cartel victims access to its files, and that the EU Courts have been given ample opportunity to interpret the provisions of the Transparency Regulation that allow for exceptions to the general obligation of transparency. While the General Court has, at least occasionally, been willing to accept the applicants' arguments in favour of granting access, the ECJ has shut the door firmly on anyone seeking access to the Commission's case files.

Chapter 7 explores the possibilities for cartel victims to seek access through national courts. Whereas section I provides a general overview of the Commission's obligation to cooperate with national courts under Article 4(3) TEU and Article 15 of Regulation 1/2003, section II is devoted to damages proceedings and the rules now laid down by the Damages Directive. The chapter shows that while the Damages Directive has the explicit aim to facilitate the collection of evidence, and introduces a number of provisions on disclosure, it explicitly limits the possibilities of national courts to request evidence from the Commission. Thus, in this respect, the Commission's obligation to cooperate has been limited through the adoption of the Damages Directive. Furthermore, despite the explicit aim to facilitate evidence gathering, the wording of the Directive has actually raised hurdles in some Member States. That is the few Member States that have traditionally had wide (pre-trial) disclosure rules, and which have now had to adjust their practices to accommodate the Directive's requirement that disclosure orders should be proportionate, banning wide or non-specific disclosure requests. Thus, while some hurdles may have been removed, others have surfaced, and the road towards a level playing field still appears bumpy. From the Commission's perspective, the limitations imposed by the Directive are most likely welcome, as this may help to keep the leniency system alive.

[37] B Balsaningham, *The EU Leniency Policy; Reconciling Effectiveness and Fairness* (Alphen aan den Rijn, Wolters Kluwer, 2017) 169.

The Commission's unwillingness to grant access to its case files by no means implies that it turns a blind eye to the difficulties that cartel victims may encounter when they seek to build their case against cartel offenders. Traditionally, the public versions of the Commission's infringement decisions have been rather succinct, but in recent years, the Commission has endeavoured to publish longer and more detailed infringement decisions. This change could potentially facilitate matters for cartel victims attempting to substantiate their claims against the infringers. Chapter 8 examines the Commission's initiative, and concludes that while it is positive from a private enforcement perspective, it does not come without drawbacks. The Commission's attempts to publish more detailed infringement decisions have met steep resistance from the addressees of those decisions, which has resulted in lengthy court proceedings concerning what information that may be published. In the case of *Evonik Degussa*,[38] many of the damages claims had already been settled by the time the court proceedings ended and the Commission could publish the full version of its decision. Furthermore, there are indications that the Commission's new practice may impact the effectiveness of the Commission's leniency programme, making cartel offenders less inclined to come forward and seek immunity.

Indeed, much of the concern expressed by the addressees of the Commission's infringement decisions revolves around the leniency documents submitted to the Commission and whether the information provided under the leniency programme should be made public. Chapter 9 explores the possibility and appropriateness of extending the leniency programme into the field of private actions, and whether this could ease the tension between the competition law enforcement system and the rules on transparency. This discussion builds on the US experience, where the rules on civil liability were amended and where leniency applicants may now escape part of the civil liability as damages are de-trebled.

Chapter 10 is the final chapter. It is here that the dots are joined. The chapter provides an analysis of the legal framework currently surrounding the Commission's cartel case files, and proposes a number of amendments to the existing rules. These proposals – including an extension of the leniency system into the sphere of private actions, requiring immunity recipients to cooperate with cartel victims and provide them with the evidence in their possession – are aimed at achieving a system that is both effective from a competition law enforcement perspective and that manages to ensure adequate procedural safeguards and a transparent EU administrative system.

[38] Case C-162/15 P, *Evonik Degussa GmbH v European Commission*, EU:C:2017:205.

PART I

The Legislative Framework

1

The Rules Governing Access

> Transparency, integrity, and accountability are the essential prerequisites of a democracy based on the rule of law. They promote good governance and build trust in the policy-making process, thereby enhancing the legitimacy and credibility of public institutions.[1]

The Commission's cartel case files are beginning to take on the value of the One Ring in *The Lord of the Rings*. However, unlike in the epic novel by JRR Tolkien, cases concerning access to the Commission's cartel files do not necessarily depict a fight between good and evil forces. Although cartel activity is sometimes referred to as a form of theft, few would go as far as to liken a company suspected of cartel participation to Dark Lord Sauron, and both the companies targeted by the Commission's cartel investigations and third parties may have a legitimate interest in accessing the file or in keeping it out of reach of others. This chapter outlines and presents the rules that may come into play when access is sought from the Commission's file by someone other than the parties under investigation, be it by a third party or an NCA. The rules on party access are presented in chapter 2 on EU fundamental rights protection. While the present chapter aims at providing a general overview of the rules that may be invoked to seek access from the Commission's case files, chapters 3–7 will provide more detailed descriptions and analyses of each set of rules.

I. Public Access to Documents Held by the EU Institutions

The Treaty on the European Union opens with a bold statement, declaring that it marks a new stage in the process of creating an ever-closer union among the peoples of Europe, in which decisions are taken as openly as possible and as close to the citizen as possible.[2] The principle of transparency is thus established already

[1] R Panizza, *Transparency, integrity and accountability in the EU institutions*, Briefing for the PETI Committee, European Parliament, March 2019.

[2] Art 1 TEU.

in the opening paragraph of the TEU, suggesting that it is of fundamental importance to the EU and its legal system. Indeed, and as noted by Buijze, the principle is thought not only to contribute to good governance, but also to be essential to the legitimacy of the EU, and as such it is of fundamental value.[3] The goals envisioned in Article 1 of the TEU are confirmed by Article 15(1) TFEU, which declares that 'In order to promote good governance and ensure the participation of civil society, the Union institutions, bodies, offices and agencies shall conduct their work as openly as possible.' The wording suggests that the principle of transparency does not reflect an individual right but is rather considered as a means of safeguarding democracy and ensuring an administration that works effectively. However, this is only part of the truth. The principle of transparency is a composite term and serves to protect a number of interests. As Buijze notes, it has also been derived from the principle of effective judicial protection and the rights of the defence, and has been used in conjunction with the principles of legal certainty and sound administration. In those cases, transparency is essential to safeguard individual rights of all sorts.[4] In addition, the right of access to documents has been written into the Charter, and is thus considered a fundamental right in and of itself. As such, it belongs to the individual. Transparency can thus be a means of safeguarding the public interests of democracy and legitimacy, but also to protect individual rights. The following section provides a brief presentation of how the principle of transparency and the rules on public access to documents have emerged and developed in the EU legal order.

A. Historic Background to the Principle of Transparency and the Right of Public Access

As noted by Lenaerts, the Founding Treaties were silent on issues concerning democratic legitimacy, and the early days of the European cooperation were weak in terms of democracy, accountability and accessibility to public scrutiny. Over time, the absence of any reference to the concept of democracy led some scholars to argue that the Community suffered from a 'democratic deficit'.[5] However, while the concept has its roots in the 1970s, it was two decades later that the debate on the perceived democratic deficit really gathered speed.[6] Without analysing the debate

[3] A Buijze, 'The Six Faces of Transparency' (2013) 9(3) *Utrecht Law Review* 3, 3.

[4] Ibid.

[5] K Lenaerts, 'The Principle of Democracy in the Case Law of the European Court of Justice' (2013) 62(2) *International and Comparative Law Quarterly* 271, 273. See also P Craig, *EU Administrative Law*, 2nd edn (Oxford, Oxford University Press, 2012) 357.

[6] See eg A Moravcsik, 'In Defence of "the Democratic Deficit": Reassessing Legitimacy in the European Union' (2002) 40(4) *Journal of Common Market Studies* 603; P Kratochvíl and Z Sychra, 'The End of Democracy in the EU? The Eurozone Crisis and the EU's Democratic Deficit' (2019) 41(2) *Journal of European Integration* 169. See also P Craig and G de Búrca, *The Evolution of EU Law*, 2nd edn (Oxford, Oxford University Press, 2011).

in detail, the criticism mainly consisted in a concern that the EU suffered from a lack of accountability, democracy and accessibility of the ordinary EU citizens to the EU institutions. The debate was fuelled by a number of events that took place at both Member State and institutional level during the 1990s.

The first of these events concerned European integration and the public reception of the Maastricht Treaty, which had been agreed by the Member State governments in 1991. As noted by Føllesdal, European governments had long pursued European integration, assuming that the public gave them a 'permissive consensus' toward deeper cooperation.[7] The popular and legal reception of the Maastricht Treaty challenged this assumption. Referendums on the Treaty were held in Denmark, France and Ireland, and the results of these referendums sent shock waves across the Union and led to a heated public debate on the proper ends and institutions of the EU. In Denmark, the Danish people voted against the treaty in 1992. After the defeat in the first referendum, Denmark negotiated and received an opt-out from the single currency, and the Maastricht Treaty was accepted by another referendum the following year. In France the treaty created serious cleavages within political parties, and barely passed in a referendum 51 to 49 per cent, prompting Mitterand to suggest that a long-term oversight of the EU institutions lay in the lack of talking to the people.[8] In the UK, the treaty was passed only with great difficulty in 1993.

Second, when allegations of corruption forced the Commissioners to resign in March 1999, this added fuel to an already heated debate. In the media, the EU was described as having been decapitated:

> Europe was left decapitated last night as the entire European Commission resigned *en masse* after a devastating report by an independent committee of inquiry which found that they had 'lost control of the administration'.[9]

Tomkins provides an illustrative presentation of the events leading up to this 'decapitation'. In 1998, the Commission's own anti-fraud unit, known as UCLAF,[10] disclosed that £600 million of the Commission's humanitarian aid budget for the years 1993 through 1995 could not be accounted for. According to UCLAF, this had not come to light previously because the Commission had failed to keep the European Court of Auditors (ECA) properly informed. Furthermore, Tomkins notes, in its report for the financial year 1997, published in November 1998, the

[7] A Føllesdal, 'Legitimacy Theories of the European Union', *Centre for European Studies, University of Oslo, Arena Working Papers WP 04/15*, 3.

[8] L Rossi and P Vinagre e Silva, *Public Access to Documents in the EU* (Oxford, Hart Publishing, 2017) 1.

[9] *The Guardian* (16 March 1999).

[10] In 1988, the Task Force 'Anti-Fraud Coordination Unit' (UCLAF) was created as part of the Secretariat-General of the European Commission. UCLAF worked alongside national anti-fraud departments and provided the coordination and assistance needed to tackle transnational organised fraud. Following the fall of the Santer Commission, a new anti-fraud body was established, known as OLAF. For further information, see https://ec.europa.eu/anti-fraud/about-us/history_en.

ECA stated that approximately £3 billion (representing 5 per cent of the EU's budget) had 'gone walkabout'. This included some £600 million that had been allotted to repairing and making safe the nuclear power plants of the old Soviet bloc. This money, the ECA declared, had been 'either wasted, lost, embezzled or unspent'. There were also allegations that Commission officials had attempted to suppress any investigations into fraud, and that some of them were in the habit of awarding lucrative contracts to family members.[11] These events were closely monitored by the media, which no doubt added fuel to any criticism of the EU machinery.

Third, in 2001, it was Ireland's turn to vote against a treaty proposal. In a referendum on the adoption of the Treaty of Nice, the Irish voters said no, and it was only after the negotiation of a number of amendments that the treaty was approved by the Irish people in October 2002.

These developments sparked a number of actions at EU level. In response to the bitter criticism following the Danish referendum, where the EU institutions were accused of 'institutional autism', the Council and the Commission produced non-binding codes of conduct on public access to documents, and in 1995, the first European Ombudsman was appointed. The Ombudsman was entrusted with the task of ensuring accountability and empowered to investigate complaints of maladministration against the EU institutions. Furthermore, the right of access to documents and openness in decision-making were both formally introduced by the Treaty of Amsterdam.[12] As to the 'principle of openness', the treaty modified Article 1 TEU so as to make clear that the EU institutions are bound to take their decisions 'as openly as possible'.[13]

Another response to the perceived democratic deficit and lack of accountability was the Commission's own White Paper on European governance presented in 2001,[14] in which it proposed a number of measures aimed at regaining the citizens' confidence in the EU and its institutions. The White Paper declared that it was now time to take action and that the Union should – already within the existing treaties – start adapting its institutions and establishing more coherence in its policies so that it would become easier to see what the Union was doing and what it stood for. A more coherent Union would be stronger at home and a better leader in the world, the Commission declared. It further acknowledged that many Europeans felt alienated from the Union's work. According to the Commission, this feeling of alienation reflected particular tensions and uncertainty about what the Union was and what it aspired to become, about its geographical boundaries, its political objectives and the way these powers were shared with the Member

[11] A Tomkins, 'Responsibility and Resignation in the European Commission' (1999) 62(5) *MLR* 744, 745.

[12] The Treaty of Amsterdam was signed in October 1997 and entered into force in May 1999.

[13] Lenaerts, 'The Principle of Democracy' (n 5) 277.

[14] European Commission, *European Governance: A White Paper*, COM(2001) 428 final.

States. Reforming governance addressed the question of how the EU used the powers given by its citizens, and the goal was thus to open up policy-making to make it more inclusive and accountable. A better use of powers should connect the EU more closely to its citizens and lead to more effective policies, the White Paper declared. The White Paper thus stressed the importance of inclusion, participation, and a deeper knowledge among the citizens about the EU and its goals.

At European level, the principle of transparency and the rules on public access were developed as a response to a perceived democratic deficit, where the EU administration was considered alienated from the EU citizens and where the people of Europe not only felt distant from the power, but also lacked trust in the EU institutions. The rules on public access should bring the EU closer to the citizens and ensure accountability. The efforts to implement the principle of transparency within the EU legal order had been done in two ways, first by granting citizens a right of access to documents and second by shedding some light on the traditionally opaque EU decision-making process.[15] As will be discussed further in chapter 2, the principle of transparency is applied not only to bring EU citizens closer to the decision-making process. The right of access to documents is now also a fundamental right protected by the Charter, and the principle of transparency operates as a prerequisite to the effective exercise of the rights of defence in administrative proceedings in fields such as competition law.[16] As noted by Spahiu, in less than two decades, the right of access to documents was upgraded from a right at the mere discretion of public officials to a fundamental right protected by the Charter and Treaty provisions.[17] The following section presents the legal framework surrounding public access. The rules on information exchange between competition authorities are discussed briefly in section I.D.

B. The Legal Framework Surrounding Public Access to the Commission's Case Files

After years of debate on issues such as democratic deficit and the Union's lack of legitimacy, the notion of openness has become one of the guiding principles of the functioning of the EU machinery. While Article 1 TEU declares that the decisions of the EU institutions should be taken as openly as possible and as close to the citizen as possible, the principle of transparency is set out in Article 15 TFEU.

[15] As noted by Craig, transparency now features within the legislative process. Art 16(8) TEU imposes an obligation on the Council to meet in public when it deliberates and votes on draft legislative acts. Art 15(2) renders the European Parliament subject to the same duty. See P Craig, *EU Administrative Law*, 2nd edn (Oxford, Oxford University Press, 2012) 359.

[16] Lenaerts, 'The Principle of Democracy' (n 5) 277.

[17] I Spahiu, 'Courts: An Effective Venue to Promote Government Transparency? The Case of the Court of Justice of the European Union' (2015) 31(80) *Utrecht Journal of International and European Law* 5.

As will be discussed further in chapter 2, Article 42 of the Charter grants any EU citizen, and any natural or legal person residing or having its registered office in the EU, a right of access to European Parliament, Council and Commission documents. The modalities of the right to public access are laid down in the Transparency Regulation.

i. The Treaties

Article 15 TFEU reflects the concerns voiced during the 1990s and declares that in order to promote good governance and ensure the participation of civil society, the Union institutions, bodies, offices and agencies shall conduct their work as openly as possible. While Article 15(2) declares that the European Parliament and the Council shall meet in public,[18] Article 15(3) grants every citizen of the Union, and any natural or legal person residing or having its registered office in a Member State, the right of access to documents of the Union institutions, bodies, offices and agencies, whatever their medium, subject to the principles and the conditions to be defined in accordance with what is stipulated in that paragraph.

The Article further provides that general principles and limits on grounds of public or private interest governing the right of access to documents shall be determined by the European Parliament and the Council, by means of regulations, acting in accordance with the ordinary legislative procedure. Each institution, body, office or agency shall ensure that its proceedings are transparent and shall elaborate in its own Rules of Procedure specific provisions regarding access to its documents, in accordance with the regulations referred to in Article 15(2). The ECJ, the European Central Bank and the European Investment Bank are subject to Article 15(3) and the right of public access only when exercising their administrative tasks. The European Parliament and the Council shall ensure publication of the documents relating to the legislative procedures under the terms laid down by the regulations referred to in Article 15(2).

Another Treaty article of relevance is Article 298 TFEU, which marks the first explicit reference to the EU's administration in the Treaties. It sets out three guiding principles for administrative action: openness, efficiency and independence. The Article declares that in carrying out their missions, the institutions, bodies, offices and agencies of the Union shall have the support of an open, efficient and independent European administration. Article 298(2) provides a legal basis for adopting secondary legislation to that end.[19]

[18] The Council shall meet in public when considering and voting on a draft legislative act.

[19] Prior to the Lisbon Treaty there were doubts as to whether the EU had competence to adopt a general code concerning administrative law. These doubts were removed with the adoption of the Lisbon Treaty, according to which legislative regulation can be enacted to attain the objective of an open, efficient and independent European administration. See Craig, *EU Administrative Law* (n 15) 26.

ii. The Charter

Whereas Article 41 of the Charter establishes a right to good administration, Article 42 reaffirms the right of public access laid down in Article 15 TFEU, declaring that any citizen of the Union, and any natural or legal person residing or having its registered office in a Member State, has a right of access to European Parliament, Council and Commission documents. As noted in the explanations, the Article shall be read together with Article 52(2) of the Charter, meaning that the right of access to documents is exercised under the conditions and within the limits for which provision is made in Article 15(3) TFEU.

iii. The Transparency Regulation

The modalities governing third parties' access to the Commission's cartel case files are laid down in the Transparency Regulation. The second recital of the Regulation's preamble sets out the motives behind its adoption, declaring that openness enables citizens to participate more closely in the decision-making process and guarantees that the administration enjoys greater legitimacy and is more effective and more accountable to the citizen in a democratic system. It is clear from both the recitals of the Transparency Regulation and other EU rules on transparency that they serve to secure the legitimacy and effectiveness of the EU institutions. As noted by the ECJ, a lack of information and debate is capable of giving rise to doubts in the minds of the citizens, not only as regards the lawfulness of an isolated act, but also as regards the legitimacy of the decision-making process as a whole.[20] The right of access to documents allows the citizens to monitor the work of the EU institutions.

However, and this is important to note for the sake of this study, Recital 2 of the Transparency Regulation contains a second sentence, in which it is declared that openness contributes to strengthening not only the principles of democracy, but also respect for fundamental rights as laid down in Article 6 of the TEU and in the Charter.[21] Thus, the explicit aim of the Regulation is not only to secure legitimacy and accountability, but also to safeguard the fundamental rights of individuals. Furthermore, although not explicitly recognised in the Transparency Regulation, transparency is argued to increase economic performance and market efficiency, two goals that are also achieved through the application of the competition rules.[22]

[20] Joined Cases C-39/05 and C-52/05 P, *Kingdom of Sweden and Maurizio Turco v Council of the European Union*, EU:C:2008:374.

[21] This sentence was not part of the initial proposal presented by the Commission in January 2000 but was added during the legislative process. See Proposal for a Regulation of the European Parliament and of the Council regarding public access to European Parliament, Council and Commission documents (2000/C 177 E/10).

[22] See eg Buijze, 'The Six Faces of Transparency' (n 3), with reference to JE Stiglitz, 'Information and the Change in Paradigm in Economics' (2002) 92(3) *The American Economic Review* 460.

The recitals define the purpose of the Regulation, which is to give the fullest possible effect to the right of public access to documents and to lay down the general principles and limits on such access in accordance with Article 255(2) of the EC Treaty.[23]

Documents are defined in Article 3 as 'any content whatever its medium (written on paper or stored in electronic form or as a sound, visual or audiovisual recording) concerning a matter relating to the policies, activities and decisions falling within the institution's sphere of responsibility'. Like Article 15 TFEU and Article 42 of the Charter, the Regulation provides citizens and legal persons of the Union with the right of access to the documents of the EU institutions. This right does not only cover documents that have been drawn up by the institutions themselves. Article 2 stipulates that the Regulation also applies to documents that fall into their possession. Thus, documents submitted to the Commission during the course of a cartel investigation are covered by its scope, and no distinction is made between documents that have been submitted voluntarily or through the use of force.[24]

While neither Article 15 TFEU nor Article 42 of the Charter makes any distinction between different types of documents held by the EU institutions, the Transparency Regulation's recitals do so by declaring that wider access should be granted to documents in cases where the institutions are acting in their legislative capacity.[25] As is discussed further in chapter 6, this approach has also been confirmed by the Court in *EnBW*, where it declared that the Commission's administrative practice does not require such extensive access to documents as required by the legislative activity of the EU institutions.[26] Although this differentiation is not supported by the wording of either Article 42 of the Charter or Article 15 TFEU, it may still be in line with the legislation in place. Article 52(2) of the Charter stipulates that rights for which provision is also made in the Treaties shall be exercised under the conditions and within the limits defined by those Treaties. The right of access to documents is provided for by both Article 42 of the Charter and Article 15(3) TFEU. The latter declares that general principles and limits on grounds of public or private interest governing the right to access shall be determined by the Council and the European Parliament – by means of regulations – acting in accordance with the ordinary legislative procedure. The two institutions have availed themselves of this opportunity and adopted the Transparency Regulation.

[23] Now Art 15(2) of the TFEU. The Treaty Article forms the legal basis for the Transparency Regulation.

[24] While the Commission lacks the powers to use any force during its dawn raids, it may require assistance from national law enforcement authorities, which may then use the powers vested in them under national legislation. See Art 20(6) of Regulation 1/2003.

[25] Recital 6. This wording is not found in the original regulation proposal. See Proposal for a Regulation (n 21).

[26] Case C-365/12 P, *European Commission v EnBW Energie Baden-Württemberg AG*, EU:C:2014:112, para 91. This was acknowledged by the Court already in the Grand Chamber ruling in Case C-139/07 P, *European Commission v Technische Glaswerke Ilmenau GmbH*, EU:C:2010:376, see ch 6, section II.C.

The aim of the Regulation is to ensure the fullest possible effect to the right of public access to documents, but this right is by no means absolute. Article 4 of the Transparency Regulation provides for a number of exceptions, which can be divided into two different categories. The first category comprises absolute exceptions, covering cases where access is automatically refused. This may be for reasons of public security, defence, international relations, economic, monetary or financial policy, or the privacy and integrity of individuals. The second category consists of relative exceptions, where access is refused unless there is an overriding public interest in disclosure. This may include denying access to protect the commercial interests of a firm or a private individual, legal advice, the decision-making process or ongoing investigations. When the Commission receives requests for access to its cartel case files, it often invokes the relative exceptions that are found in Article 4(2) and (3) of the Transparency Regulation. Article 4(2) reads:

> The institutions shall refuse access to a document where disclosure would undermine the protection of:
>
> - commercial interests of a natural or legal person, including intellectual property,
> - court proceedings and legal advice,
> - the purpose of inspections, investigations and audits,
>
> unless there is an overriding public interest in disclosure.

Article 4(3) reads:

> Access to a document, drawn up by an institution for internal use or received by an institution, which relates to a matter where the decision has not been taken by the institution, shall be refused if disclosure of the document would seriously undermine the institution's decision-making process, unless there is an overriding public interest in disclosur[e].

Thus, while the Regulation aims at providing the fullest possible access to documents, and while any limitations to this right should be interpreted narrowly, Article 4 provides leeway to institutions that, for one reason or another, wish to keep certain documents out of reach to the general public. This was also noted by the former European Ombudsman Jacob Söderman. When he commented on the draft regulation, he made the following remark:

> Last week, the Commission published its proposal for a Regulation. I am sorry to say that this document seems to consist mainly of a long and obscure list of possible reasons to deny access to documents. This cannot be what was intended when the Treaty of Amsterdam was drafted.[27]

The exceptions listed in the draft were essentially the same as those in the final version of the Regulation. As will be discussed further in chapter 6, the Commission

[27] Available at www.ombudsman.europa.eu/sv/speech/en/355.

has been prone to invoke these exceptions when receiving requests for access to its files, be it requests to access the entire file or just the statement of contents.[28]

C. Third Party Access Through National Courts

As is further explored in chapter 7, third parties may also seek access to documents from the Commission's case files through national courts. These courts can either order disclosure from the cartelists themselves or, in follow-on actions, from the competition authorities. While national rules govern any disclosure orders directed towards national competition authorities, Regulation 1/2003 governs the relationship with the Commission and provides national courts with the possibility to request documents from the Commission.

More precisely, Article 15 of Regulation 1/2003 governs the Commission's cooperation with national courts, and the Commission has also issued a Notice where it describes its procedures in these matters.[29] Cooperation between the Commission and national courts may take various forms, but Article 15(1) of Regulation 1/2003 governs transmission of information. The Article stipulates that, in proceedings for the application of Article 101 or 102 TFEU, the courts of the Member States may ask the Commission to transmit to them information in its possession. National courts may also ask for the Commission's opinion on questions concerning the application of the two antitrust provisions. The provision thus only grants the courts the right to request documents or opinions from the Commission, but imposes no obligation on the part of the Commission to actually grant such requests. As will be explored in more detail in chapter 7, case law from the EU Courts sheds light on the issue, establishing that the principle of sincere cooperation under Article 4(3) of the TEU requires the Commission to assist national courts, save for in those situations where a national court cannot guarantee the protection of confidential information or business secrets or where the disclosure of the requested information would be capable of interfering with the functioning and independence of the Union.[30] This view is also reflected in the Commission's Notice.[31]

The possibilities for national courts to rely on Article 15 of Regulation 1/2003 has been limited through the adoption of the Damages Directive. Article 6(10) of the Directive imposes an obligation on the Member States to ensure that – within the frame of damages proceedings – national courts may only request documents from the Commission when the evidence cannot reasonably be obtained from

[28] See eg Case T-437/08, *CDC Hydrogen Peroxide v Commission*, EU:T:2011:752.

[29] Commission Notice on the cooperation between the Commission and the courts of the EU Member States in the application of Articles 81 and 82 EC [2004] OJ C101/04.

[30] The duty of sincere cooperation laid down in Art 4(3) TEU includes a mutual legal obligation for the EU and its Member States to assist each other in carrying out the tasks that flow from the Treaties.

[31] Commission Notice (n 29) paras 21–26.

anyone else. Furthermore, certain types of evidence, such as leniency statements and settlement submissions, should never be disclosed.[32] While the wording of the Article does not explicitly prevent national courts from making requests for these types of documents, the Commission is not likely to receive any such requests, given that the evidence may not be used in court.

D. Information Exchange between the Commission and the NCAs

Cartel victims in pursuit of evidence will have to rely on rules that were, at least originally, motivated by a desire to ensure an EU administration characterised by notions such as accountability, democracy and legitimacy. The rules presented under this section pursue another goal: to ensure effective application of the EU competition rules.

In 2004, the powers to apply Articles 101 and 102 TFEU were decentralised. As from 1 May 2004, several NCAs can thus simultaneously investigate the same infringement, and apply Articles 101 and 102 TFEU in parallel. In order to ensure not only consistency and coherency, but also effective and efficient application of the EU competition rules, the enforcement system is based on coordination and close cooperation between the competition authorities. This was also envisaged by the legislator, and the cooperation between the Commission and the NCAs is governed by Regulation 1/2003 and the Network Notice. The rules on information exchange are presented in sections I.D.i and I.D.ii. The present study is not limited to information exchange between members of the ECN. The EU has also negotiated bilateral cooperation agreements with a number of third country governments. These cooperation agreements are briefly presented in section I.D.iii, while a more in-depth discussion on the information exchange carried out under these agreements is found in chapter 3.

i. Regulation 1/2003

The need for close cooperation among the competition authorities is stressed already in the recitals to the Regulation. Recital 15 requires the Commission and the NCAs to 'form together a network of public authorities applying the Community competition rules in close cooperation'. For that purpose, the recitals declare, 'it is necessary to set up arrangements for information and consultation. Further modalities for the cooperation within the network will be laid down and revised by the Commission, in close cooperation with the Member States.'

[32] Art 6(6). Other evidence, such as information that was prepared by a natural or legal person specifically for the proceedings of a competition authority, may be disclosed only after the competition authority has closed its proceedings.

Recital 16 governs information exchange, and declares that notwithstanding any national provision to the contrary, the exchange of information and the use of such information in evidence should be allowed between the members of the network even where the information is confidential. This information may be used for the application of the two Treaty articles, as well as for the parallel application of national competition law, provided that the latter application relates to the same case and does not lead to a different outcome. The recital further declares that when the information exchanged is used by the receiving authority to impose sanctions on undertakings, there should be no other limit to the use of the information than the obligation to use it for the purpose for which it was collected. This given the fact that the sanctions imposed on undertakings are of the same type in all systems, and that the rights of defence enjoyed by undertakings in the various systems can be considered as sufficiently equivalent. However, as regards natural persons, the recitals take note of the fact that they may be subject to substantially different types of sanctions across the various systems. Where that is the case, it is necessary to ensure that information can only be used if it has been collected in a way that respects the same level of protection of the rights of defence of natural persons as provided for under the national rules of the receiving authority.

The statements made in the recitals are mirrored in the operative parts of the Regulation. Article 11 requires the Commission and the NCAs to apply Articles 101 and 102 TFEU in close cooperation. The Commission has an obligation to transmit to the NCAs copies of the most important documents it has collected with the view to applying Articles 7, 8, 9, 10 and Article 29(1) of the Regulation.[33] At the request of an NCA, the Commission shall provide it with a copy of other existing documents necessary for the assessment of the case.

Article 12 is dedicated to the exchange of information between competition authorities. It grants the Commission and the NCAs the power to, for the purpose of applying Articles 101 and 102 TFEU, 'provide one another with and use in evidence any matter of fact or of law, including confidential information'. Article 12(2) imposes limits on the use of the information exchanged, stating that it shall only be used in evidence for the purpose of applying Article 101 or Article 102 TFEU and in respect of the subject matter for which it was collected by the transmitting authority. However, where national competition law is applied in the same case and in parallel to EU competition law and does not lead to a different outcome, information exchanged under the Article may also be used for the application of national competition law. As some but not all Member States may impose sanctions on natural persons, there are further restrictions on the use of information exchanged in Article 12(3). The provision stipulates that information

[33] Art 7 deals with the finding and termination of infringements, Art 8 governs interim measures and Art 9 concerns commitments. Art 10 lays down the procedure for the finding of inapplicability of Article 101 TFEU. Art 29(1) governs withdrawals of exceptions.

exchanged can only be used in evidence to impose sanctions on natural persons where:

- the law of the transmitting authority foresees sanctions of a similar kind in relation to an infringement of Article 101 or 102 TFEU or, in the absence thereof,
- the information has been collected in a way which respects the same level of protection of the rights of defence of natural persons as provided for under the national rules of the receiving authority. However, in this case, the information exchanged cannot be used by the receiving authority to impose custodial sanctions.

This in order to make sure that the defence rights of the individuals are duly safeguarded.

Furthermore, Article 28 limits the use of information collected by the Commission during an investigation, declaring that it shall be used only for the purpose for which it was acquired. The Commission is also prevented from disclosing information covered by professional secrecy. However, these obligations are without prejudice to Article 12, and the Commission is thus allowed to share information – including business secrets and other confidential information – with the NCAs. However, the Article imposes an obligation on the officials of the NCAs not to disclose information acquired that constitutes business secrets or is protected by professional secrecy. Thus, while confidential information may be shared with the NCAs, it may not reach any further.

ii. The Network Notice

The Network Notice presents the main principles of the functioning of the network. It declares that the NCAs and the Commission act in the public interest and cooperate closely in order to protect competition. The ECN is a forum for discussion and cooperation in the application and enforcement of EU competition policy. According to the Notice, it provides a framework for the cooperation of European competition authorities in cases where Articles 101 and 102 TFEU are applied, and is the basis for the creation and maintenance of a common competition culture in Europe. The ECN should ensure both an efficient division of work and an effective and consistent application of the EU competition rules.

Paragraph 26 of the Network Notice acknowledges that a key element of the functioning of the network is the power of all the competition authorities to exchange and use information that has been collected by them for the purpose of applying Articles 101 and 102 TFEU. This power is a precondition for efficient and effective allocation and handling of cases, the Commission declares. While information exchange is considered key to a well-functioning enforcement system in the EU, the Network Notice acknowledges that not all exchanges of information will lead to an effective and consistent application of the EU competition rules. As discussed in chapter 3, the Network Notice contains certain provisions dealing with information obtained by leniency applicants, and which to some extent limit the possibilities to exchange of information.

iii. Bilateral Relations with Non-EU Governments

In today's global economy cartels often cross the boundaries of jurisdictions, and these international cartels tend to be even more complex, broader in scope, larger in terms of affected volumes of commerce and more harmful to consumers than their domestic counterparts.[34] This development towards 'sophisticated multinational' cartels has made competition authorities more dependent on one another. At bilateral level, the Commission has engaged in a wide range of cooperation activities with competition authorities in a number of third countries on the basis of bilateral agreements or memoranda of understanding. The nature of such cooperation varies between countries and can cover coordination of enforcement actions, sharing of information on cases of mutual interest, dialogue on competition policy issues and, in some cases, also capacity-building support.[35] In its *Manual of Procedures*, the Commission declares that dedicated cooperation agreements in competition matters have been concluded with the United States, Canada, Japan, Korea and Switzerland. Principal elements of these agreements are mutual information, coordination of enforcement activities and exchange of non-confidential information. The agreements also contain provisions on the possibility for one party to request the other to take enforcement action, and for one party to take into account the important interests of the other party in the course of its enforcement activities.[36] They usually allow for exchange of non-confidential information, consultations, periodic visits and exchange of staff between the signatories.[37] However, as will be discussed in chapter 3, the bilateral agreement concluded with Switzerland allows for deeper cooperation, as confidential information may be exchanged without prior consent from the undertakings targeted by the authorities' investigations. The agreement is a so-called 'second generation agreement'.

[34] www.justice.gov/atr/speech/international-cartels-intersection-between-fcpa-violations-and-antitrust-violations. An OECD report of 2014 shows that in recent years, more than 90% of fines against cartels by the US authorities have been international. The number of cartel cases investigated in the EU involving a participant from outside the Union had increased by over 450% since 1990. See *Challenges of International Cooperation in Competition Law Enforcement* (OECD, 2014).

[35] https://ec.europa.eu/competition/international/overview/index_en.html.

[36] *Antitrust Manual of Procedures, Internal DG Competition Working Documents on Procedures for the Application of Articles 101 and 102 TFEU* (March 2012) 55.

[37] F Jenny, *International Cooperation on Competition: Myth, Reality and Perspective*, The University of Minnesota Law School Conference on Global Antitrust Law and Policy, Minneapolis, 20–21 September 2002, available at www.iilj.org/wp-content/uploads/2017/02/Jenny-International-Cooperation-on-Competition-2002.pdf.

2

Fundamental Rights Protection in the EU

In the previous chapter, the principle of transparency and the rules governing access to documents were presented. As was discussed in section I.A, openness and transparency became buzzwords in the wake of the Danish rejection of the Maastricht Treaty, and this in turn lead to a number of legislative changes aiming at greater transparency and accountability. To the general public, the principle of transparency thus gained its way into the EU legal order as an attempt to remedy a perceived democratic deficit and to guarantee the legitimacy of the EU by allowing citizens to monitor the decision-making process. However, as noted by Prechal and de Leeuw, the principle of transparency also plays an important role at a more concrete administrative level, and is then often related to individual rights, such as the right to be heard and the right of the defence.[1] At this level, the principle dates back to the early days of European cooperation, and was first applied by the ECJ in the field of competition law as far back as in the 1960s, when the Court recognised the right of access to the file as part of the rights of the defence.[2] The principle is thus not only aimed at securing the public goals of democracy and legitimacy, it also aims at safeguarding the fundamental rights of individuals.

The present chapter will serve as a basis for the discussion of fundamental rights issues throughout this work. It opens with a presentation of the history behind EU fundamental rights protection in section I. This is followed by a discussion in section II of the role of the ECHR in the EU legal system, which will allow the reader to understand the relevance of any references made in this work

[1] S Prechal and M de Leeuw, 'Transparency: A General Principle of EU Law?' in U Bernitz, J Nergelius and C Cardner (eds), *General Principles of EC Law in a Process of Development* (Alphen aan den Rijn, Kluwer Law International, 2008) 201, 204.

[2] See eg Case 56/64, *Établissements Consten SàRL and Grundig-Verkaufs-GmbH v Commission of the European Economic Community*, EU:C:1966:41 (*Consten and Grundig*), where Consten and Grundig claimed that there had been a breach of their defence rights in that the Commission had not communicated to them the entire contents of the case file. Acknowledging that the applicants must be informed of the facts upon which the Commission's complaints are based, it was not considered necessary that the entire content of the file should be communicated to them. As the Commission's statement included all the facts the knowledge of which was necessary to ascertain which complaints had been taken into consideration, the ECJ did not consider there to be a violation of the applicants' defence rights in that respect.

to the ECHR or the case law of the European Court of Human Rights (ECtHR or 'the Strasbourg Court'). As will be further explored in this chapter, the ECHR has entered EU law more or less through the back door, leaving the ECJ with the rather difficult task of reconciling its integrationist agenda with ECHR fundamental rights protection. A further issue addressed in this chapter is the criminal nature of the sanctions imposed in competition law cases. As is shown in section III, the Strasbourg Court considers the ECHR to be a living instrument, and over the years it has gradually broadened the scope of the notion 'criminal sanction' under Article 6 ECHR. At the same time, it has set different standards of protection depending on whether or not a sanction is to be considered as criminal within the core meaning of the term. Thus, in order to establish the right of protection to be afforded to companies targeted by the Commission's cartel investigations, it is necessary first to determine whether the sanctions are of a criminal nature, and if so, if they are considered hard-core criminal sanctions. In section III it is concluded that the fines imposed on competition law offenders are of a criminal nature but come within the wider meaning of the term. Section IV of this chapter briefly presents the fundamental rights affecting targeted companies' possibilities to access the documents in the Commission's case file. These rights will be examined in more detail in chapter 4.

I. Historic Background to EU Fundamental Rights Protection

When the Treaty of Rome entered into force in January 1958, no mention was made of fundamental rights. In fact, it is unlikely that the founding fathers even considered these issues while drafting the Treaty. Much has happened since then. Today fundamental rights feature prominently in the EU legal order, and are reflected in almost every area of EU law. This work, and the areas of law that it covers, constitutes no exception. Decisions on access to documents involve a number of fundamental rights considerations, and the Charter plays an important role in this aspect. Not only does it provide EU citizens with a right to good administration and a right of access to documents,[3] it also protects the right to privacy and the right of the defence, encompassing the principle of equality of arms and the right to be heard. This section gives a brief background to the development of fundamental rights protection in the EU, in order to illustrate how the rules have gained in importance over the years and are now playing in the same division as the EU competition rules.

In the early days of European integration there was a clear dividing line between the different routes taken to achieve lasting peace in Western Europe. The European peace project was standing on two separate but equally important

[3] Arts 41 and 42 respectively.

limbs, both seeking greater unity between the Western European states.[4] One was the EEC, striving for market integration, the other the Strasbourg-based European Council and Court, safeguarding fundamental rights protection. It soon became apparent that it was not possible to maintain a strict division between the two regimes, and over the years the ECJ has had to develop its own fundamental rights jurisdiction, the initial reason being the adoption of the doctrines of direct effect and supremacy in the 1960s, allowing individuals to invoke EU law provisions before national courts and requiring those courts to let all EU rules take precedence over national rules of any type.[5] By adopting these doctrines, the ECJ soon faced opposition from especially the German and Italian constitutional courts. These courts did not accept such supremacy, as it implied that the fundamental rights protected by their constitutions would be at stake. Facing an ever-growing criticism, the Court had to find a solution to the problem created by the dichotomy between EU law and national constitutions. The solution opted for by the ECJ was to let fundamental rights become general principles of Community law. Thus, in *Stauder v City of Ulm*, the Court declared that the provision at issue contained nothing capable of prejudicing the fundamental human rights enshrined in the general principles of Community law and protected by the Court.[6]

What Vajda describes as 'the discovery of general principles of Community law'[7] was developed further by the ECJ in the well-known case of *Internationale Handelsgesellschaft*,[8] where the Court held fundamental rights to form part of the general principles of EU law. It further declared that it was not only obliged to uphold and safeguard these rights. When doing so, it should be guided by the constitutional traditions of the Member States.[9] The subsequent *Nold* ruling reinforced the stance taken by the Court and added a little more flesh to the bones. Here, the ECJ explicitly referred to international treaties that Member States had ratified as guidelines to be followed within the framework of EU law.[10] In safeguarding the fundamental rights, the Court considered itself bound to draw inspiration from the constitutional traditions common to the Member States and the international treaties for the protection of human rights on which the Member States had collaborated or to which they were signatories.[11] Although

[4] The Treaty of Rome declared in its preamble that the Member States were determined to lay the foundations of an ever-closer union among the peoples of Europe and, according to the preamble of the ECHR, the Council of Europe aimed at achieving greater unity among its members.

[5] The case *Costa v ENEL* being considered as the landmark ruling; Case 6/64, *Flaminio Costa v ENEL*, EU:C:1964:66.

[6] Ibid para 7.

[7] C Vajda, 'The Application of the EU Charter of Fundamental Rights; Neither Reckless nor Timid?' *Edinburgh School of Law Research Paper, 2014/47, Europa Working Paper No 2014/99* (November 2014) 2.

[8] Case 11/70, *Internationale Handelsgesellschaft mbH v Einfuhr- und Vorratsstelle für Getreide und Futtermittel*, EU:C:1970:114.

[9] Ibid para 4.

[10] Case 4/73, *Nold KG v European Commission*, EU:C:1974:51.

[11] Ibid para 13.

referring to international treaties, the Court did not explicitly mention the ECHR. It was not until all Member States had ratified the ECHR that the Court made explicit mention of the Convention.[12] In *Rutili* the Court acknowledged that it drew inspiration from the ECHR, and even referred to specific provisions of the Convention.[13]

Although not at the same pace, the Court's jurisprudence has been accompanied by legislative measures. Political initiatives by the EU institutions to introduce fundamental rights protection have centred mainly on two possible methods: accession to the ECHR or the adoption of a separate EU bill of rights. Eventually, the Member States opted for both methods, as the Lisbon Treaty has not only committed the EU to accede to the ECHR but has also made the Charter legally binding and has given it the same legal status as the Treaties.[14] That said, the way towards a proper bill of rights and ECHR accession has been – and still appears to be – a painstaking expedition. While keeping alive the debate on human rights in the EU, early initiatives to legislate foundered, largely through lack of an adequate legal basis for accession to the ECHR, but also due to a lack of consensus among the Member States on the principle or the form of EU human rights guarantees.[15] In 1973, the European Parliament adopted a Resolution concerning the protection of the fundamental rights of Member States' citizens when EU law is drafted,[16] and in 1977 it adopted another on the granting of special rights to the citizens of the European Community.[17] The European Parliament issued a declaration of political principle on the definition of fundamental rights in February 1977, which was subsequently adopted by the Council and the Commission.[18] At the Copenhagen European Council in 1978, the Heads of State and Government issued the 'Declaration on Democracy', which confirmed their will

> [t]o ensure that the cherished values of their legal, political and moral order are respected and to safeguard the principles of representative democracy, of the rule of law, of social justice and of respect for human rights.[19]

In a 1979 resolution, the European Parliament urged accession by the EU to the ECHR and envisaged the drafting of a European Charter of Civil Rights. Further resolutions in 1983 and 1984 emphasised the need to incorporate fundamental rights into the EU in a constitutional manner, and in 1989 the European

[12] Case 36/75, *Roland Rutili v Ministre de l'intérieur*, EU:C:1975:137, para 32.

[13] Ibid.

[14] Art 6 TEU. See also V Miller, 'Human Rights in the EU: The Charter of Fundamental Rights', *Research Paper 00/32*, House of Commons Library, 9.

[15] Ibid.

[16] European Parliament Resolution concerning the protection of the fundamental rights of Member States' citizens when EU law is drafted [1973] OJ C26/32.

[17] European Parliament Resolution on special rights to be granted to the citizens of the European Community [1977] OJ C299/23.

[18] V Miller, 'Human Rights in the EU' (n 14) 3.

[19] Summit Conclusions, 7–8 April 1978.

Parliament proposed the adoption of a declaration of fundamental rights as part of a 'Constitution' for the EU.[20]

Treaties and amending instruments since the Treaty of Rome have made explicit references to the basis of democratic principles for all Union action. The preamble to the Single European Act of 1986 expressed the determination of the Member States to work together to promote democracy on the basis of the fundamental rights recognised in the constitutions and laws of the Member States, in the ECHR and in the European Social Charter. In November 1993, the TEU entered into force.[21] Article F[22] provided an express reference to the ECHR, stating that the Union

> [s]hall respect fundamental rights, as guaranteed by the European Convention for the Protection of Human Rights and Fundamental Freedoms … and as they result from the constitutional traditions common to the Member States, as general principles of Community law.

Subsequently, the Treaty of Amsterdam introduced the possibility of imposing sanctions on Member States that fail to respect fundamental rights.[23] This possibility was further strengthened by the Treaty of Nice, which provided that the very existence of a serious and persistent breach would be sufficient for the EU to take action to suspend the voting rights of or to impose other types of sanctions on the Member State violating fundamental rights.[24]

Despite these Treaty amendments, a widespread belief remained that more was needed, and that the Union should have its proper bill of rights. This need was not necessarily perceived as stemming from insufficient levels of protection in legal practice. It was rather at political level that the desire for codification and strengthened democratic legitimacy was strongest.[25] Consequently, in June 1999, the European Council met in Cologne and decided to draw up a charter for fundamental rights. A convention was later convened to deal with the issue of a bill of rights for Europe,[26] and to draw up a draft document in advance of the European Council in December 2000.[27] The convention took on the task, but the work

[20] European Parliament Resolution adopting the Declaration of fundamental rights and freedoms [1989] OJ C120/51.

[21] The TEU was signed in Maastricht on 7 February 1992, and entered into force on 1 November 1993, see eg http://eur-lex.europa.eu/legal-content/EN/TXT/?uri=uriserv:xy0026.

[22] Now Art 6(3) TEU.

[23] Art 7 TEU.

[24] The Treaty of Nice added the first paragraph to Art 7 TEU.

[25] See eg C McCrudden, 'The Future of the EU Charter of Fundamental Rights', available at SSRN at https://ssrn.com/abstract=299639 or http://dx.doi.org/10.2139/ssrn.299639; Ö Zetterqvist, 'The Charter of Fundamental Rights and the European Res Publica' in G Di Federico (ed), *The EU Charter of Fundamental Rights: From Declaration to Binding Instrument* (Dordrecht, Springer, 2011) 6.

[26] The convention was composed of representatives of the Heads of State and Government and of the President of the Commission, as well as of members of the European Parliament and national parliaments. Representatives of the ECJ participated as observers. Representatives of the Economic and Social Committee, the Committee of the Regions and social groups, as well as experts, were invited to give their views.

[27] Zetterqvist, 'The Charter of Fundamental Rights' (n 25) 6.

did not proceed effortlessly. Opinions differed on the purpose and value of the charter. Whereas the Member States tended towards a declaratory text that would, at most, be politically binding, the Commission and the European Parliament had the intention to draft a more significant document.[28] Despite these internal conflicts, a draft bill of rights was presented in June 2000, and the Charter was signed and proclaimed in December 2000 by the European Parliament, the Commission and the Council. As for its legal status, the Member States seem to have won the battle – the Charter was not made legally binding. The Charter is the first formal EU document that in a single text combines the whole range of civil, political, economic and social rights, as well as certain 'third generation' rights such as the right to good administration.[29] The Charter's prime objective is not to create new rights but to make existing rights more visible. Despite all the efforts put into the drafting and adoption of he Charter, it played a rather insignificant role during its first decade, being undermined by its lack of binding legal effect.

With the entry into force of the Lisbon Treaty in December 2009, the legal landscape of fundamental rights protection was redesigned. The most significant changes lie in the amendments to Article 6 TEU. The Article now protects fundamental rights under three diverse and complementary perspectives: as general principles of the EU; as defined by the Charter; and as protected by the ECHR. Article 6(1) TEU not only makes the Charter legally binding, it gives the Charter the same legal value as the treaties; Article 6(2) commits the EU to accede to the ECHR; and Article 6(3) confirms general principles as a source for fundamental rights. As accession to the ECHR is still a question for the future, the most important change at this stage is the altered legal status of the Charter. Since the entry into force of the Lisbon Treaty, the Charter has gained widespread application, and it now operates as the primary source of fundamental rights in the EU.[30]

II. The Role of the ECHR within the EU Fundamental Rights Regime

As discussed in the previous section, the ECJ has been willing to accept the rights enshrined in the ECHR as general principles of EU law ever since *Rutili*.[31] However, the Court has traditionally seen itself as free to use the ECHR as a source of inspiration rather than as a set of binding rules. In *SPUC*,[32] Advocate General

[28] D Anderson and CC Murphy, 'The Charter of Fundamental Rights: History and Prospects in Post-Lisbon Europe' *EUI Working Paper Law, 2011/08* 2.

[29] G Di Federico, 'Fundamental Rights in the EU: Legal Pluralism and Multi-Level Protection After the Lisbon Treaty' in Di Federico (ed), *The EU Charter* (n 25) 15, 40.

[30] S Douglas-Scott, 'The European Union and Human Rights After the Treaty of Lisbon' (2011) 11(4) *Human Rights Law Review* 645, 645.

[31] *Rutili* (n 12).

[32] Case C-159/90, *The Society for the Protection of Unborn Children Ireland v Stephen Grogan and Others*, EU:C:1991:378 (*SPUC*).

Van Gerven noted that the ECJ did not confer direct effect on the ECHR provisions but regarded the Convention, together with the constitutional traditions common to the Member States, as the Court's aid in determining the content of the general principles of EU law. This stance, he noted, enabled the Court, in establishing general principles of EU law, also to take into account the imperatives of the fundamental freedoms and of the EU market organisations.[33] Since then, things have changed, and the ECHR may no longer serve only as a source of inspiration to the ECJ.

An important feature of the Charter is Article 52(3). This article stipulates that, to the extent that the Charter affords rights that correspond to ECHR rights, the meaning and scope of those rights shall be the same as those laid down by the ECHR. European Union law may only derogate from the ECHR if such derogation means more extensive protection. As a result, the ECHR and the case law of the ECtHR now lay down a floor in the protection of fundamental rights by the EU.[34] More or less through the back door, the EU has thus not only committed itself to ensuring a minimum standard of protection, but has also indirectly left it to the ECHR to determine what that standard should be. To use the words of Groussot and Stavefeltdt, Article 52(3) creates a situation of 'informal accession' to the ECHR.[35] According to Weiss, Article 52(3) not only requires harmony between Charter rights and corresponding ECHR rights, but absorbs these rights into the EU legal order.[36] The obligation to observe the standards of fundamental rights protection that flow from ECHR has a constitutional status in the EU. Defining or interpreting the framework for EU fundamental rights protection can no longer be done without closely studying the ECHR. Determining the ECHR standard is necessary to determine the scope of protection afforded under EU law. Such study will no longer be a traditional comparative one but rather applied to determine how the EU law stands.

III. The Criminal Nature of Competition Law Proceedings

Chapter 4 examines targeted companies' right to access the case file. However, any assessment of the scope and standard of their rights must by necessity be

[33] Opinion of AG van Gerven in *SPUC*, EU:C:1991:249.

[34] See eg the explanations to the Charter stating that the scope of the rights are determined not only by the wording of the ECHR but also by the case law of the Strasbourg Court, and Case C-400/10 PPU, *JMcB v LE*, EU:C:2010:582, where the ECJ held that where Charter rights correspond to those in the ECHR, the Court should follow the clear and consistent jurisprudence of the ECtHR.

[35] X Groussot and E Stavefeldt, 'Accession of the EU to the ECHR: A Legally Complex Situation' in J Nergelius and E Kristoffersson (eds), *Human Rights in Contemporary European Law* (Oxford, Hart Publishing, 2015) 7, 14.

[36] W Weiss, 'Human Rights in the EU: Rethinking the Role of the European Convention on Human Rights After Lisbon' (2011) 7(1) *European Constitutional Law Review* 67.

preceded by a discussion of the nature of the sanctions imposed in cartel proceedings. As is shown in the following, these fines are considered criminal in nature both under the ECHR and the Charter. This in turn means that the standard of protection granted to companies suspected of cartel participation is higher than had the fines been considered purely administrative.

A. The View of the ECtHR

Article 23(5) of Regulation 1/2003 declares that the sanctions imposed by the Commission under the Regulation are not of a criminal law nature. The paragraph is placed at the very end of the Article, which may suggest that it is of less importance. However, from a due process perspective, the question whether cartel fines are to be considered criminal or not is of great significance. The reason is that where an offence is considered to be of a criminal nature, the procedural safeguards surrounding the matter are higher than would otherwise be the case. Thus, the question whether competition law infringements and/or the sanctions imposed on competition law offenders are of a criminal nature will determine the extent of the rights provided to companies involved in cartel cases.

To give an example, Article 6(1) ECHR establishes the right to a fair trial. The Article reads as follows:

> In the determination of his civil rights and obligations or of any criminal charge against him, everyone is entitled to a fair and public hearing within a reasonable time by an independent and impartial tribunal established by law. …[37]

Judging from its wording, the rights afforded under Article 6(1) ECHR appear to apply indistinctly to both civil rights cases and criminal cases. However, the Strasbourg Court has declared that the standard of protection will vary depending on whether or not the charge is criminal. Over the years, it has thus come to ensure different levels of protection depending on whether the procedure in question is of a civil or criminal nature, allowing Contracting States a greater margin of appreciation in civil rights cases. Procedural rights are broader and apply much more strictly when 'criminal sanctions' are imposed than when civil remedies or administrative sanctions are provided. Thus, in order to determine the level of protection to be afforded in competition law matters, it is necessary to first define the nature of the procedure under Regulation 1/2003, and the sanctions imposed by the Commission.

Contrary to what Article 23(5) of Regulation 1/2003 indicates, the sanctions imposed by the Commission do not necessarily fall outside the scope of the notion 'criminal' within the meaning of Article 6(1) ECHR. In order to ensure a

[37] See at www.hri.org/docs/ECHR50.html#C.Art6.

uniform application of the ECHR,[38] the Strasbourg Court considers the indications furnished by domestic law to have only a relative value, with the notion of 'criminal' as conceived under Article 6 ECHR being an autonomous concept.[39] This was first established in the seminal case of *Engel v the Netherlands*.[40] There the Strasbourg Court was requested to determine whether a 'charge' that the national legislator counted as disciplinary could in fact be of a criminal character under the ECHR. The question was answered in the affirmative by the Strasbourg Court, which declared that the notion of 'criminal' was autonomous and presented three criteria to be applied when deciding whether an offence is criminal in the sense of Article 6 ECHR. These criteria are:

(a) the classification of the offence in the law of the respondent state;
(b) the nature of the offence; and
(c) the nature and degree of severity of the penalty that the person concerned risked incurring.[41]

The first criterion is crucial, in that if the applicable national law classifies an offence as criminal, it automatically takes the same classification for the purposes of Article 6 too. It is only when the offence is not classified as criminal that a problem arises and the second and third criteria will come into play. As to the nature of the offence, Treschel notes that there does not appear to be any definition of the notion 'criminal offence' in case law, but that a charge is criminal in nature if it concerns a norm that is basically addressed to everyone rather than to a limited group of persons and if the sanction imposed pursues a retributive goal.[42] The third criterion concerns the possible punishment. Here, the sanction must be deterrent and punitive and not compensatory. The Strasbourg Court tends to consider the nature and severity of the possible, not the actual, punishment. A possible punishment of a modest fine that may be converted into imprisonment for more than a minimal period for non-payment may fall within Article 6, as may a substantial fine that cannot be converted into imprisonment.[43] The criteria are alternative and

[38] In *Engel*, the Strasbourg Court declared that if the Contracting States were given the powers to define the notion themselves, there was a risk that they would circumvent the rules in Art 6 ECHR by classifying an offence as disciplinary instead of criminal, or to prosecute the author of a 'mixed' offence on the disciplinary rather than criminal plane. A latitude extending thus far might lead to results incompatible with the purpose and object of the Convention. See *Engel and Others v the Netherlands* App nos 5100/71; 5101/71; 5102/71; 5354/72; 5370/72 (Judgment) (ECtHR, 8 June 1976) para 81.

[39] *Öztürk v Germany* App no 22479/93 (Judgment) (ECtHR, 21 February 1984) paras 50 and 52.

[40] See *Engel* (n 38).

[41] Ibid para 82. This basic ruling has been confirmed by the Strasbourg Court on many occasions over the years, see eg *Campbell and Fell v the United Kingdom* App nos 7819/77; 7878/77 (Judgment) (ECtHR, 28 June 1984); *Ezeh and Connors v the United Kingdom* App nos 39665/98 and 40086/98 (Judgment) (ECtHR, 9 October 2003); *AP, MP and TP v Switzerland*, App no 19958/92 (Judgment) (ECtHR, 29 August 1997); *EL, RL and JO-L v Switzerland* App no 20919/92 (Judgment) (ECtHR, 29 August 1997); and *Öztürk* (n 39).

[42] S Treschel, *Human Rights in Criminal Proceedings* (Oxford, Oxford University Press, 2006) 19.

[43] DJ Harris, M O'Boyle, EP Bates and CM Buckley, *Harris, O'Boyle and Warbrick: Law of the European Convention on Human Rights*, 4th edn (Oxford, Oxford University Press, 2018) 376.

not cumulative. It is thus sufficient to establish that either the offence or the sanction is criminal in nature.[44]

The *Engel* criteria were established already in 1976 and they still apply. There is little doubt that, for the purpose of the ECHR, the sanctions imposed by the Commission in competition cases are criminal in nature. This view was first supported in *Société Stenuit v France*,[45] where the European Commission of Human Rights considered the criminal head of Article 6 to be applicable to competition cases. In a more recent judgment, the Strasbourg Court did actually get the opportunity to consider the question of the compatibility of competition law enforcement regimes with the requirements of the ECHR. The case of *A Menarini Diagnostics SRL v Italy*[46] concerned the imposition of fines by the Italian Competition Authority, and its compatibility with Article 6 ECHR and the right to a fair trial enshrined therein.[47]

Without venturing to deeply into the matter, the case may be described as follows. A Menarini Diagnostics SRL (AMD) had been fined by the Italian Competition Authority for cartel participation under the Italian Competition Act. The structure of the Italian Competition Act and the penalties available to the Italian Competition Authority bear a striking resemblance to the EU system. AMD unsuccessfully appealed the decision to the Italian courts and then turned to Strasbourg, complaining about the limited review performed by the courts. The question that the Strasbourg Court had to answer was whether the judicial review carried out by the Italian courts fulfilled the requirements in Article 6(1) ECHR. In its ruling, it confirmed that competition law could be considered penal and subject to the protections afforded by the criminal head of Article 6(1), given the severity and repressive character of the fines imposed. However, as in earlier judgments,[48] it made a further distinction between hard-core criminal cases, requiring the decision at first instance to be made by a tribunal, and criminal cases within the wider meaning of the term. As for the latter category, decisions in such cases may be made by an administrative authority at first instance as long as they can be appealed to a tribunal with full jurisdiction.[49] The Strasbourg Court considered competition cases to belong to the latter category. Furthermore, the Court rejected AMD's main contention that there had been a breach of Article 6(1) ECHR. Instead it considered that the Italian courts – which had

[44] This, however, does not exclude a cumulative approach where separate analysis of each criterion does not make it possible to reach a clear conclusion as to the existence of a criminal charge (see *Jussila v Finland* App no 73053/01 (Judgment) (ECtHR, 23 November 2006) paras 30 and 31, and *Zaicevs v Latvia* App no 65022/01 (Judgment) (ECtHR, 31 July 2007) para 31).

[45] *Société Stenuit v France* App no 11598/85 (Judgment) (ECtHR, 27 February 1992).

[46] *A Menarini Diagnostics SRL v Italy* App no 43509/08 (Judgment) (ECtHR, 27 September 2011).

[47] Interesting to note is that the nature of the offence is not necessarily criminal in nature, see *Produkcija Plus Storitveno Podjetje DOO v Slovenia* App no 47072/15 (Judgment) (ECtHR, 23 October 2018).

[48] See eg Janosevic v Sweden App no 34619/97 (Judgment) (ECtHR, 23 July 2002); and *Bendenoun v France* App no 12547/86 (Judgment) (ECtHR, 24 February 1994).

[49] *Menarini* (n 46) para 59.

declared that they were only empowered to carry out a legality review – did in fact have full jurisdiction, because they could examine the elements of proof, verify whether the administration used the powers in an appropriate manner,[50] verify the reasonableness and proportionality of the choices within a decision, verify the technical matters[51] and change the sanction.[52]

Based on the ruling in *Menarini*, some conclusions can be drawn. First of all, the Commission's procedure in Articles 101 and 102 TFEU cases is of a criminal law nature. Second, competition cases fall outside the core meaning of the term 'criminal charge', and therefore the standard of protection required is not as high as if they would have been considered hard-core criminal cases.

B. The View of the ECJ

Despite the wording of Article 23(5) of Regulation 1/2003, the Court did not await the ruling in *Menarini* before it offered certain procedural guarantees normally reserved for criminal cases. Already in *Hüls*, the Court acknowledged that given the nature of the infringements in question and the nature and degree of severity of the ensuing penalties, the principle of the presumption of innocence should apply to competition cases that may result in the imposition of fines or periodic penalty payments.[53] The Court even referred to the case law of the Strasbourg Court, and the two cases of *Özturk*[54] and *Lutz*, the latter concerning the application of Article 6 ECHR and the principle of the presumption of innocence.[55] That said, traditionally the Court has not been willing to refer to competition cases as criminal cases but rather as administrative.[56]

Just a few months after the Strasbourg Court had delivered its ruling in *Menarini*, the ECJ delivered its rulings in the *Chalkor*[57] and *KME* cases,[58] where the parties had challenged the judicial review carried out by the General Court, claiming that it fell short of the standard required by the ECHR. The cases originated from the copper tubes cartel, where the Commission had imposed heavy fines on several companies for their participation in cartels on the two markets of copper

[50] Ibid para 63.
[51] Ibid para 64.
[52] Ibid para 65.
[53] Case C-199/92 P, *Hüls AG v European Commission*, EU:C:1999:358, para 150.
[54] *Öztürk* (n 39).
[55] *Lutz v Germany* App no 9912/82 (Judgment) (ECtHR, 25 August 1987).
[56] See eg Joined Cases 46/87 and 227/88, *Hoechst AG v Commission of the European Communities*, EU:C:1989:337, para 15, where the Court discusses the right of the defence in competition cases, stating that 'the right of the defence must be observed in administrative procedures which may lead to the imposition of fines'.
[57] Case C-386/10 P, *Chalkor v Commission*, EU:C:2011:815.
[58] Case C-272/09 P, *KME v Commission*, EU:C:2011:810; and Case C-389/10 P, *KME v Commission*, EU:C:2011:816.

industrial tubes and copper plumbing tubes respectively. Both companies were unsuccessful in their appeals against the decisions to the General Court. Turning to the ECJ, KME and Chalkor criticised the General Court's willingness to grant the Commission a margin of discretion when it came to the calculation and imposition of fines – an area where the Commission has traditionally enjoyed a wide margin of discretion, when it comes both to the choice of factors to be taken into account when calculating fines and the assessment of such factors. The companies argued that the Commission should not enjoy any margin of discretion in this area as the EU Courts have full jurisdiction to review the fines imposed. According to them, the General Court had infringed their right to a full and effective judicial review under Article 47 of the Charter by failing to examine their arguments closely and thoroughly, and had deferred, to an excessive and unreasonable extent, to the Commission's discretion.

In her Opinion, Advocate General Sharpston simply chose to apply the *Engel* criteria.[59] When doing this, she had

> little difficulty in concluding that the procedure whereby a fine is imposed for breach of the prohibition on price-fixing and market-sharing agreements in Article 81(1) EC falls under the 'criminal head' of Article 6 ECHR as progressively defined by the European Court of Human Rights.[60]

The Advocate General based her conclusion on the arguments that

> the prohibition and the possibility of imposing a fine are enshrined in primary and secondary legislation of general application; the offence involves engaging in conduct which is generally regarded as underhand, to the detriment of the public at large, a feature which it shares with criminal offences in general and which entails a clear stigma; a fine of up to 10% of annual turnover is undoubtedly severe, and may even put an undertaking out of business; and the intention is explicitly to punish and deter, with no element of compensation for damage.[61]

The Court was more hesitant in its approach towards the ECHR, making no reference to either the *Engel* criteria or the Convention itself. However, declaring that the principle of effective judicial protection is a general principle of EU law to which expression is now given by Article 47 of the Charter, the Court declared that the General Court should not allow the Commission any margin of discretion when determining the fines. Instead, the General Court should carry out a full review, both in law and fact, of the Commission's decision to impose fines. By doing so, the Court implicitly ensured that the General Court's standard of review meets the standard of review required by the Strasbourg Court in competition cases, or more generally in criminal cases within the wider meaning of the term.

[59] Opinion of AG Sharpston in Case C-272/09 P, *KME v European Commission*, EU:C:2011:63, para 63.

[60] Ibid para 64.

[61] Ibid.

The foregoing allows us to conclude not only that fundamental rights are firmly established at the top of the EU norm hierarchy, but also that competition cases are considered criminal in nature, and companies targeted by the Commission's investigation should therefore be afforded a higher standard of fundamental rights protection than had these cases been considered purely administrative. The following section provides a brief presentation of the rights that may come into play when parties to an investigation seek access to the Commission's case file. A more in-depth analysis is provided in chapter 4.

IV. The Legal Framework Surrounding Party Access

A company targeted by the Commission's investigation has an obvious and legitimate interest in accessing the Commission's case file. As any sanctions imposed are of a criminal nature, failure to grant the company access to the file may violate a number of fundamental rights. Whereas the following sections provide a brief presentation of the rules surrounding party access, a more in-depth analysis of these rights is provided in chapter 4.

A. The Treaties

Unlike the right of public access, there is no treaty article explicitly acknowledging a right to party access. This does not mean that no such right can be derived from the treaties. While Article 2 TEU declares that the Union is founded on the respect for human rights, Article 6 TEU adds some flesh to the bones, declaring that the Union recognises the rights, freedoms and principles set out in the Charter, and acknowledging that the fundamental rights, as guaranteed by the ECHR and the constitutional traditions of the Member States, constitute general principles of EU law. Before the Charter was made legally binding, general principles such as the right of the defence and the right to be heard formed the basis for any right to access the file. While the Court has acknowledged these rights as general principles of EU law ever since the early days of European cooperation, the Maastricht Treaty was the first treaty explicitly acknowledging that the Union shall respect fundamental rights as guaranteed by the ECHR and as they result from the constitutional traditions common to the Member States, as general principles of EU law.[62] Today, the right to be heard, the right of the defence and the right to access one's file are all laid down in the Charter.

[62] Art F(2)

B. The Charter

As noted by Leino-Sandberg, the balance in EU administration has traditionally weighed in favour of institutional interests, allowing the institutions to emphasise efficiency, flexibility and both substantive and procedural discretion.[63] The idea of good administration as a right of citizens was introduced at EU level during the drafting of the Charter. In a public hearing on the draft, Jacob Söderman, the European Ombudsman at the time, argued that a right to good administration should be included in the Charter based on the idea that the citizen has a right to have his or her affairs dealt with properly, fairly and promptly by an open, accountable and service-minded administration.[64] The final version of Article 41 came to include many of the elements suggested, as the Article establishes the right for every person to have his or her affairs handled impartially, fairly and within reasonable time by the EU institutions. Article 41(2) declares that this right includes the right to be heard and the right to have access to one's file. Furthermore, the administration must state the reasons for its decisions. Thus, the right ensures that the individual is involved and duly informed of the actions taken by the administration, reflecting also the principle of transparency. However, in competition matters, it also ensures that targeted companies' defence rights are safeguarded.

C. Regulation 1/2003

Regulation 1/2003 contains a number of provisions that aim to guarantee the right of access to the file. Already Recital 32 addresses the matter by acknowledging that the undertakings concerned should be accorded the right to be heard by the Commission and that it is essential to ensure the right of the defence of the undertakings concerned, in particular the right of access to the file. Article 27(2) governs access to the file. The article declares that the rights of defence of the parties concerned shall be fully respected in the proceedings. They shall be entitled to have access to the Commission's file, subject to the legitimate interest of undertakings in the protection of their business secrets. The right is subject to further limitations as the article declares that the right of access to the file shall not extend to confidential information or internal documents of the Commission or NCAs. In particular, the right of access shall not extend to correspondence between the Commission and the NCAs, or between the latter.

[63] P Leino, 'Efficiency, Citizens and Administrative Culture. The Politics of Good Administration in the EU' (2014) 20(4) *European Public Law* 681, 681.

[64] Ibid 682, where reference is made to a speech given on 2 February 2000, available at www.ombudsman.europa.eu/sv/speech/en/355.

D. Regulation 773/2004

Regulation 773/2004 ('the Procedural Regulation')[65] governs the conduct of the Commission's proceedings in more detail. Articles 15 and 16 lay down the Commission's procedures for granting access to the file and treatment of confidential information. It follows from Article 15 that access to the file is only granted upon request from the parties and following the notification of the statement of objections. There are certain exceptions. Article 15(1)(a) stipulates that after the initiation of proceedings pursuant to Article 11(6) of Regulation 1/2003 and in order to enable the parties to introduce settlement submissions, the Commission shall disclose to them the objections envisaged against them and non-confidential versions of any specified accessible document listed in the case file at that point in time. When introducing their settlement submissions, the parties shall confirm to the Commission that they will only require access to the file if the statement of objections does not reflect the contents of their settlement submissions. Where settlement discussions have been discontinued with one or more of the parties, such party shall be granted access to the file when a statement of objections has been addressed to it. Furthermore, Article 15(1)(b) declares that access to leniency statements and settlement submissions shall only be granted at the premises of the Commission. The parties and their representatives may not copy the leniency corporate statements or settlement submissions by any mechanical or electronic means.

Article 15(2) mirrors Article 27 of Regulation 1/2003 and declares that the right of access shall not extend to business secrets or confidential information. However, this does not mean that the Commission is prevented from disclosing or using information necessary to prove an infringement of Article 101 or 102 TFEU.[66]

As will be discussed in chapter 4, there are a number of soft law instruments, such as the Commission's Notice on access to the file and its *Manual of Procedures*, that provide further guidance on the Commission's practices in these cases.[67]

[65] Commission Regulation (EC) No 773/2004 of 7 April 2004 relating to the conduct of proceedings by the Commission pursuant to Articles 81 and 82 of the EC Treaty [2004] OJ L123/18.

[66] Art 15(3).

[67] Commission Notice on the rules for access to the Commission file in cases pursuant to Articles 81 and 82 of the EC Treaty, Articles 53, 54 and 57 of the EEA Agreement and Council Regulation (EC) No 139/2004, [2005] OJ C325/07; and *Antitrust Manual of Procedures, Internal DG Competition Working Documents on Procedures for the Application of Articles 101 and 102 TFEU* (March 2012).

PART II

National Competition Authorities

3

Information Exchange between Competition Authorities

The words 'no man is an island' can also be applied to competition authorities. In today's global economy, cartels often cross the boundaries of jurisdictions, and these international cartels tend to be even more complex, broader in scope, larger in terms of affected volumes of commerce and more harmful to consumers than their domestic counterparts.[1] This development towards 'sophisticated multinational' cartels has made competition authorities more dependent on one another. Today, proving a competition law infringement often requires cooperation with other competition authorities. The European Commission is no exception. In a speech made by the Director General of DG COMP in the autumn of 2018, he assured the audience that the Commission not only talks the talk, it also walks the walk:

> As far as the European Commission is concerned, this is not merely talking the talk. We now cooperate with sister agencies in all cases with significant implications beyond our jurisdiction. Between 2010 and 2017 – to give you some figures – we cooperated with competition agencies outside of the EU in 65% of all cartel cases and in 54% of complex merger cases. There is no doubt that we also walk the walk.[2]

A valuable component in the cooperation between competition authorities is information exchange. The Commission considers that the power of all the competition authorities within the ECN to exchange and use information is a key element of the functioning of the network.[3] On a similar note, the OECD encourages its member countries to support information exchange between competition authorities, and the ICN has manuals for the management of information exchange.[4]

[1] www.justice.gov/atr/speech/international-cartels-intersection-between-fcpa-violations-and-antitrust-violations. An OECD report of 2014 shows that in recent years, more than 90% of fines against cartels by the US authorities have been international. The number of cartel cases investigated in the EU involving a participant from outside the Union had increased by over 450% since 1990. See *Challenges of International Cooperation in Competition Law Enforcement* (OECD, 2014).

[2] J Laitenberger, 'Developments in EU Competition Control in the Global and Digital Age', speech made at the Fordham Antitrust Law and Policy Conference, New York, September 2018.

[3] Commission Notice on cooperation within the Network of Competition Authorities [2004] OJ C101/43.

[4] ICN, *Anti-Cartel Enforcement Manual*, ch 9, 'International Cooperation and Information Sharing', available at www.internationalcompetitionnetwork.org/wp-content/uploads/2018/05/CWG_ACEMInternationalCooperationInfosharing.pdf.

However, information exchange between competition authorities requires careful manoeuvring. Not only is there a risk that the fundamental rights of targeted undertakings and their employees are not adequately protected when information is transmitted from one authority to another, there is also a risk that leniency systems are negatively affected if information that has been submitted to a competition authority within the frame of a leniency programme is later exchanged with other authorities pursuing parallel proceedings under their domestic laws.

Whereas the competition authorities' interest in close cooperation and information exchange may be evident, it is nonetheless of interest to discuss whether such cooperation must necessarily involve an exchange of information collected during the course of cartel investigations, or whether other, less intrusive forms can also provide effective and meaningful cooperation. This is followed by a discussion of fundamental rights. The concern needs to be addressed that fundamental rights – such as the right of the defence, but also the right to privacy – are not adequately safeguarded when information is exchanged. This chapter provides a brief exposé of the rights in question, and discusses the risks involved in failing to ensure adequate fundamental rights protection. This is followed by a presentation of the Commission's information exchange with other authorities within the ICN. The work carried out within the network is more policy orientated, and any information exchange is governed by bi- or multilateral agreements between individual members of the ICN. For this reason, the bilateral relations with the USA and Switzerland have been selected and are examined in sections IV.C and IV.D. The agreement between the EU and the US was concluded already in 1991, and is a so called 'first generation agreement', which excludes the exchange of confidential information from its scope of application. The agreement between the EU and Switzerland on the other hand is a 'second generation agreement', also allowing the parties to exchange confidential information. The chapter concludes with a more detailed analysis of the rules governing information exchange within the ECN.

I. Information Exchange – A Sine Qua Non of Effective Cartel Enforcement?

In its report on challenges of international cooperation in competition law enforcement, the OECD notes that while international trade has increased dramatically since 1990, the enforcement of competition law has remained primarily a domestic exercise.[5] Historically, only a limited number of authorities have engaged in international cooperation, but this number has increased over time. Until the 1990s, the need for cooperation was relatively limited as few states had competition rules

[5] OECD, *Challenges of International Cooperation* (n 1) 9.

in place, and only a handful authorities around the world actually did enforce competition laws in a cross-border context. Moreover, the OECD report notes, the bilateral relationship between Brussels and Washington covered most of the need for cooperation in those days.[6] Since then, the picture has changed. In today's global economy, cartels and mergers often cross the boundaries of jurisdictions, and competition law has gone global. The OECD notes that during the period 1990 to 2014, the number of jurisdictions enforcing competition rules increased from fewer than 20 to about 120.[7]

In 2012, the OECD and the ICN carried out a joint survey on international enforcement cooperation, with the aim to better understand experiences of competition agencies in case-related enforcement activities.[8] The survey showed that while many of the newer agencies tended to use cooperation broadly, as a way to build enforcement capacity, exchange experiences and share methodologies, more experienced agencies pursued international cooperation in order to facilitate investigations, by exchanging case-specific information and evidence and providing each other with investigatory assistance. A vast majority of the respondents found that international cooperation had been useful to their enforcement strategies, and many highlighted the benefits from informal case cooperation. These informal contacts often occurred at an early stage of a case and included consultation among agencies on matters such as the timeline of the investigation, the theory of harm and potential remedies in the case of merger reviews. Agencies underscored how even exchanging non-confidential information and general views on a case could be very useful in an investigation, and might also be sufficient in many cases. That said, when instruments were available for the exchange of confidential information, this was perceived as extremely beneficial.[9]

The report also took note of the fact that legal protection on the disclosure of information often was a requirement for agencies to be able to compel information in competition cases. As such, confidentiality rules are fundamental components of an agency's ability to obtain information, and ultimately are key underpinnings that facilitate international cooperation. The survey showed that exchange of non-confidential information was generally allowed and occurred frequently. Agencies typically engaged in case discussions on analytical methods for a particular case (eg product and geographic market definition) or assessment of the competitive effects of the case, and potential remedies that could be accepted. While the exchange of confidential information relied on formal mechanisms for

[6] Ibid 14.

[7] Ibid 5.

[8] The survey was addressed to 120 competition authorities of which 57% responded. The response rate among OECD members and observers was around 90%. See the executive summary of the *Report on the OECD/ICN Survey on International Enforcement Cooperation*, available at www.oecd.org/competition/globalforum/InternationalCooperationExecutiveSummaryEN.pdf.

[9] Ibid 2. A few words should be said about the notion of 'confidential'. The ICN *Manual of Procedure* defines confidential information as information that is defined as such by national law.

cooperation, the exchange of non-confidential information and internal agency information often occurred on an informal basis.[10] Yet many respondents considered that legal limitations on the exchange of confidential information were a primary impediment to international cooperation, and the survey thus identified exchanges of (confidential) information as a key area for improvement.

Following the joint survey, the Japan Fair Trade Commission submitted a proposal to the ICN on how to promote information sharing between competition authorities within the network. Acknowledging that a competition authority receiving a request for information from another authority may only transmit information to the extent permitted under its own legislation, it would be possible that information on on-going cases is not available for disclosure. In the absence of waivers or information gateways, non-confidential information exchanges may still be very useful within the framework, the proposal declared.[11]

It is not surprising that competition authorities aspire to closer cooperation and the power to exchange confidential information with sister agencies. However, cooperation may be useful even without such exchange, and – perhaps partly given the strict procedural safeguards that need to surround the exchange of confidential information – those authorities that were empowered to exchange confidential information with one or several agencies only rarely availed themselves of this possibility. Instead, the report from the joint survey shows that what the agencies considered to be the most useful form of cooperation was the informal case cooperation. As will be discussed in section III, such cooperation may never involve the exchange of confidential information, as this would infringe targeted companies' defence rights. Thus, while it may be desirable in theory, the exchange of confidential information may in practice not be the most valuable or useful form of cooperation between competition authorities.

II. The Territorial Reach of EU Competition Law

Trade flows and globalisation of competition law are not the only factors relevant to assess the need for international cooperation or, more precisely, the need for exchange of case-specific information. Also of relevance is the territorial reach of the competition rules in place. If the rules only catch activities that take place within the state in question, there may be a need for international cooperation, but such need is not likely to arise in all or even a majority of the cases pursued by the competition authority. If, on the other hand, the rules reach outside the

[10] Ibid 8.

[11] Proposal for Establishing the ICN Framework for Promotion of Sharing Non-Confidential Information for Cartel Enforcement, available at www.internationalcompetitionnetwork.org/wp-content/uploads/2018/05/CWG_nonConfidentialInfoFramework.pdf. See also P Horna, *Fighting Cross-Border Cartels – The Perspective of the Young and Small Competition Authorities* (Oxford, Hart Publishing, 2020) 72.

boundaries of the state then there is greater need for cooperation and exchange of case-specific information. Not only may the competition authority need assistance or wish to coordinate enforcement activities in individual cases, there may also be a greater interest in aligning rules and enforcement practices, and in avoiding conflicts with other enforcement authorities. As for the EU competition rules, their application reaches beyond the boundaries of the EU and catches activities that take place in third countries. Perhaps the most commonly referred Court case on extraterritorial application is *Wood Pulp*,[12] where a majority of the companies engaging in the cartel were resident outside the Union. This did not prevent the Commission from establishing an infringement of Article 101 TFEU, and imposing sanctions on the companies in question. The Commission's view was later endorsed by the Court, which declared that an agreement concluded between undertakings located outside the EU is caught by Article 101 TFEU if the agreement is 'implemented' within the Union.[13] More recently, the geographical remit of the EU competition rules became a question for the Court in *Intel*,[14] concerning the American computer chip maker's alleged abuse of dominance. In that case, neither Intel nor its rival AMD – which was also the target of Intel's exclusionary practices – was resident in the EU. Part of the Commission's case against Intel concerned its sales of chips to the Chinese computer manufacturer Lenovo, resident in Beijing. The computers implicated by those sales were relatively few, and accounted for a small share of the world market for the chips. Furthermore, it was not clear if any of them, and if so, how many, had actually reached the European Economic Area (EEA). This made Intel question the Commission's power to apply Article 102 TFEU. The Court did not accept the arguments put forward by Intel, and established jurisdiction.[15]

Thus, following *Intel*, it is now clear that the EU competition rules can reach agreements concluded outside the EU between companies also located outside the EU, and where it has not been established that the products in question have actually reached the European market. Given the wide territorial scope of the EU competition rules, it is fair to assume that situations will arise where the Commission would require the assistance from third country authorities in order

[12] Joined Cases 89, 104, 114, 116, 117 and 125 to 129/85, *A Ahlström Osakeyhtiö and Others v Commission of the European Communities*, EU:C:1988:447.

[13] Ibid para 16. See also AS Papadopoulos, *The International Dimension of EU Competition Law and Policy* (Cambridge, Cambridge University Press, 2010) 68.

[14] Case C-413/14, *Intel Corp v European Commission*, ECLI:EU:C:2017:632.

[15] Ibid paras 45–55. The Court accepted the General Court's application of a 'qualified effects test', declaring that it pursues the same objective as the implementation test, ie preventing conduct that has anticompetitive effects likely to impact the EU market. Second, the Court held that public international law allows jurisdiction when it is foreseeable that the conduct in question will have an immediate and substantial effect in the EU. For a further discussion of the jurisdictional issues raised in the *Intel* case, see EM Fox, 'Extraterritorial Jurisdiction, Antitrust, and the EU Intel Case: Implementation, Qualified Effects, and the Third Kind' (2019) 42(3) *Fordham International Law Journal* 981, Art 8. See also G Monti, 'The Global Reach of EU Competition Law' in M Cremona and J Scott (eds), *EU Law Beyond Borders: The Extraterritorial Reach of EU Law* (Oxford, Oxford University Press, 2019) 174, 186.

to be able to ensure an effective application of the EU competition rules. Likewise, other jurisdictions, with equally extensive scope of application, would want the assistance from the Commission, be it through the transmission of information or coordination of enforcement activities. Any such exchange of information requires careful manoeuvring in order to safeguard the fundamental rights of targeted companies. It is thus likely that, when investigating international cartels, the Commission may and will lawfully gather information also of relevance to the investigations of third country authorities. Cooperation between the Commission and third country competition authorities is gaining in importance, and we are likely to witness the conclusion of more cooperation agreements allowing for the exchange of case-specific information between competition authorities. When negotiating such agreements, the Commission must tread carefully and make sure that the fundamental rights of targeted undertakings are duly safeguarded.

III. Safeguarding Fundamental Rights

Article 28 of Regulation 1/2003 governs the Commission's handling of information acquired during its investigations. The first paragraph limits the use of information gathered by the Commission during the course of its investigations, and the second prevents Commission officials from disclosing information acquired pursuant to the regulation and of the kind covered by professional secrecy. Article 28(1) stipulates that, without prejudice to Articles 12 and 15, any information collected pursuant to Articles 17 to 22 shall be used only for the purpose for which it was acquired. As for the latter articles, they govern the Commission's fact-finding powers and provide the Commission with means to collect the information necessary for it to carry out its duties under the Regulation, be it through requests for information, interviews or on-the-spot inspections.[16]

When sending out a request for information under Article 18 or carrying out an inspection under Article 20, the Commission is required to state the purpose of the request or the inspection. This requirement may seem insignificant, but it actually fulfils a very important objective, and that is to safeguard the right of the defence of targeted undertakings and their employees. An inspection extending beyond the scope of the subject matter or purpose of the inspection decision will not only be deemed to infringe the right of the defence, it may also violate the undertaking's right to privacy. The requirement in Article 28 reflects the obligations in Articles 17 to 22, and ensures that the Commission does not act beyond the scope of its powers and use the information collected for purposes other than those indicated in the inspection decision or the request for information.

If the Commission cooperates with other competition authorities and transmits information collected during the course of a competition law investigation, such

[16] Interviews performed under Art 19 are voluntary.

transmission may therefore infringe both the right of the defence and the right to privacy. While the Commission and the third country competition authority may investigate the same actions or factual circumstances, the infringement investigated by the third country authority will by necessity concern restrictions of competition outside the remits of the EU and rules other than Article 101 or 102 TFEU. As the Commission's powers are limited to enforcing the EU competition rules, any inspection decision or request for information should be limited in scope to infringements of these rules and to examining the effects of any anticompetitive behaviour in the EU.[17] This in turn means that information transmitted under these premises should be considered used for another purpose than that for which it was acquired. The following sections present the Court's view on the relationship between the duty of the Commission to state and act within the purpose of an investigation and the right of the defence and the right to privacy.

A. The Right of the Defence

The right of the defence is a composite term that encompasses a number of rights, including the right to be heard, the principle of equality of arms and the right to have access to the evidence on which any accusations are based. Of particular relevance to the issues discussed in this chapter is the Court's case law concerning the scope of the Commission's powers to search for information and use the information gathered during the course of its investigations, as these cases discuss the rationale behind any limitations on the Commission's power to use such information.

Articles 17 to 22 of Regulation 1/2003 provide the Commission with a set of investigatory tools. Among these, the unannounced inspection – or dawn raid – is by far the most powerful. It is therefore not too surprising that the Court has been given ample opportunity to interpret and define the Commission's powers during dawn raids. In many of these cases, targeted companies have argued that the Commission failed to respect their right of the defence. One of the early cases is *Hoechst*, where the Court declared that the Commission's obligation to state both the purpose and subject matter of the inspection in its inspection decision was necessary in order for the undertaking to be able to assess the scope of its duty to cooperate while at the same time safeguarding the rights of the defence.[18]

Another of the early cases dealing with companies' defence rights is *Dow Benelux*,[19] where the Court stipulated that the right of the defence constitutes a fundamental principle of EU law, which must be ensured not only at the adversarial

[17] Art 4 of Regulation 1/2003.

[18] Joined Cases 46/87 and 227/88, *Hoechst AG v the Commission of the European Communities*, EU:C:1989:337, para 29. The duty to state the subject matter and purpose was also necessary in order for the company to assess whether the inspection was *justified* (emphasis added).

[19] Case C-85/87, *Dow Benelux v Commission of the European Communities*, EU:C:1989:379.

stage of a competition case, but also during preliminary inquiry procedures.[20] In the case at hand, Dow Benelux had challenged the Commission's inspection decision, arguing that it should be annulled due to the defective nature of the statement of reasons, the lack of reasonable or proper evidence as to whether or not the inspection was well-founded and, in the alternative, an infringement of the fundamental right to the inviolability of the home.[21] In its ruling, the Court acknowledged that the duty to state the subject matter and purpose of the inspection in its decision is a fundamental requirement to show that the investigation is justified, but also to enable the targeted company to assess the scope of its duty to cooperate while at the same time safeguarding its right of the defence.[22] Dow Benelux had also claimed that the evidence relied on by the Commission when adopting its inspection decision either did not constitute reasonable evidence or had been unlawfully obtained.[23] It had been established that the decision was based on information obtained during two earlier inspections, which were both unrelated to the subject matter of the challenged inspection decision. The Court acknowledged that the right of the defence prevents the Commission from relying on evidence obtained during another investigation unrelated to the subject matter or purpose of the ongoing investigation. However, the Court noted, this does not mean that the Commission is barred from initiating a new inquiry in order to verify or supplement information it happened to obtain during a previous investigation, if such information indicates the existence of anti-competitive practices.[24] This submission was thus also rejected by the Court.

A more recent case concerning the consequences of acting beyond the scope of the investigation, and using the information collected for purposes other than those stated in the inspection decision, is *Deutsche Bahn*.[25] Before the launch of a dawn raid at the premises of the German railway company, the agents who were to perform the inspection had been specifically informed that a second complaint had been received, this time against one of Deutsche Bahn's subsidiaries (DUSS). The agents had also been apprised of the subject matter of that complaint. However, the alleged actions of DUSS were not covered by the inspection decision. During the dawn raid, documents relating to DUSS were collected, and while the inspection based on the first decision was still underway, the Commission adopted a second and later also a third inspection decision concerning the suspected actions by DUSS. Deutsche Bahn unsuccessfully challenged the inspection decisions before the General Court, and then turned to the ECJ.

In its ruling, the Court declared that although the efficacy of an inspection requires the Commission to provide the agents responsible for the inspection

[20] Ibid para 26.
[21] Ibid para 5.
[22] Ibid para 26.
[23] Ibid para 11.
[24] Ibid para 19.
[25] Case C-583/13 P, *Deutsche Bahn AG and Others v European Commission*, EU:C:2015:404.

with all the information that could be useful, such information must relate solely to the subject matter of the decision.[26] The Court acknowledged that under Article 28(1) of Regulation 1/2003, information obtained during investigations must not be used for purposes other than those indicated in the inspection decision. This limitation is aimed at preserving – in addition to business secrecy, expressly referred to in Article 28 – the undertakings' rights of defence, which also Article 20(4) is intended to safeguard, the Court continued.[27] Those rights would be seriously endangered if the Commission were able to rely on evidence that was obtained during an investigation but not related to the subject matter or purpose thereof.[28] The Court therefore found that the Commission had acted unlawfully during the first inspection when it had collected material that lacked such connection. As a consequence, the Commission was not able to rely on the material collected as a basis for the second and third inspection decisions. The Court thus set aside the judgment of the General Court in so far as it dismissed the actions brought against the two subsequent inspection decisions, and also annulled those decisions.[29]

To conclude, the obligation on the part of the Commission to inform targeted companies of the purpose and subject matter of its investigations is necessary in order for them to assess the scope of their duty to cooperate while at the same time safeguarding their rights of the defence. Article 28 of Regulation 1/2003 provides an additional safeguard in this respect, as it prohibits the Commission from using the information gathered for any purposes other than those indicated in its inspection decision or request for information. Whereas the cases presented above concern the Commission's own use of the information gathered during the course of its investigations, this chapter concerns the transmission of information to other competition authorities and their subsequent use of the information gathered by the Commission. However, the cases are still of relevance, as Article 28 simply declares that information collected pursuant to Articles 17 to 22 shall be used only for the purpose for which it was acquired, thereby catching the transmission of as well as the other authorities' use of such information. Second, and perhaps more importantly, the underlying rationale behind Article 28 is to safeguard the companies' right of the defence. The risk that those rights are not protected properly appears even more pertinent where information is transmitted to third country authorities, that is, authorities that will not even use the information for the purpose of investigating infringements of Article 101 or 102 TFEU, and which are located in countries where the possibilities for the companies to effectively exercise their fundamental rights may be limited.

[26] Ibid para 62.

[27] Ibid para 58. Art 20(4) requires the Commission to specify the subject matter and purpose of the inspection.

[28] *Deutsche Bahn* (n 25) para 58.

[29] Ibid.

B. The Right to Privacy

Any transmission of evidence gathered during the course of a cartel investigation may thus infringe targeted companies' defence rights. However, it may also be argued that such measures could affect their right to privacy. In a number of rulings, both the ECJ and the Strasbourg Court have declared that in order for an inspection or request for information to be considered compliant with Article 7 of the Charter or Article 8 ECHR, it needs to be justified and surrounded by adequate procedural safeguards against abuse or arbitrariness. As will be further discussed in the following, the procedural safeguards surrounding the Commission's evidence gathering may be considered inadequate if it is allowed to transmit the information collected to third country competition authorities.

The right to privacy is laid down in Article 7 of the Charter. The Article mirrors Article 8 ECHR. Article 7 of the Charter states:

> Everyone has the right to respect for his or her private and family life, home and communications.

The corresponding provision in the ECHR reads:

> 1. Everyone has the right to respect for his private and family life, his home and his correspondence.
> 2. There shall be no interference by a public authority with the exercise of this right except such as is in accordance with the law and is necessary in a democratic society in the interests of national security, public safety or the economic well-being of the country, for the prevention of disorder or crime, for the protection of health or morals, or for the protection of the rights and freedoms of others.

An initial reflection concerns the personal scope of the right. The wording of the two provisions may be taken to suggest that only natural persons are protected by the right to privacy, as they contain express references to the notions of 'home' and 'family life'. However, the right to privacy has been gradually broadened under both EU and ECHR law, and the two articles now afford protection to legal persons. Over the years, a number of cases concerning the right to privacy during the course of competition law investigations have been brought before both the EU and the Strasbourg Courts. From these cases it is clear that the Commission's investigatory methods may interfere with targeted undertakings' right to privacy, and that in order for such interference to be lawful, it must be in accordance with the law, serve a legitimate aim and be necessary in a democratic society.[30]

[30] *Wieser and Bicos Beteiligungen GmbH v Austria* App no 74336/01 (Judgment) (ECtHR, 16 October 2007) para 12. For a more detailed discussion of undertakings' right to privacy, see H Andersson, *Dawn Raids Under Challenge – Due Process Aspects on the European Commission's Dawn Raid Practices* (Oxford, Hart Publishing, 2018) 53–64.

Most of these cases concern the collection of evidence, and whether the methods used by competition authorities meet the standards of the ECHR or the Charter. From these cases it can be concluded that dawn raids carried out in accordance with the terms of Regulation 1/2003 are considered to be in accordance with the law and to serve a legitimate aim – to ensure effective application of the competition rules.[31] As for the question whether an investigation carried out without reasonable grounds for suspicion would be considered necessary in a democratic society, both the ECJ and the Strasbourg Court appear to share the view that this question should be answered in the negative. In *Robathin*, the Strasbourg Court examined in particular whether the inspection warrant was based on reasonable suspicions,[32] and the ECJ has consistently held that the duty on the part of the Commission to state the subject matter and purpose of the inspection or the request for information serves to ensure that the measures taken are justified.[33] In *Nexans*, the General Court explicitly stated that the Commission must have reasonable grounds to suspect the infringement stated in the inspection decision, and that a search carried out with the ultimate aim of detecting any infringement – and not just the one indicated in the inspection decision – would be incompatible with the company's right to privacy.[34] This was also the view taken in *France Télécom*[35] and in *HeidelbergCement*, where the Court declared that the obligation to state the purpose of the request for information relates to the Commission's obligation to indicate the subject matter of its investigation and therefore to identify the alleged infringement of the competition rules. It further stated that a request for information is only considered necessary when there is a relationship between the information requested and the alleged infringement, and where the Commission has reason to believe that the information will help it determine whether or not the alleged infringement has taken place.[36] Likewise, in *České dráhy*, the General Court acknowledged that, under the right to privacy, the terms of an inspection decision must not exceed the scope of the infringement, 'which may be suspected on such grounds'.[37]

[31] As for the legitimate interests listed in Art 8(2) ECHR, the Strasbourg Court declared in *Vinci Construction* that dawn raids in competition cases serve the aims of ensuring the economic well-being of the country and preventing disorder and crime. See *Vinci Construction et GTM Génie Civil et Services v France* App nos 63629/10 and 60567/10 (Judgment) (ECtHR, 2 April 2015) para 72.

[32] *Robathin v Austria* App no 30457/06 (Judgment) (ECtHR, 3 July 2012) para 44.

[33] See eg Case C-247/14 P, *HeidelbergCement AG v European Commission*, EU:C:2016:149, para 19, where the Court also refers to its rulings in Joined Cases 97/87 to 99/87, *Dow Chemical Ibérica and Others v Commission of the European Communities*, EU:C:1989:380, Case C-94/00, *Roquette Frères*, EU:C:2002:603, Case C-37/13 P, *Nexans SA and Nexans France SAS v European Commission*, EU:C:2014:2030, and Case C-583/13 P, *Deutsche Bahn* (n 25).

[34] Case T-135/09, *Nexans France SAS and Nexans SA v European Commission*, EU:T:2012:596, para 65.

[35] Case T-340/04, *France Télécom SA v Commission of the European Communities*, EU:T:2007:81, para 53, where the General Court refers to *Roquette Frères* (n 33).

[36] *HeidelbergCement* (n 33) paras 23 and 24.

[37] Case T-325/16, *České dráhy a.s. v European Commission*, EU:T:2018:368, para 37.

Thus, an investigation carried out without reasonable suspicion would constitute a breach of Article 7 of the Charter, as would an investigation going beyond the scope of the suspected infringement of the EU competition rules. It is only when the Commission has reason to suspect an infringement that the investigatory measures taken by the Commission are considered justified and not arbitrary or disproportionate, and the Commission will then have to limit its investigation to the purpose and subject matter stated in the inspection decision or the request for information. If the Commission ventures outside these limits, the measures taken are no longer considered necessary or justified. This procedural safeguard serves to strike a proper balance between the opposing interests of adequate fundamental rights protection and effective competition law enforcement.

In order for the measures taken by the Commission during an investigation to be considered justified and in accordance with Article 7 of the Charter, they must be surrounded by adequate procedural safeguards against abuse or arbitrariness. This has been a question for the Court in relation to dawn raids. Regulation 1/2003 allows the Commission to carry out dawn raids without prior judicial authorisation, and this order has been challenged by targeted companies on numerous occasions. One of the more recent cases is *Deutsche Bahn*, where the German railway company argued that the inspections carried out without prior judicial authorisation infringed its right to privacy under Article 7 of the Charter.

The General Court did not accept this argument, dismissing the applications on all grounds and fully confirming the legality of the Commission's inspection decisions. As for the requirement for prior judicial authorisation, the General Court declared that this requirement was not absolute, and that other procedural safeguards may compensate for the lack of ex ante control. It explicitly referred to the case law of the Strasbourg Court,[38] stating that effective ex post control should compensate for the lack of ex ante control.[39] It further recognised five types of procedural safeguards provided under Regulation 1/2003, the first being the requirement on the part of the Commission to provide reasons for its decision, the second the restrictions governing the inspectors during the dawn raid, the third the fact that the Commission may not use any force during inspections, the fourth concerning intervention by national authorities, and the fifth and final being the possibility of a subsequent judicial review.[40] The General Court considered these safeguards to be protected under the EU system. As for the subsequent judicial review, it declared that the EU Courts may carry out a review in full of the

[38] The General Court referred to the cases of *Harju v Finland* App no 56716/09 (Judgment) (ECtHR, 15 February 2011) and *Heino v Finland* App no 56720/09 (Judgment) (ECtHR, 15 February 2011).

[39] Joined Cases T-289 and 290/11 and T-521/11, *Deutsche Bahn and Others v European Commission*, EU:T:2013:404, para 66.

[40] Ibid para 74.

inspection decisions, and that the system thus complied with the Charter and the ECHR.[41] The ECJ later upheld the General Court's ruling in this part.[42]

The Strasbourg Court does also carry out an overall assessment of the procedural safeguards when it examines the applicability of Article 8 ECHR. In *Bernh Larsen Holding*, a case concerning the measures taken by the Norwegian tax authorities during the course of an audit, it examined whether there were adequate procedural safeguards against any abuse or arbitrariness, and made an overall assessment of the safeguards available in order to determine whether or not the measures taken were considered compliant with Article 8 ECHR.[43] That said, while the Strasbourg Court carries out an overall assessment, one procedural safeguard appears to be mandatory, and that is the possibility of effective judicial review. In order for the procedural safeguards to be considered adequate, the company must be able to challenge any measures taken before a tribunal, and such right should not only be guaranteed, it should also be timely.[44]

It can be concluded from these cases that the investigatory measures taken by the Commission, including the collection and use of information, need to be surrounded by adequate procedural safeguards against abuse and arbitrariness. Otherwise, the measures taken will be considered contrary to Article 7 of the Charter. The adequacy of any procedural safeguards must be considered carefully before any transmission of information gathered by the Commission is transferred to third country authorities, as it appears evident that the risks involved in such transmission are high. What if the Commission is allowed to transmit the evidence gathered during an investigation to a competition authority outside the EU without first adopting a challengeable decision? Should the procedural safeguards surrounding the Commission's investigatory measures then be considered adequate? Judging from the foregoing, this question should be answered in the negative.

The Commission is not allowed to carry out an inspection without reasonable suspicion, as the inspection would then not be considered justified. However, which requirements are or should be imposed on the receiving authority? Will it be considered sufficient that it is conducting its own investigation against the company in question, or will it be required to show that it actually has reason to suspect the company of any wrongdoing before the transmission takes place? Which procedural safeguards should be available under the third country legislation? Should the authority in question be required to limit the use of the

[41] Ibid para 97.

[42] The Strasbourg Court has also confirmed that investigatory measures taken without a judicial warrant may be compliant with Art 8 ECHR, provided the procedural safeguards surrounding such measures are considered adequate. See eg *Bernh Larsen Holding AS and Others v Norway* App no 24117/08 (Judgment) (ECtHR,14 March 2013).

[43] In the case at hand, the Norwegian authorities had made copies of the server (belonging to a company other than the applicant) for review at the authorities' premises.

[44] See eg the Strasbourg Court's reasoning in *Société Canal Plus and Others v France* App no 29408/08 (Judgment) (ECtHR, 21 December 2010) and *Compagnie des Gaz de Pétrole Primagaz v France* App no 29613/08 (Judgment) (ECtHR, 21 December 2010).

information and/or ensure possibilities for judicial review, and what if the authority fails to adhere to the agreement or meet the requirements otherwise dictated by the Commission? If the receiving authority decides to forward the information to other authorities or uses the information in other investigations, the harm caused to the targeted company is irremediable.

There are many aspects to consider, and while there may be no clear-cut answers to these questions, it is nevertheless important to discuss these practices from a fundamental rights perspective, and make sure that the procedural safeguards available can guarantee protection from disproportionate or arbitrary measures in these cases too. For this purpose, any exchange of information between competition authorities must be (i) surrounded by clear rules, (ii) challengeable before the EU Courts, and (iii) not allowed unless it can be guaranteed that the third country authority has reason to suspect the company of an infringement of its own competition rules, and only uses the information for the purpose of its own investigation against that company. The authority should thus not be allowed to use the information for any other investigation or forward it to other authorities. However, no matter which guarantees that are given, the risks involved are still high, as any damage caused may be irreparable. What is more, and as will be discussed in the following, it appears that the requirements listed are not always met. The agreement with Switzerland allows for the exchange of case-specific and confidential information, and while the parties have not yet availed themselves of this possibility, the Commission takes the view that any such transmission may occur without the adoption of a challengeable decision.

C. Fundamental Rights – Concluding Remarks

The foregoing shows that while cooperation between competition authorities may be necessary in order to tackle international cartels and ensure effective competition law enforcement, the Commission will have to tread carefully whenever such cooperation involves the exchange of information gathered during the course of its investigations. It is argued that such exchange of information may infringe both the rights of the defence and the right to privacy, especially if there is no possibility for companies to challenge the transmission before national or EU courts. In the following sections, the information exchange with US and Swiss authorities will be examined in more detail, followed by a discussion on the information exchange carried out within the frame of the ECN.

IV. Cooperation Reaching Outside the EU

The Commission cooperates with a number of third country authorities, and such cooperation is based on bilateral agreements or memoranda of understanding. The nature of the cooperation activity varies between countries and can cover coordination of enforcement actions, sharing of information on cases of mutual interest, dialogue on competition policy issues and, in some cases, capacity building support.[45] Dedicated cooperation agreements in competition matters have been concluded with the United States, Canada, Japan, Korea and Switzerland. The principal elements of these agreements are mutual information, coordination of enforcement activities and exchange of non-confidential information. The agreements also contain provisions on the possibility for one party to request the other to take enforcement action (positive comity), and for one party to take into account the important interests of the other party in the course of its enforcement activities (traditional comity).[46] The bilateral agreements usually allow for exchange of non-confidential information, consultations, periodic visits and exchange of staff between the signatories.[47] However, as will be discussed in section IV.D, the bilateral agreement concluded with Switzerland allows for deeper cooperation, as confidential information may be exchanged without prior consent from the source of such information. The agreement is a so-called 'second generation agreement'. Before examining the bilateral agreements in more detail, a few words need to be said about the legal status of such agreements, and where they are to be placed in the EU norm hierarchy.

A. The Status of International Agreements Within the EU Legal Order

The cooperation agreement between the EU and the US was initially concluded between the Commission and the Government of the United States. However, following complaints from the French Government, the ECJ later found that the Commission was not competent to enter into the agreement, which prompted the Council to step in and sign the agreement on behalf of the EU.[48] This turn of events prompts discussion not only of the division of competences between the EU institutions, but also, and more importantly to this work, of the placing of international agreements within the EU legal order. More specifically, in the event that an agreement concluded with a third country is deemed contrary

[45] https://ec.europa.eu/competition/international/overview/index_en.html.

[46] *Antitrust Manual of Procedures, Internal DG Competition Working Documents on Procedures for the Application of Articles 101 and 102 TFEU* (March 2012) 55.

[47] F Jenny, *International Cooperation on Competition: Myth, Reality and Perspective*, The University of Minnesota Law School Conference on Global Antitrust Law and Policy, Minneapolis, 20–21 September 2002, available at www.iilj.org/wp-content/uploads/2017/02/Jenny-International-Cooperation-on-Competition-2002.pdf.

[48] Case C-327/91, *French Republic v Commission of the European Communities*, EU:C:1994:305. See also the Exchange of Interpretative Letters with the Government of the United States of America attached to the cooperation agreement, at https://eur-lex.europa.eu/legal-content/EN/TXT/PDF/?uri=CELEX:21995A0427(01)&from=EN.

to EU fundamental rights protection, it will need to be determined which legal instrument should prevail, the Charter or the international agreement. In *ATAA* the Court declared that 'by virtue of Article 216(2) TFEU, where international agreements are concluded by the European Union they are binding upon its institutions and, consequently, they prevail over acts of the European Union'.[49] On numerous occasions the Court has declared that international treaties binding the EU are ranked between secondary and primary law.[50] In the Grand Chamber ruling of *Kadi*,[51] the Court declared that the primacy of international treaties over secondary EU legislation could not extend to primary EU law, in particular to the general principles of which fundamental rights form a part.[52] The obligations imposed by an international agreement cannot have the effect of prejudicing the constitutional principles of the EC Treaty, the Court declared.[53] On the same note, Lenaerts and Gutiérrez-Fons take the stand that secondary EU legislation must, as far as possible, be interpreted in a manner that is consistent with international agreements binding the Union.[54] Where an international obligation is incompatible with the constitutional tenets of the EU, the duty of consistent interpretation should not apply,[55] and the agreement will then have to give way also to secondary EU legislation. Thus, according to these authors, it is only when an international obligation is compatible with the constitutional tenets of the EU that the primacy of the international treaties applies. In any event, in a conflict between an international agreement and the Charter or a general principle of EU law, the latter will prevail. It is in this setting that we now examine the bilateral cooperation agreements concluded with the United States and Switzerland respectively.

B. Bilateral Relations – General

Bilateral enforcement cooperation agreements are agreements that do not harmonise the competition laws of the contracting parties but that provide for

[49] Case C-366/10, *ATAA and Others*, EU:C:2011:864, paras 50–56.

[50] W Weiss, 'Human Rights in the EU: Rethinking the Role of the European Convention on Human Rights After Lisbon' (2011) 7(1) *European Constitutional Law Review* 72.

[51] Joined Cases C-402/05 P and C-415/05 P, *Yassin Abdullah Kadi and Al Barakaat International Foundation v Council of the European Union and Commission of the European Communities*, EU:C:2008:461, paras 307–308.

[52] As Kokott and Sobotta point out, the EU is not a member of the UN, and therefore it was not clear whether the EU was at all bound by the UN Security Council measures in question; see J Kokott and C Sobotta, 'Constitutional Core Values and International Law – Finding the Balance?' (2012) 23(4) *The European Journal of International Law* 115. This fact was also recognised by the ECJ in *Kadi*. However, the statement relating to any conflict between international treaties and EU primary legislation was based on the assumption that the EU was bound by an obligation to submit to the international treaty in question under Art 300(7) EC (now Art 216(2) TFEU). See *Kadi* (n 51) paras 306–309.

[53] *Kadi* (n 51) para 285.

[54] K Lenaerts and J Gutiérrez-Fons, 'To Say What the Law of the EU Is: Methods of Interpretation and the European Court of Justice', *EUI Working Papers, AEL 2013/9*, 30.

[55] The principle of consistent interpretation means that secondary EU legislation should, as far as possible, be interpreted in accordance with the international agreements concluded by the EU.

mechanisms of enforcement cooperation.[56] As noted by Kiriazis, it is obvious that the effectiveness of cooperation on specific cases pursuant to any bilateral agreements depends upon the ability of the agencies involved to exchange different types of information and use it as needed in their respective internal procedures.[57] To be allowed unlimited access to other competition authorities' case files when investigating international cartels would no doubt be a dream come true for many case handlers around the world. However, as was discussed in the previous section, a free exchange of information would be contrary to the fundamental rights enjoyed by targeted companies. While the EU is a member of a number of international organisations such as the ICN and the OECD, it has entered into bilateral cooperation agreements with only five governments. Out of these five agreements, only one – that with Switzerland – is a so-called 'second generation agreement', also allowing for the exchange of confidential information between the competition authorities in the absence of a written consent by targeted undertakings. Second generation agreements are also in preparation with Canada and Japan.[58] However, according to Demedts, a second generation agreement with the US is currently not considered necessary in view of the needs of the case handlers and a lack of political support due to the divergence of the competition law systems with regard to data protection.[59]

Demedts further notes that while reciprocity is not an explicit condition for the conclusion of a second generation agreement with the EU, both the Explanatory Memorandum as well as the preamble to the agreement between the EU and Switzerland strongly underline the similarities between Swiss and EU substantive and procedural rules, declaring that they are based on the same principles and provide for similar rules. This might indicate that de facto reciprocity is a requirement for the EU to enter into a second generation agreement. It represents a reassurance for the EU Member States that their interests will earn equal protection in the partner country.[60]

C. Bilateral Relations – The US Agreement

The EU and US competition cooperation agreement dates back to 1991. As discussed in section IV.A, it was initially concluded between the Commission and the United States Government. Following a ruling from the Court according to

[56] AS Papadopoulos, *The International Dimension of EU Competition Law and Policy* (Cambridge, Cambridge University Press, 2010) 52.

[57] G Kiriazis, 'Jurisdiction and Cooperation Issues in the Investigation of International Cartels', speech made in June 2001, available at https://ec.europa.eu/competition/speeches/index_2001.html.

[58] See https://ec.europa.eu/competition/international/news.html.

[59] V Demedts, *The Future of International Competition Law Enforcement* (Leiden, Brill Nijhoff, 2018) 164.

[60] Ibid 173.

which the Commission lacked the powers to enter into the agreement, the Council had to step in and conclude the agreement instead. This was done through the exchange of interpretative letters, which contained a number of provisions on the interpretation of the agreement. In addition to the agreement of 1991, the parties have also concluded a specific agreement on positive comity.[61]

Article I of the agreement sets out its purpose and declares that the agreement aims at promoting cooperation and coordination and at lessening the impact of any differences between the two parties in the application of their competition laws. Each party shall notify the other whenever its competition authority/-ies become aware that their enforcement activities may affect important interests of the other party.

As for the exchange of information, this is governed by Article III, which declares that it is in the parties' common interest to share information that will (i) facilitate effective application of their respective competition laws, or (ii) promote better understanding by them of economic conditions and theories relevant to their enforcement activities. To promote these common interests, they agree to meet at least twice a year to (i) exchange information on their current enforcement activities and economic sectors of common interest, and (ii) discuss policy changes or any other matters of mutual interest.[62] Furthermore, the parties agree to provide each other with significant information about anticompetitive activities that they believe is relevant to or could warrant enforcement activity by the other party. Article III.4 is perhaps the most interesting, as it obliges the parties, upon request from the other party, to provide the latter with such information in their possession as the requesting party 'may describe that is relevant to an enforcement activity being considered or conducted by the requesting party's competition authorities'. This obligation is, however, surrounded by a number of limitations provided in Articles VIII and IX.

According to Article VIII, neither party is required to provide information to the other party if such disclosure is prohibited by the law of the party possessing the information or would be incompatible with important interests of that party. Furthermore, Article IX stipulates that nothing in the agreement shall be interpreted in a manner inconsistent with the existing laws or as requiring any change in the laws of the United States or the EU. When the Council agreed to substitute the Commission as party to the agreement, it required the US Government to accept that the above provisions should be understood to mean that the information covered by the provisions of Article 20 of Regulation 17/62,[63] or by equivalent provisions in other regulations in the field of competition law, should 'not under any circumstances be communicated by the Commission to the US antitrust

[61] Agreement between the European Communities and the Government of the United States of America on the application of positive comity principles in the enforcement of their competition laws.

[62] Art III.2.

[63] Art 20 of Regulation 17/62 corresponds to Art 28 of Regulation 1/2003.

authorities, save with the express agreement of the source concerned'. The Council further required all information provided in confidence by either party to be considered confidential by the receiving party, which should oppose any request for disclosure to a third party unless such disclosure was either authorised by the undertaking concerned or required under the law of the receiving party. The corrigendum effectively prohibits any transmission of information collected by the Commission pursuant to Articles 17 to 22 of Regulation 1/2003, unless the source of the information expressly agrees to such transmission. This clause is perhaps not promoting a more effective cartel enforcement, but it does address and remedy any fundamental rights concerns.

As for the application of the cooperation agreement, Demedts notes that the Commission and the US authorities work closely together on merger cases, as parties are then often willing to waive any confidentiality, but it is not equally clear to what extent the authorities cooperate in cartel cases.[64] Cooperation is said to take place regularly and from the very early stages of the case, and Demedts notes that important aspects of such cooperation are the timing and scope of initial investigative actions. Often cooperation serves to prepare or coordinate inquiries or inspections, such as simultaneous inspections to preserve the element of surprise, but it may also include more general discussions on the timing of inspections and the scope of the actions.[65] Thus, while the cooperation agreement prevents the Commission from disclosing the information contained in its case files, it may still serve as a valuable tool to further international cartel enforcement.

D. Bilateral Relations – The Swiss Agreement

In May 2013, the EU and Switzerland signed a cooperation agreement in competition matters. While the agreement was the fifth cooperation agreement signed by the EU, it was the first 'second generation agreement'. By this is meant that, unlike the agreements previously concluded, this agreement also allows for the exchange of confidential information absent any consent from the source of such information. Before the conclusion of the agreement, the authorities only had limited possibilities to coordinate their enforcement activities, and as several cartels had affected both the EU and Swiss markets, there was a perceived need for further and closer cooperation between the two jurisdictions.

The agreement provides a framework for coordination and cooperation of enforcement activities. It aims at enhancing cooperation for effective implementation of competition rules and, like the US agreement, it provides for regular contact in order to discuss policy issues and enforcement efforts and priorities. Whereas the purpose of the US agreement is 'to promote cooperation and coordination

[64] Demedts, *The Future of International Competition Law Enforcement* (n 59) 147.
[65] Ibid.

and to lessen the impact of any differences between the two parties in the application of their competition laws', the agreement concluded with Switzerland goes further and aims at contributing to the effective enforcement of the competition laws of each party through cooperation and coordination, including the exchange of information. Thus, the Swiss agreement explicitly acknowledges that its aim is to achieve more effective competition law enforcement. Like in the agreement with the United States, the competition authorities shall notify each other with respect to enforcement activities they consider may affect important interests of the other party. Article 4 of the agreement allows the parties to coordinate their enforcement activities when they are investigating related matters. They may in particular coordinate the timing of their inspections.

The core element of the agreement concerns the exchange of information between the competition authorities, and this matter is dealt with in Article 7. The article allows the Commission to transmit evidence from its case files even without the consent of the source of such information. Such transmission requires that a number of conditions are met. First, information may only be transmitted where both parties are investigating the same or related conduct or transaction. Second, the request shall be made in writing and include a general description of the subject matter and the nature of the investigation or proceedings to which the request relates and the specific legal provisions involved. It shall also identify the undertakings subject to the investigation or the procedure whose identity is available at the time of the request. Finally, the requested authority shall determine, in consultation with the requesting authority, what information is in its possession that is relevant and may be transmitted. The article further declares that neither party is under any obligation to transmit any information obtained during the investigative process, especially not if the transmission would be incompatible with the authority's important interests or unduly burdensome. Furthermore, the parties are prevented from transmitting or discussing information obtained during a leniency or settlement procedure, unless the undertaking that has provided such information has given its express consent in writing. The exchange of information is also subject to strict conditions protecting business secrets and personal data. Thus, whereas the agreement allows for exchange of case-specific information even without the consent of targeted undertakings, such transmission is surrounded by a number of restrictions, and there is no obligation on the part of the authorities to transmit information obtained during an investigation.

Important to note is the fact that the competition authorities are only allowed to exchange information already in the possession of the respective authority. This limitation underlines that the agreement is not a basis for the collection of information solely on behalf of the other authority. Rather, the information qualifying for being shared with the other authority must have been collected within the framework and for purposes of domestic proceedings. While the Commission may thus not carry out a dawn raid on behalf of the Swiss authorities, it may nevertheless collect information that is also of relevance to other authorities during the course of its own investigations. Worth mentioning in relation to this requirement is the case of *Nexans*,[66] which concerned the Commission's powers to collect information relating to projects outside the Union.

In the case at hand, the Commission's inspection decision indicated that the alleged cartel probably had a global reach. Nexans challenged the Commission's inspection decision on several grounds, one being that the geographic scope of the decision was overly broad. Nexans argued that the Commission should have indicated how projects outside the EU were relevant to the cartel investigation in question. In terms of jurisdiction, the Commission's remit extends only to protecting the EU internal market from distortions of competition. However, the Court declared that it did not follow from this that the Commission is limited – during its dawn raids – to reviewing business records relating solely to projects that have an effect in the EU. In the current case, the Commission was on the trail of a cartel that 'probably had a global reach'. In this instance, even documents linked to projects located outside the EU were therefore likely to provide relevant information regarding the suspected infringement, for example, relating to the modus operandi of the cartel or a possible agreement to divide up the global market.[67] The ECJ therefore dismissed the appeal. The ruling confirms the Commission's broad discretion to review and seize information relating to non-EU countries during dawn raids, particularly where it suspects that the cartel is global in nature or may be wholly or partially operated from outside the EU. It is therefore likely that, while the Commission is prevented from collecting information on behalf of the Swiss authorities, some of the information collected will still be of use to those authorities.

Article 8 regulates the use of the information exchanged. According to that article, information that the competition authority of a party discusses with or transmits to the other competition authority shall be used only for the purpose of enforcing that party's competition laws by its competition authority. Information obtained by investigative process and discussed with or transmitted to the competition authority of the other party shall only be used by the receiving competition authority for the enforcement of its competition laws with regard to the same or related conduct or transaction. Furthermore, information transmitted without the consent of the source of the information may only be used by the receiving authority for the purpose defined in the request. No information disclosed may be used to impose sanctions on natural persons, and the competition authorities are at all times free to require that the information transmitted shall be used subject to the terms and conditions defined by the transmitting authority. Furthermore, the competition authorities of the two parties may not discuss, request or transmit information obtained by investigative process if the use of such information would be prohibited under the procedural rights and privileges guaranteed under their respective laws and applicable to their enforcement activities, including the privilege against self-incrimination and the legal professional privilege.

[66] *Nexans* (n 33).
[67] *Nexans* (n 33) para 40.

There are thus a number of safeguards in place that should ensure that the information disclosed by the Commission to the Swiss authorities is used only for the purpose of investigating the conduct covered by the Commission's own inspection decision or information request. However, the agreement does not contain any provision on judicial review. Given the far-reaching scope of the information that may be exchanged and in light of the criminal nature of competition law fines, it is surprising that the agreement does not foresee any right to appeal a decision to exchange information absent consent by the undertaking concerned. To date, there has been no transmission of confidential information without a waiver, and we do not know whether or not the Commission would decide to transmit such information by way of a challengeable decision. Unless that is the case, this omission will jeopardise the lawfulness of the agreement, as the procedural safeguards against abuse and arbitrariness would then not be considered adequate.[68]

V. Information Exchange Within the ECN

In May 2004, Regulation 1/2003 entered into force with the explicit aim of decentralising the enforcement of the EU competition rules. Not only were national competition authorities now empowered to apply these rules in full, as from this date they are also required to do so whenever an anticompetitive agreement or conduct is capable of affecting trade between Member States.[69] To ensure the proper functioning of this new enforcement system, the Regulation provides for close cooperation between the Commission and the NCAs. Thus, Recital 15 declares that the Commission and NCAs should form together a network of public authorities applying the EU competition rules in close cooperation. For that purpose, the recital declares, it is necessary to set up arrangements for information and consultation. Further modalities for the cooperation within the network should be laid down and revised by the Commission, in close cooperation with the Member States. On the same day as the Regulation was adopted, the Commission and the Council made a joint statement setting out the envisaged framework for such network.[70] In April the following year, the Commission issued the Network Notice.

Since the adoption of the Regulation, cooperation between the competition authorities has developed considerably. In its communication to the European

[68] In an e-mail dated 21 January 2020, the International Team at DG Comp points to the fact that the agreement does not require a decision, nor define the formality of the transfer itself any more closely, indicating that it may be willing to transfer confidential information without adopting a formal decision or receiving prior consent from the source of the information in question.

[69] Arts 3 and 5 of Regulation 1/2003.

[70] See Communication from the Commission to the European Parliament and the Council, Ten Years of Antitrust Enforcement under Regulation 1/2003: Achievements and Future Perspectives, COM(2014) 453.

Parliament and the Council on the first 10 years with Regulation 1/2003, the Commission acknowledges that the Regulation has brought about a landmark change in the way in which EU competition law is enforced.[71] As noted by the Commission, the EU competition rules have to a large extent become the 'law of the land' throughout the Union. The NCAs have become a key pillar of the application of the rules, and the work carried out in the ECN has become increasingly important to ensure coherent enforcement and to allow stakeholders to benefit from a more level playing field.

On its website, the Commission declares that the objective of the ECN is to build an effective legal framework to enforce EU competition law against companies who engage in cross-border business practices that restrict competition and are therefore anti-consumer. Furthermore, the Commission declares, the ECN should ensure an efficient division of work and effective and consistent application of the EU competition rules. The Commission and the NCAs cooperate with each other through the ECN by:

- informing each other of new cases and envisaged enforcement decisions;
- coordinating investigations, where necessary;
- helping each other with investigations;
- exchanging evidence and other information; and
- discussing various issues of common interest.[72]

Relevant to this study is the exchange of evidence and other information. Article 26 of the Network Notice states that a key element of the functioning of the network is the power of all authorities to exchange and use information, including documents, statements and digital information, which has been collected by them for the purpose of applying Article 101 or 102 TFEU. In the following section, the rules and procedures on information exchange are examined more closely.

A. The Rules Surrounding Information Exchange Within the ECN

As mentioned previously, the recitals to Regulation 1/2003 provide for the setting up of a network among the competition authorities within the Union. However, the Regulation does not only anticipate a network for cooperation, it also contains provisions expressly aimed at facilitating such cooperation by allowing for the exchange of information between the Commission and the NCAs.

[71] ibid.
[72] https://ec.europa.eu/competition/ecn/more_details.html.

Article 12 of Regulation 1/2003 governs information exchange between competition authorities. Article 12(1) stipulates that for the purpose of applying Articles 101 and 102 TFEU, the Commission and the competition authorities of the Member States shall have the power to provide one another with and use in evidence any matter of fact or of law, including confidential information. Information exchanged shall only be used in evidence for the purpose of applying the two treaty articles and in respect of the subject matter for which it was collected by the transmitting authority. However, where national competition law is applied in the same case and in parallel to EU competition law and does not lead to a different outcome, information exchanged under Article 12 may also be used for the application of national competition law. Accordingly, the limitations provided for in Article 28 governing the use of information and professional secrecy, do not apply to information exchange between the Commission and the NCAs.

The Regulation contains one important limitation on information exchange between competition authorities, and that concerns the use of transmitted information for the purpose of imposing sanctions on natural persons. According to Article 12(3), information exchanged between competition authorities may only be used to impose such sanctions if the law of the transmitting authority foresees sanctions of a similar kind in relation to an infringement of Article 101 or 102 TFEU or, in the absence thereof, the information has been collected in a way that respects the same level of protection of the rights of defence of natural persons as provided for under the national rules of the receiving authority. However, in this case, the information exchanged cannot be used by the receiving authority to impose custodial sanctions.

In addition to the provisions in Regulation 1/2003, the Commission's practices are also governed by the Network Notice, where the Commission imposes further limitations on the information exchange between the Members of the ECN, in particular as concerns information gathered within the frame of leniency programmes. Recognising the importance of safeguarding the effectiveness of the various leniency programmes applicable throughout the Union, the Network Notice declares that the transmission of information voluntarily submitted by a leniency applicant to another ECN member requires the consent of the leniency applicant. This also applies to information obtained during or following an inspection, or by means of or following fact-finding measures that could not have been carried out except as a result of the leniency application. Members of the ECN will encourage leniency applicants to give their consent, especially in relation to disclosure to authorities that could grant leniency to the applicant. Once consent to disclosure has been given by an undertaking, it cannot be withdrawn.[73] The issue is also addressed in the Leniency Notice, which declares that the Commission will transmit corporate statements to the NCAs only provided that (i) the conditions set out in the Network Notice are met, and (ii) the level of protection

[73] Para 40 of the Network Notice.

against disclosure awarded by the receiving competition authority is equivalent to the one conferred by the Commission.[74]

The ban on transmission is not absolute, as paragraph 41 of the Network Notice declares that no consent is required where:

- the receiving authority has also received a leniency application relating to the same infringement and from the same applicant as the transmitting authority, provided that, at the time the information is transmitted, it is not open to the applicant to withdraw the information it has submitted to the receiving authority (paragraph 41(1));
- the receiving authority has provided a written commitment that the information will not be transmitted, nor will any other information that the receiving authority may obtain following the transmission be used by it or any other authority to which the information is subsequently transmitted, to impose sanctions on the leniency applicant, on any other natural or legal person covered by favourable treatment offered due to the leniency application, on any employee, or former employee of any person who has been offered leniency (paragraph 41(2));
- information has been collected by an ECN member under Article 22(1) of Regulation 1/2003 on behalf of the authority to whom the leniency application was made (paragraph 41(3)).
- information has been submitted to the Commission by an NCA and relates to cases initiated as a result of a leniency application, which will only be made available to those NCAs that have committed to respecting the principles set out in the Commission Notice. The same principle applies where a case has been initiated by the Commission as a result of a leniency application made to the Commission (paragraph 42 of the Network Notice).

National competition authorities in all Member States have signed a statement committing themselves to these principles.

An additional limitation concerning the use of information acquired from sister agencies is found in paragraph 39 of the Network Notice. Where an NCA initiates an investigation involving the application of Article 101 or 102 TFEU, it is required under Article 11(3) of Regulation 1/2003 to inform the Commission and make information available to the other NCAs. If the case originates from a leniency application, other members of the network will not use the information as a basis for starting their own investigation.[75] This is without prejudice to any power of a competition authority to open an investigation on the basis of information received from other sources, or to request information under Article 12 of Regulation 1/2003 from any member of the ECN (including the authority to whom the leniency application was submitted).

[74] Para 37 of the Leniency Notice.

[75] Whether under the EU competition rules, national competition or other laws.

As noted by the OECD and ICN in their joint survey, the ECN provides a unique experience in terms both of the number of participating agencies and the availability of formal instruments for cooperation (allowing for exchange of confidential information and investigatory assistance in antitrust and cartel cases). The survey showed that many ECN respondents considered the ECN to provide a unique setting for cooperation, in that its members applied the same substantive rules and the framework provided very powerful instruments for cooperation.[76] Indeed, the information exchange within the ECN cannot be compared to any other cooperation between competition authorities. The Member State authorities are all empowered to apply and enforce Articles 101 and 102 TFEU, and will then not have to limit their findings to the remit of their own jurisdiction. In such a system, where competition authorities may investigate the same case and apply the same rules in parallel, the information exchange is a necessary feature and a precondition to the effective and consistent application of the rules. Although the requirements in Article 28 of Regulation 1/2003 do not apply to information exchanged within the ECN, one can assume that some information transmitted to NCAs will be used for the same purpose as that for which it was collected. This is unlikely to happen in any other cooperation between competition authorities.

VI. Information Exchange – Concluding Remarks

For obvious reasons, there is a clear dividing line between the cooperation that takes place between the Commission and the NCAs and the cooperation that takes place between the Commission and authorities outside the EU. Today, the EU enforcement regime is based on parallel powers and decentralisation. This requires close cooperation between the competition authorities of the EU, which is also foreseen by the legislator. Article 12 of Regulation 1/2003 explicitly allows for information exchange between competition authorities, but requires the recipients of transmitted information to use it for the purpose of applying Articles 101 and 102 TFEU and in respect of the subject matter for which it was collected by the transmitting authority. The article can thus be seen as a necessary extension of Article 28. However, it contains one additional element, as it allows the NCAs also to use the information for the application of their domestic rules where they are applied in the same case and in parallel to EU competition law.

While there may be certain elements in the information exchange within the ECN that may raise concerns, the exchange as such must be considered rather unproblematic. However, the cooperation and information exchange with third country authorities is not necessarily equally unproblematic. According to

[76] Executive summary of the Report on the OECD/ICN Survey on International Enforcement Cooperation, available at www.oecd.org/competition/globalforum/InternationalCooperationExecutiveSummaryEN.pdf.

Article 28 of Regulation 1/2003, information collected by the Commission during its cartel investigations shall be used only for the purpose for which it was acquired. The wording of the article prompts two reflections. First, it is the information collected that is protected. This means that it is not only the physical documents collected that are protected from being used for another purpose, but also their contents. Second, there is no limitation to 'confidential' information. Thus, a bilateral agreement that prohibits exchange of confidential information, requiring the source of the information to consent to such transfer, does not satisfy the requirements in Article 28. The agreement with the US explicitly prohibits the Commission from transmitting information gathered during the course of its investigations, and the agreement with Switzerland governs 'evidence obtained by investigative process' rather than confidential information, but other bilateral agreements, such as the one with Canada, do not restrict the Commission's actions in a similar way. Nor does the agreement with Canada define the notion of 'confidential information'. As will be further discussed in chapters 6 and 8, the General Court has declared that, in order for a piece of information to be considered confidential: (i) it should be known only to a limited number of persons, (ii) its disclosure should be liable to cause serious harm, and (iii) the interests liable to be harmed by disclosure must be worthy of protection.[77] It is likely that some information gathered during the course of a cartel investigation, while not being in the public domain, fails to meet the criteria in (ii) or (iii). The question is then whether the cooperation agreement should prevail and the Commission should thus be allowed to transfer case-specific information that is not technically considered confidential to third country authorities. An international agreement may trump a regulation but it does not prevail over the Charter or the general principles of EU law. Furthermore, the bilateral agreements all have one thing in common, the parties are only required to assist each other to the extent permitted by their laws and regulations. As the requirement in Article 28 of Regulation 1/2003 serves to protect targeted companies' defence rights, it could be argued that the Commission should be prevented from transmitting any information from its case files to third country authorities, at least unless such transmission was already foreseen in the request for information or the inspection decision. The targeted companies should already have been informed of this possibility at the time the information was gathered and had the chance of challenging the inspection decision or such transmission without the fear of repercussions.

As for the agreement with Switzerland, which allows for the exchange of information obtained during the investigatory process without prior consent, the Commission has not yet exchanged such information without a waiver. However, it has pointed to the fact that the agreement does not require a decision, nor define the formality of the transfer itself any more closely, indicating that it would be willing to transfer confidential information without adopting a formal decision or

[77] Case T-198/03, *Bank Austria Creditanstalt v. Commission*, EU:T:2006:136.

receiving a prior consent from the source of the information in question.[78] This can of course be questioned from a due process perspective, at least if there is no mention of a possible exchange of information in the inspection decision or the decision to request information, allowing targeted companies to challenge those decisions and thereby also the possible exchange of information.

A further concern is related to a risk inherent in all close contacts, and that is the risk of accidental or 'off the record' sharing of information. As mentioned already at the beginning of this chapter, Laitenberger declared in 2018 that the Commission cooperated with competition agencies outside of the EU in 65 per cent of all cartel cases. While there may be strict regulations governing such cooperation, and while the cooperation referred to may not concern the exchange of information gathered during the course of investigations, there is always a risk that too close contacts have the effect that too much information is shared during meetings or in other informal contacts.[79]

A final point to be addressed, or rather briefly touched upon, concerns the application of the principle of *ne bis in idem*. When the Commission gathers information under Regulation 1/2003, it is not allowed to broaden the scope of its search or information request to gather evidence not of relevance to its own investigation. Thus, if transmitted to third country authorities, the same information will be used to establish an infringement in both jurisdictions, and it is likely that the same actions by the targeted undertakings will be condemned in both jurisdictions. Under the ECHR and the Charter, the principle of *ne bis in idem* protects both natural and legal persons from being punished twice for the same criminal offence. As discussed in chapter 2, cartel infringements and the sanctions imposed by the Commission are considered criminal in nature, albeit within the wider meaning of the term. However, the ECHR requires the double jeopardy to take place within one and the same jurisdiction, and the methods applied by cooperating authorities are therefore unlikely to be formally caught by the principle. Another important aspect is of course that the Commission's cooperation with Korea, Japan, Canada and the US is not caught by the ECHR in the first place. That said, there are nevertheless merits to any criticism of a system where the competition authorities are allowed to cooperate closely while they pursue parallel investigations against the same companies, gather evidence used by both authorities to sanction these companies for the same factual circumstances, and where the only dividing line between the two offences is the territory affected by the companies' anticompetitive practices, especially given the broad territorial reach of many competition rules, as evidenced by the *Intel* case discussed in section II. Furthermore, it should be noted that the Charter does not limit the application of the principle to individual Member States. Any concern becomes

[78] This according to the International Team of DG COMP in an e-mail dated 21 January 2020.
[79] Laitenberger, 'Developments in EU Competition Control' (n 2).

even more relevant within the frame of the ECN, where up to three NCAs can impose sanctions on the same companies, for the same unlawful behaviour and for the infringement of the same rules – Article 101 or 102 TFEU.[80] However, any closer scrutiny of the merits to such criticism would be the subject of another study. Suffice it to say that these concerns should not be neglected when drafting and concluding 'second generation' cooperation agreements.

[80] Technically, there is nothing in Regulation 1/2003 to prevent 27 NCAs from investigating the same offence, however the Network Notice provides a structure for the division of cases between the Commission and the NCAs, according to which up to three NCAs may pursue an investigation of the same unlawful behaviour.

PART III

Parties and Complainants

4

Targeted Companies' Right to Access the File

Anyone suspected of cartel participation will know that much is at stake. Should the Commission find the company guilty, it will most certainly have to pay a hefty fine. There is also the risk that parallel proceedings concerning infringements of national competition rules may result in prison sentences or other individual sanctions. Furthermore, the company may have to face damages claims from alleged victims both throughout the EU and outside its borders. While this development towards tougher sanctions and corrective justice may be welcome from a competition law perspective, it highlights the need to safeguard the fundamental rights of those targeted by the Commission's investigations. One such right is the right of the defence. Access to the file is one of the procedural safeguards intended to protect this right and to ensure, in particular, that the right to be heard may be exercised effectively.[1] As discussed in the preceding chapter, the ECJ has declared that the right of the defence may not only be invoked during court proceedings or at the adversarial stage of a competition case, but must also be respected during preliminary inquiry procedures, including in particular investigations that may be decisive in providing evidence of infringements of the competition rules.[2] While the right of the defence is now explicitly laid down in Article 48(2) of the Charter, that provision applies to anyone who has been charged, implying that it may only be invoked when a case has reached the courts.[3] However, the right of the defence is also reflected in the procedural guarantees listed under the principle of good administration pursuant to Article 41 of the Charter. This is so particularly with respect to the right to have a case handled impartially, fairly and within reasonable

[1] Case T-65/89, *BPB Industries Plc and British Gypsum Ltd v Commission of the European Communities*, EU:T:1993:31, para 30; and Joined Cases T-191/98, T-212/98 to T-214/98, *Atlantic Container Line AB and Others v Commission of the European Communities*, EU:T:2003:245, para 334.

[2] Joined Cases 46/87 and 227/88, *Hoechst AG v the Commission of the European Communities*, EU:C:1989:337, para 15.

[3] According to the Charter explanations, the right laid down in Art 48 shall have the same meaning and scope as the rights guaranteed under the ECHR. As discussed in section VII, the right of the defence forms part of the right to a fair trial under the ECHR, and may thus only be invoked when a case has reached the courts.

time, the right to be heard and the right of access to one's file.[4] This chapter will focus on the last of these.

As will be discussed further in the following, the Commission has never been able to adopt infringement decisions without first allowing the parties a right to be heard. However, the right – as we know it – to access the file was first introduced by the Directorate-General Competition (DG COMP) in the early 1980s. The EU Courts considered, and to some extent still consider, the Commission's obligation to grant full access to be self-imposed. In the case of *Solvay*, the Court declared in a Grand Chamber ruling that the right of access to the file means that the Commission must provide the undertaking concerned with the opportunity to examine all the documents in the investigation that might be relevant for its defence.[5] That said, the EU Courts have declared that it is not for the Commission alone to determine which documents may be useful for the defence, thereby limiting the Commission's scope of discretion.[6] Should the Commission fail to grant full access to its case file and rely on documents that have not previously been disclosed to the parties, the evidence in question will be struck out by the EU Courts, but it is only when such failure is considered to constitute a violation of the companies' defence rights that it may lead to the annulment of the infringement decision. Thus, to quote the General Court in *Cimenteries*, 'Access to the file is not an end in itself but is intended to protect the rights of the defence.'[7]

I. Access to the File – Emergence of the Right

A company targeted by a Commission investigation will have a clear and obvious interest in accessing the Commission's case file. As cartel cases are by definition pursued against more than one company, the granting of access may sometimes not be as straightforward as initially thought. In its *Manual of Procedures*, the Commission takes note of the fact that access to file work requires legal and procedural knowledge and implies a substantive assessment of confidentiality claims. This, the Commission declares, is often a complex exercise given the tension between two fundamental interests: on the one hand, the rights of defence of the parties targeted by the investigation; and on the other hand, the protection of confidential information by the author or owner of the document.[8] Article 27(2) of

[4] HP Nehl, 'Article 48 Presumption of Innocence and Right of Defence (Administrative Law)' in S Peers et al (eds), *The EU Charter of Fundamental Rights; A Commentary* (Oxford, Hart Publishing, 2014) 1277, 1289.

[5] Case C-109/10 P, *Solvay SA v European Commission*, EU:C:2011:686, para 54.

[6] See P Craig, *EU Administrative Law*, 2nd edn (Oxford, Oxford University Press, 2012) 355.

[7] Joined Cases T-25/95, T-26/95, T-30/95 to T-32/95, T-34/95 to T-39/95, T-42/95 to T-46/95, T-48/95, T-50/95 to T-65/95, T-68/95 to T-71/95, T-87/95, T-88/95, T-103/95 and T-104/95, *Cimenteries CBR and Others v Commission of the European Communities*, EU:T:2000:77, para 156.

[8] *Antitrust Manual of Procedures, Internal DG Competition Working Documents on Procedures for the Application of Articles 101 and 102 TFEU* (March 2012), module 12, 'Access to File and Confidentiality', section 1, point (1).

Regulation 1/2003 provides targeted companies with a right to access the case file, and in its notice on access to the file ('the Access Notice'),[9] the Commission further defines its duties to provide access as an obligation on its part to 'give the persons, undertakings or associations of undertakings an opportunity of making known their views on the objections against them and to give them access to the case file in order to fully respect their rights of the defence in the proceedings'.[10] While the Access Notice reflects the Commission's current practice, targeted companies have not always been allowed to access the file. In the early cases, the ECJ took the view that while the parties should be allowed to exercise their right to be heard, there was no need for the Commission to communicate the evidence in its case files to them.

A. The Early Cases – No Right to Access the Entire Case File

As with so many other rights guaranteed under EU law, the right to access one's case file was not initially part of the statutory framework. That said, the first regulations on the application of the EU competition rules already contained provisions that reflected the principle of equality of arms and served to protect targeted companies' right to be heard. Thus, Article 19 of Regulation 17/62 required the Commission to give the parties a right to be heard before any infringement decisions were adopted, and Regulation 99/63 governed the procedure of such hearings.[11] The latter Regulation imposed an obligation on the Commission to inform the parties in writing of its objections against them, and allow them a right to make known their views on the Commission's objections. According to Article 4 of the Regulation, the Commission's infringement decisions could only contain objections upon which the parties had been given an opportunity to give their view.

Already in the case of *Consten and Grundig*, the two applicants complained that their defence rights had been infringed as the Commission had failed to communicate the contents of the case file to them. The Court acknowledged that the proceedings before the Commission were administrative, and that this meant that the parties concerned should be put in a position before the decision was issued to present their observations on the Commission's objections, thereby implicitly acknowledging that the principle of equality of arms applied in these cases. For that purpose, the Court continued, they must be informed of the facts upon

[9] Commission Notice on the rules for access to the Commission file in cases pursuant to Articles 81 and 82 of the EC Treaty, Articles 53, 54 and 57 of the EEA Agreement and Council Regulation (EC) No 139/2004, [2005] OJ C325/7.

[10] Ibid.

[11] Regulation No 99/63/EEC of the Commission of 25 July 1963 on the hearings provided for in Article 19(1) and (2) of Council Regulation No 17 [1963] OJ L127/2268.

which the complaints were based. However, the Court did not consider it necessary for the Commission to communicate the entire case file to the applicants. Finding that the statement of objections included all the facts knowledge of which was 'necessary to ascertain which complaints were taken into consideration', the Court found that there had been no violation of the companies' defence rights.[12] In another of the early cases, *Francolor*, the Court once again held that targeted companies lacked a right to access the case file. Acknowledging that the right of the defence also applied during the administrative procedure, the Court declared that it was sufficient for the Commission to inform the parties of the essential elements of fact on which the Commission based its objections. The Court did not consider it necessary for the contents of the file to be made available in their entirety. Finding that the statement of objections clearly stated all the facts taken into consideration against the applicant, the Court found no infringement of the right of the defence.[13]

In *Hoffmann-La Roche* the applicant complained that the Commission's infringement decision referred to documents that had not been discussed or even mentioned at the oral hearing. According to the applicant, its right to be heard had thus been violated and there had also been an infringement of Article 4 of Regulation 99/63. Furthermore, the applicant objected that the decision was based on information that had not been brought to its attention and that it could not check, as the Commission relied on its duty to observe the principle of professional secrecy. The Commission, on the other hand, argued that the right to be heard should not be confused with any right to production of the entire case file. In its ruling, the Court acknowledged that in earlier cases it had held that the requirements concerning the right to be heard were satisfied if the notification set forth, clearly albeit succinctly, the essential facts upon which the Commission relied. However, the Court further declared, this statement had been subject to the proviso that 'in the course of the administrative procedure it supplies the details necessary to the defence'.[14] The Court then continued:

> Thus it emerges from the provisions quoted above and also from the general principle to which they give effect that in order to respect the principle of the right to be heard the undertakings concerned must have been afforded the opportunity during the administrative procedure to make known their views on the truth and relevance of the facts and circumstances alleged and on the documents used by the Commission to support its claim that there has been an infringement of Article 86 of the Treaty.[15]

[12] Case 56/64, *Établissements Consten S.à.R.L. and Grundig-Verkaufs-GmbH v Commission of the European Economic Community*, EU:C:1966:41, [1966] ECR 299, 338.

[13] Case 54/69, *SA Française des Matières Colorantes (Francolor) v Commission of the European Communities*, EU:C:1972:75, paras 22–26.

[14] Case 85/76, *Hoffmann-La Roche & Co AG v Commission of the European Communities*, EU:C:1979:36, para 10.

[15] Ibid para 11.

In that particular case, the Court found that there had been no breach of this obligation since the target company had seen and inspected all of the documents on which the Commission relied in its infringement decision. Since then, the Court has been given ample opportunity to rule on these issues, and has consistently held that the right of the defence prevents the Commission from relying on objections to which the parties have not been able to reply, and that the parties must be provided with all the information necessary for them to defend themselves effectively and to comment on the allegations made against them. However, it was not the Court but the Commission that first introduced a right for companies to access the case files in their entirety.

B. The Commission's Revision of its Policy

In its Eleventh Report on Competition Policy, published in 1981, the Commission acknowledged that a wide-ranging discussion had been going on in Parliament and in 'interested legal and economic circles' on the administrative procedures relating to restrictive agreements and practices. On the one hand, the Commission noted, there were suggestions for a simplification and acceleration of procedures, and on the other hand suggestions for increased procedural guarantees, which would have the effect of prolonging and slowing down the Commission's procedures.[16] While the Commission did not see a need for any substantial amendments, it nevertheless aimed at allaying the principal apprehensions that had emerged in talks with stakeholders, and reported that it had taken a number of steps to reinforce the objectiveness of its procedures. These measures concerned investigations carried out at undertakings, access to the Commission's files and proceedings at oral hearings.[17]

As for the question of access to the case files, the Report made reference to a number of rulings, including *Consten and Grundig* and *Hoffmann La Roche*, and declared that according to these rulings, the Commission was not obliged to send the firms all the documents on which it had based its arguments in the statement of objections. It was sufficient to forward only the documents concerning the essential facts. The Commission noted further that it already gave undertakings the opportunity of commenting on all documents and all factual information it put forward against them in the statement of objections. Furthermore, the Commission declared, where firms submitted requests, justified by the need for a better understanding of the file, it allowed them to inspect the documents themselves. According to the Report, the Commission consistently informed the firms concerned, in so far as possible, of the relevant parts of formal complaints. In its

[16] *Eleventh Report on Competition Policy*, Commission of the European Communities, 1981, point 34.

[17] Ibid point 16.

Report it declared that it was now even considering going beyond the requirements laid down by the Court to allow, in principle, firms involved in a procedure to have access to the file on the particular case.[18] Such inspection, the Commission declared, must be limited by the Commission's obligation not to disclose business secrets and the need to preserve the confidential nature of the Commission's internal or working documents.

The Commission soon turned words into deeds. Already the following year, it reported that it had put into effect the proposal mentioned in the previous Report, to go beyond the requirements laid down by the Court and improve the exercise of the right of the defence in the course of its administrative procedures.[19] Thus, it now permitted the undertakings involved in a procedure to inspect the file on their case. According to the Report, companies were informed of the contents of the Commission's file by means of an annex to the statement of objections listing all the documents in the file and indicating documents or parts thereof to which they were allowed access. The undertakings were then invited to come and consult these documents on the Commission's premises. If a company wished to consult only a few documents, these were instead sent to the company. As stated in its Eleventh Report, certain categories of documents were not considered accessible, namely internal Commission documents and documents containing business secrets or other confidential information. From now on, companies could thus review the documents in the Commission's file.

C. The Case Law after the Commission's Change of Practice

The same year as the Commission published its *Twelfth Report on Competition Policy*, a case was brought before the ECJ in which the parties complained of the limited possibilities to access the Commission's case files. In the Joined Cases of *VBVB and VBBB v Commission*,[20] the Court observed that although regard for the rights of the defence required that the undertaking concerned was effectively enabled to make known its point of view on the documents relied upon by the Commission, there were no provisions that required the Commission to divulge the contents of its files to the parties concerned. As the Commission had not made use of any document unavailable to the parties and on which they had not had the opportunity to make their views known, the submission was dismissed. The Commission's change of practice was thus not reflected in the Court's case law.

[18] Ibid point 24.

[19] *Twelfth Report on Competition Policy*, Commission of the European Communities, 1982, point 34.

[20] Joined Cases 43/82 and 63/82, *Vereniging ter Bevordering van het Vlaamse Boekwezen, VBVB, and Vereniging ter Bevordering van de Belangen des Boekhandels, VBBB v Commission of the European Communities*, EU:C:1984:9.

It would not take long before the EU Courts took notice of the Commission's new policy and made it stand by its words. In the case of *Hercules*, the General Court referred to the Court's ruling in *VBVB and VBBB v Commission* and declared that regard for the rights of the defence did not require the Commission to divulge the contents of its files to the parties concerned.[21] However, the General Court also noted that the Commission had changed its practice as described in the *Twelfth Report on Competition Policy*. By establishing a procedure for providing access to the file in competition cases, the Commission had imposed on itself rules exceeding the requirements laid down by the ECJ, from which it was not permitted to depart, the General Court declared.[22] This led it to conclude that the Commission was required to make available to the parties all documents it had obtained during the course of the investigation, whether in the companies' favour or otherwise, save where business secrets, the Commission's internal documents or other confidential information were involved.[23] The right to access one's file was now also confirmed by the EU judiciary. Notably, the General Court's reasoning suggests that it did not consider the Commission's failure to constitute a breach of the companies' defence rights as much as a violation of their legitimate expectations or right to equal treatment. Interesting to note is that the General Court has later referred to its own reasoning in *Hercules* and declared that it is in order to allow the undertakings in question to defend themselves effectively against the objections raised in the statement of objections that the Commission is required to make available the investigation file.[24] This, however, is not what was established in *Hercules*.

Another interesting observation is that while the General Court considered the Commission's obligation to grant access to be self-imposed, it was not equally willing to let the Commission change its practice and adopt a more restrictive approach. In *ICI*,[25] the Commission suspected the two companies ICI and Solvay of a market-sharing arrangement. During the administrative procedure, it refused to grant ICI access to documents emanating from Solvay.[26] When the matter reached the General Court, the Commission referred to its *Eighteenth Report*

[21] Case T-7/89, *SA Hercules Chemicals NV v Commission of the European Communities*, EU:T:1991:75, para 52.

[22] Ibid para 53. The General Court referred to Case 148/73, *Raymond Louwage and Marie-Thérèse Louwage, née Moriame v Commission of the European Communities*, EU:C:1974:7, where the Court established that 'Although an internal directive has not the character of a rule of law which the administration is always bound to observe, it nevertheless sets forth a rule of conduct indicating the practice to be followed, from which the administration may not depart without giving the reasons which have led it to do so, since otherwise the principles of equality of treatment would be infringed.'

[23] *Hercules* (n 21) para 54.

[24] See eg Case T-23/99, *LR AF 1998 A/S, formerly Løgstør Rør A/S v Commission of the European Communities*, EU:T:2002:75, para 170; and Joined Cases T-109/02, T-118/02, T-122/02, T-125/02, T-126/02, T-128/02, T-129/02, T-132/02 and T-136/02, *Bolloré SA and Others v Commission of the European Communities*, EU:T:2007:115, para 45.

[25] Case T-36/91, *Imperial Chemical Industries plc v Commission of the European Communities*, EU:T:1995:118 (*ICI*).

[26] Likewise, it had rejected Solvay's request to access the documents emanating from ICI.

on Competition Policy, where it had addressed the problems of disclosing documents in procedures involving several competing firms. The Report stated that in cases where proceedings were instituted against several competing firms, the Commission had to, for reasons of public interest, ensure that the access to files did not lead to an exchange of commercially sensitive information between the companies under investigation. The Commission now claimed that, given the statements in its Report, no one could have had any reason to expect it to grant access to the documents in question.[27] The General Court did not accept this new stance taken by the Commission and declared that while undertakings may have a right to protection of business secrets, this right must be balanced against the right of the defence. Furthermore, the General Court declared, the Commission could not justify its outright refusal to make disclosure by claiming that Solvay had requested confidential treatment of the documents provided. Instead, the Commission should have endeavoured to find ways to disclose as much information as possible by, for example, deleting sensitive passages in the documents at hand or at least providing ICI with a list of the documents in the file, and then allowed ICI to request access to specific documents in the file.[28]

The General Court's view in these cases till stands. Over the years, both the EU Courts and the legislator have confirmed that in order to allow undertakings to defend themselves effectively against the objections raised against them in the statement of objections, the Commission has an obligation to make available the investigation file, except for documents containing business secrets of other undertakings, other confidential information and internal documents. In addition, the right to the protection of business secrets must be weighed against the safeguarding of the right of the defence. Therefore, if the Commission takes the view that certain documents in its file contain business secrets or other confidential information, it should prepare non-confidential versions of those documents or have them prepared by the undertakings providing the documents in question. If the preparation of non-confidential versions of all the documents proves difficult, it should send the parties concerned a sufficiently precise list of the documents posing problems so as to enable them to ascertain whether it is appropriate to seek access to specific documents. In the following, the legislative framework now surrounding the Commission's procedures will be presented.

II. Access to the File – The Legislative Framework

As discussed in section I, the right of access to the file in competition cases was first introduced by the Commission. Once there, the EU judiciary has made the Commission stick to its words, and has interpreted and clarified the scope and

[27] *ICI* (n 25) para 58. The Commission had rejected the principle that there is an obligation to disclose its files.

[28] Ibid para 103.

meaning of the right. Today it is firmly established in the Charter and is also protected by the Antitrust Regulations. The Commission's procedures surrounding access to the file are outlined in a number of soft law instruments: notices, best practices and a manual of procedures.

A. The Charter Provisions

As stated in the introductory part of this chapter, access to the file is one of the procedural safeguards intended to protect the right of the defence and to ensure, in particular, that the right to be heard may be exercised effectively. A company experiencing problems in accessing its case file may seek to rely on two Charter provisions. The first is Article 41, which establishes a right to good administration. It provides a right for every person to have his or her affairs handled impartially, fairly and within reasonable time by the institutions and bodies of the Union. Article 41(2) declares that the right to good administration includes the right of every person to have access to his or her file, while respecting the legitimate interests of confidentiality and of professional and business secrecy. As discussed in the preceding sections, this right was initially developed in the context of competition law enforcement, but through the Charter it has now gained general application.[29]

The second Charter provision that may be of relevance to cases concerning access to the file is Article 48(2), which explicitly provides for the right of the defence. However, the Article contains a limitation, as it declares that respect for the right of the defence shall be guaranteed to anyone who has been charged, implying that the provision may not be invoked until the Commission has adopted an infringement decision.

Like the undefined legal notion of the right to good administration, the right of the defence is an umbrella concept encompassing a number of procedural safeguards essentially developed through the hands of the ECJ.[30] When the right of access to the file was first acknowledged by the ECJ, it was rationalised as being part of the right of the defence.[31] As will be discussed further in this chapter, while the right is now laid down in Article 41 of the Charter, the underlying rationale behind the right is still to ensure that the parties may properly exercise their defence rights. Thus, the ECJ has consistently held that the right of the defence applies already during the investigatory stage of a cartel case, and that targeted companies' right to access their case file constitutes one of its key components. In *Solvay*, Advocate General Kokott reiterated the statement made by the Court that in all proceedings that may lead to the imposition of penalties, in particular

[29] See eg P Craig, 'Article 41; Right to Good Administration' in S Peers et al (eds), *The EU Charter of Fundamental Rights; A Commentary* (Oxford, Hart Publishing, 2014) 1069, 1073.

[30] Nehl, 'Article 48 Presumption' (n 4) 1289.

[31] See eg Craig, 'Article 41' (n 29) 1073.

fines or penalty payments, protection of the rights of the defence is a fundamental principle of EU law. She then noted that the right had now also been codified in Article 41(2)(a) and Article 48(2) of the Charter, suggesting that the Commission's administrative procedures may be governed by both provisions.[32] In the Grand Chamber ruling following upon the Advocate General's Opinion, the Court made no mention of Article 48, declaring:

> Observance of the rights of the defence in a proceeding before the Commission, the aim of which is to impose a fine on an undertaking for infringement of the competition rules requires that the undertaking under investigation must have been afforded the opportunity to make known its views on the truth and relevance of the facts alleged and on the documents used by the Commission to support its claim that there has been an infringement of the Treaty. Those rights are referred to in Article 41(2)(a) and (b) of the Charter of Fundamental Rights of the European Union.[33]

Thus, while the Court still acknowledges that the obligation to grant access serves to protect the right of the defence, companies will have to rely on Article 41 of the Charter rather than Article 48(2) should the Commission fail to fulfil its obligation to grant access to the documents in its case file. This was also the view taken by the General Court in *Shell v the Commission*, where it declared that Article 41 of the Charter establishes the observance of the rights of the defence as a fundamental right and as a consubstantial element of the right to good administration.[34] Article 48 on the other hand, may be applicable at the stage where the fine has been imposed and the case reaches the courts.

B. Access under Regulation 1/2003

Article 27(2) of Regulation 1/2003 establishes a right for the parties concerned to have their right of defence fully respected in proceedings governed by the Regulation. The article further states that the parties shall be entitled to have access to the Commission's file, subject to the legitimate interests of undertakings in the protection of their business secrets. It sets out further limits to the right of access, declaring that it shall not extend to confidential information and internal documents of the Commission or the NCAs. In particular, the right shall not cover correspondence between the Commission and NCAs, or between the latter, including documents drawn up pursuant to Articles 11 or 14 of the Regulation.[35] However, Article 27(2) also makes it clear that nothing in the article shall prevent the Commission from disclosing and using information necessary to prove an

[32] Opinion of AG Kokott in Case C-109/10 P, *Solvay SA v European Commission*, EU:C:2011:256, para 152.

[33] *Solvay* (n 5) para 53.

[34] Case T-343/06, *Shell Petroleum NV and Others v European Commission*, EU:T:2012:478, para 82.

[35] Art 11 governs cooperation between the Commission and the NCAs, and Art 14 consultations with the Advisory Committee.

infringement. This also means that confidentiality may have to give way to targeted companies' defence rights.

C. Access under Regulation 773/2004

Regulation 773/2004 governs the conduct of the Commission's proceedings in more detail. Article 15 lays down the Commission's procedures for granting access to the file. There are important limitations and conditions governing the granting of access. First of all, Article 15 stipulates that access is granted upon request by the parties. The file is thus not automatically submitted to them. Second, not everyone targeted by the Commission's investigations has a right to access the file. It is only where the investigation results in the adoption of a statement of objections against one or several companies that those companies are granted access to the case file. If there is no statement of objections, or if it is not addressed to a company, there is thus no right for that company to access the file.

Article 15(1)(a) and (b) contain further exceptions. Article 15(1)(a) stipulates that after the initiation of proceedings pursuant to Article 11(6) of Regulation 1/2003, and in order to enable the parties to introduce settlement submissions, the Commission shall disclose to them the objections envisaged against them and non-confidential versions of any specified accessible document listed in the case file at that point in time. When introducing their settlement submissions, the parties shall confirm to the Commission that they will only require access to the file if the statement of objections does not reflect the contents of their settlement submissions. Where settlement discussions have been discontinued with one or more of the parties, such party shall be granted access to the file when a statement of objections has been addressed to it. Furthermore, Article 15(1)(b) declares that access to leniency statements and settlement submissions shall only be granted at the premises of the Commission. The parties and their representatives may not copy the leniency corporate statements or settlement submissions by any mechanical or electronic means.

Article 15(2) provides further limits to the right. Echoing the Court's case law and Regulation 1/2003, it declares that the right shall not extend to business secrets, other confidential information or internal documents of the Commission or of the NCAs.[36] Neither shall it extend to correspondence between the Commission and the NCAs or between the latter. Like Article 27(2) of Regulation 1/2003, Article 15(3) declares that nothing in the Regulation prevents the Commission from disclosing and using information necessary to prove an infringement of

[36] The wording of the article suggests that targeted companies may gain access to documents that the Commission has received from competition authorities outside the EU. However, it is clear from point 15 of the Access Notice that the Commission will not grant access to such documents. In the case of Lantmännen, the EU rejected the claim that documents originating from settlement discussions should benefit from a presumption of confidentiality on the sole ground that they originated from such discussions. See Case C-318/19 P(R).

Article 101 or 102 TFEU. Article 15(4) limits the use of the documents submitted to targeted companies, declaring that they may only be used for the application of the two treaty provisions.

D. The Access Notice

In addition to any binding legislation, the Commission has issued a number of soft law instruments laying out the details of its practices. One of these instruments is the Access Notice.[37] It was first published in 1997[38] and provides a framework for the exercise of the right in antitrust or merger cases. Interesting to note is that the 1997 Notice acknowledged that 'all documents not regarded as non-communicable [under the confidentiality criteria] are accessible to the parties concerned' and that 'thus, access to the file is not limited to documents which the Commission regards as relevant to an undertakings' right of defence'.[39] It is clear from the wording of the current Notice that it only governs situations where the addressee of a statement of objections is seeking access to its file. This is in line with the wording of Regulation 773/2004 and limits not only the personal but also the temporal scope of the right, as access will not be granted to targeted companies prior to the notification of the statement of objections. Point 26 explicitly stipulates that the parties have no right of access to the file prior to the notification of the Commission's statement of objections. However, already in point 3 the Commission declares that the term 'access to the file' is used in the Notice exclusively to mean the access granted to the addressees of the statement of objections, thereby excluding from its scope those situations where parties seek access during the investigatory stage of the administrative procedure.

According to the Notice, access will be granted upon request and normally on a single occasion, following the notification of the statement of objections. As a general rule, no access will be granted to other parties' replies to the Commission's objections.[40] A party will, however, be granted access to documents received after notification of the objections at later stages of the administrative procedure, where such documents may constitute new evidence – whether of an incriminating or of an exculpatory nature – pertaining to the allegations concerning that party in the Commission's statement of objections. This is particularly the case where the Commission intends to rely on new evidence.[41] Furthermore, the consolidated

[37] Access Notice (n 9).

[38] Commission Notice 97/C 23/03 on the internal rules of procedure for processing requests for access to the file pursuant to Articles 85 and 86 of the EC Treaty and Articles 65 and 66 of the ECSC Treaty and Council Regulation 4064/89 [1997] OJ C23/3.

[39] Ibid point 1.B. See also HP Nehl, *Principles of Administrative Procedure in EC Law* (Oxford, Hart Publishing, 1999) 54.

[40] Access Notice, point 27.

[41] Ibid.

version of the Notice refers to the Notice on the conduct of proceedings discussed in section II.E, which provides for further access to such documents when the Commission considers it useful.

The Notice not only indicates the point in time at which parties will be given access, but also provides guidance on what documents the Commission considers to be (i) part of its file, and (ii) accessible. According to Section II.B of the Access Notice, the file consists of all documents that have been obtained, produced and/or assembled by DG COMP during the course of an investigation. The Commission takes note of the fact that some documents collected during an investigation may prove to be unrelated to the subject matter of the investigation. These may therefore be returned to the company from which they were collected, and shall then no longer be considered part of the file. Mirroring the Antitrust Regulations, the Notice excludes from any disclosure obligation internal documents, correspondence with other public authorities, confidential documents and business secrets. If a party considers that, after having obtained access to the file, it requires knowledge of specific non-accessible information for its defence, it may submit a reasoned request to that end to DG COMP. If DG COMP is not in a position to accept the request, and if the party disagrees with that view, the matter will be resolved by the Hearing Officer.[42]

E. The Commission's Notice on Best Practices for Conduct of Proceedings Concerning Articles 101 and 102 TFEU

The Commission's Notice on Best Practices for Conduct of Proceedings Concerning Articles 101 and 102 TFEU ('the Conduct of Proceedings Notice'),[43] which was published in 2011, has the principal purpose to provide practical guidance on the conduct of antitrust proceedings before the Commission. It contains a number of provisions dealing with the parties' right to access the file, most of them reflecting what is stated in the Antitrust Regulations. The Conduct of Proceedings Notice declares that where required by the rights of defence, or where it may – in the Commission's view – help to further clarify factual and legal issues relevant for the case, the Commission may give parties a copy of the non-confidential version (or specific parts thereof) of other parties' written replies to the statement of objections. According to the Notice, this would normally be done prior to the oral hearing, so as to allow parties to comment on them at the hearing. The Commission may also decide to do so in appropriate cases with respect to complainants and admitted third parties. If access is granted because it is required for the rights of the defence, parties are also entitled to have sufficient additional

[42] Access Notice, point 47.

[43] Commission Notice on Best Practices for the Conduct of Proceedings Concerning Articles 101 and 102 TFEU [2011] OJ C308/6.

time to comment on these replies. For obvious reasons, the obligation to provide access when required by the rights of the defence also existed prior to the adoption of the Conduct of Proceedings Notice, albeit that it was not explicitly acknowledged in a Commission Notice. However, the Commission's declaration that it may, at its own discretion, grant parties, complainants or other third parties access when it considers it to be useful is a new feature, and this has prompted a revision of the Access Notice, which now contains a footnote referring to the Conduct of Proceedings Notice.

F. *The Manual of Procedures*

The Manual of Procedures is an internal working tool intended to give practical guidance to staff on how to conduct antitrust investigations. The *Manual* is published on the Commission's website and may therefore also serve as guidance for companies targeted by the Commission's investigations. Module 12 gives guidance on the practical modalities of managing access to files and dealing with confidentiality claims. The module provides valuable practical information on how the Commission approaches these matters, discussing, inter alia, which documents are considered part of the file and whether or not they should be considered accessible, and laying out the procedure for dealing with confidentiality claims and how the access-to-file work should be conducted by the staff of DG COMP.

G. The Commission's *Best Practices on the Disclosure of Information in Data Rooms*

The Commission's case files are voluminous, to say the least, and the access to file work implies a substantive assessment of confidentiality claims and requires legal and procedural knowledge. Granting access to the file, the Commission declares, is often a complex exercise given the tension between two fundamental interests: on the one hand the rights of defence of the parties targeted by the investigation; and on the other, the protection of confidential information by the author or owner of the document.[44]

The purpose of the Data Room Best Practices[45] is to provide practical guidance on when and how to use data rooms to disclose, in a restricted manner, business secrets and other confidential information obtained during antitrust proceedings. The document aims at increasing transparency and the predictability of the

[44] *Antitrust Manual of Procedures* (n 8) module 12, 'Access to File and Confidentiality', section 1, point (1).

[45] DG Competition, *Best Practices on the disclosure of information in data rooms in proceedings under Articles 101 and 102 TFEU and under the Merger Regulation*, available at https://ec.europa.eu/competition/mergers/legislation/disclosure_information_data_rooms_en.pdf.

process within the existing legal and procedural framework, thereby enhancing the efficiency of antitrust and merger investigations, the Commission declares.

During the course of its investigation, DG COMP obtains both quantitative and qualitative information, some of which may serve as evidence underpinning the reasoning in the statement of objections. Data collected from third parties (such as cost and price data, sales data, bidding data, margins, etc) often constitute business secrets, which are by nature confidential. The Commission acknowledges that in particular if the data are of a quantitative nature, it may not be possible to provide, in a timely manner, a meaningful non-confidential version. Exceptionally, this may also be true for qualitative information (such as internal strategy documents of competitors).[46] However, granting access to such data may be necessary in certain circumstances for an effective exercise of the rights of defence. In its best practice, the Commission declares that data rooms are an exceptional tool that can safeguard the rights of defence while respecting the legitimate interests of confidentiality of the undertakings or persons from which the Commission has obtained the information. By means of a data room, documents in the file are made accessible to an addressee of a statement of objections in a restricted manner, that is by limiting the number and/or category of persons having access and the use of the information being accessed to the extent strictly necessary for the exercise of the rights of defence.[47]

H. The Hearing Officer's Mandate

The post of the Hearing Officer was first established in 1982 to enhance impartiality and objectivity in competition proceedings. The Hearing Officer is responsible for organising and conducting oral hearings, and acting as an independent arbiter when a dispute about the effective exercise of procedural rights between parties and DG COMP arises in antitrust and merger proceedings. The powers and duties of the Hearing Officer are set out in Decision 2011/695 of the President of the European Commission on the function and the terms of the Hearing Officer ('the Hearing Officer's Mandate' or 'the Mandate').

Chapter 4, Article 7 of the Mandate deals with the situation when a party has reason to believe that the Commission has not fulfilled its obligations under Article 27(2) of Regulation 1/2003. As noted by Kellerbauer et al, the most common source of disagreement is the view taken by some undertakings that they are entitled to see documents that information providers consider to be confidential or the Commission considers to be internal.[48] The provision stipulates that where a

[46] Ibid, point 7.
[47] Ibid point 9.
[48] M Kellerbauer et al, 'Procedures to Establish the Existence of an Infringement' in L Ortiz Blanco (ed), *EU Competition Procedure*, 3rd edn (Oxford, Oxford University Press, 2013) 393, 420.

party that has exercised its right of access to the file has reason to believe that the Commission has in its possession documents that have not been disclosed to it, and that those documents are necessary for the proper exercise of the right to be heard, it may make a reasoned request for access to these documents to the Hearing Officer, subject to Article 3(7). The latter article requires the party to turn to the Director General of DG COMP before referring the issue to the Hearing Officer.

III. When Should Access be Granted?

The question on the timing of the Commission's disclosure is of great practical importance. Article 27 of Regulation 1/2003 affords the parties a right of access but is silent on when such access should be granted. Under the Commission's current practice, the right of the targeted companies to gain access to the Commission's case file begins as soon as they are notified of the statement of objections. In the Access Notice, the Commission declares that parties have no right of access prior to such notification. The parties, on the other hand, may want to access evidence at an earlier stage of the administrative procedure, and the issue has therefore been one for the EU Courts. The Courts have sided with the Commission and declared that parties should not be allowed access before the case reaches the adversarial stage. The two cases of *Dalmine* and *Orange* both illustrate the Court's reasoning and the rationale behind its stance. In *Dalmine*,[49] the applicant objected to the Commission's use of statements that had been given in a criminal case by Dalmine's former managers to the public prosecutor of Bergamo. Dalmine claimed that the Commission had seriously prejudiced the company's right of the defence by failing to inform Dalmine promptly that it was in possession of these confidential statements.[50] In its ruling, the General Court found that Dalmine had not put forward any legal basis on which it would be entitled to be informed, before receiving the statement of objections, of the fact that the Commission had in its possession minutes of statements made by some of the undertaking's former managers to the public prosecutor.[51] The General Court declared that when the Commission requests information from undertakings it suspects of having participated in an infringement, it is under no obligation to inform them of the evidence already in its possession. The communication of that information might prejudice the effectiveness of the Commission's investigation, as it would enable the undertakings in question to identify what information is already known to the Commission and therefore what information could still be concealed from it, the General Court concluded. This view was later confirmed by the ECJ, which declared that if the right of access was extended to the period preceding the notification of the statement of objections, this would

[49] Case T-50/00, *Dalmine SpA v Commission of the European Communities*, EU:T:2004:220.
[50] Ibid para 75.
[51] Ibid para 83.

prejudice the effectiveness of the Commission's investigations in the way described by the General Court.[52]

Similarly, in *Orange*, the applicant had argued that the inspection carried out by the Commission had been arbitrary, claiming that the Commission had not been in possession of reliable indicia against it when deciding to carry out the dawn raid.[53] To this the General Court responded that it should be borne in mind that the administrative procedure is divided into two distinct and successive stages: the investigation stage and the *inter partes* stage. It is not until the beginning of the second stage, when the Commission issues its statement of objections, that the company is informed of all the essential evidence on which the Commission relies and the company gets access to the file. As in *Dalmine*, the General Court declared that if those rights were extended to the investigation stage, the effectiveness of the Commission's investigation would be compromised, since the undertaking concerned would be able, at the preliminary investigation stage, to identify the information known to the Commission, hence also the information that could still be concealed from it.[54] However, the General Court continued, the measures taken during the investigation stage suggest, by their very nature, that an infringement has been committed and may have major repercussions on the situation of the undertaking under suspicion. Thus, the duty on the part of the Commission to specify the subject matter and purpose of the inspection serves to protect the company's right of the defence at the investigation stage.

The General Court declared that although the duty to specify the subject matter and purpose of the inspection is a fundamental requirement designed to safeguard the applicant's right of the defence, and which may thus not be limited due to considerations relating to the effectiveness of the investigation, the Commission cannot be required to indicate the evidence leading it to consider that Article 102 TFEU has possibly been infringed.[55] Such an obligation, the General Court declared, would upset the balance struck by the case law, between preserving the effectiveness of the investigation and upholding the rights of defence of the undertaking concerned.[56]

Thus, to conclude, it is the view of the EU Courts that during the investigation stage, the Commission should be rather secretive, not disclosing the evidence in its case file; but once the statement of objections has been notified and the case moves on into the second, adversarial stage, the parties have a right to access the case file.[57]

[52] Case C-407/07 P, *Dalmine SpA v Commission of the European Communities*, EU:C:2007:53, para 60.
[53] Case T-402/13, *Orange v European Commission*, EU:T:2014:991, para 75.
[54] Ibid para 78.
[55] Ibid para 81.
[56] Ibid paras 80–81. This line of argumentation is recognised from Case T-296/11, *Cementos Portland Valderrivas SA v European Commission*, EU:T:2014:121, where the General Court made an identical statement in para 37.
[57] Interesting to note is that in its Conduct of Proceedings Notice, the Commission declares that in the spirit of encouraging an open exchange of views, it will, in cases based on formal complaints,

IV. Which Documents are Part of the File and Accessible?

While there is now a right for parties to access their file, the scope and meaning of this right cannot be fully understood unless one knows which documents are considered to be part of the file and if there are any exceptions to the right of access. Statutory legislation is silent on the definition of the notion, leaving interpretation to the Commission and the Courts. In *ICI*, the Hearing Officer went as far as to declare that no one knew what the word 'file' meant.[58] Unfortunately, this could to some extent still be considered to hold true.

A. The Notion of the File

Since the Hearing Officer made his statement in *ICI*, declaring that the problem of access should not be discussed at the hearing, the Charter and the Antitrust Regulations have been adopted, providing parties with a statutory right to access their file. It is therefore more important than ever to define the meaning and scope of this notion. Unfortunately, the legislative provisions give only limited guidance. Article 41 of the Charter lays down the right of every person to have access to his or her file, while respecting the legitimate interests of confidentiality and of professional and business secrecy. According to the Charter explanations, the wording of the right results from the case law, and reference is made to a number of cases, including one competition case: *Orkem*.[59] However, the ruling in *Orkem* does not once mention the word 'file', let alone define its meaning. According to Article 27(2) of Regulation 1/2003, the parties concerned should be entitled to access the 'Commission's file', subject to the legitimate interest of undertakings in the protection of their business secretes. The right of access shall not extend to confidential information or internal documents of the Commission or the NCAs, the article declares.[60] Article 15 of the Procedural Regulation[61] provides a list of information and documents that should be considered inaccessible, and declares that nothing should prevent the Commission from using or disclosing information necessary

provide the parties, at an early stage (unless such is considered likely to prejudice the investigation) and at the latest shortly after the opening of proceedings, with the opportunity of commenting on a non-confidential version of the complaint. The Commission may also provide the parties, shortly after the opening of proceedings, with the opportunity to review non-confidential versions of other 'key submissions' already submitted to the Commission. That said, the review of key submissions will not be offered in the context of cartel proceedings (points 71–74 of the Notice).

[58] *ICI* (n 25) para 14.

[59] Case 374/87, *Orkem SA v the Commission of the European Communities*, EU:C:1989:387.

[60] Art 27(2) of Regulation 1/2003.

[61] Commission Regulation (EC) No 773/2004 of 7 April 2004 relating to the conduct of proceedings by the Commission pursuant to Articles 81 and 82 of the EC Treaty [2004] OJ L123/18.

to prove an infringement of Article 101 or 102 TFEU. No further guidance is provided and the notion of the file is not defined.

Regulation 1/2003 makes it clear that the parties shall be given access to the file but that some categories of information or documents may be exempted from this right. However, judging from the wording of Article 27(2), all other documents or information contained in the file should be accessible. Over the years, and admittedly already before the adoption of Regulation 1/2003, the Commission appears to have taken a narrow stance on which documents form part of the file. It is clear from its practice that it considers the documents collected during the course of the investigation and up until the notification of the statement of objections to make up the file. In the Access Notice, it declares that the 'Commission file' consists of all documents that have been obtained, produced and/or assembled by DG COMP during the investigation.[62] It states further that if the Commission finds a document to be unrelated to the investigation and returns it to the undertaking from which it was obtained, the document shall no longer be considered as part of the file. Also, documents protected by legal professional privilege should be excluded.[63]

The term 'investigation' is not further defined by the Commission in the Access Notice, but the *Manual of Procedures* confirms that it corresponds to the first of the two successive stages of a competition case,[64] declaring that the 'file' consists of all documents obtained, produced and/or assembled by DG COMP during the investigation that has led the Commission to raise its objections.[65] This in turn means that the Commission will not consider the replies to the statement of objections or the documents received during the *inter partes* stage to form part of the file. The question is of course whether Article 41 of the Charter or Article 27(2) of Regulation 1/2003 allows the Commission to make such a division, excluding from its file some of the documents received by the parties prior to the adoption of the infringement decision, and while the case is still open.

[62] Access Notice, point 8. The term 'document' is used for all forms of information support, irrespective of the storage medium, and also covers any electronic data storage device as may be or become available. This means that documents submitted to or in possession of services other than DG COMP should not be regarded as part of the file. This view is also confirmed in module 12, subsection 2.1 of the *Manual of Procedures* (n 8).

[63] Module 12, subsection 2.1 of the *Manual of Procedures* (n 8).

[64] Over the years, the EU Courts have divided antitrust procedures into two stages: the preparatory investigation stage; and the *inter partes* stage. See eg *Orkem* (n 59) para 20, and *Cimenteries* (n 7) para 45.

[65] Module 12, subsection 2.1 of the *Manual of Procedures* (n 8). In *Hercules*, the Commission argued that the applicant should not have a right of access to the replies to the statement of objections. More precisely, it denied 'that a right may be derived from a desire to glean ideas as to how to defend oneself from the arguments put forward by the other producers involved'. The Commission referred to its Twelfth Report on Competition Policy, stressing that access to the file must concern only documents obtained during the course of the investigation pursuant to Arts 11 and 14 of Regulation No 17. In that Report, the Commission in no way undertook to grant access to any replies received subsequent to the statement of objections. See Case C-51/92 P, *Hercules Chemicals NV v Commission of the European Communities*, EU:C:1999:357, para 70.

The General Court takes the view that such a division is compatible with Article 27(2) of Regulation 1/2003. In *Shell v Commission*, it sided with the Commission and declared that an obligation to give access to other parties' replies to the statement of objections applies to information on which the Commission intends to rely in its infringement decision. In the case at hand, Shell had been granted access to certain passages of one of the replies to the statement of objections, as the Commission intended to rely on those passages in order to classify the company as instigator and leader of the cartel. In its application, Shell argued that by refusing to disclose all the replies, the Commission had infringed Article 27(2) of Regulation 1/2003 and its right of the defence.[66] In its ruling, the General Court declared that the other parties' replies to the statement of objections are not in principle included in the documents of the investigation file that the parties may consult. Acknowledging that the Commission must grant access to parts of the replies to the statement of objections that may be useful for the parties' defence, it declared that it was up to the Commission to determine whether or not a piece of information could be of such use. Interesting to note is that in *Aalborg Portland*, the Court had to rule on whether the Commission could preclude certain documents from the administrative procedure, and then declared that it could not be for the Commission alone, who notifies any objections and adopts the decision imposing a penalty, to determine the documents of use in the defence of the undertaking concerned.[67] However, according to the General Court, that argument, relating to documents within the file compiled by the Commission, could not apply to the replies given by other parties concerned to the statement of objections.[68]

Likewise, in *Cimenteries*, the General Court declared that the Commission is not required to make available, on its own initiative, documents that are not in its investigation file, in that case including replies to the statement of objections, and which it does not intend to use against the parties concerned in the final decision. Consequently, an applicant who learns during the administrative procedure that the Commission has documents that might be useful for its defence must make an express request to the Commission for access to those documents.[69] The General Court's view is reflected in the *Manual of Procedures*, which states that as concerns exculpatory documents, access to documents after the notification of the objections can be granted upon a specific request of a party, where such documents may constitute new evidence and pertain to the allegations concerning that party, which are ultimately relevant for the Commission's final decision.[70]

This to some extent artificial division between documents received before or after the adoption of the statement of objections is unfortunate for a number of reasons. We know that the right of the defence prevents the Commission

[66] *Shell* (n 34) para 75.

[67] Joined Cases C-204/00 P, C-205/00 P, C-211/00 P, C-213/00 P, C-217/00 P and C-219/00 P, *Aalborg Portland A/S and Others v Commission of the European Communities*, EU:C:2004:6, para 126.

[68] *Shell* (n 34) para 89.

[69] *Cimenteries* (n 7) paras 380 and 383.

[70] Module 12, Subsection 4.1 of the *Manual of Procedures*.

from relying on evidence in its decision to which the parties have not been granted access or given the opportunity to comment upon. This means that the Commission is required to grant access to inculpatory documents received after the notification of the statement of objections, at least if it intends to rely on such evidence in its infringement decision. Furthermore, as will be further discussed in section V, the Commission is under an obligation to allow the parties access to evidence that may be useful to their defence, this irrespective of whether the Commission receives it prior to or after the adoption of the statement of objections. As mentioned in section II.V, the Commission may also grant access to the replies to statement of objections if it considers that it would help to further clarify factual and legal issues. The Commission considers this decision to be at its discretion.

This means that in some instances, the Commission has to grant access to documents received during the adversarial stage in order to safeguard the defence rights, and in some instances it may do so if it considers that it would further the investigation. It can be questioned whether it should be for the Commission to select which evidence received after the adoption of the statement of objections may be useful for the parties' defence. While the General Court was clear on this point in *Shell*, it is hard to see why the Court's reasoning in *Aalborg Portland* should not also apply to evidence received by the Commission after the adoption of the statement of objections. Furthermore, and as noted by the General Court in *Solvay*, when a party does not have access to the documents in question, it is unable likewise to decide whether or not it would use them in its defence.[71] Second, as for the Commission's possibility to grant access to certain documents if it considers that granting access would further the investigation, this practice could be questioned from an equality perspective. Are targeted companies treated alike if some are granted access to certain types of evidence and others not?

A final point concerns the reason behind the exclusion from the case file of documents received during the adversarial stage. In *Bolloré*, the Commission justified this division with the desire to avoid procedures that continue *ad infinitum*.[72] This is understandable, but not necessarily a valid argument, especially as there is nothing preventing the Commission from granting access to the documents in question prior to the oral hearing, and then having the parties comment on the evidence in question at the hearing instead of in a written submission.

B. Accessible Documents

In the Grand Chamber ruling in *Solvay*, the Court declared that the right of access required the Commission to provide the undertaking concerned with the

[71] Case T-30/91, *Solvay SA v Commission of the European Communities*, EU:T:1995:115, para 83.

[72] Joined Cases T-109/02, T-118/02, T-122/02, T-125/02, T-126/02, T-128/02, T-129/02, T-132/02 and T-136/02, *Bolloré SA and Others v Commission of the European Communities*, EU:T:2007:115, para 53.

opportunity to examine all the documents in the investigation that might be relevant for its defence. Those documents comprise both inculpatory and exculpatory evidence, with the exception of business secrets of other undertakings, internal documents of the Commission and other confidential information.[73] Both Article 41 of the Charter and Article 27 of Regulation 1/2003 grant parties a right to access their file. However, just as the Court declared in *Solvay*, this does not mean that all documents put on the file are accessible. As will be discussed in more detail in chapter 8, Article 339 TFEU and Article 28 of Regulation 1/2003 both prevent Commission officials from publishing or otherwise disclosing information covered by professional secrecy.[74] Article 27(2) of Regulation 1/2003 makes the obligation to provide access subject to the legitimate interest of undertakings in the protection of their business secrets. Furthermore, it explicitly excludes confidential information and internal documents of the Commission or the NCAs from the disclosure obligation. In particular, the article declares, the right of access shall not extend to correspondence between the Commission and the NCAs, or between the latter, including documents drawn up pursuant to Articles 11 and 14.[75] That said, nothing in Article 27(2) shall prevent the Commission from disclosing and using information necessary to prove an infringement. Article 15(2) of the Procedural Regulation mirrors the wording of Article 27(2).

Thus, while confidential information is generally not considered accessible, the Commission is not prevented from disclosing such information should this be required in order to safeguard the parties' defence rights. The Court already took this view in the case of *Hoffmann La Roche*, declaring that the Commission's obligation not to disclose information covered by professional secrecy must be reconciled with the right to be heard.[76] This is also reflected in the Access Notice, which acknowledges that in cartel proceedings, the qualification of a piece of information as confidential is not a bar to its disclosure if such information is necessary to prove an alleged infringement or could be necessary to exonerate a party. The need to safeguard the parties' rights of the defence through the provision of the widest possible access to the file may outweigh the concern to protect confidential information of other parties, the Access Notice states. It is for the Commission to assess whether those circumstances apply to any specific situation. This calls for an assessment of all relevant elements, including the relevance of the information, whether it is indispensable, the degree of sensitivity and the seriousness of the infringement.[77]

[73] *Solvay* (n 5) para 54.

[74] For discussion of the meaning of the notions of professional secrecy, confidential information and business secrets, see ch 8.

[75] Art 11 governs cooperation between the Commission and the NCAs, and Art 14 consultations with the Advisory Committee.

[76] *Hoffmann-La Roche* (n 14) para 13.

[77] Access Notice, point 24.

Internal documents, such as drafts, opinions or memos, are also considered inaccessible. The Commission takes the view that they may be neither inculpatory nor exculpatory, and do not constitute part of the evidence on which the Commission can rely in its assessment of a case.[78] Given their lack of evidential value, this restriction does not prejudice the proper exercise of the parties' right of defence, the Commission declares in the Access Notice. The Notice further states that the Commission is not required to draft any minutes of meetings with any person or undertaking. If the Commission chooses to make notes of such meetings, such documents constitute the Commission's own interpretation of what was said at the meetings, for which reason they are classified as internal documents. Where, however, the person or undertaking in question has agreed the minutes, they will be made accessible after deletion of any business secrets or other confidential information. Such agreed minutes constitute part of the evidence on which the Commission can rely in its assessment of a case.

The Commission's view that it is not required to draw up minutes of meetings reflects the view taken by the General Court in *TACA*, where the applicants had argued that the right of access to the file required the Commission to draw up minutes from meetings with complainants.[79] In its ruling, the General Court declared that there was no general duty to draw up minutes of meetings or telephone conversations with complainants, but if the Commission wished to rely on statements made during the course of such conversations, it had to create a written document to be put on the file and made accessible to the parties.[80] While it is unlikely that a complainant will provide exculpatory information, such information may be provided in meetings with others. It is unfortunate if such oral information is not recorded and made available to the parties.

This was also recognised by the European Ombudsman following a complaint by Intel alleging procedural errors by the Commission during the course of an investigation concerning possible abuse of dominance. Intel claimed that the Commission had failed to take minutes of a meeting with Dell, despite the fact that the meeting directly concerned the subject matter of the Commission's investigation. The Ombudsman adopted a decision in which he found that the Commission had gathered information relating to the subject matter of the investigation during the meeting with Dell. He also found that the Commission had failed to make a proper note of that meeting and that the investigation file did not include the agenda of the meeting. The Ombudsman concluded that the Commission had committed an instance of maladministration, but did not make any finding as to whether the Commission had infringed Intel's rights of the defence.[81] Intel had

[78] Access Notice, point 12.

[79] Joined Cases T-191/98, T-212/98 to T-214/98, *Atlantic Container Line AB and Others v Commission of the European Communities*, EU:T:2003:245, para 350.

[80] Ibid para 351.

[81] Summary of the European Ombudsman's decision on complaint 1935/2008/FOR, available at www.ombudsman.europa.eu/en/press-release/en/4403.

also claimed that the Commission had encouraged Dell to enter into an information exchange agreement with AMD,[82] which would allow AMD access to certain confidential information contained in the Commission's file. During the course of his investigation, the Ombudsman found that the possibility of Dell's entering into such agreement was first raised in a telephone call between senior representatives of Dell and senior Commission representatives. However, since the Commission had not made any notes of the content of that call, the evidence available was not sufficient for the Ombudsman to make any finding of maladministration as regards Intel's second allegation. The Ombudsman recommended that in the future, proper internal notes should be made of the content of meetings or telephone calls with third parties concerning important procedural issues.

The Conduct of Proceedings Notice, which was published two years after the Ombudsman's decision, does not accommodate the concerns expressed by the Ombudsman. That said, the Notice declares that during the investigative phase, DG COMP may hold meetings or conduct phone calls with the parties, with complainants, or with third parties. After such meetings or calls the parties, complainants or third parties may want to substantiate their statements or presentations in writing. According to point 44 of the Conduct of Proceedings Notice, any such written documentation communicated to DG COMP will be put on the file. A non-confidential version, together with a brief note prepared by DG COMP, will be made accessible to the parties when they are granted access to the file. Subject to any anonymity requests, this note will mention the undertaking(s) attending the meeting (or participating in the phone call relating to substantive issues) and the timing and topic(s) covered by the meeting (or phone call). Such a brief note will also be prepared when the meeting takes place on the Commission's initiative. The Commission will further grant access to the recordings of any interviews carried out during the investigation and included in the file. The *Manual of Procedures* acknowledges that this requires the Commission to ensure that business secrets and other confidential information is duly protected, which may include an obligation to protect the identity of the interviewee, especially in those cases where the employer is not aware that one of its employees has given an interview.

Another sensitive issue that needs to be handled by the Commission concerns corporate statements made by leniency applicants and forming part of the file. The Procedural Regulation was amended following the adoption of the Damages Directive. Reflecting Article 6(6) of the Damages Directive, Article 16(a) now explicitly limits the granting of access to both corporate statements and settlement submissions, stating that access to such documents shall be granted only for the purposes of exercising the rights of defence in proceedings before the Commission. Furthermore, the article stipulates, information taken from such statements and submissions may be used by the party having obtained access to

[82] AMD, or Advanced Micro Devices Inc, is a competitor to Intel, and was also the target of Intel's exclusionary practices.

the file only where necessary for the exercise of its rights of defence in proceedings before the European Courts reviewing Commission decisions, or before the courts of the Member States in cases that are directly related to the case in which access has been granted.

The recitals to the Leniency Notice acknowledge that the protection of corporate statements is not a bar to their disclosure to other addressees of the statement of objections in order to safeguard their rights of defence. Also the *Manual of Procedures* acknowledges a right to access such statements, as these statements describe the infringement. Subsection 4.1.2 of module 12 of the *Manual of Procedures* thus states that access to both written and oral statements will be made upon request, and will be granted at the Commission's premises following the issuing of the statement of objections. In the case of written corporate statements, access will be granted by allowing the party to read the document at the Commission's premises and to take notes or make dictation. With respect to oral statements, access will be granted by allowing the party to read the Commission transcript of the recording and to take notes. The party will also, on request, be given the opportunity to listen to (relevant parts of) a copy of the original recording in case of doubts concerning the correctness of the statement. Any direct reproduction of the statements (or their recordings/transcripts) by mechanical or electronic means is prohibited. Forrester and Berghe are critical of this order.[83] According to them, the transcript is often dictated by the leniency applicants' lawyers rather than the Commission officials. These lawyers may, for natural reasons, want to downplay the role of their clients and inculpate the co-conspirators, they note. However, their main concern appears to be that the inculpated companies do not have access to the raw material uncovered by the leniency applicant, and that there is no opportunity for the alleged co-infringers to challenge the witness whose story the confessing lawyer tells, and thus no mechanism to discover how credible unseen witnesses are.[84]

The Leniency Notice complements the *Manual of Procedures*, and declares that access to corporate statements is only granted provided that the addressees of the statement of objections commit – together with the legal counsel getting access on their behalf – not to make any copy by mechanical or electronic means of any information in the corporate statement to which access is being granted, and to ensure that the information will be used solely for the purposes of judicial or administrative proceedings for the application of the EU competition rules at issue in the related administrative proceedings. The use of such information for a

[83] I Forrester and P Berghe, 'Leniency: The Poisoned Chalice or the Pot at the End of the Rainbow?' in C Beaton-Wells and C Tran (eds), *Anti-cartel Enforcement in a Contemporary Age: Leniency Religion* (Oxford, Hart Publishing, 2015) 159, 171.

[84] Ibid. They also argue that the Commission and the EU Courts attribute too much probative value to leniency statements. They claim that the EU Courts tend to consider that leniency statements are particularly credible due to the potential adverse consequences in terms of fines, follow-on damages or reputational damages for the applicant company.

different purpose during the proceeding may be regarded as lack of cooperation within the meaning of the Leniency Notice. Other parties involved in the procedure, such as complainants, will not be granted access to corporate statements.

As discussed in more detail in section IV.A, the replies to the statement of objections and any observations to the statement of objections submitted to the Commission by third parties (such as complainants) at that stage are not considered to form part of the Commission's file. That said, if new facts or evidence appear as a result of the addressees' replies, investigation measures taken separately or a new complaint, the companies have to be given an opportunity to give their explanations of these new aspects. Again, unless the companies are not given such opportunity, the Commission cannot rely on those new aspects in its final decision. If these new elements justify raising supplementary objections in substance, or they imply a modification in the intrinsic nature of the infringement with which the company is charged, they have to be communicated to the targeted companies by a supplementary statement of objections in due form.[85] If, on the other hand, new information only corroborates the objections already raised against the companies, it is sufficient to bring them to the attention of the parties by a simple letter, giving the parties the possibility to provide written comments on the new evidence within a fixed deadline.

V. Consequences of the Commission's Failure to Grant Access

It is clear from the foregoing that both statutory legislation and the Court's case law require the Commission to adhere to the policy initially introduced by the Commission itself in 1982, and grant the parties access to the case file. If required in order to protect the parties' rights of the defence, it will have to find ways to disclose confidential information without causing unnecessary harm to the owner of such information. Furthermore, the Commission is prohibited from basing its infringement decisions on evidence that has not been communicated to the parties during the course of the administrative procedure. As will be discussed in this section, such evidence is not admissible and will be struck by the EU Courts,[86] but failure to observe the right of access or the right to be heard can also result in the annulment of the infringement decision.

In the cases of *Solvay* and *ICI*, for example, the Commission's refusal to grant access made the General Court annul the Commission's infringement decision against the two companies for breach of the rights of the defence. The General Court found that during the administrative proceedings, the Commission had

[85] *Manual of Procedures*, (n 8), module II, subsection 8.1.

[86] See eg Case C-62/86, *AKZO Chemie BV v Commission of the European Communities*, EU:C:1991:286, para 21.

not granted sufficient access to the case file, and that it should have, at the very least, supplied a list of documents coming from the other undertakings, in order to enable the applicants to ascertain their exact content as well as their usefulness to the defence.[87] The investigations against the two companies concerned both Articles 101 and 102 TFEU. Solvay had been found guilty not only of cartel participation but also of abuse of dominance, and the Commission had thus adopted two infringement decisions against the company. Finding that the Commission had failed to respect Solvay's defence rights, the General Court also annulled the decision concerning Article 102 TFEU. The Commission later adopted a new infringement decision against Solvay, but this decision was eventually annulled by the ECJ in a Grand Chamber ruling. As it turned out, the Commission had mislaid several sets of documents in the case file, and could not even provide a list of those documents as the indexes to the binders in question could not be found. Finding that the missing documents might contain information useful for Solvay's defence, the Court set aside the General Court's ruling and annulled the Commission's infringement decision.[88] The Commission thus had to see both the first and the second Article 102 decisions annulled due to its failure to grant access and respect the defence rights of Solvay.

These rulings show that failure by the Commission to grant access to the case file may have serious consequences.[89] However, as will be discussed in this section, the EU Courts will not annul an infringement decision unless the Commission's refusal to grant access constitutes an infringement of the applicant's rights of the defence. Furthermore, as noted by the General Court in *Cimenteries*,[90] even though they may constitute an infringement of the rights of the defence, Commission measures refusing access to the file often produce only limited effects. Therefore, the General Court declared, only measures immediately and irreversibly affecting the legal situation of the undertakings concerned would be of such a nature as to justify, before completion of the administrative procedure, the admissibility of an action for annulment.[91] In most cases, the Court will not establish an infringement of the applicant's defence rights, or will not consider the rights of the applicants to be immediately and irreversibly affected. This means that while evidence may be struck, most infringement decisions will remain valid.

The EU Courts' view can be illustrated by the ruling of the General Court in *Cimenteries*,[92] where it declared that, contrary to the applicants' contentions, the finding that the Commission did not give the applicants proper access to the

[87] *Solvay* (n 71) paras 83–89.

[88] *Solvay* (n 5).

[89] Also ICI's competitor Solvay managed to prove an infringement of its defence rights, which made the General Court annul the infringement decision in so far as it concerned Solvay. See *Solvay* (n 71).

[90] Joined Cases T-10/92, T-11/92, T-12/92 and T-15/92, *Cimenteries CBR and Others v Commission of the European Communities* EU:T:1992:123.

[91] Ibid para 42.

[92] *Cimenteries* (n 7).

investigation file during the administrative procedure could not in itself lead to annulment of the contested decision. Access to the file is not an end in itself but is intended to protect the rights of the defence. Thus, the right of access to the file is inseparable from and dependent on the principle of the rights of the defence, the General Court concluded.[93] Likewise, in the case of *AEG v Commission*, the ECJ found that the incriminating documents relied upon by the Commission in its infringement decision should have been mentioned in and annexed to the statement of objections.[94] As that obligation had not been observed in the case at hand, those documents were struck by the Court. However, the plea of infringement of the rights of the defence was not of a general scope, and the Court therefore concluded that the failure did not imply that the procedure as a whole was irregular. According to the Court, the Commission's exclusion of certain documents did not violate the applicant's rights of the defence except to the extent to which the Commission's objections could be proved only by reference to those documents. Consequently, the Court considered whether, after excluding the documents in question, the objections could still be regarded as having been proved.[95] Finding that to be the case, the Court did not annul the decision on this ground.

This view was confirmed by the Court in the more recent case of *Knauf*, where it found it to be settled case law that the failure to communicate a document constitutes a breach of the rights of the defence only if the undertaking concerned shows, first, that the Commission relied on that document to support its objection and, second, that the objection could be proved only by reference to that document.[96] It is for the undertaking concerned to show that the result at which the Commission arrived in its decision would have been different had the Commission not been able to rely on the document in question. *Knauf* and *AEG* both concerned the Commission's failure to communicate incriminating documents. However, it may also be that the Commission fails to communicate possibly exculpatory documents. This was a question for the General Court in the case of *Hercules*.[97] There, the applicant challenged the Commission's refusal to grant it access to the other parties' replies to the statement of objections. According to Hercules, this constituted an infringement of its rights of the defence. It claimed that access to the documents in question should have been given at the stage of the administrative proceedings, in particular in the light of the Commission's allegations that all the undertakings in question had jointly infringed Article 101 TFEU, and that the

[93] Ibid para 156.

[94] In the case of *Dalmine*, the General Court declared that the fact that a document is referred to in a statement of objections without being annexed thereto does not, in principle, constitute an infringement of the rights of the defence, provided that the addressees have access to that document before they are required to reply to the statement of objections. See *Dalmine* (n 49) para 60.

[95] Case C-107/82, *Allgemeine Elektrizitäts-Gesellschaft AEG-Telefunken AG v Commission of the European Communities*, EU:C:1983:293, para 30.

[96] Case C-407/08 P, *Knauf Gips KG v European Commission*, EU:C:2010:389, para 13.

[97] *Hercules* (n 21).

infringement of the rights of the defence could not be remedied after the conclusion of the administrative proceedings and even less once the proceedings before the EU judicature had commenced. In its assessment of Hercules' allegations, the General Court considered it unnecessary to determine whether the Commission's refusal constituted a breach of the rights of the defence, as the applicant had failed to show that the outcome of the administrative procedure could have been different if it had been granted access to the documents in question. It therefore dismissed that ground of challenge.

The General Court's ruling was later appealed to the ECJ,[98] which declared that a breach of the general principles governing right of access to the Commission's file could, in principle, cause the decision to be annulled if the rights of the defence had been infringed. In the case at hand, Hercules had, following the joinder of the cases seeking annulment of the Commission's infringement decision, been granted access to the other parties' replies to the statement of objections. Hercules had not drawn from those replies any exonerating evidence, and the Court therefore concluded that Hercules had failed to establish that those replies contained any evidence of use for its defence. Consequently, it had also failed to establish that the Commission's refusal had infringed its right of the defence. On the contrary, the Court concluded, Hercules had admitted, implicitly but unequivocally, that that was not the case. Contrary to what the General Court had found, the ECJ declared that Hercules was not required to show that the Commission decision would have been different in content had Hercules been given access to the replies during the administrative procedure; only that it would have been able to use the documents for its defence.[99]

In the Grand Chamber ruling in *Solvay*, the Court once again confirmed this stance, noting that where access to the file, and particularly to exculpatory documents, is granted at the stage of the judicial proceedings, the undertaking concerned has to show not that the Commission decision would have been different in content, but only that the documents in question could have been useful for its defence. The Court noted that a belated disclosure does not return the applicant to the situation in which it would have been had it been able to rely on those documents during the administrative procedure. Where access to the file, and particularly to exculpatory documents, is granted at the stage of the judicial proceedings, the Court concluded, the undertaking concerned therefore has to show not that if it had had access to the non-disclosed documents the Commission decision would have been different in content, but only that those documents could have been useful for its defence.[100] This was also the view taken by the ECJ in *Aalborg Portland*. There it declared that it was sufficient for the applicant to show that the exculpatory evidence might have been useful in the sense that, had the

[98] *Hercules* (n 65).
[99] Ibid para 81.
[100] *Solvay* (n 5) para 57.

applicant been able to rely on the documents in question during the administrative procedure, it would have been able to put forward evidence that did not agree with the findings made by the Commission at that stage, and would therefore have been able to have some influence on the Commission's assessment in any decision it adopted.[101]

In the case of *Shell*, the General Court declared that the distinction between exculpatory and inculpatory documents also applied in respect of documents received by the Commission subsequent to the notification of the objections, and that the applicant had therefore misinterpreted the Court's case law when asserting that the Commission automatically infringed Shell's defence rights when it, upon request, refused to communicate such documents.[102] As for exculpatory evidence received after notification of the objections, the party must request access to such documents. Should the Commission refuse to grant access, an infringement of the company's defence rights will only be established if the company can show that the non-disclosure was able to influence, to its disadvantage, the course of the proceedings and the contents of the Commission's decision. In the case at hand, the Commission had allowed the applicant to acquaint itself with the passages of KWS's reply on which it sought to rely in its final decision. The General Court also found those passages to be perfectly understandable without it being necessary to place them in a wider context. The applicant had also argued that the other replies might have contained exculpatory evidence. To this the General Court replied that it was for the applicant to provide prima facie evidence indicating that the non-disclosure was able to influence, to its disadvantage, the course of the proceedings and the contents of the Commission's decision. As Shell had only submitted, in a general and purely speculative manner, that the replies might have provided it with exculpatory evidence regarding its role as instigator and leader, the General Court found that the Commission had been right to refuse to communicate all the replies to the statement of objections and to limit disclosure of KWS's reply to certain passages. The plea was therefore rejected.[103]

To conclude, failure to grant access may result in the annulment of the infringement decision, but only if such failure constitutes a breach of the company's defence rights. As for incriminating evidence, the Commission must have relied on the evidence in question in its infringement decision, and the company must also be able to show that absent that document, the Commission would not have been able to substantiate its objections. Also the failure to grant access to exculpatory evidence received prior to or after the adoption of the statement of objections may constitute a breach of the company's defence rights. The company will then not have to show that the evidence in question would have let it off the hook, only that it would have been able to use it for its defence. The threshold is set

[101] *Aalborg Portland* (n 67), para 75.
[102] *Shell* (n 34), para 86.
[103] Ibid para 94.

quite high, and rightly so. Annulling an infringement decision for the sole reason that the Commission has failed to communicate one document, which together with a number of others formed the basis of the Commission's infringement decision, would have negative consequences that would far outweigh the rights and interests of the company in question. At the same time, it would be unfortunate if the Commission decided not to communicate exculpatory evidence received from the other parties. It may be assumed that such evidence will then not come to the attention of the company in question. The Commission is no doubt walking a fine line between the interests of efficiency and objectivity.

VI. The Parties' Use of the Information Obtained from the Commission

As discussed previously in this chapter, if necessary to protect a party's defence rights, the right of access may encompass documents or other information that is confidential or that constitutes business secrets. It is therefore important to restrict the use of the information transferred. As will be shown in the following, the Commission will not hesitate to take action should a party fail to respect the restrictions imposed.

Article 16a of the Procedural Regulation governs use of documents received. It states that documents obtained through access to the file shall only be used for the purposes of judicial or administrative proceedings for the application of Articles 101 and 102 TFEU. Furthermore, it imposes certain restrictions on the use of information taken from settlement submissions and leniency statements, declaring that such information may only be used in proceedings before the EU Courts reviewing the Commission's decision, or before national courts of the Member States in cases directly related to the case in which access has been granted.

Failure to respect the restrictions may have consequences. The Leniency Notice was revised following the adoption of the Damages Directive, and point 34 now declares that any failure during the proceedings to comply with the provisions of the Procedural Regulation on the use of information obtained through access to the file may be regarded as lack of cooperation within the meaning of points 12 and 27 of the Leniency Notice. In certain circumstances it is subject to penalties to be laid down under national law. Moreover, if any such use is made after the Commission has already adopted a prohibition decision in the proceedings, the Commission may, in addition to applicable penalties under national law, in any legal proceedings before the Union Courts, ask the Court to increase the fine in respect of the responsible undertaking. Should any of the above limitations on the use of information be breached, at any point in time, with the involvement of an outside counsel, the Commission may report the incident to the bar of that counsel, with a view to disciplinary action.

VII. Does the EU Standard Meet the ECHR Standard?

The right to good administration laid down in Article 41 of the Charter is a so-called third-generation right and lacks a corresponding provision in the ECHR. Nor does the ECHR contain any provision explicitly granting parties a right to access their case files during the course of administrative procedures. This does not mean that parties have no right to access their case files under the Convention, and that Article 52(3) of the Charter thereby allows the EU to set its own standard in these cases. The principle of equality of arms is considered to be one of the significant elements of a fair trial, and it applies both in civil and criminal cases.[104] The early cases from the Strasbourg Court already acknowledged the principle as inherent in Article 6 ECHR. In its report in the joined cases *Pataki and Dunshirn v Austria*,[105] the European Commission of Human Rights noted that in the case at hand, the problem was whether the notion of a 'fair trial' embodied any right relating to the defence beyond and above the minimum rights laid down in Article 6(3) ECHR.[106] The Commission declared that 'what is generally called "the equality of arms", that is the procedural equality of the accused with the public prosecutor, is an inherent element of a fair trial'. It did not consider it necessary to express its definite opinion on whether the rights laid down in Article 6(3) encompassed the principle of equality of arms, since in any case it was beyond doubt that the wider and general provision of a fair trial, contained in Article 6(1), embodied the notion.[107] Indeed this stance has been confirmed by the Strasbourg Court on numerous occasions.[108]

That said, there is an important distinction between the rights granted to companies during the course of a competition case and the application of the defence rights under the ECHR. As the ECHR provides no right to good administration, the right to access the file is instead considered part of the right to a fair trial.[109] This means that the Convention right does not necessarily apply before the competition authority has adopted an infringement decision and the case becomes one for the courts. While the Commission is sometimes accused of taking on the roles of investigator, prosecutor and judge, it is not a tribunal within the meaning

[104] See eg European Court of Human Rights, *Guide on Article 6 of the European Convention on Human Rights (Civil limb)* (31 August 2019) 67, available at www.echr.coe.int/Documents/Guide_Art_6_ENG.pdf.

[105] *Pataki and Dunshirn v Austria* App nos 596/59 and 789/60 (ECmHR, 28 March 1963).

[106] Art 6(3) contains a list of minimum rights afforded to anyone charged with a criminal offence. While the rights listed serve to ensure equality of arms, the principle as such is not mentioned.

[107] *Pataki and Dunshirn* (n 105).

[108] See eg *Werner v Austria*, where the Strasbourg Court declared that it would examine the complaint in the light of the whole of Art 6(1), because the principle of equality of arms is only one feature of the wider concept of a fair trial. *Werner v Austria* App no 138/1996/757/956 (Judgment) (ECtHR, 24 November 1997) para 63.

[109] The principle is considered part of Art 5 ECHR concerning the rights of persons who have been deprived of their liberty.

of the ECHR. As discussed in chapter 2, the Strasbourg Court has established that infringement decisions in cartel cases may be adopted by an administrative authority at first instance as long as such decisions can be appealed to a tribunal with full jurisdiction.[110] However, at one point in time, the Commission will have to ensure that it lives up to the ECHR standard. When an application is filed with the General Court, the Charter standard thus needs to meet the ECHR standard.

The case of *Miailhe v France*[111] can be used to illustrate this division between administrative and judicial proceedings, and the limitations of Article 6 ECHR. Mr Miailhe was the honorary consul for the Philippines in Bordeaux during the years 1960 to 1983. He had dual French and Philippine nationality, and took the view that, for tax purposes, he was to be considered resident in the Philippines. For this reason, he had not filed any tax returns in France. This eventually made the French tax authorities launch an audit against him, during which they requested him to produce a number of documents. However, a few months previously, the customs authorities had carried out an inspection at his premises and had seized 15,000 documents, some of which were the ones now requested by the tax authorities. Mr Miaihle was therefore unable to produce these documents, and the tax inspector had to examine them at the offices of his customs colleagues. He made copies of some 1,200 documents, and later also contacted the Philippine tax authorities and requested copies of certain documentation. At the end of the tax audit, four supplementary assessments were served on Mr Miailhe, and the Department of Revenue decided to institute criminal proceedings against him for tax evasion.

In April 1986, the Tax Offences Board ('the CIF') gave approval for a complaint to be lodged, seeking the imposition of criminal tax penalties. The Revenue lodged a complaint and annexed some of the documents provided by the customs authorities. It did not at that juncture append any of the documents forwarded by the Philippine authorities, although the tax inspector's summary report that had been placed in the file of the judicial investigation mentioned the correspondence between the French and the Philippine authorities. It was only upon an order from the investigating judge that the Revenue later placed in the file the documents received from the Philippine authorities, and then only some of them. Mr Miaihle was sentenced to three years' imprisonment and a fine of FRF 150,000.[112]

Mr Miailhe eventually turned to the Strasbourg Court. Relying on Article 6(1) ECHR, he complained that he had not had access to all the documents held by the Revenue, and that this had contravened the principle of equality of arms both during the administrative stage before the CIF gave its opinion and during the subsequent criminal trial. The Strasbourg Court acknowledged a duty on its part to satisfy itself that the proceedings as a whole were fair, having regard to any

[110] *A Menarini Diagonstics SRL v Italy* App no 43509/08 (Judgment) (ECtHR, 27 September 2011) para 59.

[111] *Miailhe v France (No 2)* App no 18978/91 (Judgment) (ECtHR, 26 September 1996).

[112] Ibid para 21.

possible irregularities before the case was brought before the courts of trial and appeal, and checking that those courts had been able to remedy them if there were any.[113] In the present case, the Strasbourg Court found that it appeared clear from the national courts' decisions that they had based their rulings solely on the documents in the case file, on which the parties had presented argument at hearings before them, thereby ensuring that the applicant had had a fair trial. The failure to produce certain documents already during the administrative procedure therefore did not infringe Mr Miailhe's defence rights or the principle of equality of arms. The application was dismissed.[114]

Likewise, Article 47 of the Charter, granting a right to an effective remedy and a fair trial, applies at the stage when the individual has been charged. The distinction between Articles 41 and Article 47 of the Charter was addressed by Advocate General Wathelet in the case of *MG and NR v Staatssecretaris van Veiligheid en Justitie*, where he argued that:

> Although the general term 'rights of the defence' may (although not necessarily) cover the rights affirmed in Articles 41 and 47 of the Charter, I consider that the rights protected by those provisions are quite distinct rights and apply in different contexts: the first in the pre-litigation administrative context and the second in the context of court proceedings. It follows that the rights in question cannot be merged lest the right of an individual to be heard be 'swept aside' when the administrative authorities are minded to adopt a measure which will adversely affect that individual. The EU legislature's intention to protect individuals subject to an administrative procedure throughout that procedure is clear from the relationship between Articles 41 and 47 of the Charter. Those two very different rights must not be conflated, otherwise there could be a break in the continuity of the system of rights of the defence safeguarded by the Charter.[115]

Thus, while Article 6 ECHR does not apply during the administrative stage of a cartel case, it may influence the application of Article 47 of the Charter once the case has reached the General Court. Furthermore, if there are irregularities during the administrative procedure that are not remedied during court proceedings, this may constitute a violation of the right to a fair trial. The Strasbourg Court considers a fair trial to require both adversarial proceedings and adherence to the principle of equality of arms. The latter requires that a fair balance

[113] The case of *Natunen v Finland* can be used to illustrate such a situation. Suspecting the applicant of an aggravated drug offence, the Finnish Police had recorded a number of telephone calls between the applicant and the other suspects. Some of those recordings were later used in the trial to prove the allegations against the applicant. When he claimed that the telephone calls had concerned other issues (proving that he had travelled to Estonia for reasons other than to buy drugs) and requested the prosecutor to disclose all recordings, it turned out that the Police had destroyed those recordings that were not considered relevant. Such destruction was required under Finnish legislation and had taken place prior to the court proceedings that were instituted. The Strasbourg Court found that the destruction of recordings possibly containing exonerating evidence infringed the applicant's right to a fair trial under Art 6 ECHR. See *Natunen v Finland* App no 21022/04 (Judgment) (ECtHR, 31 March 2009).

[114] *Miailhe* (n 111) para 44.

[115] View of AG Wathelet in Case C-383/13 PPU, *MG and NR v Staatssecretaris van Veiligheid en Justitie*, EU:C:2013:553, paras 46 and 47.

be struck between the parties, and applies to both criminal and civil cases. The right to an adversarial trial means in principle the opportunity for the parties to have knowledge of and comment on all evidence adduced or observations filed with a view to influencing the court's decision.[116] In addition, Article 6(1) requires that the prosecution authorities disclose to the defence all material evidence in their possession for or against the accused.[117] The right to an adversarial trial is closely related to equality of arms, and in some cases the Strasbourg Court finds a violation of Article 6(1) looking at the two concepts together. In this context, the relevant considerations can also be drawn from Article 6(3)(b), which guarantees to the applicant adequate time and facilities for the preparation of his defence. In *Leas v Estonia*, the Strasbourg Court declared that failure to disclose to the defence material evidence that could enable the accused to exonerate himself or have his sentence reduced, would constitute a refusal of facilities necessary for the preparation of the defence.[118]

The cases referred to in the foregoing all concern the rights of natural persons. For the avoidance of doubt it should be noted that these principles also apply in cases concerning legal persons. In *Yukos*,[119] the Russian Federation had launched attacks against Yukos Oil. In October 2003 a tax audit was initiated. Contrary to earlier findings, the Russian tax authorities found that Yukos owed €2.9 billion in back taxes, and ordered the company to pay this amount in two days. Without waiting for the two-day period of grace to expire, the authority had a court issue an order to freeze the assets of the company, making it impossible for Yukos to pay the alleged debt. The subsequent court proceedings left a great deal to be desired, and after a disappointing appeal by Yukos, the tax authorities moved to enforcement measures and auctioned off Yukos' assets for a fraction of their value. Yukos was later liquidated. However, before the liquidation, the company had filed an application with the Strasbourg Court. In its assessment on the applicability of Article 6 ECHR, the Court noted that the article applied under its criminal head to the tax assessment proceedings,[120] and reiterated that the principle of equality of arms was one feature of the wider concept of a fair trial that also includes the fundamental right that criminal proceedings should be adversarial.[121] Partly due to the fact that the company was not considered to have had sufficient time to study the case file at first instance, the Strasbourg Court found that there had been a violation of Article 6(1) taken in conjunction with Article 6(3)(b).[122]

[116] *Brandstetter v Austria*App nos 11170/84, 12876/87 and 13468/87 (Judgment) (ECtHR, 28 August 1991) para 67.

[117] See eg *Edwards v United Kingdom* App no 13071/87 (Judgment) (ECtHR, 16 December 1992) para 36; *Rowe and Davies v the United Kingdom* App no 28901/95 (Judgment) (ECtHR, 16 February 2000) para 60; and *Natunen* (n 113) para 39.

[118] *Leas v Estonia*, App no 59577/08 (Judgment) (ECtHR, 6 March 2012) para 81.

[119] *OAO Neftyanaya Kompaniya Yukos v Russia* App no 14902/04 (Judgment) (ECtHR, 20 September 2011; rectified 17 January 2012).

[120] Ibid para 527.

[121] Ibid para 538.

[122] Ibid para 551.

To conclude, the Strasbourg Court has established that the principle of equality of arms and the right to an adversarial trial apply both in criminal and civil cases, and that in criminal proceedings the accused has a right to access all the material evidence for or against him or her. If there have been irregularities during the procedures leading up to the court proceedings, the Strasbourg Court will have to make sure that they are remedied during the court proceedings, as there may otherwise be a violation of the right to a fair trial. Applying these principles to the current EU system, it can be concluded that the EU standard meets the ECHR standard in this respect. The Commission will grant the parties access to all documents it has drawn up or gathered before the adoption of the statement of objections. Furthermore, it is required to grant access to any inculpatory or exculpatory evidence received after such date, which would in principle comprise all material evidence. Unless necessary to protect the companies' right of the defence, the Commission will not disclose confidential information or internal documents. However, exclusion of such documents is accepted under the ECHR. The Strasbourg Court has declared that the entitlement to disclosure of relevant evidence is not an absolute right. In any criminal proceedings there may be competing interests that must be weighed against the rights of the accused. In some cases it may be necessary to withhold certain evidence from the defence so as to preserve the fundamental rights of another individual, or to safeguard an important public interest. However, only such measures restricting the rights of the defence as are strictly necessary are permissible under Article 6 ECHR.[123]

Given the above – and given that the EU Courts will not admit evidence unless it has previously been disclosed to targeted companies, and that it may annul infringement decisions if the parties' defence rights have been infringed – the EU standard meets the ECHR standard. If, in an individual case, the Commission would refuse or otherwise fail to grant access to exculpatory documents, such omission would only fail to meet the ECHR standard if the party does not get access to the evidence in question during the subsequent court proceedings. However, while there may be irregularities in individual cases, the system as such appears to meet the ECHR standard, and there is thus no need to revise the system for that reason.

VIII. Access to the File – Concluding Remarks

Already in the early cartel cases, the Court recognised that companies enjoyed a right of the defence even during the investigatory phase, and that the Commission was prevented from adopting infringement decisions without first having allowed the parties to present their observations on the Commission's objections.

[123] See eg *Natunen* (n 113) para 40; and *Rowe and Davies* (n 117) para 61.

This meant that targeted companies must be informed of the facts upon which the complaints were based. However, the Court was also clear that this did not mean that the companies had a right of access to the file. Instead, it was the Commission that committed to granting such access in the early 1980s, and which was later forced to stick by its words. Today, Article 41 of the Charter protects the right to good administration, and includes the right of every person to have access to his or her file. Article 27(2) of Regulation 1/2003 mirrors this obligation, and grants parties a right to access their file. In competition cases, the right belongs to addressees of the statement of objections, and they will be given the opportunity to access the file on one occasion, after the statement of objections has been issued but before the oral hearing is held. There is no general right to access other parties' replies to the statement of objections, but as the Commission is prevented from relying on evidence to which the parties have not had access, the Commission will inform the parties of any incriminating evidence contained in or attached to such statements. The Commission is now also considered to have a duty to grant access to any exculpatory evidence received during the adversarial stage. While the division between evidence received before and after the adoption of the statement of objections may be acceptable from an ECHR point of view – at least as long as the parties are granted access to both inculpatory and exculpatory evidence received during the adversarial stage – one may question whether it is appropriate to maintain an order where it is up to the Commission to determine whether a certain piece of information may or may not be useful for the targeted company's defence. This especially since the Court has established that this should not be for the Commission to decide when granting access to documents collected during the investigatory stage. Furthermore, the fact that the Commission may sometimes decide to transmit replies to statement of objections or other documents received during the adversarial stage – not because it is required to do so but because it considers that it would further the investigation – may be questioned from an equal treatment perspective.

That said, failure by the Commission to grant access may have several consequences. First, Article 27 of Regulation 1/2003 requires the Commission to base its decisions solely on objections to which the parties concerned have been able to comment. The Commission may not rely on evidence to which the parties have not been granted access, and such evidence will therefore be struck.[124] Furthermore, any subsequent infringement decisions may be annulled, but only if the parties' defence rights have been infringed, reflecting the EU Courts' view that access to the file is not an end in itself but intended to protect the rights of the defence.[125] As for incriminating evidence, the Commission must have relied on the evidence in question, and the company must also be able to show that absent that document, the Commission would not have been able to substantiate its objections. Also,

[124] Parties may be required to request such access both under the EU rules and the ECHR.
[125] *Cimenteries* (n 7) para 156.

the failure to grant access to exculpatory evidence received prior to or after the adoption of the statement of objections may constitute a breach of the company's defence rights. The company will then not have to show that the evidence in question would have let it off the hook, only that it would have been able to use it for its defence. The threshold is set quite high, and rightly so. Annulling an infringement decision for the sole reason that the Commission has failed to communicate one document, which together with a number of others formed the basis for the Commission's objections, would have negative consequences far outweighing the rights and interests of the company in question. However, it would be unfortunate if the Commission failed to communicate possibly exculpatory evidence received from the other parties, as it is likely that such evidence will otherwise not come to the attention of the company in question. The Commission is walking a fine line between the interests of efficiency and objectivity.

5

Third Parties' Right to Access Documents in the Capacity of Complainants or Interveners

As will be discussed further in chapter 6, third parties seeking access to the Commission's case files will have to rely on the Transparency Regulation, and keep their fingers crossed that none of the exceptions to the right of public access applies. However, there are certain circumstances where third parties may also have a right to access documents from the Commission's case file under Regulation 1/2003. That is where they have a right to be heard, either because they are complainants or because the Commission considers that they have a sufficient interest in or can contribute to the investigation. Recently, third parties have also sought leave to intervene in annulment actions before the General Court with a view to accessing the evidence relied on by the Commission.[1] This chapter presents the regulatory framework surrounding these practices, followed by an overview of existing case law.

I. The Regulatory Framework

A. Seeking Access under Regulation 1/2003

As discussed previously, Article 27 of Regulation 1/2003 governs the right of access to the file and the right to be heard, two rights that by their nature are closely linked and to some extent intertwined.[2] The article provides targeted companies with a right to be heard on matters to which the Commission has taken objection, and the Commission is only allowed to base its decision on objections to which the parties have been able to comment. As for the role and rights of third parties, the last sentence of the article stipulates that complainants shall be 'associated closely with the proceedings' – undoubtedly a rather vague and non-committing wording.

[1] B Balsaningham, *The EU Leniency Policy; Reconciling Effectiveness and Fairness* (Alphen aan den Rijn, Wolters Kluwer, 2017) 169.

[2] For a more detailed discussion of the relationship between these rights, see ch 4.

Article 27(2) declares that the right of the defence shall be fully respected during the proceedings, and grants the parties to the investigation a right of access to the file. The paragraph makes no reference to complainants or other third parties.

The Procedural Regulation governs the conduct of the Commission's proceedings in more detail, and contains a number of provisions dealing with complainants and their rights during the course of a competition law investigation. Important to note is that not everyone has the right to file an official complaint with the Commission, which in turn means that not everyone can receive the official status of 'complainant'. Article 27(2) of Regulation 1/2003 declares that those entitled to lodge a complaint are natural or legal persons who can show a legitimate interest and Member States. This limitation is mirrored in Article 5 of the Procedural Regulation, which stipulates that in order for a natural or legal person to be allowed to lodge a complaint with the Commission, that person must show a legitimate interest. Neither Regulation 1/2003 nor the Procedural Regulation defines the notion of 'legitimate interest'. When Regulation 1/2003 was adopted, the Commission drafted and issued a Notice on complaints.[3] In the Notice, the Commission declared that in its past practice, the condition of legitimate interest had seldom been a matter of doubt, as most complainants had been in a position of being directly and adversely affected by the alleged infringement. The Notice nevertheless refers to a number of cases where the General Court has addressed the issue, and from which it can be inferred that undertakings can claim a legitimate interest where they are operating in the relevant market or where the conduct complained of is liable to directly and adversely affect their interests. This, the Notice declares, confirms the established practice of the Commission, which has accepted that a legitimate interest can, for instance, be claimed by competitors whose interests have allegedly been damaged by the behaviour complained of or by undertakings excluded from a distribution system.[4] As noted by Kerse and Khan, the Commission may act on a complaint even if the person in question is not able to show a legitimate interest. However, no procedural rights will then flow from the complaint.[5]

While complainants should be given the opportunity to be closely associated with the investigation, they are thus not granted a right to access the Commission's case file. The only exception to this is where the Commission intends to reject a complaint. Article 8 of the Procedural Regulation stipulates that where the Commission intends to reject a complaint, it must inform the complainant of its intention, and the latter may then request access to the documents on which the Commission has based its provisional assessment. According to point 31 of the Access Notice, the complainant may request access to the documents on which the Commission has based its provisional assessment. The complainant will be

[3] Commission Notice on the handling of complaints by the Commission under Articles 81 and 82 of the EC Treaty [2004] OJ C101/05.

[4] Ibid paras 34–36.

[5] C Kerse and N Khan, *EU Antitrust Procedure*, 6th edn (London, Sweet & Maxwell, 2012) 59.

provided access to such documents on a single occasion, following the issuance of the letter informing the complainant of the Commission's intention to reject its complaint. For this purpose, the complainant may not have access to business secrets or other confidential information belonging to other parties involved in the proceedings.[6] Article 16a of the Procedural Regulation stipulates that any documents submitted to complainants may only be used for the purposes of judicial or administrative proceedings for the application of Article 101 and 102 TFEU, which includes damages proceedings before national courts.

Closely related to the right of access is the right to be heard, as the latter right presupposes that any person entitled to the right to be heard is granted access to the evidence collected by the investigating authority. In short, to exercise your right properly, you need information. As previously discussed in chapters 2 and 4, the right to be heard, as a fundamental right, only applies to those against whom a possible adverse measure is envisaged. However, the law has also recognised that other parties with a particular interest in a case may have a right to be heard. In antitrust matters, Articles 6 and 13 of the Procedural Regulation confer on complainants and interested third parties a right to be heard in writing. They have also been recognised as having a right to have certain access to the information available in the case file. But the intensity of this right is very different from that of the defendants themselves. Complainants are simply entitled to a non-confidential version of the statement of objections, whereas interested third parties enjoy an even more diluted right to be informed of the nature and subject matter of the procedure.[7] In most cases, they are provided with an edited version of the statement of objections for their comment, but considerations of confidentiality may militate against sending even a redacted version of the statement of objections, in which case the Commission will instead prepare and submit a summary.[8] As noted by Durande and Williams, this 'softer' version of the right to be heard is not the expression of a fundamental right but is drawn from the legislator's conviction that antitrust enforcement is strengthened through the close involvement of complainants and interested third parties in the proceedings.[9] It is in this context that the law provides the Commission with discretion to invite complainants and interested third parties upon request to express their view at the oral hearing of the defendants. In other words, this right seems to be designed, to a large extent, to primarily serve the purpose of the procedure and not the interests of the third parties concerned. This view is also reflected in the Court's case law.

[6] See also I Van Bael, *Due Process in EU Competition Proceedings* (Alpen aan den Rijn, Wolters Kluwer, 2011) 175.

[7] Art 13(1) of the Procedural Regulation only requires the Commission to inform interested third parties in writing of the nature and subject matter of the procedure.

[8] Kerse and Khan, *EU Antitrust Procedure* (n 5) 206.

[9] S Durande and K Williams, 'The practical impact of the exercise of the right to be heard: A special focus on the effect of Oral Hearings and the role of the Hearing Officers' *Competition Policy Newsletter* (Summer 2005).

B. Intervention before the General Court

Third parties may want to take part in direct actions before the General Court to support the position of one of the main parties or to protect their own interests. Article 40 of the Statute of the Court of Justice grants anyone who can establish an interest in the result of a case a right to intervene. An application to intervene shall be limited to supporting the form of order sought by one of the parties. An intervener must accept the case as he or she finds it at the time of his or her intervention. Interveners are limited to supporting the form of order sought by one of the parties. In other words, an intervener cannot ask the court to make an order that a main party has not already requested, and an intervener has no right to request an oral hearing. If admitted to a case, an intervener will receive all procedural documents served on the main parties, excluding information identified as confidential[10] Once admitted, the intervener will be invited to submit a statement in intervention by a deadline set by the Court. The other parties then have a chance to reply to that statement.[11]

II. The Courts' Case Law

A. *AKZO* – Submission of Statement of Objections to Complainant in the Process of a Damages Proceeding

The two companies AKZO Chemie BV and AKZO Chemie UK Ltd (jointly referred to as AKZO) were both part of the AKZO group, which at the time was the EU's largest supplier of benzoyl peroxide.[12] The product was also manufactured by a small undertaking, Engineering and Chemical Supplies Ltd (ECS). In June 1982, ECS filed a complaint with the Commission, accusing AKZO of abusing its dominant position through selective pricing.[13] In addition to this, ECS later commenced an action before the UK courts claiming damages against AKZO for the harm allegedly caused by its abusive conduct. In September 1984 the Commission issued a statement of objections against AKZO, in which it held that AKZO had abused its dominant position by threatening to sell benzoyl peroxide to ECS's customers at discriminatory and abnormally low prices. The statement of objections was accompanied by 127 annexes. A copy of the statement of objections was sent to ECS, together with a list of the annexes. The

[10] Art 144(7) of the Rules of Procedure of the General Court.

[11] Ibid Art 145.

[12] Benzoyl peroxide is a product used in the making of plastics and as a bleach for the treatment of flour.

[13] Case 53/85, *AKZO Chemie BV and AKZO Chemie UK Ltd v Commission of the European Communities*, EU:C:1986:256, para 3.

accompanying letter indicated that ECS could apply for access to those annexes if it considered it necessary to do so in order to submit its observations. The Commission made it clear that if any documents were made available to ECS, they could only be used for the purposes of the Commission's proceedings.

AKZO later submitted its views on the statement of objections. The reply to the statement of objections was forwarded to ECS without AKZO's knowledge. By letter of 19 November 1984, ECS sought access to the annexes in order to be able to exercise its right to be heard under Article 19(2) of Regulation 17/62. The Commission informed AKZO of ECS's application, emphasising that it would not disclose any documents that contained business secrets, with the exception of those constituting direct evidence of the competition law infringement. It emerged from the Commission's letter that ECS had already been given access to AKZO's reply to the statement of objections. In its response, AKZO expressed surprise that the Commission had forwarded the reply, and offered to summarise the annexes or, in any event, to communicate them to ECS only after deleting certain confidential passages. It enclosed a list of documents it considered should be regarded as strictly confidential.[14] On 14 December 1984 the Commission communicated to ECS certain of the annexes and only informed AKZO that it had done so in a letter of 18 December 1984. In its letter, the Commission emphasised that it was for it to decide whether or not documents were confidential. It stated that it had followed the list drawn up by AKZO, with a few exceptions in regard to which it provided a brief explanation. This prompted AKZO to bring an action for a declaration that the Commission's decision to transmit certain confidential documents to ECS was void. In its application AKZO also sought an order from the ECJ requiring the Commission to demand that ECS return the documents it had received.[15]

AKZO based its application on three pleas in law. In the first place, it alleged that by communicating to ECS certain documents that were all in some way confidential, the Commission had acted in breach of its obligation not to disclose information covered by the obligation of professional secrecy or subject to protection as a business secret. In the second place, by communicating to ECS certain documents that the latter could use in the legal proceedings pending in the UK, the Commission had infringed Article 20(1) of Regulation 17/62, which provided that information acquired by the Commission in the exercise of its powers of investigation might be used only for the purpose for which it was obtained. Finally, AKZO argued that the Commission had infringed Article 278 TFEU[16] inasmuch as, by implementing its decision before notifying it to AKZO, it had deprived the latter of the possibility of applying for an order suspending the operation of that decision at the same time as it instituted proceedings for annulment.

[14] Ibid para 10.
[15] Ibid para 12.
[16] At the time Art 185 of the Treaty.

As to the first plea, the Court acknowledged that Article 339 TFEU[17] imposed an obligation on Commission officials not to disclose information covered by the obligation of professional secrecy, and that this obligation was reflected in Article 20(2) of Regulation 17/62. However, the Court noted further, the obligation of professional secrecy was mitigated in regard to third parties on whom Article 19(2) of the Regulation conferred the right to be heard. Thus, the Court continued, the Commission could forward confidential information in so far as it was necessary to ensure the proper conduct of the investigation. However, this possibility did not extend to all confidential information. Taking note of the fact that Article 19(3), which provided for the publication of notices prior to the granting of negative clearance or exemptions, and Article 21, which provided for the publication of certain decisions, both required the Commission to have regard to the legitimate interest of undertakings in the protection of their business secrets, the Court concluded that business secrets were afforded very special protection. Although the two articles dealt with particular situations, those provisions should be regarded as the expression of a general principle that applied during the course of the administrative procedure, the Court continued. It followed that a third party who had submitted a complaint could not in any circumstances be given access to documents containing business secrets. Any other solution, the Court concluded, would lead to the unacceptable consequence that an undertaking might be inspired to lodge a complaint with the Commission with the sole aim to gain access to its competitors' business secrets.[18]

The Court noted that it was for the Commission to assess whether or not a particular document contains business secrets, but that, after giving an undertaking an opportunity to state its views, the Commission is required to adopt a decision in that connection that contains an adequate statement of the reasons on which it is based and that must be notified to the undertaking concerned.[19] Having regard to the extremely serious damage that could result from improper communication of documents to a competitor, the Commission must, before implementing its decision, give the undertaking an opportunity to bring an action before the Court with a view to having the assessments made reviewed by it and to preventing disclosure of the documents in question. As the Commission had forwarded some of the annexes without informing AKZO beforehand, the decision to communicate the annexes to ECS was declared void.[20] The Court dismissed the remainder of the application.

[17] At the time Art 214 of the Treaty.

[18] *AKZO* (n 13) para 28.

[19] Ibid para 29.

[20] Ibid para 31. AKZO had also requested the Court to demand that ECS return the documents transmitted by the Commission. The Court found this application inadmissible, declaring that it lacked jurisdiction to make such an order in relation to a legality review. See the ruling, para 23. This stance has been confirmed by the Court in later rulings, but in *Parliament v Council* it added that although it lacked such jurisdiction, the Council was nevertheless under an obligation to put an end to the infringement it had committed within a reasonable period. See Case C-21/94, *European Parliament v Council of the European Union*, EU:C:1995:220, para 33.

B. *Matra-Hachette* – Limited Procedural Rights

In February 1991, the two car manufacturers Volkswagen and Ford notified the Commission of a joint venture agreement they were about to enter into for the production of a multi-purpose vehicle, which could potentially fall within the ambit of Article 101 TFEU.[21] Matra Hachette (Matra) lodged a complaint with the Commission, to which the Director General responded that the joint venture agreement was to be exempted from the prohibition in Article 101(1) TFEU. A few weeks later, the Commission published a Notice in which it announced that it would respond favourably to the notification of the joint venture agreement.[22] Following that publication, Matra submitted its written observations, in which it requested access to the case file and an opportunity to submit oral observations. In response, the Commission declared that it intended to grant access to all the important parts of the file, but that a hearing did not seem necessary at that stage of the process. The Commission later disclosed to Matra, for its comments, copies of certain documents from the file, together with a list of documents it did not intend to disclose by reason of their confidential nature. Matra then requested that certain of the listed documents should be made available to it either directly or, if need be, through the intermediation of independent experts. The Commission refused that request.[23]

Matra submitted its observations on the documents that it had received, but did not manage to convince the Commission to take action against the joint venture. Instead, the Commission informed Matra that it was going to reject the complaint, and in December 1992 it granted the exemption requested by Ford and Volkswagen. A copy of the decision was forwarded to Matra, which soon lodged an application with the General Court, requesting it to annul the exemption decision and the decision rejecting its complaint.[24]

The allegations relating to the Commission's interpretation and application of Article 101 TFEU will not be addressed in this work. However, Matra did also challenge the formal legality of the exemption decision, arguing, inter alia, a breach of the right of the defence. More precisely, Matra maintained that the exemption decision was vitiated by breach of the rights of the defence, as Matra had not been granted access to certain essential information in the case file and had therefore not been able properly to put its views to the Commission. According to Matra, the refusal to disclose certain documents in the file should render illegal the procedure under which the exemption decision had been adopted.[25] The General Court did

[21] At the time Art 85 of the EC Treaty.

[22] Notice pursuant to Article 19(3) of Council Regulation No 17 concerning notification No IV/33.814 – Ford/Volkswagen [1991] OJ C182/8.

[23] Case T-17/93, *Matra Hachette SA v Commission of the European Communities*, EU:T:1994:89, para 10.

[24] Ibid para 17.

[25] Ibid para 31.

not agree. Referring to the ECJ's case law, it noted that the ECJ had consistently held that the principle of full disclosure in the administrative procedure before the Commission applied only to undertakings targeted by the Commission's investigations and that could be penalised by an infringement decision. The rights of third parties, as laid down by Article 19 of Regulation 17/62,[26] were limited to the right to participate in the administrative procedure.[27] It followed that the Commission enjoyed some latitude in taking account, in its decision, of the written observations and any oral observations presented by them. In particular, third parties cannot claim a right of access to the file compiled by the Commission on the same basis as the undertakings under investigation, the General Court concluded.[28] While acknowledging that complainants enjoy some procedural rights, the General Court declared that they were not as far-reaching as the right to a fair hearing of the companies that are the object of the Commission's investigation.[29] The General Court thus found Matra's plea to be unfounded.

C. *Koninklijke Luchtvaart Maatschappij* – Seeking Leave to Intervene

The case of *Koninklijke Luchtvaart Maatschappij* concerns the right to intervene before the General Court. In November 2010, the Commission imposed fines on a number of airline companies found guilty of having coordinated their pricing of freight services. One of their customers, Schenker, was considering bringing damages actions against the airlines, and sought leave to intervene before the General Court.[30] In support of its application, it claimed in essence to have a threefold legal and economic interest in the appeals:

- a legal interest in the final termination of the cartel and the prevention of its reoccurrence as a company affected by the cartel;
- an economic interest resulting from the higher prices it was forced to pay as a customer of the airlines in the cartel;
- a direct and existing interest in having the contested decision upheld, as it formed the legal basis of possible damage claims before national courts.

The General Court disagreed. First, it found that the aim of obtaining the final termination of the cartel and the prohibition of its reoccurrence was too general

[26] In parts corresponding to Art 27 of Regulation 1/2003.

[27] Reference made to Joined Cases 142/84 and 156/84, *British-American Tobacco Company Ltd and RJ Reynolds Industries Inc v Commission of the European Communities*, EU:C:1987:490, paras 19 and 20.

[28] Reference is made to *AKZO* (n 13).

[29] *Matra Hachette* (n 23) para 35, where reference is made to the ECJ's ruling in Case 60/81, *International Business Machines Corporation (IBM) v Commission of the European Communities*, EU:C:1981:264.

[30] It is fair to assume that leave to intervene was sought with the view to obtaining access to the evidence relied on by the Commission.

to be considered an interest in the meaning of Article 40 of the Statute of the Court of Justice, as it did not constitute 'a direct, existing interest in the result of the case' for the purposes of that provision.[31] Also, the obligation to refrain from price coordination in the future was already prohibited under Article 101 TFEU, notwithstanding any court decision. Second, contrary to the claim made by Schenker, the fact that an undertaking might possibly be affected by high prices caused by an alleged cartel does not mean that it has a right to intervene in a case in which the undertakings accused of participating in the cartel challenge the legality of the decision establishing and punishing the alleged cartel activity, the General Court declared.[32] Last, the General Court concluded that the purpose of the appeal proceedings is not to make possible or facilitate private damages actions before national courts but to review the legality of the contested Commission decision. In particular, it stated that damage claims could be brought independently of any prior Commission decision.[33]

III. Concluding Remarks

It is clear from the foregoing that while the right of parties to access the file is motivated by a need to protect their right of the defence, the Court's reasoning in these cases suggests that it is the interest of ensuring a proper and efficient conduct of the investigation rather than the procedural rights of the complainant that mandates disclosure.

A further observation concerns the complainants' use of any information provided under Regulation 1/2003. Already in *Akzo* the applicant argued that the Commission had violated the restrictions on the use of information collected during the course of its investigations when it transmitted information to ECS, which the latter could use in the damages proceedings pending before the UK courts.[34] Finding that the Commission's decision to transmit the information was unlawful on other grounds, the Court dismissed the applicant's plea. However, the question raised by *Akzo* is of relevance, especially following the adoption of the Damages Directive. According to Article 16a of the Procedural Regulation, any documents obtained pursuant to the Regulation may be used only for the purposes of judicial or administrative proceedings for the application of Articles 101 and 102 TFEU. Should this be considered to include cartel damages proceedings before national courts, customers or competitors might nowadays have greater incentives

[31] Order of the General Court in Case T-28/11, *Koninklijke Luchtvaart Maatschappij NV v European Commission*, EU:T:2011:624, para 15.

[32] Ibid para 18.

[33] Ibid para 27.

[34] This despite the fact that the Commission had imposed an obligation on ECS only to use the transmitted documents for the purposes of the Commission's proceedings, see *AKZO* (n 13) para 6.

to bring to the Commission's attention any signs of unlawful conduct. Recital 3 of the Damages Directive supports such interpretation, declaring that

> Articles 101 and 102 TFEU produce direct effects in relations between individuals and create, for the individuals concerned, rights and obligations which national courts must enforce. National courts thus have an equally essential part to play in applying the competition rules (private enforcement).

Furthermore, following the adoption of the Damages Directive, the Procedural Regulation has been aligned with the provisions of the Directive, and it is clear from these amendments that documents received pursuant to the Regulation may be used in cartel damages proceedings. Mirroring Article 6(5) of the Damages Directive, Article 16 of the Procedural Regulation imposes restrictions on the use of certain information, declaring that certain categories of information may not be used in proceedings before national courts until the Commission has closed its proceedings against all parties under investigation or otherwise terminated its proceedings.[35] Thus, judging from these limitations, other information received pursuant to the Procedural Regulation may be used already prior to the termination of the Commission's proceedings.

Filing a formal complaint is not without risk – the complainant becomes part of the procedure and its status as complainant is disclosed to the defending parties. Furthermore, even if the information submitted by the complainant is considered confidential, this does not prevent the Commission from disclosing and using it to prove an infringement of Articles 101 and 102 TFEU, or protecting the parties' defence rights. That said, if cartel victims may access some of the evidence required to prove their claim for damages already at an early stage of the cartel case, this would of course increase their incentives to bring illegal behaviour to the Commission's attention. Provided that they can prove a legitimate interest or in some way assist the Commission in the investigation, cartel victims can now access valuable information already following the adoption of the statement of objections.

Paradoxically, this could in turn increase the attractiveness of the leniency programme, as companies would then have to fear not only the betrayal of their co-conspirators, but also complaints from cartel victims. As will be discussed further in chapter 9, the risk of having to pay damages may deter companies from self-reporting. However, if there is a risk that cartel victims complain to the Commission, this may increase the attractiveness of the leniency system. It is better to have to pay only damages than have to pay both a hefty fine and damages.

[35] That is information that was prepared by other natural or legal persons specifically for the proceedings of the Commission, and information that the Commission has drawn up and sent to the parties in the course of its proceedings.

PART IV

Third Parties and the Role of the Leniency Programme

6

Seeking Access under the Transparency Regulation

While chapter 5 discussed the limited but still existing possibilities under Regulation 1/2003 for third parties to access certain documents from the Commission's case file, most third parties will have to seek other ways to access those documents. The typical third party seeking access is the victim of a competition law infringement, be it a cartel victim or someone suffering loss due to a dominant player's abuse of its market power. As this work evolves around the Commission's cartel files, the current chapter will focus on the former.

Cartel victims may seek a number of different routes to access the evidence required to prove their claim. Over the years, two types of requests have been particularly prominent when cartel victims seek access to documents held in the files of the Commission. Potential claimants have either relied on the Transparency Regulation and sought direct access to the Commission's files, or they have applied for disclosure in the national courts.[1] This chapter will discuss the first option, while chapter 7 will examine the second. The picture that emerges from the two chapters depicts a situation where the evidence held in the Commission's case file is safely protected from third parties, and where cartel victims may still have to fight an uphill battle to access the evidence necessary to prove their claims.

I. Seeking Direct Access to the Commission's File

As discussed in chapter 1, the right of public access to documents is set out both in Article 15(3) TFEU and Article 42 of the Charter. Thus, not only is it firmly established at the top level of the EU norm hierarchy, in that the right of access to documents can no longer be seen only as a tool to ensure democratic legitimacy or to remedy any democratic deficit, it is now also a fundamental right, and as such it belongs to the individual. This means that any limitation of the right must be proportionate, and made only if it is necessary and genuinely meets either

[1] S Peyer, 'Access to Competition Authorities' Files in Private Antitrust Legislation' (2015) 3 *Journal of Antitrust Enforcement* 58, 59.

objectives of general interest recognised by the Union or the need to protect the rights and freedoms of others.[2]

While the right of access to documents is established in primary EU legislation, the modalities governing its application are laid down in the Transparency Regulation.[3] The Regulation is designed to introduce greater transparency into the work of the Union institutions, and provides citizens and legal persons of the Union with the right of access to the documents of the institutions. As declared in its recitals, the purpose of the Regulation is to give the fullest possible effect to the right of public access to documents, and to lay down the general principles and limits on such access in accordance with Article 15 TFEU.[4] This right covers not only documents that are drawn up by the institutions themselves, but also documents that fall into their possession.[5] According to its recitals, the Transparency Regulation seeks to guarantee that the administration enjoys greater legitimacy and is more effective and more accountable to the citizen in a democratic system. The recitals further declare that openness contributes to strengthening the principles of democracy, but also the respect for fundamental rights as laid down in Article 6 TEU and in the Charter. Thus, the Transparency Regulation acknowledges the dual roles of the transparency principle in the EU legal system.

However, the right of access to documents is not absolute. While Article 2 of the Transparency Regulation establishes a right of access, Article 4 provides for a number of exceptions to this right, among which we find the protection of commercial interests of natural and legal persons, court proceedings and legal advice, as well as the protection of the purpose of inspections, investigations and audits.[6] As established by the Court, these exceptions shall be given a narrow interpretation and may also be set aside if there is an overriding public interest in disclosure.[7]

[2] Art 52(1) of the Charter.

[3] Save for the possibilities to access the file under Regulation 1/2003 discussed in the preceding chapter. As will be further discussed in this chapter, Regulation 1/2003 can be considered to govern the modalities of access to the Commission's case files in other respects too, as it is construed to ensure that only certain categories of persons may access the files.

[4] Art 255(2) of the EC Treaty.

[5] According to Art 2(3) of the Transparency Regulation, the Regulation applies to all documents held by an institution, that is to say, documents drawn up or received by it and in its possession, in all areas of activity of the EU. Furthermore, Art 3 defines a document as any content, whatever its medium (written on paper or stored in electronic form or as a sound, visual or audiovisual recording), concerning a matter relating to the policies, activities and decisions falling within the institution's sphere of responsibility.

[6] Art 4(2) of the Transparency Regulation. When the former European Ombudsman Jacob Söderman commented on the draft regulation, he made the following remark: 'Last week, the Commission published its proposal for a Regulation. I am sorry to say that this document seems to consist mainly of a long and obscure list of possible reasons to deny access to documents. This cannot be what was intended when the Treaty of Amsterdam was drafted.' The exceptions are essentially the same as in the final version of the Regulation. See www.ombudsman.europa.eu/sv/speech/en/355.

[7] The exceptions in Art 4(2) and (3) may be set aside if there is an overriding public interest. However, the exceptions in Art 4(1) are absolute exceptions, covering cases where access is automatically refused (for reasons of public security, defence, international relations, economic, monetary or financial policy, or the privacy and integrity of individuals).

The following section will take a closer look at the jurisprudence in order to determine how the rules are interpreted when cartel victims seek access to the Commission's case files, and whether Article 4 is given a narrow interpretation.

II. The Courts' Case Law

This section examines the EU Courts' case law on requests for access to documents from the Commission's cartel files. Several of these cases did never reach further than the General Court. However, they still provide valuable guidance, as they reflect the consistent approach taken by the Commission over the years, and to some extent also the reasoning behind this approach. Furthermore, the rulings show that although the General Court and the ECJ have sometimes taken opposing views on the matter, and although the reasons for accepting limitations of the right to access have varied over time, the exceptions provided for in Article 4 of the Transparency Regulation have consistently served to prevent private litigants from gaining access to the Commission's files.

A. *VKI* – The Transparency Regulation and the Principle of Proportionality

The case of *VKI* is one of the earliest on the application of the Transparency Regulation. In this case, the General Court took the view that the Commission, upon a request for access to the entire case file, should carry out a review of each and every document before adopting a decision in the matter. However, it acknowledged that in certain circumstances and in exceptional cases, the Commission was allowed to rely on the principle of proportionality and derogate from the obligation to carry out an individual examination of requested documents.

Verein für konsumenteninformation (VKI) is an Austrian consumer organisation that helps to enforce collective consumer rights. Following the Commission's decision to impose fines on a number of Austrian banks for participation in a cartel known as the Lombard Club, VKI brought several sets of proceedings against one of the banks before the Austrian courts. In June 2002, VKI requested access to the Commission's case file, declaring that consultation of the file would be of indispensable help to it in the damages proceedings. The Commission rejected the request, which prompted VKI to submit a confirmatory request in which it stated that it was not primarily interested in the Commission's internal documents. By a formal decision, the Commission also rejected this request. In the contested decision, it divided the documents in the Lombard Club file into 11 separate categories. Excluding internal documents, the file contained more than 47,000 pages. The Commission further detailed the reasons on which it based its view that each of the 11 categories was covered by one or more of the exceptions provided for by the Transparency Regulation. According to the Commission, there was no overriding interest justifying disclosure. The Commission further considered that partial disclosure was not possible, as this required a detailed examination of each document, which would have represented an excessive and disproportionate amount of work for it. The Commission's decision prompted VKI to turn to the General Court.

In its application, VKI challenged the Commission's failure to carry out a concrete examination of the documents, arguing that the Transparency Regulation required the Commission to do so. The Commission, for its part, argued that it was allowed to refuse access to various categories of documents without carrying out an individual examination of each document belonging to those categories, and that an individual examination had not taken place since the effort involved in such an operation would have been disproportionate.[8]

The General Court declared that it should first be determined whether the Commission was obliged, in principle, to carry out a concrete, individual examination of the documents referred to in the request for access, and, if so, to examine to what extent that obligation could be qualified by certain exceptions based, inter alia, on the amount of work entailed by it. Here, the General Court acknowledged that according to settled case law, the examination required must be specific in nature, and must be carried out in respect of each document covered by the request.[9] The General Court was not convinced by the Commission's arguments relating to the application of the exceptions in Article 4 of the Transparency Regulation. It considered that the Commission was bound in principle to carry out a concrete and individual examination of each document before establishing that the exceptions were applicable. Since the Commission had failed to do so, the General Court went on to determine whether it was permissible for an institution to justify a total refusal to grant access by reason of the very large amount of work that, according to that institution, is entailed by a concrete and individual examination of the requested documents.

The Commission had argued that Article 6(3) of the Transparency Regulation relieved it of any obligation to examine the documents in question. The Article stipulates that in the event of an application relating to a very long document or to a very large number of documents, the institution concerned may confer with the applicant informally, with a view to finding a fair solution. The General Court noted that the parties had met in July 2002, but that the meeting and the contacts that followed had not led to any solution. As Article 6(3) does not contain any provision expressly permitting the institution to limit the scope of examination in the absence of a solution, the General Court examined whether the principle of proportionality could instead justify such refusal.[10] Here, the General Court

[8] Case T-2/03, *Verein für konsumenteninformation v Commission of the European Communities*, EU:T:2005:125, para 60.

[9] Ibid para 69.

[10] Ibid para 98.

declared that the refusal to examine concretely and individually the documents covered by a request for access did, in principle, constitute a manifest breach of the principle of proportionality. It should be borne in mind, however, the General Court continued, that it is possible for an applicant to make a request for access relating to a manifestly unreasonable number of documents, perhaps for trivial reasons, thus imposing a volume of work on the institution that could very substantially paralyse its proper working.[11] Furthermore, as Article 6(3) of the Transparency Regulation required the parties to seek a 'fair solution', it reflected the possibility of account being taken, albeit in a particularly limited way, of the need to reconcile the interests of the applicant with those of good administration. Thus, the General Court concluded, there should be a possibility, in exceptional cases, for an institution to rely on the principle of proportionality and to refuse to carry out an individual examination of the documents covered by the request for access.[12]

The General Court held that it was only in exceptional cases and where the administrative burden proved to be particularly heavy, thereby 'exceeding the limits of what may reasonably be required', that a derogation from the obligation to examine the documents could be permissible.[13] Furthermore, the General Court continued, the burden of proof should then lie with the institution, and the institution should also consult with the applicant and try to find a solution. It was further bound to consider specifically whether and how it could adopt a measure less onerous than a concrete, individual examination of the documents. Such examination could only be avoided when the institution had genuinely investigated all other conceivable options and explained in detail in its decision the reasons for which those various options did also involve an unreasonable amount of work, the General Court concluded.[14] Finding that the Commission had not investigated all perceivable options, it annulled the Commission's decision.

B. The *CDC Hydrogene Peroxide* Case – Access to the Statement of Contents

In the *CDC Hydrogene Peroxide* case, which, like *VKI*, did not reach further than the General Court, the applicant – CDC Hydrogene Peroxide Cartel Damage Claims (CDC) – requested full access to the statement of contents of the Commission's case file in the *Hydrogen Peroxide* Decision.[15] The Commission denied access to the statement, declaring that it did not constitute a document within the meaning of Article 3(a) of the Transparency Regulation.[16] The applicant

[11] Ibid para 101.
[12] Ibid para 103.
[13] Ibid para 112.
[14] Ibid para 115.
[15] Case COMP/F/38.620 – *Hydrogen peroxide and perborate.*
[16] For the meaning of 'document' under Art 3 of the Transparency Regulation, see n 5.

then wrote to the Commission and set out the reasons why the statement should be regarded as a document. The Commission appears to have accepted those arguments as it, in its response to CDC, still refused access but this time declared that disclosure would undermine the protection of the purpose of the investigation activities and the commercial interests of the undertakings which had taken part in the cartel.[17] This led CDC to bring an action against the Commission's decision, seeking its annulment and arguing that it infringed the fundamental principles of the Transparency Regulation as well as the first and third indents of Article 4(2) of the same Regulation.[18] One of the arguments put forward by the Commission before the General Court was that, with regard to the concept of professional secrecy – which is part of the broader concept of commercial interests – the risk of an action for damages being brought is a serious disadvantage that could lead undertakings taking part in cartels to cease to cooperate with the Commission in the future. According to the Commission, it could not be accepted that the protection of professional secrecy or the commercial interests of undertakings should be affected by an application for access to documents based exclusively on private law interests.[19]

The General Court did not accept the Commission's arguments and ruled in favour of the applicant. According to the General Court, denying access to the statement of contents did not protect any commercial interest other than the interest of the cartel companies to avoid damage claims, an interest that was not protected under the Transparency Regulation.[20] Nor did the General Court accept the claim that a denial of access would protect the interests of the investigation, as it had been closed two years earlier and the appeals did not concern the issue of guilt but rather the calculation of fines. Given the above, the General Court annulled the Commission's decision. This time, the General Court thus ruled in favour of the applicant, allowing the principle of transparency to prevail.

C. *Technische Glaswerke Ilmenau* – State Aid File Safe from Disclosure

As the heading suggests, this Grand Chamber ruling from the ECJ[21] does not concern a request for access to a cartel case file. Yet it deserves a brief presentation as the Court's findings in this case also bear relevance to cartel cases. In December

[17] The first and third indents of Art 4(2) of the Transparency Regulation.

[18] Case T-437/08, *CDC Hydrogene Peroxide Cartel Damage Claims v European Commission*, EU:T:2011:752, paras 29 and 55.

[19] Ibid, para 31.

[20] This reasoning corresponds to the General Court's reasoning in *Bank Austria* (Case T-198/03), which will be further discussed in ch 8, where the General Court established that in order for a piece of information to be considered confidential, the interests liable to be harmed by disclosure must be worthy of protection.

[21] Case C-139/07 P, *European Commission v Technische Glaswerke Ilmenau GmbH*, EU:C:2010:376.

1998, the Federal Republic of Germany notified the Commission of various measures designed to consolidate the financial position of Technische Glaswerke Ilmenau (TGI). Following an investigation, the Commission later found that those measures constituted illegal state aid incompatible with the Internal Market. During the course of the proceedings, TGI had submitted its observations in respect of the formal investigation procedure, and had requested the Commission to give it access to a non-confidential version of the file and the opportunity to submit further observations. The request was rejected by the Commission, which prompted TGI to seek other ways to gain access to the case file. It soon submitted a formal request for access to the entire file on the basis of the Transparency Regulation. This request was also rejected by the Commission, which declared that not only were the documents covered by the exception in Article 4(2) of the Transparency Regulation, but they also formed part of the ongoing formal state aid procedure. The applicant brought an action before the General Court for annulment of the Commission's decision. The General Court ruled in favour of TGI and annulled the decision on the ground that the Commission had failed to carry out a concrete and individual assessment of the documents in the file. The Commission was none too pleased with the ruling, and lodged an appeal to the ECJ.

In its preliminary observations, the Court took note of the fact that the request concerned the entire case file, and that the documents therein did indeed fall within an activity of 'investigation' within the meaning of Article 4 of the Transparency Regulation.[22] However, the Court noted further, it is not sufficient that a document falls within an activity mentioned in Article 4 of the Transparency Regulation; the Commission must also explain how that document could specifically and effectively undermine the interest protected by the Article. That said, referring to its ruling in *Turco*,[23] the Court declared that it was nevertheless open to the Commission to base its decisions in that regard on general presumptions that apply to certain categories of documents, as considerations of a generally similar kind are likely to apply to requests for disclosure relating to documents of the same nature.

The Court then went on to examine the procedure surrounding state aid investigations, acknowledging that Regulation 659/1999 did not lay down any right for interested parties to access documents in the Commission's administrative file.[24] Thus, the Court continued, it followed from the Regulation that the interested parties, except for the Member State that had granted the aid, did not have any right to consult the documents on the Commission's administrative file.

[22] Ibid para 52.

[23] Joined Cases C-39/05 and C-52/05 P, *Kingdom of Sweden and Maurizio Turco v Council of the European Union*, EU:C:2008:374, para 50.

[24] Council Regulation (EC) No 659/1999 of 22 March 1999 laying down detailed rules for the application of Article 93 of the EC Treaty, repealed and replaced by Council Regulation (EU) 2015/1589 of 13 July 2015 laying down detailed rules for the application of Article 108 of the Treaty on the Functioning of the European Union.

Furthermore, the Court declared, it was important to note that, in contrast with cases where the Union institutions act in the capacity of a legislature, in which wider access to documents should be authorised pursuant to recital 6 of the Transparency Regulation, documents relating to procedures for reviewing state aid fall within the framework of the institution's administrative functions. Based on the foregoing, the Court concluded that, for the purposes of interpreting the exception laid down in Article 4(2), third indent, of the Transparency Regulation, the General Court should have taken account of the fact that no interested parties other than the Member State concerned have a right to consult the documents in the Commission's administrative file. The Court concluded that the General Court should therefore have acknowledged the existence of a general presumption that disclosure of documents in the administrative file undermines protection of the objectives of investigation activities.[25] This did not exclude the possibility for the applicant to demonstrate either that a given document was not covered by the presumption, or that there was a higher public interest justifying its disclosure. Thus upholding the Commission's appeal, the Court declared that the ruling of the General Court should be set aside.

i. *Comment on the Court's Ruling*

This Grand Chamber ruling is both interesting and relevant to this study for a number of reasons, the main one being the Court's reasoning on the relationship between the Transparency Regulation and the rules on state aid procedures. Finding that the latter do not allow disclosure to others than the Member State concerned, the Court declares that there is a general presumption that disclosure of documents in the administrative file in principle undermines the protection of the objectives of investigation activities. This reasoning does not appear to be dependent on the number or nature of the documents requested, but solely on the fact that state aid procedures are governed by secrecy. To use the words of Rossi and Vinagre e Silva, 'the Court does not refer to a presumption of association document-exception, but clearly to another type of presumption: that certain documents must, in principle, be protected from public view by dicta of sectoral law "public access is not foreseen"'.[26]

D. *The Netherlands v Commission* – Access to the Commission's Infringement Decision

In September 2006, the Commission imposed fines on a number of companies for participation in a cartel for the supply of road pavement bitumen. The Kingdom

[25] *Technische Glaswerke Ilmenau* (n 21) para 61.

[26] L Rossi and P Vinagre e Silva, *Public Access to Documents in the EU* (Oxford, Hart Publishing, 2017) 155.

of the Netherlands considered that it had been harmed by the cartel and intended to seek compensation in the national courts. It submitted a request for access to the complete version of the Commission's infringement decision ('the Bitumen Decision'), a request that was rejected by the Commission. The Kingdom of the Netherlands then made a confirmatory application in which it stated that it intended to seek compensation for the loss suffered and, for this reason, it would be useful to examine the information contained in the confidential version of the Decision. It further identified certain specific passages in the Bitumen Decision that it considered to be of particular interest, namely, those concerning:

(a) the nature and scale of the infringements;
(b) the organisation and operation of the cartel;
(c) the role of certain undertakings as instigators or leaders of the cartel;
(d) the price-fixing agreements within the cartel;
(e) the difference in the price levels of bitumen between the Netherlands and in neighbouring countries;
(f) the interest of the road builders in seeing the price of bitumen increase;
(g) the bitumen market shares and the bitumen sales turnover in the Netherlands of the participants in the cartel;
(h) the names of the people representing the participants at the cartel meetings; and finally
(i) 'other information requested'.[27]

The Commission also rejected the confirmatory application, giving the following reasons. As for the information mentioned in the first point, the Commission indicated that the public and confidential versions were identical. As for the information mentioned in points (b)–(h), the Commission considered this to be covered by the exceptions in the first and third indents of Article 4(2) of the Transparency Regulation. The information was thus liable to affect the companies' commercial interests and the purpose of the Commission's inspections or investigations. The Commission did not consider there to be any overriding public interest mandating the granting of access. As for the argument that the information would be useful when preparing the action for damages, the Commission once again declared that this interest was private and not public in nature.[28]

The Kingdom of the Netherlands filed an application with the General Court, asking it to annul the Commission's decision to refuse access.[29] In its ruling, the General Court noted that in order for the Kingdom of the Netherlands to show that the decision was vitiated by an error capable of justifying its annulment,

[27] The request explicitly identified the passages in the Bitumen Decision that contained the requested information.

[28] Case T-380/08, *The Netherlands v European Commission*, EU:T:2013:480, para 7. See also the Commission's reasoning in the *CDC Hydrogene Peroxide* case discussed in section II.B.

[29] The Commission later published a new version of the Bitumen Decision that contained less undisclosed information, prompting the Kingdom of Netherlands to revise its application.

it must establish either that the Commission committed an error in considering that it could refuse access under each one of the exceptions in Article 4(2) of the Transparency Regulation invoked by the Commission, or that an overriding public interest, the passage of time or the obligation of the Commission to respect either Article 4(3) TEU or the principle of proportionality justified disclosure of that information.

The General Court further noted that the case concerned the relationship between the Transparency Regulation and Regulation 1/2003, and that those two Regulations have different objectives. The first is designed to ensure the greatest possible transparency of the decision-making process and the information on which the public authorities base their decisions. It is thus designed to facilitate as far as possible the exercise of the right of access to documents of the institutions, and to promote good administrative practices, the General Court declared. The second Regulation, the Court continued, is designed to ensure compliance with the duty of professional secrecy in proceedings that punish infringements of EU competition law.[30]

As for the exceptions invoked, the General Court acknowledged that the contested information related to an inspection and investigation within the meaning of Article 4(2) of the Transparency Regulation. Furthermore, the General Court noted, as the underlying case concerned an investigation under Article 101 TFEU, the Commission was likely to have gathered sensitive information about the commercial strategies of the undertakings concerned, their sales figures, their market shares or their business relations, so that access to documents in such a proceeding could undermine the protection of the commercial interests of those undertakings.[31] The General Court further noted that, in principle, it is not sufficient for the Commission to invoke the exceptions in Article 4, it must also explain how access to the document in question could undermine the interest protected by those exceptions. That said, the General Court acknowledged that in cases concerning state aid and mergers, the Commission was allowed to base its decisions on general presumptions that apply to certain categories of documents, as similar general considerations are likely to apply to requests for disclosure relating to documents of the same nature.[32] In both areas, there were regulations that contained provisions concerning access to information and to documents obtained in the context of investigations and review proceedings. Referring to Articles 27 and 28 of Regulation 1/2003 as well as Articles 8 and 15 of the Procedural Regulation – provisions restricting the use of information obtained during the course of competition law proceedings – the General Court declared that such general presumptions were also applicable in proceedings

[30] *The Netherlands v European Commission* (n 28) para 30.
[31] Ibid para 34.
[32] Ibid para 35.

under Article 101 TFEU. In those proceedings, generalised access on the basis of the Transparency Regulation would jeopardise the balance that the Union legislature had sought to ensure.[33]

Moreover, the General Court held that, as regards information gathered by the Commission pursuant to the Leniency Notice, the disclosure of that information could dissuade potential leniency applicants from making statements under that Notice. Indeed, the General Court noted, they could find themselves in a less favourable position than that of other undertakings that had participated in the cartel and that had not cooperated with the investigation or that had cooperated to a lesser extent.[34] Referring to the Court's ruling in *Éditions Odile Jacob*, the General Court declared that the Commission should be able to rely on a general presumption, regardless of whether the application for access concerned a proceeding that had already been closed or a proceeding that was pending. The publication of sensitive information concerning the economic activities of the undertakings involved is likely to harm their commercial interests, regardless of whether or not a proceeding is pending, the General Court declared. Furthermore, it continued, the prospect of such publication after the proceeding is closed runs the risk of adversely affecting the willingness of undertakings also to cooperate at the stage when such a procedure is still pending.[35]

However, the General Court noted, the presumption may be rebutted if the applicant can show that a given document is not covered by the exceptions in Article 4 of the Transparency Regulation, or that there is a higher public interest justifying its disclosure.[36] The Kingdom of the Netherlands had argued that the protection of commercial interests in Article 4(2) only covered lawful and legitimate commercial interests, which would exclude not only the commercial interests of cartel participants but also their interest in evading damages claims. This argument was not accepted by the General Court. Referring to Articles 27 and 28 of Regulation 1/2003, it concluded that the commercial interests did deserve protection. While acknowledging that the interest in non-disclosure to the public of the details of the offending conduct does not merit any particular protection, the General Court emphasised that there was a need to respect the reputation and dignity of the undertakings concerned so long as they had not been found guilty of an infringement. In the present case, a number of judicial proceedings concerning the Bitumen Decision were still pending before the Court. Furthermore, the General Court continued, the public version of the Bitumen Decision contained the details necessary for cartel victims to bring action before the national courts.[37]

[33] Ibid para 39.

[34] Ibid para 41.

[35] Ibid para 43, where the General Court refers to Case C-404/10 P, *European Commission v Éditions Odile Jacob SAS*, EU:C:2012:393, para 124.

[36] *The Netherlands v European Commission* (n 28) para 45.

[37] Ibid para 55.

The Kingdom of the Netherlands had also argued that since it did not request access to the documents in the Commission's case file but only to certain confidential passages in the infringement decision, it was not possible for the Commission to rely on the third indent of Article 4(2) of the Transparency Regulation governing the protection of inspections and investigations. To this the General Court responded that the provision would be deprived of all its practical effectiveness if its scope were limited to documents collected in the context of an investigation and could not be used to refuse the parties access to documents drafted subsequently by that institution containing information from protected documents.[38] The General Court dismissed the application in its entirety.

i. *Comment on the General Court's Ruling*

In this case, the Commission justified its refusal not to grant access by referring to several passages in Article 4(2) of the Transparency Regulation. While a document may very well be covered by several exceptions, it nevertheless makes the task of challenging such decision an even steeper uphill battle. Not only does the applicant lack knowledge of the contents of the document in question, it will then have to argue that the information contained therein (which it has not seen) is not protected by any of the exceptions in Article 4 of the Transparency Regulation. This is of course an impossible task in most cases. It remains for the applicant to seek to convince the Court that there is an overriding public interest in the granting of access.

Furthermore, and as pointed out by the applicant, the request did not concern documents from the file but the Commission's infringement decision. The applicant had also made it clear that it was not the entire decision but certain passages that it considered to be of interest. The requested information was in most parts closely connected to or describing the infringement. The applicant sought information on the organisation and the operation of the cartel, the price-fixing agreements, the role of certain companies as instigators or leaders of the cartel, etc. This prompts a number of reflections. First of all, the General Court bases its findings on a need to reconcile the interests of the Transparency Regulation and the Antitrust Regulations. It refers to Articles 27 and 28 of Regulation 1/2003 and to Articles 8 and 15 of the Procedural Regulation.[39] While it is true that the Commission should protect information covered by professional secrecy or constituting business secrets, the General Court could also have mentioned Article 30 of Regulation 1/2003, which requires the Commission to publish its infringement decisions. Thus, whereas it may be argued that third parties should

[38] Ibid para 60.

[39] The Procedural Regulation has been amended following the adoption of the Damages Directive, and the rules on the use of information accessed under the Regulation previously found in Arts 8 and 15 are now found in Art 16a of the Procedural Regulation.

not be given access to the case file, the Regulation is built on the principle that the public have a right to be informed of the infringement, and this already at the time of its adoption and not when the ECJ has ruled on any appeals. Thus, allowing the Commission to rely on a presumption that the information in the infringement decision is covered by the exceptions in Article 4 of the Transparency Regulation may be to draw things a bit too far.

Second, while the information requested in points (b)–(h) referred to above could potentially jeopardise the Commission's investigation(s), it is hard to see how it can affect the cartel companies' commercial interests in ways other than the interest in keeping the details of their unlawful behaviour protected from third parties. It can be questioned whether this interest is worthy of protection. In *CDC Hydrogene Peroxide* the General Court declared that it was not.

Furthermore, and as will be discussed in chapter 8, the EU Courts take a slightly different stance when it comes to the Commission's right to choose which information is to be included in the public versions of its infringement decisions. In those cases, the EU Courts accept and endorse the publication of more detailed versions of the infringement decisions, and do not accept targeted companies' arguments that the information contained in these decisions should be protected from the public eye. They thus allow the Commission a broad margin of discretion in drafting the public versions of its infringement decisions, and leave any balancing of diverging interests to the Commission. That said, and as is further discussed in chapter 8, it is understandable, and to some extent also appropriate, that the Commission is put in the driver's seat and allowed to control which information is to be disclosed to third parties. When the Commission drafts its infringements decisions it can choose what information to disclose, focusing on the infringement and on what is of relevance to describe the unlawful actions, leaving irrelevant information aside and balancing the interests of the parties involved against one another. It is undoubtedly easier to carry out a balancing exercise when drafting an infringement decision than when reviewing thousands of documents covered by an application for access. However, in the present case, the request concerned one document – the infringement decision – and the Commission could have been required to at least go through the document and assess whether certain parts could be disclosed to the applicant. As will be further discussed in chapter 8, information on the operative parts of the infringement should not be considered confidential.

E. *EnBW* and the Presumption of Confidentiality

The case of *EnBW* concerns the Commission's refusal to grant access to its cartel case file and the possibilities to rely on a general presumption of confidentiality when doing so. In 2007, the Commission imposed fines on a number of companies for taking part in a cartel related to gas insulated switchgear (GIS), a power substation device. Following the decision, EnBW claimed that it had been harmed by the GIS cartel and sought to receive compensation for such loss. Relying on the Transparency Regulation, EnBW requested access to all documents in the Commission's case file. Following discussions with the Commission, EnBW later withdrew its application and made a fresh application from which it excluded three categories of documents, namely, all documents dealing exclusively with the structure of the undertakings concerned, all documents relating exclusively to the identity of the addressees of the cartel decision and all documents that were drawn up wholly in Japanese.[40] The Commission rejected the request through a formal decision where it classified the documents in the file according to five categories:

1. Documents provided during the course of a leniency application; that is the leniency statements as well as documents provided in connection with the leniency application.
2. Requests for information and the parties' replies to those requests.
3. Documents obtained during inspections.
4. The statement of objections and the parties' replies thereto.
5. Internal documents.

The fifth category was further divided into (a) documents relating to facts, and (b) procedural documents. According to the Commission, each of these five categories fell within the exception provided for in the third indent of Article 4(2) of the Transparency Regulation,[41] and some of the documents in category 5 also belonged to the exception laid down in Article 4(3).[42] The Commission saw no overriding public interest in disclosure. According to the Commission, all the documents in the file were fully covered by the exceptions listed in the Transparency Regulation, and partial access could therefore not be granted. An action for annulment of the Commission's decision was brought by EnBW before the General Court.

i. The Ruling of the General Court

In its ruling, the General Court considered whether the conditions were met for dispensing with the obligation to undertake a concrete, individual examination of the content of the documents requested. On this point, it concluded that the general presumption on which the Commission had relied applied only

[40] Case C-365/12 P, *European Commission v EnBW Energie Baden Württemberg AG*, EU:C:2014:112, para 14.

[41] According to which the institutions shall refuse access where disclosure would undermine the protection of the purpose of inspections, investigations and audits, unless there is an overriding public interest in disclosure.

[42] Access to a document drawn up by the institution or received by an institution, which relates to a matter where the decision has not been taken by the institution, shall be refused if disclosure of the document would seriously undermine the institution's decision-making process, unless there is an overriding public interest in disclosure.

while the procedure concerning the documents in question was still ongoing. Once the procedure was closed, as in that case, it was instead necessary to undertake a concrete, individual examination of each of the documents concerned. The General Court then focused on the question whether the Commission had acted correctly in examining the documents by category. It found that categories 1, 2, 4 and 5(a) were not useful for the purposes of processing the request for access, since no real difference could be detected between the documents allocated to each category. Only category 3 (documents obtained during dawn raids) was useful for the purposes of ascertaining whether the exception laid down in the third indent of Article 4(2) applied, since it comprised documents obtained against the will of the undertaking. The General Court therefore annulled the contested decision in so far as it refused access to the documents falling within categories 1, 2, 4 and 5(a). However, for the sake of completeness, the General Court examined the refusal of access to the documents falling within categories 1, 2, 4 and 5(a), and concluded that the protection of the purpose of investigations could not justify refusing access to the documents because the case concerned a procedure that had already been completed and there was no reason to give special treatment to competition law proceedings. Nor, according to the General Court, had the Commission shown that access was likely to undermine the commercial interests of the undertakings concerned. Lastly, the General Court found that the Commission was wrong to apply, in a general and abstract way, the exception laid down in Article 4(3) to documents in category 5(a). Based on the above, the General Court annulled the contested decision in its entirety.[43]

ii. The Ruling of the ECJ

Turning to the ECJ, the Commission challenged the General Court's ruling, claiming that the General Court should have taken account of the Antitrust Regulations and their provisions on access to the file. By failing to do so, the General Court reached the erroneous conclusion that the Commission was not entitled, without carrying out a specific and individual analysis of each document in the file, to take the view that all such documents were covered by a general presumption of confidentiality.[44] Furthermore, it was the Commission's view that the judgment under appeal jeopardised the leniency mechanism and the proper implementation of the competition rules more generally.[45] According to the Commission, the General Court had failed to have regard to the fact that the documents provided in connection with a request for leniency deserve special protection, even at the time when all proceedings have concluded. In particular, the fact that undertakings fear

[43] Case T-344/08, *EnBW Energie Baden-Württemberg AG v European Commission*, EU:T:2012:242.
[44] *EnBW* (n 40) para 60.
[45] Opinion of AG Cruz Villalón in Case C-365/12 P, *European Commission v EnBW Energie Baden Württemberg AG*, EU:C:2013:643, para 30.

public disclosure of such documents is liable to make them less inclined to cooperate, the Commission argued. Irrespective of the contribution made by the private enforcement system to the enforcement of EU competition law, such a contribution cannot justify or counteract the threat to the public interest. Any useful purpose such actions might serve is also dependent on the Commission's ability to unearth infringements of the competition rules, the Commission argued.[46]

The ECJ commenced by acknowledging that Article 255 EC[47] provided that any citizen of the Union, and any natural or legal person residing or having its registered office in a Member State, was to have a right of access to the documents of the EU institutions.[48] The Court further recalled that the Transparency Regulation is designed to confer on the public as wide a right of access as possible to documents of the institutions. Having established the main rule, the Court moved on to the exceptions. Here, it declared that where the exceptions in Article 4 applied, the institutions must refuse access unless there is an overriding public interest in disclosure. The Court further declared that according to well-established case law, the institution concerned must provide explanations as to how access to a certain document could specifically and actually undermine the interest protected by an exception in Article 4. Having said that, the Court nevertheless declared that it is open to the EU institution concerned to base such decisions on general presumptions that apply to certain categories of documents, as considerations of a generally similar kind are likely to apply to requests for disclosure relating to documents of the same nature.[49] The Court declared that it had already acknowledged the existence of such presumptions in four particular cases, and that all four cases were characterised by the fact that the request for access covered not just one document but a set of documents.[50]

In that type of situation, the Court continued, the recognition that there is a general presumption that the disclosure of documents of a certain nature will, in principle, undermine the protection of one of the interests listed in Article 4 of the Transparency Regulation enables the institution concerned to deal with a global application and to reply thereto accordingly. The present case entailed that type of situation, the Court noted.[51] As the Commission was likely to gather commercially sensitive information during the course of a competition law investigation, and as the protection of commercial interests was closely linked to protecting the purpose of the investigation in these cases, the Court declared that a general presumption should apply to requests for access to a set of documents in a file relating to a proceeding under Article 101 TFEU.[52] Furthermore, the Court noted, the case was

[46] *EnBW* (n 40) para 47.
[47] Now Art 15 TFEU.
[48] See *EnBW* (n 40) para 61.
[49] Ibid para 65.
[50] Ibid para 67.
[51] Ibid para 69.
[52] Ibid para 81.

still pending before the General Court. According to the ECJ, and contrary to the General Court's finding, a proceeding under Article 101 TFEU cannot be regarded as closed once the Commission's final decision has been adopted irrespective of any possible future judgment by the EU judicature annulling that decision.[53] Given that the annulment of such decision may lead the Commission to resume its investigation with a view to adopting a new decision, investigations relating to a proceeding under Article 101 TFEU may be regarded as completed only when the decision adopted by the Commission is final.

In its appeal, the Commission had argued for a harmonious interpretation of the Transparency Regulation and the Antitrust Regulations. The Court agreed with the Commission on this point. It reasoned that the Antitrust Regulations and the Transparency Regulation are on the same footing in the EU legal order, and that accordingly they should be applied consistently. The Transparency Regulation does not operate in a vacuum but should be reconciled – both in terms of its interpretation and its application – with the specific regulatory schemes governing access to documents in particular areas. Thus, if the purpose of the Transparency Regulation is to confer a right of access to the EU institutions' documents, the extent of such access should depend on the activities of the institution. While the Transparency Regulation sought to ensure the widest possible access, the Antitrust Regulations instead had the aim of securing that the rights of the parties to the investigation were respected, and that complaints were dealt with diligently, while at the same time ensuring compliance with the duty of professional secrecy.[54]

According to the ECJ, the Commission's activity in antitrust proceedings does not require the same level of disclosure as compared to the legislative activities of the Union.[55] Moreover, the exceptions set forth in Article 4 of the Transparency Regulation cannot be interpreted without taking account of the Antitrust Regulations' specific rules on access to the file. Here, the ECJ noted that, according to the Antitrust Regulations, in principle it is only the parties to cartel proceedings that have a right to access the Commission's files. The ECJ thus found that if third parties, such as EnBW, were able to access the Commission's files through the Transparency Regulation, the specific system put in place by the Antitrust Regulations would be jeopardised. More specifically, a generalised access would jeopardise the balance the legislator sought to ensure in the Antitrust Regulations, between the obligation on the undertaking concerned to submit to the Commission possible sensitive information to enable it to ascertain whether a concerted practice was in existence and to determine whether that practice was

[53] Ibid para 99. The General Court had found that it could not apply the reasoning in *Technische Glaswerke Ilmenau* as, contrary to the situation in that case, the Commission had already adopted its infringement decision and the investigation was thus terminated.

[54] *EnBW* (n 40) para 83.

[55] Ibid para 91. The Court's statement is not restricted to antitrust proceedings, as it declares that the administrative activity of the Commission does not require such extensive access to documents as that required by the legislative activity of an EU institution.

compatible with Article 101 TFEU.[56] Thus, the Commission's investigative powers, which mostly rely on the information given by companies, would be undermined by the lack of guarantee that the documents submitted (voluntarily or not) by investigated companies would be treated with the highest degree of confidentiality.

Consequently, the ECJ concluded that the Commission was entitled to rely on a general presumption, stemming from the Antitrust Regulations, that the documents in a cartel file fell within one or more of the exceptions in Article 4 of the Transparency Regulation. The Commission could thus apply a blanket approach to a third party's broad and unspecified request, thereby sparing itself a fastidious document-by-document review of its voluminous cartel files.

The Court did take notice of the fact that this presumption may be rebutted, and that EnBW sought access to the documents in question with the intention of later filing a damages claim. While acknowledging that any person is entitled to claim compensation for the loss caused by breach of the competition rules, and that such rights strengthen the enforcement of Article 101 TFEU, the Court did not consider such general considerations to be capable of prevailing over the reasons justifying the refusal to disclose the documents in question.[57] Furthermore, the Court noted that in order to ensure effective protection of the right to compensation, there is no need for every document relating to a cartel proceeding to be disclosed to a claimant 'on the ground that that party is intending to bring an action for damages, as it is highly unlikely that the action for damages will be based on all the evidence in the file relating to that proceeding'.[58] Thus, in order for the Commission to be obliged to weigh the interests of disclosure against those listed in Article 4 of the Transparency Regulation, the person seeking access must first show that the documents in question are necessary for a successful damages claim. If this is not shown, the Court concluded, the interest in obtaining compensation for the loss suffered as a result of a breach of Article 101 TFEU cannot constitute an overriding public interest.[59]

iii. Comment on the Ruling of the ECJ

The case of *EnBW* is interesting for a number of reasons. First of all, it confirms the Court's conclusion in *Technische Glaswerke Ilmenau* that the right of access has different meanings depending on the context in which the requested documents were drawn up. It is safe to assume that when the Member States agreed on the wording of Article 15 TFEU and Article 42 of the Charter, it was not the present situation that they had in mind. Yet the two articles are in place, and they do not make any difference between cases where an EU citizen is seeking access

[56] Ibid para 90.
[57] Ibid para 105.
[58] Ibid para 106.
[59] Ibid para 108.

to a protocol from a Council meeting or when an alleged cartel victim requests access to the entire case file. However, the recitals to the Transparency Regulation declare that wider access should be granted to documents in cases where the institutions are acting in their legislative capacity, and this is also confirmed by the Court in *EnBW*, where it declares that the Commission's administrative practice does not require such extensive access to documents as required by the legislative activity of the EU institutions.[60] Although such interpretation is not supported by the wording of either Article 42 of the Charter or Article 15 TFEU, it may still be in line with the legislation in place. Article 52(2) of the Charter stipulates that rights for which provision is also made in the Treaties shall be exercised under the conditions and within the limits defined by those Treaties. As for the right to public access, this right is provided for by Article 15(3) TFEU, which in turn declares that the right shall be subject to the principles and the conditions determined by the European Parliament and the Council, by means of regulations – the Transparency Regulation. As noted, the recitals of the Regulation acknowledge two different standards of protection, and while it would have been preferable if this had been acknowledged in the operative parts of the Regulation, the Court cannot be accused of judicial activism when establishing a double standard, and letting the scope of protection depend on whether the institution is acting in its legislative or administrative capacity.

Second, and this is of course also of great relevance, through this ruling the Court now establishes that the possibility to rely on general presumptions extends to requests for documents from the Commission's cartel files. The applicant, EnBW, had requested access to a set of documents – more or less the entire case file – and the Court declared that when the Commission receives a global application for documents of a certain nature, it must be able to reply thereto accordingly.[61] The finding is not only based on the fact that the Commission is acting in its administrative capacity, but is also based on the relationship between the Transparency Regulation and the Antitrust Regulations. The three Regulations stand on an equal footing, and while one has the aim of granting the widest access possible to the documents of the institutions, the two others have explicitly limited the number of persons who may access the Commission's files to parties and complainants. This allows the Court to draw the conclusion that the documents in the Commission's case file are of such a nature as to justify the application of a general presumption.

Interesting to note is that while *EnBW* concerns a 'global application for access', the Court's reasoning on the relationship between the Transparency Regulation and the Antitrust Regulations would also allow for a presumption of confidentiality where the applicant seeks access to only one document from the case file. If you are neither a party nor a complainant then you do not have a right of access under the Antitrust Regulations, and the granting of access under the Transparency

[60] Ibid para 91. This was acknowledged by the Court already in the Grand Chamber ruling in *Technische Glaswerke Ilmenau* (see section II.C).

[61] *EnBW* (n 40) para 68.

Regulation would fail to ensure coherence between the three legal instruments. This would be in line with the Court's reasoning in *Technische Glaswerke Ilmenau*, which although it did also concern a request for access to the entire case file, is not based on the number of documents requested but rather on the relationship between the Transparency Regulation and the rules on state aid procedures.

A third observation concerns the temporal scope of protection. In *EnBW*, the Court now declares that the exceptions in Article 4 of the Transparency Regulation shall also apply after the Commission has adopted its infringement decision. Given that the annulment of such decision may lead the Commission to resume its investigation with a view to adopting a new decision, investigations relating to a proceeding under Article 101 TFEU may be regarded as completed only when the decision adopted by the Commission is final, the Court concludes.

Finally, in several of the cases presented in this chapter, the Commission argued that the protection of professional secrecy or the commercial interests of undertakings should not be affected by an application for access to documents based exclusively on private law interests, that is these interests could not constitute an overriding public interest in the meaning of Article 4 of the Transparency Regulation. It is clear from this case that the Court does not accept this argument, as it acknowledges that documents can be disclosed if necessary to ensure effective protection of the right to compensation. That said, the Court requires the person seeking access to show that the documents in question are necessary for a successful damages claim, a potentially challenging task.

Anyone seeking access to the Commission's case file will thus have to fight an uphill battle. All documents in the file are presumed to be covered by the exceptions in Article 4 of the Transparency Regulation, and either that presumption will need to be rebutted or it will have to be successfully argued that there is an overriding public interest in favour of disclosure, with explanation of how granting access to particular documents would serve such public interest.

F. *Axa Versicherung* – The Presumption of Confidentiality and its Application to a Request for a Single Document

In November 2008, the Commission adopted an infringement decision against a number of companies active in the car glass sector, imposing fines totalling more than €1.3 billion.[62] In February 2012, Axa Versicherung AG (Axa), a company active in the motor insurance sector, submitted a request under the Transparency Regulation for access to the complete version of the table of contents in the Commission's case file. Axa based its request on the need to support an action for damages before a German court against one of the cartel members.

[62] Decision C(2008) 6815 final of 12 November 2008 relating to a proceeding pursuant to Article 101 TFEU and Article 53 of the EEA Agreement (COMP/39.125 – *Car glass*).

The Commission granted Axa partial access to the requested document, stating that the other parts could not be disclosed as they were covered by certain exceptions to the right of access laid down in Article 4 of the Transparency Regulation. Axa later submitted a second request for access, this time for the complete version of a set of documents. The request was refused by the Commission.

Axa then submitted two confirmatory applications for access to the documents in question, which prompted the Commission to adopt a decision whereby it granted more extensive access to the table of contents but refused the two confirmatory applications as to the remainder.[63] In reaching that conclusion, the Commission found that several actions for annulment had been brought before the General Court against the *Car glass* decision and that those actions were still pending. In addition, it stated that actions for annulment were also pending before the General Court against decisions of the Hearing Officer relating to the publication of a final non-confidential version of the *Car glass* decision.[64] The Commission then clarified the scope of the applicant's two requests. It essentially found that the first request concerned the complete version of the table of contents, and in particular three categories of information that had not previously been disclosed to Axa: (i) references to correspondence exchanged with leniency applicants; (ii) the names of natural persons, third-party undertakings and law firms that had participated in the proceeding; and (iii) some non-public, potentially sensitive, commercial information.

As regards the second request, the Commission stated that it concerned a large set of documents included in its case file, and that those documents were covered by a general presumption of inaccessibility under the Transparency Regulation. According to the Commission, it should be presumed, in a general way, that all of the documents covered by the second request fell within the exceptions laid down in the third indent of Article 4(2) of the Regulation, relating to the protection of the purpose of inspections, investigations and audits, and the first indent of Article 4(2), relating to the protection of commercial interests. Lastly, the Commission argued that all of the internal documents of the Commission also fell within the exception laid down in the second subparagraph of Article 4(3) of the Transparency Regulation, relating to the protection of opinions for the internal use of the institution concerned.[65] As for the table of contents, the Commission stated that it was now able to disclose information from which the identity of the law firms that had represented the undertakings could be ascertained, since such information was already in the public domain. However, it maintained that the other information to which it had refused access in its earlier decision could still not be disclosed, be it references to correspondence exchanged with leniency applicants,

[63] Case T-677/13, *Axa Versicherung AG v European Commission*, EU:T:2015:473, para 5.

[64] For a further discussion on the Commission's decision to publish a longer and more detailed version of the *Car glass* decision, see ch 8, section IV.

[65] *Axa* (n 63) para 8.

the names of natural persons and third-party undertakings that were involved in the proceeding, or various items of commercially sensitive information.

Axa was not best pleased with the Commission's decision and filed a complaint with the General Court. In its application it argued, inter alia, that the Commission had erred in law when it relied on a general presumption that the documents in the second request were covered by the exceptions in Article 4. Acknowledging that the purpose of the Transparency Regulation is to confer on the public as wide a right of access as possible, the General Court noted that such right is nevertheless subject to a system of exceptions laid down in Article 4, albeit that such exceptions should be interpreted and applied strictly. Referring to *EnBW*, the General Court declared that, as a rule, the institution to which the request is addressed must also provide explanations as to how access to that document could specifically and actually undermine the interest protected by the exception or exceptions relied on. Moreover, the risk of the interest being undermined must be reasonably foreseeable and must not be purely hypothetical.[66]

i. The Request Concerning a Set of Documents

Once again referring to *EnBW*, the General Court acknowledged that in the case of requests relating to a set of documents, the Commission was entitled to presume that their disclosure would undermine the protection of the purpose of inspections and investigations, as well as the protection of the commercial interests of the parties to the proceedings. Furthermore, the General Court declared, such presumption was not restricted to requests concerning all documents in the file but could also be relied upon by the Commission in cases where the request concerned a more specific set of documents, identified by reference to their common characteristics or the fact that they fell within one or more general categories.[67] In the present case, the General Court noted that the number of documents covered by the request amounted to 3,948, which represented approximately 90 per cent of the documents in the case file, and that all the requested documents clearly related to an 'inspection and investigation' within the meaning of Article 4(2). Moreover, the documents were likely to contain commercially sensitive information. The Commission, the General Court concluded, had therefore been right to rely on a general presumption that the documents in question were fully covered by the exceptions in Article 4 of the Transparency Regulation.[68]

Axa had also argued that any presumption of confidentiality should be considered rebutted given that the documents dated from more than five years previously and were therefore too old to warrant protection. To this the General Court

[66] Ibid para 93.

[67] Ibid para 40, where the General Court makes reference to the ECJ's ruling in *Éditions Odile Jacob* (n 35) paras 10 and 123.

[68] *Axa* (n 63) para 57.

responded that the exceptions laid down in the Transparency Regulation may apply for 30 years, or even longer if necessary, and that the fact that the documents were more than five years old could not in or of itself rebut the presumption of confidentiality.[69] Neither did the General Court accept Axa's argument that there was an overriding public interest warranting the granting of access. Axa had argued that the public interest in allowing victims of anticompetitive practices to exercise their right to compensation should trump the interests protected by the exceptions in Article 4 of the Transparency Regulation, and that this required the Commission to disclose the requested documents. To this the General Court replied that while Axa had marked the 3,948 documents as either 'relevant' or 'possibly relevant', it had merely made general claims that these documents were of interest and that it had to inspect them to be able to substantiate its claim for damages. By contrast, the General Court noted, Axa had not explained why it needed these documents, even if only by setting out the specific factual or legal arguments that securing those documents might help it substantiate its claim before the national court.[70]

Axa had argued that there were no appropriate rules under German civil procedure law permitting the documents to be requested *inter partes*, suggesting that this was the only possible route available to Axa. However, as Axa had not elaborated on this argument, and had not demonstrated that it had no other ways of obtaining the documents, the General Court did not consider the Commission to have erred in law when relying on Article 4 of the Transparency Regulation in regard to the second request.[71]

ii. The Request Concerning the Table of Contents

Axa had also challenged the Commission's decision not to disclose the table of contents in its entirety. Declaring that it is open to an EU institution to base its decision on a general presumption even though the request at issue covers only one single document, the General Court nevertheless held that the institution must then first establish that the general considerations normally applicable to a particular type of document do apply to the document in question.[72] As the request concerned the table of contents only, the Commission should not have claimed, as it did in its defence, that it was part of the case file and was therefore in its entirety covered by the general presumption of inaccessibility.[73]

As previously noted, the Commission had found that the first request concerned the complete version of the table of contents, and in particular three categories of information that had not previously been disclosed to Axa, (i) references to correspondence exchanged with leniency applicants; (ii) the names of natural persons,

[69] Ibid para 63.
[70] Ibid paras 71–73.
[71] Ibid para 76.
[72] Ibid para 94, where the General Court referred to *Turco* (n 23).
[73] *Axa* (n 63) para 96.

third-party undertakings and law firms that had participated in the proceeding; and (iii) some non-public, potentially sensitive, commercial information. As for the first category, references to leniency documents, the General Court noted that the Commission had removed these references completely from the table of contents, and that such removal *en bloc* was driven by general considerations, according to which disclosure of such references could jeopardise the effectiveness of the leniency system. According to the Commission, leniency applicants expected the information they provided to be treated as confidential, and these expectations were worthy of protection in order to safeguard the effectiveness of the leniency programme, which is a useful tool to detect and prevent infringements. The General Court did not accept the Commission's reasoning. Referring to the Court's ruling in *Donau Chemie*, it declared that it is only where there is a risk that a given document may actually undermine the public interest relating to the effectiveness of the leniency programme that non-disclosure of the document may be justified.[74] The General Court further noted that it was settled case law that where the Commission or the national courts are called upon to take a decision on whether to grant access to documents collected under the leniency programme, they must refrain from taking an inflexible and absolute stance liable to undermine either the effective application of the competition rules by the public authorities entrusted with ensuring their observance or the effective exercise of individuals' rights flowing from these rules. They must therefore weigh up, on a case-by-case basis, the different interests in favour of disclosure and in favour of the protection of the documents in question. The General Court considered these considerations to be even more relevant in the present case, where Axa had already brought an action for damages before a national court and had asked the Commission for access not to the 'leniency documents' included in the file, but only to the references to those documents contained in the table of contents.

The General Court further found that in the present case, the presumption of confidentiality had been based on general and speculative considerations, none of which had proved that there was any specific or actual harm to the interests invoked by the Commission warranting an absolute refusal to disclose the dates, headings or other references to the leniency documents included in the table of contents. In short, the General Court continued, such refusal negated the effects of the principle that the exceptions to the right of access to documents must be interpreted and applied strictly. Furthermore, in so far as the Commission had relied on the need to protect its leniency programme and the documents relating to it in all cases, the General Court found it necessary to make two observations. It acknowledged that the case law recognised the value of the leniency programme, but at the same time pointed out that the public interest in preserving its effectiveness could not be considered to take precedence, in a general and absolute way,

[74] Ibid para 122, where the General Court refers to Case C-536/11, *Bundeswettbewerbsbehörde v Donau Chemie AG and Others*, EU:C:2013:366, para 48.

over the other public and private interests at stake, which were also worthy of protection and must be reconciled with it on a case-by-case basis. In addition, the General Court noted, recital 20 in the preamble to and Article 6(2) of the Damages Directive expressly state that the Directive is without prejudice to the rules on public access to documents laid down in the Transparency Regulation. Given the above, the General Court concluded that the contested decision was not substantiated to the requisite legal standard in so far as it had found it possible to presume, in a global, complete and absolute way, that the granting of access to references to the 'leniency documents' in the table of contents would undermine the interests protected by Article 4 of the Transparency Regulation.[75] As for the two other categories in the table of contents, the General Court did not accept the arguments put forward by Axa, and upheld the Commission's decision.

iii. Comment on the General Court's Ruling

The case of *Axa* concerns both a request for a single document and a set of documents. In addition, the single document is not really part of the case file but merely the table of contents. Thus, it could be argued that the ECJ's reasoning on the relationship between the Transparency Regulation and the Antitrust Regulations does not apply in this situation.

As for the second request, the General Court applies the ECJ's reasoning in *EnBW* and allows the Commission to deal with a global application by replying thereto accordingly, and thus to rely on a general presumption that the requested documents are covered by the exceptions in Article 4 of the Transparency Regulation. However, as for the first request, the General Court does not accept the argument that the table of contents should be treated in the same way. Nor does it allow the Commission to rely on a general presumption that all references to leniency material in a table of contents should be covered by a general presumption of confidentiality in order to preserve the effectiveness of the leniency programme. Rightly so. The Transparency Regulation does require exceptions to be interpreted narrowly, and if only parts of a document are covered by the exceptions in Article 4 then the remaining parts should be disclosed. In the absence of the requirement to ensure the harmonious interpretation between two Regulations standing on equal footing, it is fair to require the Commission to go through the table of contents, and to determine whether all references to leniency documents will actually harm the effectiveness of the leniency programme. This by no means prevents the Commission from deleting references to leniency documents in those cases where it deems it necessary and justifiable under the Transparency Regulation.

[75] *Axa* (n 63) para 136.

III. The Right to Public Access – A Right in Theory but not in Practice?

Judging from the case law presented in this chapter, the Commission is consistent in its attitude towards third parties seeking access to its case files, rejecting requests no matter whether they concern one document or the entire case file. In *VKI*, the main argument for such refusal was that an examination of the 47,000 pages of documents would require too much work; and in the case of *EnBW*, the Commission also argued that the review of the documents requested would take a disproportionate amount of time.[76] However, this does not appear to be the only or even the main reason behind the Commission's unwillingness to open the doors to its archives. As is apparent from all the cases referred to in this chapter, it is instead the Commission's concern for the leniency programme and the effectiveness of its enforcement activities that appears to be the main reason behind the Commission's consistent refusals. Even in the case of *VKI*, the Commission sought to justify its refusal by declaring that a large number of the documents had been submitted under the leniency programme.[77]

While the Commission is consistent in its view on the interpretation of the Transparency Regulation, the case law of the EU Courts has developed over the years. In *VKI*, the General Court found that the Commission was under an obligation to review all documents in the file before adopting its decision. It was only in exceptional cases – where (i) a concrete, individual examination would entail an unreasonable amount of administrative work, (ii) the Commission had genuinely investigated all other conceivable options, and (iii) it had explained in detail why those options also involved an unreasonable amount of work – that the Commission was allowed to rely on the principle of proportionality and adopt a decision refusing access to its case file without having first examined the documents therein.

A decade later, and following a number of rulings in areas such as state aid and merger control, the Commission could instead 'respond to a global application in a global way' – just as it argued that it should be able to do in *VKI*. As long as the request concerns a 'set of documents', there is no need to investigate 'all other conceivable options', as the exceptions in Article 4 of the Transparency Regulation are presumed to apply to the documents in the Commission's case file. In fact, the Court's reasoning in *Technische Glaswereke Ilmenau* allows for an even more restrictive approach towards requests for access. Presumably, these findings are also the result of a proportionality analysis. However, the weights put in the balance are no longer the same as those in *VKI*. First, since the General Court's ruling in *VKI*, the ECJ has acknowledged that the Commission's administrative

[76] *EnBW* (n 43) para 65.
[77] *VKI* (n 8) para 81.

practice does not require such extensive access to documents as is required by the legislative activity of the EU institutions.[78] Second, it is now established that the Transparency Regulation cannot be seen or applied in isolation but should be interpreted in harmony with the Antitrust Regulations in order to secure coherence and consistency in the EU legal system.

As for the finding that the Commission is not required to ensure the same access to its administrative files as to it legislative files, this is in line not only with the historical background to the transparency rules but also with the legislation actually in place. As noted by Ashton, the purpose of the Transparency Regulation was to create more transparent public administration, not to facilitate discovery of documents in civil litigation.[79] That said, while the rules have sprung from an ambition to do away with a perceived democratic deficit and an aspiration to bring EU citizens closer to the EU and its decision-making process, neither Article 15 TFEU nor Article 42 of the Charter makes any distinction between administrative files or files relating to the legislative process. Yet, and as discussed in section II.E, the Court's interpretation is in line with both the Charter and the TFEU. Article 52(2) of the Charter stipulates that rights for which provision is also made in the Treaties shall be exercised under the conditions and within the limits defined by those Treaties. As regards the right of access to documents, it is also provided for by Article 15(3) TFEU, which in turn declares that the right shall be subject to the principles and the conditions determined by the European Parliament and the Council, by means of regulations. It is clear from the recitals to the Transparency Regulation that wider access should be granted to documents in cases where the institutions are acting in their legislative capacity. While it would have been preferable if this limitation had been provided for in the operative parts of the Regulation, the Court can thus not be accused of judicial activism when establishing a double standard.

Second, as for the role played by the Antitrust Regulations, the Court is right in acknowledging that the Transparency Regulation cannot be seen in isolation but must be interpreted in harmony with the two Regulations governing the enforcement of the competition rules. Regulation 1/2003 was adopted two years after the Transparency Regulation had entered into force, and is built not on the principle of transparency, but rather on principles of efficiency, effectiveness and confidentiality. As is discussed in chapters 4 and 5, and partly due to the companies' duty to cooperate and submit information, access to the file is only granted to the parties and to those who are given the status of complainants. If third parties could circumvent these rules and access the case file through the Transparency Regulation, this would undoubtedly upset the order established by the Antitrust Regulations. Furthermore, as Article 4 of the Transparency Regulation is framed – acknowledging the interest of protecting commercial

[78] *EnBW* (n 40) para 91; and *Technische Glaswerke Ilmenau* (n 21) para 60.
[79] D Ashton, *Competition Damages Actions in the EU – Law and Practice*, 2nd edn (Cheltenham, Edward Elgar, 2018) 102.

interests, inspections and investigations – such interpretation would not go against the wording of the Regulation. That said, it can of course be questioned whether the system put in place by Regulation 1/2003 is optimal, and whether the limited access to the Commission's case files is necessary to ensure effective competition law enforcement. However, as long as the rules are framed the way they are, they will by necessity affect companies' willingness to cooperate with the Commission and create legitimate expectations.

Furthermore, recital 6 of the Damages Directive explicitly acknowledges the need to coordinate private and public enforcement of the EU competition rules, declaring that in order to ensure effective private enforcement actions under civil law and effective public enforcement by competition authorities, both tools are required to interact to ensure maximum effectiveness of the competition rules. It is necessary to regulate the coordination of those two forms of enforcement in a coherent manner, for instance in relation to the arrangements for access to documents held by competition authorities. Such coordination at Union level will also avoid the divergence of applicable rules, which could jeopardise the proper functioning of the internal market. While the recital concerns disclosure in national courts, it still points to the necessity of coordinating the granting of access to evidence under public and private enforcement. That said, and as pointed out by the General Court, the Damages Directive applies without prejudice to the Transparency Regulation.[80]

Harmonious interpretation does not mean that one Regulation shall at all times give way to the other. Thus, while it may be reasonable to let the Commission rely on a general presumption when it receives a request for a large number of documents, it is not necessarily equally appropriate to allow it to rely on such presumption when the request only concerns a limited number. It could then be argued that the Commission should review the documents requested and assess whether they are actually to be kept confidential. This is in line with the Court's reasoning in *EnBW*, where it declares that the general presumption applies to requests for 'sets of documents'. It remains to be seen where the line should be drawn, as a 'set of documents' could just as well comprise three documents as 1,000 documents.

It is interesting to note in this respect is that in *EnBW* the Court builds its reasoning on the fact that the applicant had sought access not to one document but to a set of documents. Thus, the Court declared that when the Commission receives a request for access to documents, identified globally, it must be able to respond accordingly and rely on a general presumption that the documents in its case file are covered by the exception in Article 4(2). This line of reasoning is recognised from the Court's ruling in the case of *LPN*,[81] which concerned a

[80] Recital 20 of the Damages Directive.

[81] Joined Cases C-514/11 P and C-605/11 P, *Liga para a Protecção da Natureza (LPN) and Republic of Finland v European Commission*, EU:C:2013:738.

dam construction project in Portugal and whether this project infringed EU legislation on the conservation of natural habitats and wild fauna and flora. A non-governmental organisation, LPN, had lodged a complaint with the European Commission against the project, and later it requested access to certain documents drawn up by the Commission's working group and exchanged with the Portuguese Government. In that case, the Court acknowledged that the existence of a general presumption that the disclosure of documents of a certain nature would, in principle, undermine the protection of one of the interests listed in Article 4 of the Transparency Regulation enabled the institution concerned to deal with a global application and to reply thereto accordingly. In the case at hand, the documents formed part of the pre-litigation stage of the infringement proceeding and were therefore considered to be of such nature as to warrant the application of a general presumption. In *LPN* there is no other regulation mandating a harmonious interpretation, and the Court therefore had to build its reasoning on the fact that the request was 'global' in character. In the case of *Technische Glaswerke Ilmenau*, on the other hand, the Court does not build its reasoning on the size of the request but rather on the relation with the rules on state aid procedure. It could therefore be argued that there was no need for the Court in *EnBW* to follow the line of reasoning in *LPN*. Yet the choice appears deliberate, as the Court refers to *Technische Glaswerke Ilmenau* and declares that a similar general presumption applies to a request for access to a set of documents in a file relating to a proceeding under Article 101 TFEU.[82]

Important to note is that the Court's case law does not formally force the Transparency Regulation to give way to the Antitrust Regulations. It is therefore appropriate that the Court, while referring to the case of *Technische Glaswerke Ilmenau*, still declares that the general presumption applies in cases where the Commission receives a set of documents. A set of documents may comprise 10 or 10,000 documents, but it still prevents the Commission from applying a blanket refusal to all requests for access.

This especially since the general presumption that one or more of the exceptions in Article 4 of the Transparency Regulation applies makes it more or less impossible for an applicant to gain access to the Commission's case files. To give an example, in *Netherlands v Commission*, the Commission considered that the contested information was covered by the exceptions set out in both the first and third indents of Article 4(2) of the Transparency Regulation. This meant that in order to succeed in showing that the contested decision was vitiated by an error capable of justifying its annulment, the Kingdom of the Netherlands had to establish either that the Commission had committed an error in considering that it could refuse access to that information under each one of those exceptions, or that an overriding public interest, the passage of time or the obligation of the

[82] *EnBW* (n 40) para 81.

Commission to respect the principle of proportionality justified at the very least partial disclosure of that information. This is undoubtedly a challenging task for an applicant who has not accessed the documents and can thus not verify whether the Commission's justifications are valid or not.

Thus, while the Transparency Regulation establishes an order that in theory should ensure the fullest possible access to the documents held by the EU institutions, requiring them to disclose all documents in their possession 'falling in to their sphere of responsibility', and where any limitations to this obligation should be narrowly construed and not apply where there is an overriding public interest in disclosure,[83] the reality is otherwise. While the Court's case law may be in line with applicable legislation, it nevertheless creates or endorses an order where the interests of preserving a well-functioning public enforcement system are allowed to prevail. It is therefore important that the interest of ensuring effective private enforcement is secured in some other way. The following chapters will examine the possibilities of accessing evidence through national courts and the possibility for the Commission to adopt more detailed infringement decisions, in order to determine whether these two mechanisms can help restore the balance between public and private enforcement of the EU competition rules.

[83] Article 4(2) and (3).

7

Seeking Access Through National Courts

As is shown from the previous chapter, the Commission and the ECJ have more or less shut the door on anyone attempting to access evidence directly from the files of the Commission. Most third parties seeking to substantiate their claims against competition law offenders are therefore left with the option of trying to access such evidence through the hands of the national courts. In follow-on actions, these courts can order disclosure either from the cartelists themselves or from the competition authorities. National courts may also want to seek access to the Commission's case files. Such requests are governed by Article 15 of Regulation 1/2003, which provides national courts with the possibility to request documents or other forms of evidence from the Commission.

This chapter will discuss the relationship between the Commission and national courts, and how it has been affected by the adoption of the Damages Directive. As is shown in the following, the Commission has previously left this door ajar, agreeing to hand over documents from its files to national courts. However, the Commission's cooperative approach has met with steep resistance from the companies targeted by the Commission's infringement decisions, and the Damages Directive has now more or less prohibited national courts from seeking access to the Commission's case files.

This chapter will first examine the Court's and the Commission's approach prior to the Damages Directive, after which there will be a presentation of the Damages Directive's provisions governing disclosure of evidence held by competition authorities, and how the Directive is likely to affect and limit the Commission's cooperation with national courts.

I. The Commission and the National Courts before the Damages Directive

When the enforcement of the EU competition rules was decentralised in 2004, it was not only necessary to establish a structure for the cooperation between the Commission and the NCAs. The relationship with national courts also needed structure. Thus, Article 15 of Regulation 1/2003 governs the Commission's cooperation with national courts, and the Commission has also issued a Notice in which it describes its procedures in these matters.[1] Cooperation between the Commission and national courts may take various forms. Article 15(1) of Regulation 1/2003 governs transmission of information or opinions. It stipulates that, in proceedings for the application of Article 101 or 102 TFEU, Member State courts may ask the Commission to transmit to them information in its possession. They may also ask for the Commission's opinion on questions concerning the application of the two antitrust provisions. The Article thus only grants national courts the right to request documents or opinions from the Commission; it imposes no obligation on the Commission to actually cooperate. Case law from the EU Courts sheds light on the issue. The principle of sincere cooperation under Article 4(3) TEU requires the Commission to assist national courts, save for in those situations where a national court cannot guarantee the protection of confidential information or business secrets or where the disclosure of the requested information would be capable of interfering with the functioning and independence of the Union.[2] This view is also reflected in the Commission's Notice.[3] Thereupon follows a presentation of cases governing the Commission's duty to assist national courts in their application of EU legislation.

A. *Zwartveld* – The Duty to Transmit Information during an Ongoing Commission Investigation

While *Zwartveld*[4] is not a competition case, it illustrates the Commission's duty to assist national courts in the application of EU legislation. In August 1988, the *rechter-commissaris* at the *Arrondissementsrechtbank* Groningen submitted a request for judicial cooperation to the ECJ. The request was made within the frame of an investigation concerning possible forgery contrary to Article 225 of the Dutch Penal Code. More precisely, the *rechter-commissaris* suspected the managers of the fish market in Lauwersoog of having introduced a second market – or a black market – in addition to the official fish market, which would constitute a breach of national provisions adopted to implement the EU rules on fishing quotas. As the Commission had carried out inspections in the Netherlands with regard to sea fisheries, the *rechter-commissaris* now sought access to the reports drawn up following those inspections. The Commission refused access, declaring that the documents formed part of a file on legal matters pending in the Commission. The *rechter-commissaris* then turned to the ECJ, challenging the Commission's decision to refuse access.

[1] Commission Notice on the cooperation between the Commission and the courts of the EU Member States in the application of Articles 81 and 82 EC [2004] OJ C101/54.

[2] The duty of sincere cooperation laid down in Art 4(3) TEU includes a mutual legal obligation for the EU and its Member States to assist each other in carrying out the tasks that flow from the Treaties.

[3] Commission Notice (n 1) paras 21–26.

[4] Case C-2/88, *Imm, JJ Zwartveld and Others*, EU:C:1990:440.

The Commission argued that there were imperative reasons relating to the need to avoid any interference with the functioning and independence of the EU that precluded the reports from being transmitted to the Dutch judge.[5] According to the Commission, the refusal was motivated by the need to (i) preserve the division of powers between the Commission and national authorities, (ii) avoid interference with the functioning and the independence of the Communities, and (iii) protect the rights of third parties who might be liable to disciplinary or legal proceedings under national law if communication of private information was forwarded to the national judge.[6]

As for the first argument, the Court declared that no risk of interference with the division of powers had been established. Moving on to the second and third arguments, the Court stressed that the EU institutions were under a duty of sincere cooperation with the judicial authorities of the Member States. While the Court acknowledged that the Commission could justify a refusal to produce documents to a national judicial authority on legitimate grounds connected with the protection of the rights of third parties, or where the disclosure of this information would be capable of interfering with the functioning and independence of the Community,[7] the Commission had adduced no evidence to show that the production of individual particulars contained in the reports or the granting of permission to Commission officials to give evidence thereon would be likely to adversely affect those interests.[8] Consequently, the Court found that the Commission had failed to establish the imperative reasons that would justify the refusal to produce the reports or the refusal to permit its officials to be examined as witnesses on the information contained in those reports.[9]

The Court thus made it clear that the Commission is bound by a duty of sincere cooperation, and that this duty requires it to assist the national courts in applying the EU rules by transmitting information, providing opinions and/or appearing as witnesses. A refusal to cooperate may only be accepted if the Commission can show that it is justified by imperative reasons, such as if the assistance would jeopardise the accomplishment of the duties assigned to the Commission by the Union legislature.

B. *Delimitis* – The Duty of Sincere Cooperation in Competition Cases

The *Delimitis*[10] case concerned a beer supply agreement and its compatibility with the EU competition rules. Following the termination of the agreement, there was

[5] Ibid para 5.
[6] Ibid para 6.
[7] In particular by jeopardising the accomplishment of the tasks entrusted to it.
[8] *Zwartveld* (n 4) para 11.
[9] Ibid paras 12 and 13.
[10] Case C-234/89, *Stergios Delimitis v Henninger Bräu AG*, EU:C:1991:91.

a dispute between the two parties as regards outstanding payments. During the proceedings before the national court, the reseller claimed that the agreement was contrary to Article 101 TFEU, and the national court therefore decided to stay its proceedings and seek guidance from the ECJ. One question submitted to the Court concerned the national court's powers to apply Article 101 TFEU to an agreement that did not satisfy the conditions for application of Regulation 1984/83, and which would thus require an individual exemption.[11] In its reply, the ECJ reminded the national court that it is always open to national courts to contact the Commission in situations where the concrete application of Article 101 or 102 TFEU raises particular difficulties, in order to obtain the economic and legal information that institution can supply to it. Under Article 4(3) TEU,[12] the Court concluded, the Commission is bound by a duty of sincere cooperation with the judicial authorities of the Member States, who are responsible for ensuring that EU law is applied and respected in the national legal systems.[13]

C. *Postbank* – The Duty to Protect Professional Secrecy

In July 1991, the Netherlands Association of Banks (the NVB) notified an agreement to the Commission under Article 4 of Regulation 17/62. The agreement, also known as the GSA agreement, established a common procedure for processing payment and transfer orders on the basis of pre-printed transfer forms. Following notification of the GSA agreement, the Commission received a number of complaints from users of the transfer forms, and chose to send out requests for information to the NVB and a number of Dutch banks that were parties to the agreement. In June 1993, the Commission sent a statement of objections concerning the GSA agreement to the NVB and arranged for an oral hearing to be held in October that year.

In parallel, NUON and Mega Limburg – both users of the transfer forms – had initiated proceedings against the two Dutch banks Postbank and ABN Amro before a Dutch court, challenging the legality of the new scale of charges for the use of the transfer forms. Despite not formally being complainants in the administrative procedure pending before the Commission, the Commission chose to authorise NUON and Mega Limburg to attend the oral hearing. In order to enable the two companies to prepare for the hearing, the Commission forwarded to them the complete and unredacted version of the statement of objections. The cover letter explicitly stated that the information contained in the statement of objections should only be used in preparation for the hearing and

[11] Commission Regulation (EEC) No 1984/83 of 22 June 1983 on the Application of Article 85(3) of the Treaty to Categories of Exclusive Purchasing Agreements [1983] OJ L173/5. At the time, the Commission and the EU Courts had exclusive competence to apply Art 101(3) TFEU.

[12] Article 5 of the EC Treaty.

[13] *Delimitis* (n 10) para 53.

certainly 'not for any other purpose, especially in legal proceedings'.[14] As it turned out, the Commission had failed to notify the NVB of its intention to disclose the statement of objections, and thus had not given it an opportunity to oppose the transmission or to indicate the passages that should be regarded as constituting business secrets. NUON and Mega Limburg later asked the Commission for an authorisation to submit the statement of objections and the minutes from the oral hearing to the Dutch court hearing their case, arguing that the Commission had no power to prohibit the production of those documents in national legal proceedings. The Commission appears to have accepted their arguments, as it informed the two companies that the earlier restriction appeared unfounded and was therefore inoperative. NUON and Mega Limburg forwarded a copy of the statement of objections to the Dutch court and informed Postbank of its actions.[15]

Postbank asked the Commission to reverse its decision to authorise the production of the statement of objections before the Dutch court, stating that the objections were based directly or indirectly on information that the Commission had received in the administrative procedure and that both the NVB and Postbank had 'expressly described as constituting business secrets'.[16] According to Postbank, this meant that the information could be disclosed to third parties only if it was necessary for the conduct of the procedure initiated by the Commission. The Commission did not agree and saw no reason to depart from its position, declaring that as the parties were already in possession of the documents in question, they could not be prevented from producing them to the national court.[17] Postbank then lodged a complaint with the General Court, requesting it to annul the Commission's decision.

In its first plea, Postbank had argued that the authorisation constituted an infringement of Article 20(1) of Regulation 17/62, which prohibited the use of information acquired during a competition law investigation for a purpose other than that for which it was sought.[18] The General Court did not accept this argument, declaring that Article 20(1) should be interpreted in the light of the principle of sincere cooperation governing the relationship between the Member States and the EU institutions. The case at hand, the Court noted, concerned cooperation between the Commission and a national court in so far as that court, through the production of the statement of objections, would use it as guidance when interpreting the antitrust provisions.[19] Furthermore, the General Court declared, the principle of sincere cooperation requires the EU institutions, and above all the

[14] Case T-353/94, *Postbank NV v Commission of the European Communities*, EU:T:1996:119, para 10.
[15] Ibid para 14.
[16] Ibid para 15.
[17] Ibid para 16.
[18] Art 20(1) corresponds to Art 28(1) of Regulation 1/2003. However, unlike Art 28(1), which expressly declares that the restrictions contained therein shall be without prejudice to Arts 12 and 15, Regulation 17/62 did not govern the relationship with national courts, and did thus not make any exceptions for transmission of information to those courts.
[19] *Postbank* (n 14) para 63.

Commission, which is entrusted with the task of ensuring the effective application of the Treaty provisions, to give active assistance to any national judicial authority dealing with an infringement of the EU rules. That assistance, the Court noted, may consist of disclosing to the national courts documents acquired by the institutions in the discharge of their duties.[20] In proceedings concerning the EU competition rules, the General Court continued, the national courts are entitled to seek information from the Commission on the state of any procedure the Commission may have set in motion, and to obtain from that institution such economic and legal information as it may be able to supply. The Court then declared that such cooperation between the Commission and the national court fell outside the scope of Regulation 17/62 and, consequently, the Court noted, Article 20(1) of the said Regulation could not be interpreted as imposing on the Commission an obligation to prohibit undertakings from producing documents from the administrative procedure in national legal proceedings.[21]

The General Court acknowledged that the obligation imposed by Article 20(1) could provide protection for undertakings having an interest in non-disclosure of confidential information, in particular business secrets, forwarded to the Commission during the administrative procedure. However, the Court noted, the need for such protection should not override the right of undertakings to argue their case in national legal proceedings. Moreover, the General Court declared, that prohibition is not necessary to protect confidential information and business secrets. Once documents from the administrative procedure are produced in national legal proceedings, there is a presumption that the national courts will guarantee the protection of confidential information, in particular business secrets, since, in order to ensure the full effectiveness of the provisions of EU law in accordance with Article 4(3) TEU, they are required to uphold the rights those provisions confer on individuals.[22] In conclusion, the General Court found no breach of Article 20(1) of Regulation 17/62.

The applicant had also argued that by allowing the transmission of the statement of objections to the Dutch court, the Commission had infringed Article 339 TFEU[23] as well as Article 20(2) of Regulation 17/62, both provisions requiring the Commission not to disclose information covered by professional secrecy.[24] Acknowledging that confidential information and business secrets may be covered by professional secrecy, the General Court noted that the applicant and the other banks had indicated on several occasions that the statement of objections contained confidential information as well as business secrets, and had protested against (i) its transmission to NUON and Mega Limburg, and (ii) the authorisation to

[20] Ibid para 65.

[21] Ibid para 66. Regulation 17/62 did not contain a provision corresponding to Art 15(1) of Regulation 1/2003, and there was thus no exception with regard to information transmitted to national courts; cf the reference to Art 15 in Art 28(1) of Regulation 1/2003.

[22] *Postbank* (n 14) para 69.

[23] At the time Art 214 of the Treaty.

[24] The latter article corresponds to Article 28(2) of Regulation 1/2003.

forward the statement of objections to the Dutch court.[25] The Commission, on the other hand, did not consider that the version sent to the two companies contained any business secrets since its annexes had not been included. The General Court noted that even if Article 339 TFEU or Article 20(2) of Regulation 17/62 prevented the Commission from transmitting such documents to third parties, this did not in any way prevent their disclosure to the national courts.[26] The General Court then declared that Article 20(2) was inapplicable in the present case, and that Article 339 TFEU should not be interpreted as prohibiting the Commission from producing to national courts any documents received during the course of the administrative procedure, as such prohibition might compromise the cooperation between the national judicial authorities and the Union institutions. However, the General Court continued, in offering its cooperation to the national courts, the Commission may at no time undermine the guarantees given to individuals concerning professional secrecy.

This means that the Commission – faced with a request to authorise the production to national courts of documents containing confidential information and business secrets – must take all necessary precautionary measures to ensure that the protection of such information is not undermined by or during the transmission of the documents to the national courts. In particular, the General Court declared, in a case like the present, where the undertakings concerned gave notice of the existence of business secrets, the Commission should have given them the opportunity to state their views. They should also have been allowed to point out the passages in the documents that might cause them harm if no precautions were taken before the transmission to the national court, and to indicate the nature and scope of such damage.[27]

The General Court further held that the Commission does not, in principle, infringe Article 339 TFEU by failing to prohibit the disclosure to national courts of documents protected by professional secrecy. However, it continued, it should nevertheless be possible for the Commission to refuse such disclosure in certain circumstances. That is where the Commission, despite having taken all the necessary precautions, cannot fully ensure the protection of rights of third parties. Such refusal is justified, the General Court continued, only where there are no other ways of ensuring protection, which in principle is a matter for the national courts, or 'where the disclosure of that information would be capable of interfering with the functioning and independence of the Community'.[28] In the present case, the Commission should have closely examined the views of the applicants concerning the production of the documents, and should have taken all the necessary precautions to ensure that their interests were protected. This means, the General Court continued, that the Commission should have informed the applicants of the

[25] *Postbank* (n 14) para 88.
[26] Ibid para 89.
[27] Ibid para 91.
[28] Ibid para 93, where the General Court makes reference to *Zwartveld* (n 4), and Case 145/83, *Stanley George Adams v Commission of the European Communities*, EU:C:1985:448.

request from NUON and Mega Limburg regarding production of the documents in national legal proceedings. Moreover, having regard to any observations by the banks concerning the presence of business secrets in those documents, it should immediately have notified a duly reasoned decision to those banks.[29]

In the context of transmitting the statement of objections and the minutes of the hearing to third parties, the Commission should have (i) given the banks the opportunity to state their views on the confidential nature of the information in question, (ii) adopted a decision in that connection containing an adequate statement of the reasons on which it was based, and (iii) notified the applicants of the decision. As the Commission had failed to do so, after receiving a subsequent request for 'authority' to produce those documents in national legal proceedings, it was, *a fortiori*, required to take the necessary measures to obviate any risk of disclosure of any business secrets that might be contained in those documents. However, the General Court noted, it was clear from the documents before the Court that the Commission had not informed the applicant of the request from NUON and Mega Limburg, and had thus not given notice to NVB of its positive response to that request until four days after sending it to those undertakings. On that basis, the General Court concluded that the Commission had failed its obligation of professional secrecy, and annulled the Commission's decision.

D. *Alstom* – Transmission of Replies to the Statement of Objections

In March 2004, ABB Ltd informed the Commission of the existence of anti-competitive practices in the gas insulated switchgear (GIS) sector and filed an application for immunity from fines. On the basis of the information supplied by ABB, the Commission launched an investigation and later adopted an infringement decision against Alstom and 19 of its competitors for participation in a cartel on the GIS market, imposing fines totalling €750 million.[30] National Grid Electricity Transmission ('National Grid') owns and maintains the high-voltage electricity system in England and Wales, and operates the system across Great Britain. Alleging that it had excessively overpaid for its GIS purchases, National Grid brought an action for damages before the High Court of Justice of England and Wales ('the High Court'), seeking £249 million in damages from the cartel members. During the course of these proceedings, National Grid made applications for disclosure of evidence held by the defendants and the Commission.

After extensive discussion, and 'not without some disagreement between the parties', there was substantial disclosure.[31] Despite the substantial disclosure,

[29] *Postbank* (n 14) para 94.
[30] At the time, the fine was the largest ever total fine imposed on a cartel.
[31] *National Grid Electricity Transmission Plc v ABB Ltd and Others* [2012] EWHC 869 (Ch) [8].

National Grid had managed to obtain only very limited disclosure from two of the defendants, Alstom and Areva, since they were French companies and had contended that the French 'blocking statute' prevented them from making disclosure.[32] However, during the course of the Commission's investigation, ABB and Siemens had obtained, by exercising their right of access to the file, copies of documents and replies to information requests submitted to the Commission by Alstom and Areva. In July 2011, the High Court ordered ABB and Siemens to disclose certain of those documents within a confidentiality ring. National Grid also wished to gain access to certain documents held by the Commission, and had made an application for disclosure of, inter alia, Alstom's reply to the statement of objections. The High Court made a request to the Commission pursuant to Article 15 of Regulation 1/2003, asking the Commission to transmit Alstom's reply to the statement of objections together with some other documents, expressly excluding any leniency material from the request. The Commission informed the High Court that it intended to accede to the request for cooperation, but stated that it had first to inform Alstom of its intent to forward the reply to the UK court. Perhaps not too surprisingly, Alstom declared that it would challenge any decision to share the reply with the UK court.

Alstom later brought an action before the General Court seeking the annulment of the Commission's decision to accede to the request for cooperation, in so far as it involved disclosure, first, of information in the reply to the statement of objections, which by its nature was covered by the obligation of professional secrecy, and, second, of information provided by other companies in connection with the Leniency Notice, which appeared in Alstom's reply.[33] On the same date, it lodged an application for interim measures, seeking the suspension of the operation of the contested decision.[34] Alstom complained that despite the express exclusion of leniency material from the scope of the request, the version of Alstom's reply to the statement of objections that the Commission had decided to communicate included such material. The Commission appears to have accepted these arguments, as it informed Alstom that it no longer intended to communicate that material to the High Court.[35] This made Alstom amend the form of order sought, now only requesting the General Court to annul the Commission's decision in so

[32] French Law No 68-678 of 26 July 1968 (as subsequently modified). Alstom had objected against the order to disclose certain documents, claiming that compliance with such order would violate a French statute usually referred to as 'the French blocking statute', and expose it to a risk of criminal prosecution in France. Alstom argued that because of the risk of prosecution, the order should not have been made, and it asked the court to set it aside. The Court of Appeal dismissed Alstom's appeal, holding that the English courts have full jurisdiction to apply their procedural rules to parties in proceedings before them, which includes a discretion to make directions that would entail the parties' potentially breaching a foreign law.

[33] Case T-164/12, *Alstom v European Commission*, EU:T:2014:1089, para 14.

[34] Case T-164/12 R, *Alstom v European Commission*, EU:T:2012:637. The application for interim measures was granted by the President of the General Court.

[35] *Alstom* (n 33).

far as it involved the disclosure of information protected by professional secrecy. Following the development in the proceedings before the national court, the High Court later withdrew its request for cooperation, and the Commission agreed also to formally withdraw the contested decision. The General Court then found it unnecessary to adjudicate on the action, and ordered the parties to bear their own costs.

E. The Court's Case Law – Concluding Remarks

It is clear from the Court's case law that Article 4(3) TEU, and the principle of sincere cooperation enshrined therein, requires the Commission to assist national courts in their application of EU law, be it through the transmission of documents or by providing *amicus curiae* letters. In competition cases, this obligation is reinforced by Article 15(1) of Regulation 1/2003, which although it does not impose any legal obligations on the Commission, nevertheless encourages cooperation by explicitly allowing national courts to ask for assistance in the application or interpretation of the antitrust provisions. The *Alstom* case illustrates the Commission's commitment to assist national courts. As discussed in chapter 4, parties will not be granted access to other parties' replies to the statement of objections unless such documents may constitute new evidence pertaining to the allegations concerning that party; and they may then be given access to only parts of the reply if that is considered sufficient to safeguard the defence rights. Thus, while these documents are not considered part of the Commission's case file and therefore not covered by the right of access to the file, and while the Commission would not grant third parties access to such documents under the Transparency Regulation, it sees no problem in transmitting them to national courts. Perhaps rightly so. Through the adoption of Regulation 1/2003, national courts are empowered to apply the EU competition rules in full, and may therefore need the Commission's assistance to a greater extent than earlier. This may also be the only channel available for private litigants to access the evidence required to prove their case. Furthermore, and more importantly, the obligation to cooperate and assist the national courts is not absolute. The Commission may refuse to produce documents if such refusal can be justified on legitimate grounds connected with the rights of third parties, or where the disclosure would be capable of interfering with the functioning and independence of the Union. National courts are also required to ensure that information covered by professional secrecy is duly protected. Important to note is that it is the Commission that will have to justify the refusal and show that it is motivated by imperative reasons. If the Commission fails to do so, it is thus under a legal obligation to transmit the requested documents to the national court applying or interpreting EU law. As will be discussed in section II, the possibilities for national courts to avail themselves of the opportunity to seek assistance from the Commission has to some extent been limited through the adoption of the Damages Directive.

F. The EU Courts' Case Law Reflected in the Commission's Notice

When the application of the EU competition rules was decentralised in 2004, the Commission issued a Notice on its cooperation with national courts.[36] The Commission acknowledges that the duty to assist national courts in the application of EU competition law is mainly reflected in the obligation for the Commission to transmit information to these courts. Recognising that the EU Courts have found Article 4(3) TEU to impose on the European institutions and the Member States mutual duties of loyal cooperation, Articles 21–26 of the Notice govern the Commission's duties to transmit information to national courts. While acknowledging that Article 339 TFEU obliges the EU institutions not to disclose information 'of the kind covered by the obligation of professional secrecy, in particular information about undertakings, their business relations or their cost components', the Commission declares that a combined reading of Article 339 TFEU and Article 4(3) TEU does not lead to an absolute prohibition on the Commission's transmission of information covered by the obligation of professional secrecy. Referring to the case law of the EU Courts, the Notice declares that the duty of loyal cooperation requires the Commission to provide the national court with whatever information the latter asks for, even information covered by professional secrecy. However, the Notice declares, in offering its cooperation, the Commission may not in any circumstances undermine the guarantees laid down in Article 339 TFEU.[37]

Consequently, before transmitting information covered by professional secrecy to a national court, the Commission will remind the court of its obligation under Union law to uphold the rights that Article 339 TFEU confers on both natural and legal persons, and it will ask the court if it can and will guarantee protection of confidential information and business secrets. If the national court cannot offer such guarantee, the Commission will not transmit the information covered by professional secrecy. Only when the national court has offered a guarantee that it will protect the confidential information and business secrets will the Commission transmit the information requested, indicating those parts that are covered by professional secrecy and those that are not, and which can therefore be disclosed.[38]

The Notice acknowledges that the case law of the EU Courts allows for further exceptions to the disclosure of information. Referring to *Zwartveld* and *Postbank*,[39] the Notice explicitly mentions the situation where the transmission

[36] Commission Notice on the co-operation between the Commission and the courts of the EU Member States in the application of Articles 81 and 82 EC [2004] OJ C101/54.

[37] Ibid para 24.

[38] Ibid para 25.

[39] *Zwartveld* (n 4) and *Postbank* (n 14).

could jeopardise the interests of the Union, or where a refusal is necessary to avoid any interference with the Union's functioning or independence, in particular by jeopardising the accomplishment of the tasks entrusted to it.[40] According to the original Notice, this implied that the Commission would not transmit information voluntarily submitted by a leniency applicant without the consent of the applicant. The Notice was amended in 2015 to align the provisions on disclosure with the Damages Directive. Today, the Notice explicitly acknowledges that disclosure must not unduly affect the effectiveness of the Commission's application of the competition rules, in particular so as not to interfere with pending investigations or with the functioning of the leniency programme or the settlement procedures. For that purpose, Article 26(a) of the Notice declares that the Commission will at no time transmit leniency statements or settlement submissions. According to Article 26(b), the Commission will only be able to transmit certain information after it has closed its proceedings, and that is (i) information drawn up by natural or legal persons specifically for the proceedings before the Commission, and (ii) information drawn up by the Commission and sent to the parties during the proceedings. These obligations mirror Article 6(5) and (6) of the Damages Directive. Section II further addresses the impact of the Damages Directive on the cooperation between the Commission and the national courts.

II. The Commission and the National Courts after the Directive

The previous sections have addressed the Commission's obligation to cooperate with national courts and assist them through, inter alia, the transmission of documents or submission of *amicus curiae* letters. However, as will be discussed in this section, while the obligation still applies, the Damages Directive can be seen as something of a game changer, limiting the possibilities for national courts to request documents from the Commission and other competition authorities. Important to bear in mind is that these limitations apply only to damages proceedings, and that the Commission's duty to cooperate with national courts remains unaffected in other types of competition cases.

The preamble to the Damages Directive acknowledges that actions for damages in antitrust cases do not only require a complex factual and economic analysis; competition law litigation is also characterised by information asymmetry, where the evidence necessary to prove a claim is often held exclusively by the opposing party. Recognising that access to evidence is key to achieving effective private enforcement, the Damages Directive contains a number of provisions that seek to remedy the problem of information asymmetry. Chapter II, covering

[40] Commission Notice (n 36) para 26.

Articles 5–8, governs disclosure of evidence. Article 5 deals with disclosure in general, while Article 6 adds further requirements in situations where the evidence is included in the file of a competition authority.[41] As noted by Wils, the competition authorities' case files are obvious locations for potentially relevant evidence.[42] Yet both Recital 29 and Article 6(10) of the Damages Directive make competition authorities the last possible resort for obtaining evidence. According to Article 6(10), competition authorities only have to disclose evidence where such evidence 'cannot possibly be obtained from another party or from a third party'. The rationale behind this approach is that competition authorities have limited resources, and should focus those resources on the core task of detecting and punishing competition law infringements.[43] Thus, the national court hearing a damages claim may only request documents from the Commission if it is practically impossible to obtain the evidence elsewhere. In addition, in those situations where national courts are allowed to make requests to the Commission, the Damages Directive contains provisions that affect the size and nature of any such requests.

First of all, it is now clear that certain evidence may never be sought from the Commission, or may be sought only after the case has been closed. Article 6(5) of the Damages Directive declares that, as regards the following types of documents, the national court may order disclosure only after the competition authority, by adopting a decision or otherwise, has closed its proceedings:

(a) information that was prepared by a natural or legal person specifically for the proceedings of the competition authority;
(b) information that the competition authority has drawn up and sent to the parties in the course of its proceedings; and
(c) settlement submissions that have been withdrawn.

While the wording of the article appears to allow for disclosure orders after the authority has adopted a decision but before the case has been finally adjudicated by the courts, it cannot be ruled out that the ECJ will interpret the prohibition as also encompassing the period when the case is pending before the EU Courts.[44]

[41] According to Art 2 of the Damages Directive, 'competition authority' shall mean the Commission or an NCA or both, as the context may require. It is not altogether clear which situations are governed by Art 6, as some of the paragraphs govern evidence held by parties while others govern information in the hands of the competition authority.

[42] WPJ Wils, 'Private Enforcement of EU Antitrust Law and its Relationship with Public Enforcement: Past, Present and Future' (2017) 40(1) *World Competition* 3, 31. See also the Commission's Proposal for a Directive of the European Parliament and of the Council on certain rules governing actions for damages under national law for infringements of the competition law provisions of the Member States and of the European Union, COM(2013) 404 Final, at 14.

[43] Wils, 'Private Enforcement' (n 42).

[44] Cf its case law in relation to the Transparency Regulation, discussed in ch 6. In the case of *EnBW*, the ECJ held that a proceeding under Art 101 TFEU cannot be regarded as closed once the Commission's final decision has been adopted irrespective of any possible future judgment by the EU judicature annulling that decision. Given that the annulment of such decision may lead the Commission to resume its investigation with a view to adopting a new decision, investigations relating to a proceeding under

It is further clear from Article 16a of the Procedural Regulation, governing the use of documents provided to parties and third parties, that the Commission should have closed its proceedings against all parties before the documents may be used in proceedings before national courts. As for leniency statements and settlement submissions, they should at all times be kept out of reach, and Article 6(6) thus imposes a blanket ban on disclosure of these documents.[45]

Second, there are also certain limitations when it comes to other types of evidence. While the Damages Directive acknowledges that the evidence necessary to prove a claim is seldom sufficiently known or accessible to the claimant, thereby aiming at providing a remedy to the problem of information asymmetry, it nevertheless contains provisions that may actually limit the possibilities for national courts to order disclosure. For instance, parties are required to request disclosure of specified items of evidence or categories of evidence. According to Article 5, national courts should only be allowed to order disclosure where a claimant has made a plausible assertion, on the basis of facts reasonably available to that claimant, that the claimant has suffered harm, and that such harm was caused by the defendant. Where a request for disclosure aims to obtain a category of evidence, that category should be identified by reference to common features of its constitutive elements, such as the nature, object or content of the documents in question, the time during which they were drawn up, or other criteria, provided that the evidence falling within the category is relevant within the meaning of the Damages Directive. Such categories should be defined as precisely and narrowly as possible on the basis of reasonably available facts.

Furthermore, Article 5(3) declares that national courts should limit the disclosure of evidence to that which is proportionate. According to Recital 23, the requirement of proportionality should be carefully assessed when disclosure risks unravelling the investigation strategy of a competition authority by revealing which documents are part of the file, or risks having a negative effect on the way in which undertakings cooperate with the competition authorities. Particular attention should be paid to prevent 'fishing expeditions', that is, non-specific or overly broad searches for information that is unlikely to be of relevance for the parties to the proceedings. Disclosure requests should therefore not be deemed to be proportionate where they refer to the generic disclosure of documents in the file of a competition authority relating to a certain case, or the generic disclosure of documents submitted by a party in the context of a particular case. Such wide disclosure requests would not be compatible with the requesting party's duty to specify the items of evidence or the categories of evidence as precisely

Art 101 TFEU may be regarded as completed only when the decision adopted by the Commission is final. Case C-365/12 P, *European Commission v EnBW Energie Baden Württemberg AG*, EU:C:2014:112, para 99.

[45] As reflected in the Commission's Notice on cooperation with national courts, see section I.F. Likewise Art 16a of the Procedural Regulation prevents parties and third parties from using these documents in national court proceedings.

and narrowly as possible. In the initial proposal for the Damages Directive, the Commission noted that the willingness of undertakings to supply such evidence exhaustively or selectively when cooperating with competition authorities may be hindered by disclosure requests that identify a category of documents by reference to their presence in the file of a competition authority rather than their type, nature or object. Therefore, such global disclosure requests for documents should normally be deemed by the court to be disproportionate and as not complying with the requesting party's duty to specify categories of evidence as precisely and narrowly as possible. The UK litigation against the Dutch truck manufacturer DAF illustrates the Commission's view on this.

As discussed in chapter 4, parties to the investigation have a right to access the file, and as addressees of the Commission's infringement decisions, they will also get a copy of the confidential version of those decisions. During the course of a damages litigation, it is likely that the claimant will want to seek access to these documents. In a UK litigation launched by Royal Mail against DAF, the judge ordered the defendant to disclose to Royal Mail a substantial part of the Commission's case file. The High Court judge ruled that DAF should disclose the entire file, bar leniency material, privileged material and certain categories of data. This meant that 32,000 documents out of a total of 39,000 documents were to be disclosed.[46] In subsequent and parallel proceedings brought by various distribution, logistics and utility companies, a number of claimants applied to the High Court for disclosure from DAF of the same version of the Commission case file that had previously been disclosed to Royal Mail. While Royal Mail had obtained disclosure prior to the transposition of the Directive into UK law, the subsequent requests were made under the new rules. The broad request prompted the Commission to issue a letter to the English court, raising concern that the requirements of the Damages Directive were not being complied with.[47] DAF had raised similar concerns, and had argued that if the court were to allow the request for broad disclosure, this would force defendants to disclose a considerable amount of information that was irrelevant and unnecessary to the damages claim. The High Court judge ultimately ordered DAF to hand over the confidential version of the Commission's decision and related documents from the Royal Mail litigation, subject to redaction of irrelevant material.[48] The ruling ordering broad disclosure of documents appears to have been influenced by the fact that the documents in question had already been disclosed to Royal Mail, and that disclosure in the subsequent cases would therefore add very little burden or cost.

Thus, to conclude, while the Commission has traditionally seen itself as required to cooperate with national courts, the Damages Directive limits the possibilities

[46] www.mlex.com/GlobalAntitrust/DetailView.aspx?cid=1018650&siteid=190&rdir=1.

[47] *Suez Groupe SAS & Ors v Fiat Chrysler Automobiles NV & Ors* [2018] EWHC 1994 (Ch) [10]–[11]. In the letter the Commission expressed its concern '[t]hat the very broad scope of the disclosure of evidence requested by the claimants in the proceedings referred to above may not fulfil the proportionality requirements introduced by the Damages Directive'.

[48] Ibid.

for these courts to seek assistance from the Commission. It is to be hoped that national courts will not hesitate to make requests to the Commission in those cases where it appears impossible to access the evidence elsewhere. It must not be forgotten that the Member States are also bound by the duty of sincere cooperation in Article 4(3) TEU and must take any appropriate measures to ensure an effective application of EU legislation.

III. International Aspects

In today's global economy, cartels and other competition law infringements often cross the boundaries of jurisdictions and reach beyond the borders of the EU. Rules on disclosure and access to evidence may vary between jurisdictions, and the consequences of such deviations may be that the policy of the Commission and the EU legislator is set aside, and that the protection afforded under EU law cannot be guaranteed. The ongoing *Qualcomm* case illustrates the practical problems associated with international antitrust enforcement. In January 2018, the Commission imposed a fine of €997 million on Qualcomm for abuse of dominance.[49]

The Commission was not the only competition authority investigating the business practices of Qualcomm. Early in 2017, the Federal Trade Commission (FTC) lodged a complaint against Qualcomm before the US District Court of the Northern District of California, arguing that it had refused to license standard essential patents to its competitors on fair, reasonable and non-discriminatory terms. As part of the discovery process, Qualcomm requested access to the confidential versions of certain third party responses to the requests for information (RFIs) issued by the Commission during the course of its investigation against Qualcomm.[50] The respondents had not only submitted their responses to the Commission; they had also sent them to the FTC. Qualcomm's disclosure request led the Commission to write two *amicus curiae* letters to the US court, arguing that Qualcomm had responded to the Commission's RFI in the expectation that confidential information would be safeguarded and that the disclosure of such confidential information would likely harm the Commission's law enforcement capabilities.

In August 2017, the US District Court sided with Qualcomm and ordered the FTC to disclose the RFI responses. The court held that a party may in principle obtain discovery regarding any non-privileged matter that is relevant for its defence under federal civil procedural rules. Discovery may be limited on several grounds, including for reasons of international comity. In this case it was already

[49] Case AT.40220 – *Qualcomm (exclusivity payments)*, Commission decision of 24 January 2018. No public version available.

[50] Qualcomm had only received the non-confidential versions during the course of the Commission's investigation.

doubtful whether comity played a factor, as the documents in question had also been provided to the FTC and were thus already located in the United States. In any event, the doctrine of international comity did not apply here as Qualcomm's request would have had to undermine important, sovereign interests of the EU. This was not the case as no foreign law or privileges would be violated by the production of relevant documents, the court concluded.

While the US District Court acknowledged that it had discretion to limit discovery on several grounds, including international comity, and while it recognised as valid the Commission's concerns that the disclosure of RFI responses might harm its enforcement efforts, it ultimately found the Commission's arguments not to be legally persuasive, partly due to Qualcomm's right to obtain relevant, proportionately needed information in discovery to aid its defence.[51] The case shows that what is considered confidential or otherwise protected under EU law may not necessarily be considered worthy of protection in other jurisdictions. Once the information has crossed the Atlantic, the Commission may no longer guarantee its protection.[52]

IV. Concluding Remarks

It is clear from the foregoing that the Commission has a general obligation under Article 4(3) TEU to assist national courts when they apply EU legislation. In competition matters, this obligation is further reinforced by Article 15 of Regulation 1/2003, which allows national courts to ask the Commission to transmit to them information in its possession or its opinion on questions concerning the application of the EU competition rules. Over the years, the Commission has taken this obligation seriously and cooperated with national courts. The *Alstom* case discussed in section I.D shows that the Commission has even been willing to hand over documents to which not even the parties normally have access, and which the Commission would not disclose under the Transparency Regulation. When challenging the Commission's decision, Alstom had argued that the information was protected by professional secrecy and contained material submitted under the leniency programme. As for the argument concerning professional secrecy, it is clear from the case law of the EU Courts that Article 4(3) TEU also requires the Commission to transmit confidential information. However, in order to ensure that the obligation of professional secrecy is protected, the Commission's cooperation is conditioned upon the national court's assurance that it will maintain and safeguard the confidentiality of any information transmitted from the Commission.

[51] US District Court, Northern District of California, Case 5:17-cv-00220-LHK, *Federal Trade Commission et al v Qualcomm Incorporated.*

[52] See https://riskandcompliance.freshfields.com/post/102egdn/document-disclosure-in-international-antitrust-investigations.

It can also be concluded that while the Damages Directive aims at providing a remedy to the problem of information asymmetry, it contains provisions that make it harder for national courts to access information directly from the Commission. Not only are they prevented from requesting documents from the Commission if the documents can reasonably be accessed elsewhere, they may never order or request disclosure of leniency statements or settlement submissions. Other types of evidence, such as information drawn up by a competition authority and sent to the parties in the course of its proceedings, may only be disclosed once the case is closed. Furthermore, the Commission does not consider broad disclosure orders encompassing a large number of documents from its case files to be compatible with the provisions of the Damages Directive. In 2015, the Commission amended its Notice on cooperation with national courts, which now explicitly acknowledges that disclosure must not unduly affect the effectiveness of the Commission's application of the competition rules, in particular so as not to interfere with pending investigations or with the functioning of the leniency programme or the settlement procedures. This means that the Commission will at no time transmit leniency statements or settlement submissions. It can thus be concluded that the Commission's practices have changed following the adoption of the Damages Directive, and that the concern for the leniency programme is affecting its cooperation with national courts, bringing its practices closer to its stance in other areas, such as the application of the Transparency Regulation.

8

More Detailed Infringements Decisions – The Way Forward?

When cartel victims seek access to the documents held in the Commission's case files, it is not necessarily that they wish to access the physical documents but rather that they seek the information contained therein – information that, at least in part, is also found in the Commission's infringement decisions. Article 339 TFEU and Article 28 of Regulation 1/2003 impose an obligation on the Commission not to disclose any information covered by the obligation of professional secrecy.[1] At the same time, Article 30 of Regulation 1/2003 requires the Commission to publish its infringement decisions, and Article 15 TFEU obliges it to ensure the transparency of its proceedings. The Commission has the delicate task of reconciling these potentially conflicting obligations when drafting the public versions of its infringement decisions. Traditionally, these versions have been rather succinct, but in recent years the Commission has endeavoured to publish longer and more detailed infringement decisions. This change in the Commission's practice could potentially facilitate matters for cartel victims attempting to substantiate their claims against the infringers. Although more detailed versions of the decisions will not necessarily provide an amount of evidence sufficient to substantiate the victims' claims, they may at least help victims limit their requests in such a way that the Commission may actually grant access and/or the national courts may order disclosure of the evidence necessary to support their case.[2] Perhaps not too surprisingly, the Commission's

[1] Art 339 TFEU imposes an obligation on the members of the EU institutions not to reveal any information covered by professional secrecy: 'The members of the institutions of the Union, the members of committees, and the officials and other servants of the Union shall be required, even after their duties have ceased, not to disclose information of the kind covered by the obligation of professional secrecy, in particular information about undertakings, their business relations or their cost components.'

[2] In the case of *AKZO* discussed in section III, it is clear that the Commission's choosing to publish a more detailed version of the infringement decision was at least partly motivated by a request for access to a confidential version of the decision. See para 38, where the General Court refers to a letter sent from the Commission to the applicants, according to which the proposed publication of the decision had to be understood in the light of a request for access to the confidential version of the infringement decision, made on the basis of the Transparency Regulation. Another example is the UK damages case of *Daimler AG v MOL Ltd and others* [2019] EWHC 3197 (Comm). In July 2019, the German car manufacturer Daimler AG won a UK court order for Mitsui OSK Lines and other cartelist shipping companies to disclose a redacted copy of the Commission's cartel decision. According to Daimler, the disclosure of the decision would allow it to make a more focused disclosure request at a later stage of the cartel proceeding (ibid [13]).

attempts to publish longer and more detailed versions of cartel decisions have met with steep resistance from their addressees. As expected, they are challenging the Commission's decisions to publish these versions, arguing that they contain confidential information and should be protected from the public. In addition, and as will be discussed further in chapter 9, there are indications that the Commission's new approach may have a negative impact on cartel members' willingness to self-report and apply for leniency.

This chapter examines five cases dealing with the level of detail allowed in the Commission's infringement decisions. While the rulings support the Commission's endeavours to provide more information to the public, they do not necessarily address or acknowledge the risk that cartel members will become less inclined to apply for leniency. On the contrary, it is clear from the rulings that not only does the Court consider the granting of immunity from or the reduction in fines to be the sole purpose of the leniency programme,[3] it also takes the view that the Commission's obligation to publish infringement decisions serves the aim of achieving a more effective private enforcement system. For this reason, the Court has established that while the public versions of the decisions may not contain verbatim quotations from any leniency statements, they may reproduce the information contained therein. It is also the Court's view that to the extent that the publication of more detailed public versions may impact the effectiveness of the leniency system, any such balancing act is to be carried out by the Commission when drafting the version to be published on its website.

Furthermore, companies targeted by the Commission's cartel investigations may find it hard to protect information that has been exchanged within the frame of the cartel, as the General Court then considers the cartel members to have renounced the confidentiality of any such information. Another conclusion to be drawn from these rulings is that while the EU Courts used to interpret Article 30 of Regulation 1/2003 in the light of Article 4 of the Transparency Regulation, this can no longer be done. It is now established that as there is a right for the Commission to rely on a general presumption that all documents in the Commission's case files are covered by the exceptions in Article 4 of the Transparency Regulation, that Regulation may no longer be used as guidance when determining what information to include in the public versions of the Commission's infringement decisions. Finally, the Court has confirmed that information that is more than five years old shall, due to the passage of time, be presumed to have lost its commercial importance and thereby also its confidential nature.

Before examining the case law on the publication of infringement decisions in more detail, a short presentation of the rules surrounding these procedures will be given.

[3] Thereby excluding protection from civil liability from the scope of the leniency programme.

I. The Procedure

The principle of transparency is already established in Article 1 TEU, which declares that decisions of the Union shall be taken as openly and as closely to the citizen as possible. Article 15 TFEU declares that in order to promote good governance and ensure the participation of civil society, the Union institutions shall conduct their work as openly as possible. In the spirit of the two articles, Article 30 of Regulation 1/2003 requires the Commission to publish its cartel decisions.[4] Such publication shall state the names of the parties and the main content of the decision, including any penalties imposed. The Commission should pay regard to the legitimate interests of the undertakings in the protection of their business secrets. As noted by Van Bael, and as evidenced from the reasoning in both *AKZO* and *Pilkington*, the aim of the provision is not to limit the Commission's freedom to publish public versions that contain more information than the minimum necessary. Longer and fuller decisions may thus be published, as long as the information contained therein is not inconsistent with the protection of professional secrecy.[5]

In addition to the aims acknowledged in Article 1 TEU, the obligation to publish infringement decisions serves a number of other aims. In the Grand Chamber ruling in *Evonik Degussa*, the Court recognised that one of those aims is to facilitate private enforcement of the competition rules, declaring that

> [t]he provision reflects considerations concerning the effectiveness of the application of EU competition law in so far as, in particular, such publication enables victims of infringements of Article 101 TFEU to be provided with support during their actions for damages against those who have committed those infringements.[6]

However, in the same ruling the Court also acknowledged that those interests must be weighed against the protection of rights conferred by EU law, in particular on the undertakings concerned, such as the right to protection of professional secrecy or business secrecy, or on the individuals concerned, such as the right to the protection of personal data.

As for the procedure to be followed, the Commission will ask the addressees of the infringement decision to provide a non-confidential version of the

[4] That is decisions made pursuant to Art 23 of Regulation 1/2003.

[5] I Van Bael, *Due Process in EU Competition Proceedings* (Alphen aan den Rijn, Wolters Kluwer, 2011) 212, where reference is made to Case T-198/03, *Bank Austria Creditanstalt v Commission*, EU:T:2006:136, para 78. There, the General Court declares that '[t]he interest of an undertaking which the Commission has fined for breach of competition law in the details of the offending conduct of which it is accused not being disclosed to the public does not warrant any particular protection, given the public interest in knowing as fully as possible the reasons behind any Commission action, the interest of the economic operators in knowing the sort of behaviour for which they are liable to be penalised and the interest of persons harmed by the infringement in being informed of the details thereof so that they may, where appropriate, assert their rights against the undertakings punished, and in view of the fined undertaking's ability to seek judicial review of such a decision'. See also Case T-462/12, *Pilkington Group Ltd v European Commission*, EU:T:2015:508, para 45.

[6] Case C-162/15 P, *Evonik Degussa GmbH v European Commission*, EU:C:2017:205, para 78.

decision. The Commission takes the view that in general, an undertaking cannot claim confidentiality for an entire document or whole sections thereof, as it is normally possible to protect confidential information with limited redactions.[7] Should the company and DG COMP disagree on whether or not certain information should be protected, the matter will be referred to the Hearing Officer, who then has the task of striking a balance between the addressee's interest in confidentiality and the public's interest in being fully informed of the infringement. If the Hearing Officer finds it necessary to disclose certain information – either because it does not constitute a business secret or other confidential information, or because there is an overriding interest in its disclosure – the addressee will be informed accordingly in a reasoned decision made on behalf of the Commission.[8] The decision is challengeable before the EU Courts, and interim measures may be requested in order to prevent disclosure pending the appeal proceedings before the EU Courts.

A. Confidential Information

The two notions 'professional secrecy' and 'business secrets' play a particularly important role when determining what information may be included in the public version of an infringement decision, and the interpretation of these notions therefore merits some reflection. While Article 339 TFEU and Article 28 of Regulation 1/2003 both prevent Commission officials from publishing or otherwise disclosing information covered by professional secrecy, Article 30 of Regulation 1/2003 requires the Commission to have regard to the interests of undertakings in the protection of their business secrets. Thus, while the Commission shall at all times make sure that information covered by professional secrecy is protected, it shall pay particular regard to the companies' business secrets when publishing its infringement decisions, suggesting that the two notions are not identical. The question then is what determines whether a certain piece of information is to be considered a business secret, covered by professional secrecy, or fair game?

Article 339 TFEU does not define the notion of 'professional secrecy' but it nevertheless provides some guidance, stating that protection should cover, in particular, information about undertakings, their business relations or their cost components. While the notion of cost components is rather specific, 'information about undertakings and their business relations' may cover a wide variety of information, and the application of Article 339 TFEU thus requires careful assessment. In *Postbank*, discussed in chapter 7, the General Court addressed the relationship

[7] In 2015, the Commission published Guidance on the preparation of public versions of Commission Decisions adopted under Articles 7 to 10, 23 and 24 of Regulation 1/2003. The Guidance provides detailed instructions on how to claim confidentiality, see at http://ec.europa.eu/competition/antitrust/guidance_on_preparation_of_public_versions_antitrust_04062015.pdf.

[8] Art 8 of the Hearing Officer's Mandate.

between Article 339 TFEU and Article 30 of Regulation 1/2003. There, it concluded that the notion of professional secrecy is broader in scope than the notion of business secrets, declaring that information protected by professional secrecy may encompass both business secrets and other confidential information, and that the notion of business secrets covered information of which not only disclosure to the public but also mere transmission to a person other than the one that provided the information may seriously harm the latter's interests.[9] In *AKZO*, a case concerning the Commission's decision to communicate certain information in its case file to a complainant, the Court made a distinction between information covered by professional secrecy and information constituting business secrets. Noting that Article 30 of Regulation 1/2003 requires the Commission to protect business secrets, the Court declared that they should be afforded 'very special protection', indicating that the protection may be stronger for business secrets than for other confidential information.[10] This seems reasonable given how the General Court defined the notion of business secrets in *Postbank*.

The Commission's Guidance on the preparation of public versions of its infringement decisions provides examples of information that may qualify as business secrets. According to the Guidance, the term may include technical and/or financial information relating to an undertaking's know-how; margins calculations and price structure; production secrets and processes; supply sources; quantities produced and sold; market shares; customers and distributors lists; marketing plans; cost and methods of assessing costs; and sales strategies.[11] As for other confidential information, the Guidance declares that, depending on the specific circumstances of each case, the notion may cover information that would enable the parties to identify complainants or other third parties where they have a justified wish to remain anonymous.[12] The Guidance also provides examples of information that the Commission normally considers not to be confidential. This includes:

(a) the Commission's own assessment;
(b) information relating to an undertaking that is publicly available or made known outside the undertaking, or outside the association to which it has been communicated by that undertaking (including information such as price targets, price increases, dates of implementation of such increases and customer names). For information to lose its confidential nature, it is

[9] Case T-353/94, *Postbank v Commission*, EU:T:1996:119, paras 86–87.

[10] Case C-53/85, *AKZO Chemie BV and AKZO Chemie UK Ltd v Commission of the European Communities*, EU:C:1986:256, para 28. The Court further declared that 'Although they [Arts 19 and 21 of Regulation 17/62] deal with particular situations, those provisions must be regarded as the expression of a general principle which applies during the course of the administrative procedure. It follows that a third party who has submitted a complaint may not in any circumstances be given access to documents containing business secrets.'

[11] Guidance (n 7) 10.

[12] Ibid.

sufficient for it to be available to specialist circles or capable of being inferred from publicly available information;

(c) information that has lost its commercial importance, for instance due to the passage of time:

(d) data from or about another undertaking (such as price announcements, sales data, etc). Exceptionally, data received pursuant to a contract with that undertaking that envisages confidentiality might be considered as confidential. General references to a non-disclosure agreement are insufficient to justify the confidentiality of such data; and

(e) statistical or aggregate information.[13]

The Guidance also lists a number of conditions that need to be met in order for information to be considered worthy of protection. Thus, according to the Guidance, it emerges from the case law that[14] for information to be regarded as confidential, all the following conditions must be met: (i) the information must be known only to a limited number of persons, (ii) its disclosure must be likely to cause serious harm to the person who has provided it or to third parties, and (iii) the interests liable to be harmed by the disclosure must be objectively worthy of protection.

Following this brief presentation of the procedure surrounding the publication of infringement decisions and the notions of professional secrecy and business secrets, the following sections will present the case law from the EU Courts. The number of cases is still limited and only a few have reached the ECJ. Nevertheless, it is possible to draw some conclusions on what type of information the EU Courts deem should be protected from disclosure, and thus excluded from the public versions of the infringement decisions.

II. *Pergan Hilfsstoffe* – Professional Secrecy and the Presumption of Innocence

The General Court's ruling in *Pergan Hilfsstoffe* dates back to 2007 and concerns the role played by fundamental rights – or more specifically the presumption of innocence – in the determination of which information the Commission may publish in its infringement decisions. In 2002, the Commission launched an investigation against a number of organic peroxide producers suspected of cartel participation. Some of the companies involved were suspected of having participated in these market-sharing and price-fixing arrangements for nearly three decades – from 1971 to 1999. In March 2003, the Commission opened formal proceedings and adopted a statement of objections, which was subsequently notified to the

[13] Ibid 13.

[14] Notably *Bank Austria* (n 5) para 71.

companies under investigation, including the German producer Pergan Hilfsstoffe für industrielle Prozesse GmbH (Pergan). Pergan contested both the scope and the duration of its participation in any cartel activity, stating that it had only had sporadic contact with two of the other parties to the investigation, and that such contact had taken place during the period of 1994 to 1996 only, which meant that, in any event, any infringement was time-barred. By letter of 10 December 2003, the Commission informed Pergan of its decision to close the proceedings against it.[15] By another decision of the same date, the Commission imposed fines on a number of its competitors for breach of Article 101 TFEU. The infringement decision was addressed to those companies but not to Pergan.[16]

While the operative part of the infringement decision did not mention Pergan, the recitals described the company's involvement in the cartel, and declared that the Commission had been prevented from imposing any fines on Pergan due to lack of sufficient evidence concerning its involvement in the cartel after 31 January 1997. The Commission later informed Pergan of its intention to publish a non-confidential version of the decision, inviting Pergan to identify any passages it considered to contain business secrets or other confidential information. In its reply, Pergan asked the Commission to remove all references to Pergan and its involvement in the cartel from the public version of the decision on the ground that it was not an addressee of the decision and had therefore not had the possibility to challenge the Commission's findings before the General Court.

As DG COMP and Pergan failed to reach an agreement on what information was to be included in the non-confidential version, Pergan turned to the Hearing Officer, asking him to remove all references to Pergan in the non-confidential version of the infringement decision. However, the Hearing Officer refused to remove such references on the ground that they contained no business secrets.[17] As noted by the Hearing Officer, the concept of a business secret presupposes that disclosure of the information in question will cause serious harm to the interests of the person concerned. As regards the risk of actions for damages under national law, the Hearing Officer found that such risk could not in itself cause serious and unjust harm such as to justify protection of the disputed information. In the event that they are well-founded, actions for damages before national courts are in fact the acceptable consequence of committing an infringement of Community and national competition law, the Hearing Officer concluded. He further noted that Pergan was not the addressee of the infringement decision and that this decision, in the absence of a finding that Pergan had infringed Article 101 TFEU, was

[15] Case T-474/04, *Pergan Hilfsstoffe für industrielle Prozesse GmbH v Commission of the European Communities*, EU:T:2007:306, para 9.

[16] The decision was also addressed to a number of companies within the AKZO group, but as AKZO had received immunity, no fines were imposed.

[17] Save for the name of Mr S, information relating to the detailed assessment of Pergan and the reference to its market share, which were to be replaced by a band of market shares, see para 21 of the ruling.

therefore not legally binding on national courts. This prompted Pergan to turn to the General Court.

A. The View of the General Court

In its ruling, the General Court took note of the fact that the operative part of the infringement decision did not mention Pergan and that this prevented Pergan from challenging the decision.[18] It further declared that the scope of the Commission's power to adopt and publish infringement decisions, and the scope of the protection of professional secrecy must both be interpreted in the light of the general principles and fundamental rights of the EU, and in particular of the principle of presumption of innocence – as reaffirmed in Article 48 of the Charter.[19] This principle, the General Court continued, implied that every person accused is presumed to be innocent until his guilt has been established according to law. Adherence to the principle precludes any formal finding, and even any allusion to the liability of an accused person for a particular infringement in a final decision, unless that person has enjoyed all the usual guarantees accorded for the exercise of the rights of defence. Furthermore, the General Court continued, the guilt of a person accused of an infringement is established definitively only where the decision finding that infringement has acquired the force of *res judicata*.[20] Thus, the General Court continued, findings the person charged with an infringement has not had the opportunity to contest before the Community judicature cannot be regarded as established in law. The fact that such findings evade any review by the courts, and therefore, in the event that they are unlawful, any correction by the Community judicature, is manifestly contrary to the principle of the presumption of innocence, the General Court concluded.[21]

Since the Commission's findings relating to Pergan's infringement of Article 101 TFEU were thus capable of infringing the principle of the presumption of innocence, those findings must, in principle, be regarded as confidential, and therefore as being of the kind covered by the obligation of professional secrecy, the General Court continued. This principle stems, inter alia, from the need to respect the reputation and dignity of the person concerned as that person has not been finally found guilty of an infringement, the General Court stated further. It also considered the confidentiality of such information to be confirmed by Article 4(1)(b) of the Transparency Regulation, which provides that information disclosure of which would harm the protection of privacy and the integrity of the individual, is to be protected.

[18] *Pergan Hilfsstoffe* (n 15) para 74.
[19] Ibid para 75.
[20] Ibid para 76.
[21] Ibid para 77.

In the present case, Pergan had lacked standing to bring an action against the infringement decision, despite the fact that it contested the merits of the grounds of that decision in which its participation in the infringement was mentioned. Such a situation is contrary to the principle of the presumption of innocence and infringes the protection of professional secrecy, which require that respect for the reputation and dignity of the applicant be ensured, the General Court declared. It therefore concluded that the disputed information must be held to be covered by the obligation of professional secrecy within the meaning of Article 339 TFEU. In that regard, the General Court pointed out that the Commission itself had accepted, during the hearing, that it could have published the infringement decision by limiting itself to finding that Pergan had participated in the administrative procedure but that the investigation had been closed by reason of the limitation period. Against this background the General Court concluded that there was no overriding public interest in publishing the disputed information capable of prevailing over Pergan's legitimate interest in having such information protected. Thus, the General Court concluded that the Hearing Officer, in finding that the disputed information was not worthy of protection and that its publication would not cause serious and unjust harm to Pergan's interests, misapplied the protection of professional secrecy in the present case. As a consequence, the contested decision was annulled in so far as it rejected Pergan's request for confidential treatment.[22]

B. Comment on the General Court's Ruling

In its decision, the Hearing Officer had sided with DG COMP and considered that the information could be published as it did not contain any business secrets. While the General Court saw no difficulty in establishing that the Commission's finding of an infringement in the recitals of the decision was 'manifestly' contrary to the presumption of innocence,[23] it still had to explain why the information was considered confidential and why the publication of such findings would thus also infringe Article 339 TFEU.

The ruling was delivered in October 2007, two years before the Charter became legally binding. This by no means implies that the principle of the presumption of innocence did not stand on firm ground at the time, but it may, at least partially, indicate why the General Court made such an effort to explain why any references to Pergan in the non-confidential version of the infringement decision were not only contrary to Article 48 of the Charter, but were also covered by the obligation of professional secrecy established in Article 339 TFEU. It is true that any allusion

[22] Ibid para 81.
[23] Ibid para 76.

to Pergan as a cartel member might tarnish its reputation, and might thus disregard the need to respect its reputation and dignity. However, today it would have sufficed to find that the Commission's actions violated Article 48 of the Charter. The fact that neither Article 28 nor Article 30 of Regulation 1/2003 makes any reference to the Charter does not relieve the Commission from the obligation to pay due regard to the Charter provisions when drafting or publishing its decisions. Furthermore, if the reasoning is built on the fact that the information should be considered confidential, this may cause problems in those situations where the Commission's view is already known to more than a limited group of persons. While it is then clearly not confidential, the Commission should still be prevented from including it in the public version of the infringement decision.

In any event, and irrespective of whether or not the information is covered by Article 339 TFEU, it is clear that the General Court's ruling has gained widespread application. In its Guidance on the preparation of public versions of infringement decisions, the Commission declares that, 'irrespective of any claims for confidentiality', it may redact 'information relating to undertakings participating in the infringement that are not mentioned in the operative part of the Decision. This information is covered by the presumption of innocence and the obligation of professional secrecy within the meaning of Article 339 TFEU'.[24]

Furthermore, at least the UK courts appear to have recognised what is sometimes referred to as the 'Pergan principle' when deciding on which parts of the Commission's infringement decisions that should be made available during the course of any actions for damages. In October 2015, the Court of Appeal handed down judgment in *Air Canada & Ors v Emerald Supplies Limited & Ors* on how domestic courts should give effect to the principles set out in *Pergan Hilfsstoffe*.[25] Following the Commission's decision to impose fines on a number of airlines, including British Airways, some of their customers brought an action for damages before the UK courts. During the course of these proceedings, the applicants had sought disclosure from British Airways of the confidential version of the Commission's infringement decision. Addressee and non-addressee airlines sought redaction of material in the infringement decision that they contended fell within the principle established in *Pergan Hilfsstoffe*. The High Court ordered that a largely unredacted copy of the decision, including material covered by the Pergan principle, should be disclosed into a confidentiality ring. The defendants then turned to the Court of Appeal, which ruled in their favour, holding that the domestic court was obliged to ensure the same protection to Pergan material as is accorded at EU level, and that it was insufficient to disclose such material into a confidentiality ring.[26]

[24] Guidance (n 7) 22 b).
[25] *Air Canada & Ors v Emerald Supplies Limited & Ors* [2015] EWCA Civ 1024.
[26] Ibid.

III. *AKZO* – (Non-) Protection of Leniency Applicants

In May 2006, the Commission adopted an infringement decision against a number of companies active in the hydrogen peroxide and perborate sector found guilty of cartel participation.[27] Among these companies were AKZO Nobel, AKZO Nobel Chemicals Holding and Eka Chemicals (jointly referred to as the AKZO companies or the applicants), all three of which had applied for leniency and had received a 40 per cent reduction in their fine. During the course of 2007, a first non-confidential version of the infringement decision ('the PHP Decision') was published on the Commission's website. Four years later, the Commission informed the AKZO companies of its intention to publish a new, more complete, non-confidential version of the PHP Decision, setting out the entire content of that decision save for any confidential information. The Commission asked the applicants to identify the information that they considered confidential, and which should thus be excluded. The version the Commission now proposed to publish contained information that had been submitted by the AKZO companies in the context of their leniency applications, and the three companies opposed the publication of such information, arguing that it would considerably and irreversibly harm their interests.

The applicants asked the Commission to reconsider its intention to publish the proposed version of the PHP Decision and, in the alternative, to leave out of such publication certain information they regarded as confidential. The Commission agreed to omit all information that would allow direct or indirect tracing of the sources of the information submitted under the Leniency Notice. By contrast, it took the view that there was no justification in treating the other information as confidential. The AKZO companies turned to the Hearing Officer, asking him to exclude from the non-confidential version all the information they had provided under the Leniency Notice. Hiding behind his mandate, the Hearing Officer rejected the applicants' claim, declaring that his terms of reference only permitted him to determine whether the information was confidential, not whether the Commission had breached the applicants' legitimate expectations. He also pointed to the fact that the applicants had opposed the publication on the sole ground that it contained information provided under the leniency programme. The Hearing Officer did not consider them to have shown that they would suffer serious harm from the publication. In any event, a competition law offender's interest in non-disclosure of details of the offending conduct did not warrant any particular protection, the Hearing Officer continued. Furthermore, actions for damages were part and parcel of the Union's competition policy, and therefore the applicants

[27] Decision C(2006) 1766 final relating to a proceeding pursuant to Article 81 [EC] and Article 53 of the EEA Agreement against Akzo Nobel NV, Akzo Nobel Chemicals Holding AB, Eka Chemicals AB, Degussa AG, Edison SpA, FMC Corporation, FMC Foret SA, Kemira OYJ, L'Air Liquide SA, Chemoxal SA, Snia SpA, Caffaro Srl, Solvay SA/NV, Solvay Solexis SpA, Total SA, Elf Aquitaine SA and Arkema SA (Case COMP/38.620 – *Hydrogen Peroxide and Perborate*).

could not claim to have a legitimate interest in being protected against any actions for damages, he concluded.

The AKZO companies did not accept these findings and lodged an application with the General Court, requesting it to annul the contested decision. In support of their claims, they put forward three pleas in law, alleging (i) breach of the duty to state reasons under Article 296 TFEU and the right to good administration enshrined in Article 41 of the Charter, (ii) breach of the duty of confidentiality under Article 339 TFEU and Article 28 of Regulation 1/2003, and (iii) frustration of the applicants' legitimate expectations and breach of the principles of legal certainty and good administration.[28]

A. The View of the General Court

As for the first plea concerning the duty to state reasons, the applicants claimed that they were unable to understand the reasons for the rejection of their arguments concerning legitimate expectations, and that the decision did not address their claim that the Commission had departed from its previous administrative practice when deciding to publish information from the leniency application. Referring to the Court's case law,[29] the General Court responded that it is not necessary for the statement of reasons to specify all the relevant matters of fact and law, since the question whether the statement of reasons meets the requirements laid down in that provision must be assessed with regard not only to its wording but also to its context, and to all the legal rules governing the matter in question.[30] Here, the General Court noted that the applicants had claimed, in their communication with the Commission, that the publication of information submitted in the context of the leniency application would frustrate their legitimate expectations, as such publication would depart from the Commission's previous practice. Also noting that the Hearing Officer did not respond to each of those arguments as he would then have exceeded the Mandate, the General Court declared that the contested decision had been adopted following an administrative procedure in which the Commission, in several letters to the applicants, had explained why it now intended to publish the information in question.[31] Thus, the General Court concluded, the contested decision, viewed in the context in which it had been

[28] Case T-345/12, *AKZO Nobel NV and Others v European Commission*, EU:T:2015:50, para 27.

[29] Case 322/81, *NV Nederlandsche Banden Industrie Michelin v Commission of the European Communities*, EU:C:1983:313, para 14; and Case T-49/95, *Van Megen Sports Group BV v Commission of the European Communities*, EU:T:1996:186, para 51.

[30] *AKZO* (n 28) para 31.

[31] In a letter dated 28 November 2011, the Commission had justified its intention to publish the decision by reference to an objective of transparency, and in a letter dated 20 December 2011, the Commission stated, in essence, that the proposed publication had to be understood in the light of a request for access to the confidential version of the infringement decision, made on the basis of the Transparency Regulation.

adopted, provided enough information to allow the applicants to understand why the Commission had decided to depart from its previous administrative practice in the present case.[32]

As for the second plea, alleging a breach of the duty of confidentiality, the applicants argued that (i) it was clear from previous case law that information voluntarily submitted to the Commission deserves protection from disclosure, (ii) the Commission must have regard to the legitimate interest of undertakings in non-disclosure of their business secrets, and (iii) the information that they submitted under the leniency programme was covered by the obligation of professional secrecy. According to the applicants, the 2002 Leniency Notice, in particular paragraphs 29, 32 and 33 thereof, provided for the confidential treatment of information contained in leniency applications.[33] Furthermore, the applicants claimed, it was necessary to take into account that the information at issue had been provided to the Commission in its official capacity, that it was known only to a limited number of persons and that its disclosure would cause them serious harm, since it would place them in a significantly worse position in actions for damages compared with the other cartel members that had not cooperated with the Commission.[34] The applicants challenged, in that context, the Commission's approach of offering protection only to documents submitted in the context of the leniency applications or to declarations made by a leniency applicant, and not to the information contained therein. According to them, that approach infringed the fundamental right to the protection of professional secrecy guaranteed by Article 339 TFEU. At the hearing, the applicants had added that the publication envisaged by the Commission circumvented the exceptions to the right of public access laid down in the Transparency Regulation, as well as the specific rules on access to the Commission's files laid down in Regulation 1/2003. As a final argument, the applicants claimed that the non-confidential version of the PHP Decision that was published in 2007 fulfilled the purpose of informing the general public of the reasons for the decision, and that the real reason behind the Commission's decision to publish a new and more detailed version of the decision was to facilitate the action for damages brought by the company CDC Cartel Damages Claims (CDC) before the Dortmund Regional Court.[35]

The General Court noted that the applicants did not deny having participated in the cartel but that they claimed that the information should be considered confidential simply because it had been given to the Commission voluntarily in the context of the leniency programme, and that the proposed publication was

[32] Should the Commission's decision prove to be a departure from its previous practice.

[33] According to the applicants, the protection of that information was confirmed by para 6 of the 2006 Leniency Notice.

[34] We here recognise the criteria laid down in *Bank Austria* (n 5).

[35] CDC Cartel Damages Claims had purchased the claims from 32 companies active in the pulp and paper industry and purchasers of hydrogen peroxide, see at www.carteldamageclaims.com/competition-law-damage-claims/hydrogen-peroxide-cartel/.

therefore liable to undermine the protection of the purpose of the Commission's investigations. Given that the notion of professional secrecy extends beyond business secrets, the General Court found it necessary to determine whether information could enjoy protection for the sole reason that it had been voluntary submitted by a company applying for leniency.

The General Court declared that while the ECJ has interpreted Article 4 of the Transparency Regulation as meaning that it is open to the Commission to base its decisions on general assumptions regarding certain categories of documents, this does not mean that the Commission is prevented from publishing any information to which it would be entitled to refuse access under the Transparency Regulation, as this would deprive Article 30 of Regulation 1/2003 of its meaning. The General Court then assessed the criteria applying to confidential information laid down in *Bank Austria*, that is, that in order for a piece of information to be considered confidential (i) it should be known only to a limited number of persons, (ii) its disclosure should be liable to cause serious harm, and (iii) the interests liable to be harmed by disclosure must be worthy of protection. The Commission had argued that the first criterion was not met because the contested information had been taken from the Commission's case file to which the other addressees of the infringement decision had also been given access. That argument was rejected by the General Court, which considered the first criterion to be fulfilled.

As regards the second criterion, the applicants had argued that the publication of the information would put them in a much worse situation than the cartel members that had not filed for leniency. Here, the General Court noted that the information at issue essentially consisted in the description of the constituent elements of the infringement. This in turn meant that the publication of a more detailed version of the infringement decision, and in particular the part of that decision relating to the description of the way in which the cartel operated, would allow the intervener – CDC – more easily to establish the civil liability of the applicants than of the other cartel participants.[36] As such information is capable of facilitating the demonstration of harm as well as the causal link between such harm and the cartel activity, the General Court saw no problem in establishing that the proposed publication was liable to cause the applicants serious harm.[37] The second criterion was thus also fulfilled.

As for the third and final criterion, the General Court declared that when the confidentiality of a piece of information was assessed, the individual legitimate interests opposing disclosure must be weighed against the public interest that the activities of the institutions take place as openly as possible. In that respect, the interest of a competition law offender in the non-disclosure to the public of the details of the offending conduct does not merit particular protection, the General Court declared. Thus, it continued, the applicants could not legitimately oppose

[36] *AKZO* (n 28) para 74.
[37] Ibid para 77.

the publication of information revealing the details of their own illegal action.[38] The applicants had also claimed that the publication of the information would render the Commission's leniency programme less attractive, thereby undermining the effectiveness of the EU competition law enforcement system. To this the General Court responded that it was for the Commission alone to balance these interests against each other, and it rejected the second plea in law as unfounded.

By their third plea in law, the applicants argued that the publication of an infringement decision containing information voluntarily submitted under the leniency programme would frustrate their legitimate expectations, and thereby also breach the principle of legal certainty and the right to good administration guaranteed by Article 41 of the Charter. According to them, both the 2002 and the 2006 Leniency Notices gave them specific assurances that the information provided would be protected from disclosure. Those assurances arose both from the wording of the Notices and from the Commission's previous practice, the applicants argued.[39]

The General Court acknowledged that paragraphs 32 and 33 of the 2002 Leniency Notice did indicate that (i) written leniency statements may not be disclosed or used for any purposes other than the enforcement of Article 101 TFEU, (ii) the disclosure of documents received in the context of a leniency application would undermine the purpose of inspections and investigations within the meaning of Article 4(2) of the Transparency Regulation, and (iii) the initiative to provide the Commission with voluntary presentations of their knowledge of the cartel and of their participation therein, should not be discouraged by discovery orders issued in civil litigation. However, the General Court sided with the Commission, and declared that these commitments concerned only the disclosure of certain documents and statements, not the information contained therein. Nor did the General Court consider the Commission's own practice to give rise to any legitimate expectations. While acknowledging that the protection of legitimate expectations is one of the fundamental principles of EU law, it declared that economic operators are not justified in having a legitimate expectation that an existing situation that is capable of being altered by the EU institutions in the exercise of their discretion will be maintained.[40] The General Court further held that the Commission enjoys a broad margin of discretion in determining whether or not to publish non-confidential information. Article 30 of Regulation 1/2003 should therefore not be interpreted as limiting the Commission's power to publish the full text, or at the very least a highly detailed version of its decisions, if it considers it appropriate to do so. That conclusion is all the more pertinent in the present case, the General Court continued, as the publication of detailed information of the infringement

[38] Ibid para 81.

[39] Ibid para 98. The applicants explicitly referred to the fact that the notices acknowledged the risk that potential leniency applicants might be dissuaded from cooperating if this could impair their position in civil proceedings.

[40] Ibid para 120.

was liable to facilitate the establishment of the civil liability of the undertakings responsible and thereby reinforce the application of EU law in the civil sphere.[41] The General Court thus also considered the third plea in law to be unfounded and dismissed the action in its entirety.

B. Comment on the General Court's Ruling

The General Court's ruling prompts a number of reflections. It is clear that the General Court acknowledges that the publication of information provided within the frame of a leniency application may undermine the attractiveness of the leniency programme and thereby also weaken the public enforcement pillar. However, it is equally clear that it leaves it to the Commission to carry out any balancing exercise. As long as the Commission considers it appropriate to publish such information, the General Court encourages the Commission's practices, because the publication of detailed infringement decisions serves the general interests of informing the public of the Commission's actions and of strengthening the private enforcement pillar. Acknowledging that a leniency applicant may be seriously harmed if the information that it has provided describing the illegal action is made public, the General Court does not consider the company's interests in the non-disclosure of its offending conduct to be worthy of protection. This means that apart from business secrets, no information describing the illegal action will be considered to meet the third criterion of the confidentiality test set up in *Bank Austria* and applied by the Commission.

IV. *Pilkington* – Information Shared between Cartel Members No Longer Confidential

In November 2008, the Commission adopted an infringement decision against a number of companies active in the car glass sector, imposing fines totalling more than €1.3 billion, of which Pilkington's share amounted to €370 million.[42] In February 2009, it informed Pilkington and the other cartel members of its intention to publish a non-confidential version of the decision on its website, and asked the companies to identify any confidential information or information that constituted business secrets. After having considered the companies' requests for confidential treatment, the Commission published a provisional, non-confidential version of the infringement decision in February 2010.

[41] Ibid para 125.

[42] Commission Decision C (2008) 6815 final of 12 November 2008 relating to a proceeding under Article 81 [EC] and Article 53 of the EEA Agreement (COMP/39.125 – *Car glass*).

A year later, the Commission informed Pilkington of its intention to publish – for reasons of transparency – a fuller non-confidential version of the infringement decision, and to reject several requests for confidential treatment that it had previously received and that concerned three different categories of information. The first category of information concerned customer names, product names or descriptions of products, and other information that might identify individual customers (Category I information). The second category included information on the number of parts supplied by Pilkington, the share of the business of particular car manufacturers, pricing calculations, price changes, etc (Category II information). The third and last category allegedly contained information that might identify individual members of the staff involved in the implementation of the cartel (Category III information). Pilkington informed the Hearing Officer that it objected to the publication of this information, maintaining that Category I and II information had to be protected since it constituted business secrets, whilst the publication of Category III information would make it possible to identify the natural persons who had allegedly been involved in the cartel. A publication of such information would, according to Pilkington, constitute an infringement of the Commission's duty to protect personal data under Article 8 of the Charter. In the contested decision,[43] signed for the Commission, the Hearing Officer, whilst accepting the confidential nature of certain information, rejected the majority of Pilkington's requests. Pilkington challenged the decision rejecting its claim for confidentiality, arguing that the publication of a decision containing the contested information would constitute an infringement of Article 339 TFEU as well as the duty to protect personal data enshrined in Article 8 of the Charter.

In the contested decision, the Hearing Officer had found, in essence, that the Category I and II information (i) was by its very nature known to third parties, (ii) was historical, and (iii) constituted the very essence of the infringement, while, moreover, the interests of the persons harmed required its publication.[44] In its application for annulment, Pilkington claimed that the Commission had infringed Article 339 TFEU, Article 28 of Regulation 1/2003 and Article 8 of the Mandate, arguing, inter alia, that the Hearing Officer had failed to assess whether the contested material was inherently confidential. According to Pilkington, the contested decision also infringed a number of general principles, such as the principles of equal treatment and legitimate expectations.

[43] Commission Decision C(2012) 5718 final of August 2012 rejecting a request for confidential treatment submitted by Pilkington Group, pursuant to Article 8 of Decision 2011/695/EU of the President of the European Commission of 13 October 2011 on the function and terms of reference of the hearing officer in certain competition proceedings (Case COMP/39.125 – *Car glass*).

[44] *Pilkington* (n 5) para 10. Regarding the Category III information, the Hearing Officer relied on Art 5 of Regulation 45/2001 (on the protection of individuals with regard to the processing of personal data by the Community institutions and bodies and on the free movement of such data) and accepted the confidential treatment of the information in question.

A. The View of the General Court

In its ruling, the General Court noted that under Article 8(2) of the Mandate there are two different situations when the Hearing Officer may find that information should be disclosed, and that is either because the information does not constitute a business secret or other confidential information, or because the Hearing Officer considers that there is an overriding interest in its disclosure.[45] As for the notion of professional secrecy, the General Court acknowledged that it extends beyond business secrets to information that is known to only a limited number of persons and the disclosure of which is liable to cause serious harm – either to the person who has provided it or to third parties. Last, the interests liable to be harmed by disclosure must, objectively, be worthy of protection.[46] This led it to conclude that the assessment of confidentiality requires the legitimate interests that opposes disclosure to be weighed against the public interest that the activities of the EU institutions take place as openly as possible. The General Court also noted that the possibility for the Commission to rely on a general presumption that the exceptions in Article 4 of the Transparency Regulation apply to requests for sets of documents, should not affect its ability to publish longer and more detailed versions of its infringement decisions.[47]

As for the information contained in the contested decision, the General Court first addressed the possible publication of the Category I information.[48] Here, it noted that Pilkington had already decided to share this information with its competitors during the course of their cooperation within the cartel. The publication of the contested decision would thus only provide Pilkington's customers with the opportunity to learn the identity of Pilkington's other customers. The competitors were already in possession of this information. Furthermore, the General Court took note of the fact that, according to standard practice in the car glass industry, the glass installed in cars bears a visible indication of its trade origin. Given that the market was characterised by such a degree of transparency, the Category I information could not be considered confidential, the General Court concluded. Further, as the information was more than five years old, it was presumed to have lost its confidential nature due to the passage of time. Pilkington had failed to rebut that presumption, the General Court declared.

Last, the General Court sided with the Hearing Officer and acknowledged that the Commission is entitled, with due regard for the obligation of professional secrecy, to take account of the interests of persons harmed by the infringement and to facilitate their actions for damages. The Commission may accordingly publish a version of its infringement decision that is fuller than the minimum required by Article 30 of Regulation 1/2003.

[45] Ibid para 22.
[46] Ibid para 45.
[47] Ibid para 47.
[48] Information that might allow the reader to identify Pilkington's customers.

As for the Category II information, relating inter alia to the quantities of car parts supplied, allocation of market shares, agreements on prices and price calculations, the General Court acknowledged that this type of information is generally of such a nature as to fit the notion of business secrets. However, due to a number of reasons, the General Court reached another conclusion in relation to the contested information. First of all, it noted that Pilkington had chosen to communicate this type of information 'precisely to the persons and entities from whom that information is supposed to be secret'.[49] Pilkington had thus itself decided to renounce the secrecy of that information by communicating it directly to its competitors in exchange for an unlawful agreement as to their future conduct. Consequently, the General Court concluded, there was no basis for Pilkington's claim that the effect of the information's publication would be improperly to enlarge the circle of persons privy to that information, as it was Pilkington itself that had decided to share it with its competitors.[50] What is more, the General Court found the information in question to constitute the very essence of the infringement. Thus, the General Court declared, the Hearing Officer had not erred in law by emphasising the character of that information in order to rule out the possibility of its being known by only a limited number of persons.

Pilkington had also argued that it would be possible to extrapolate from the disclosed prices in order to determine the company's current price levels. This argument was not accepted by the General Court, which stressed that those levels had been set in the context of a cartel arrangement and that, in the absence of a specific explication of what interest that kind of information could have as part of attempting to deduce current price levels, Pilkington's argument must be rejected.[51]

The third and fourth pleas in law concerned alleged breach of the principles of equal treatment and legitimate expectations. Here Pilkington argued that the Commission had changed its policy concerning the publication of confidential information, thereby failing to respect the two principles. To this the General Court once again responded that the Commission is entitled to publish, with due regard to the rules governing the protection of professional secrecy, decisions that are fuller than the minimum required by Article 30 of Regulation 1/2003. Furthermore, the General Court noted, the Commission is entitled to adjust its approach as to the publication of its decisions to the needs of its competition policy. The supervisory task conferred on the Commission not only includes the duty to investigate and punish individual infringements, it also includes a duty to pursue a general policy designed to apply, in competition matters, the principles laid down by the Treaty and to guide the conduct of undertakings in the light of those principles. Consequently, even if the contested decision might lead one

[49] *Pilkington* (n 5) para 60.
[50] Ibid.
[51] Ibid para 66.

to believe that there was a change in the Commission's policy, that alone is not capable of affecting the lawfulness of the contested decision, the General Court concluded.[52] It also pointed to its previous finding that the contested material was not protected by professional secrecy, and thus rejected the two pleas.

As a final plea, Pilkington had claimed that the publication of the contested decision would constitute an infringement of the principles governing the protection of the identity of individuals, arguing that it would allow some of its employees to be identified on the basis of reference to the posts held by them and the reference by name to its customers. This plea was also rejected. The General Court observed that when the Commission publishes an infringement decision, the customers will necessarily deduce that some of the undertaking's employees have been parties to the discussions and/or concluded the agreements under investigation. It is equally inevitable, the General Court continued, that those same customers would assume that the employees concerned were those responsible for the commercial relations with them. The customers would make those deductions even if the Commission published an extremely summary version of its decision, and Pilkington could therefore not require that the names of its customers be redacted from the contested decision. Pilkington had apparently relied on the lack of trust on the part of its customers vis-à-vis some members of its staff, but to this the General Court simply responded that any lack of trust would be the consequence of Pilkington's anticompetitive behaviour and not the publication of the contested decision.[53] Given the foregoing, the General Court declared that the Hearing Officer had been correct to state that only information giving rise to the positive identification of an individual ought to be redacted. Based on the foregoing, the General Court dismissed Pilkington's action.[54]

B. Comment on the General Court's Ruling

The General Court's ruling in Pilkington was delivered only a few months after the ruling in *AKZO*. The judges are the same, as are two of the three agents acting on behalf of the Commission. It is therefore not too surprising that many of the findings in *AKZO* are reiterated in *Pilkington*. The General Court thus once again emphasises the right of the Commission to acknowledge the interests of cartel victims through the publication of more detailed versions of its infringement decisions. The General Court also takes the view that the possibility under the Transparency Regulation to rely on general presumptions and refuse access to the case file, should not affect the Commission's right to disclose the information contained therein. Furthermore, the General Court declares that any information

[52] Ibid para 77.
[53] Ibid para 83.
[54] Save for the publication of information contained in recital 115 of the *Car glass* decision (n 43), which DG COMP had agreed not to publish.

that dates back more than five years shall by default be considered to have lost its confidential nature due to the passage of time.

However, in *Pilkington*, the General Court not only reiterates earlier findings, it also raises additional obstacles to any attempts by cartel members to circumscribe the Commission's power to publish longer and more detailed versions of its infringement decisions. It does not accept the argument that the information relating, inter alia, to the quantities of car parts supplied, allocation of market shares, agreements on prices and price calculations should be considered confidential, and the reason why it takes this stance is that Pilkington had, by its own decision, shared this information with its competitors, thereby voluntarily renouncing any confidentiality. The information in question was also of such a nature as to lie at the heart of the cartel activity. This could be compared with the General Court's stance in *AKZO*, where the Commission had argued that the contested information should not be considered confidential given that it was derived from the Commission's case file to which the other co-conspirators had access in accordance with their right of access to the file.[55] Here the General Court did not agree with the Commission, declaring that information does not lose its confidential character simply because the other parties to the investigation can access it by exercising their right of access to the file.

A first observation concerns the consistency of the Commission's own reasoning. As noted by the Commission itself in the Access Notice,[56] the parties will be granted access to all documents making up the Commission file, with the exception of internal documents, business secrets of other undertakings or other confidential information. Thus, at least according to the Commission's own practice, the right of access to the file does not extend to confidential information, and any information disclosed between the parties has thus been deemed not to be of a confidential character. The General Court does not address this issue but deems that the confidentiality shall depend on who has shared this information with the parties under investigation. If it is the parties themselves who have voluntarily exchanged it during the course of the cartel, it is fair game. If, on the other hand, it is the Commission that has gathered it during the course of the investigation, it shall be deemed to maintain (any) confidential character.

V. *Evonik Degussa* – Protection of Leniency Statements

In May 2006, the Commission adopted an infringement decision against 16 hydrogen peroxide and perborates producers found guilty of cartel participation.[57]

[55] *AKZO* (n 28) paras 66–67.

[56] Commission Notice on the rules for access to the Commission file in cases pursuant to Articles 81 and 82 of the EC Treaty, Articles 53, 54 and 57 of the EEA Agreement and Council Regulation (EC) No 139/2004.

[57] *Hydrogen Peroxide and Perborate* (n 27).

Evonik Degussa had been the first company to report on the cartel, and had thus received immunity from fines. In the course of 2007, a first non-confidential version of the infringement decision ('the PHP Decision') was published on the Commission's website. Four years later, the Commission informed Evonik Degussa of its intention to publish a new and more complete non-confidential version of the PHP Decision, setting out the entire content of that decision save for any confidential information. The Commission asked Evonik Degussa to identify the information that it considered confidential, and which should thus be excluded from the public version. Perhaps not too surprisingly, Evonik Degussa considered that the PHP Decision contained both confidential information and business secrets, and objected to the proposed publication. In support of the objection, it claimed that the extended version of the PHP Decision contained a significant amount of information provided in relation to the leniency application, including the names of a number of its collaborators as well as information concerning its business relations. Evonik Degussa argued that the proposed publication would infringe the principles of legitimate expectations and equal treatment, and would be liable to have an adverse effect on the Commission's investigations.

The Commission agreed to delete all the information that would allow – directly or indirectly – the identification of the source of the information communicated pursuant to the 2002 Leniency Notice[58] as well as the names of Evonik Degussa's collaborators. As for the rest of the information covered by the objection ('the contested information'), the Commission did not consider it to be confidential. Evonik Degussa referred the matter to the Hearing Officer. As in the case of *AKZO*, the Hearing Officer pointed to the limits of his mandate, declaring that he only had the power to consider whether the contested information was confidential and not to remedy an alleged breach of Evonik Degussa's legitimate expectations. The Hearing Officer also noted that the only reason behind the objection was that the new version contained information submitted pursuant to the 2002 Leniency Notice, and that its publication would most likely be detrimental to Evonik Degussa in the context of any actions for damages. The Hearing Officer declared that the Commission had a wide discretion to publish more than the essential parts of its decisions. Furthermore, Evonik Degussa had failed to show that the proposed publication would cause it serious harm. In any event, the interest of a competition law offender in protecting details of its unlawful conduct from disclosure does not merit special protection, the Hearing Officer continued. In its application, Evonik Degussa had argued, like the AKZO companies, that the disclosure would undermine the leniency system, and thereby also the effectiveness of the public enforcement system. Just as in *AKZO*, the Hearing Officer declared that this balancing act was for the Commission to carry out, not him. Acting on behalf of

[58] Commission Notice on immunity from fines and reduction of fines in cartel cases (2002/C 45/03). The notice was replaced by a new on in 2006 (2006/C 298/11).

the Commission, the Hearing Officer thus rejected the application. This decision was challenged before the General Court.[59]

A. The View of the General Court

In support of its action, Evonik Degussa had raised five pleas in law: (i) breach of the Hearing Officer's Mandate and the right to good administration, (ii) failure to state sufficient reasons, (iii) breach of the professional secrecy protected under Article 339 TFEU and Article 8 ECHR, (iv) breach of the principles of legitimate expectations, legal certainty and equal treatment, and (v) breach of the specific purpose principle in Article 28 of Regulation 1/2003.

As for the first plea, the General Court noted that it consisted, in essence, of two parts. In the first part, Evonik Degussa took issue with the Hearing Officer for having examined neither the substance of the arguments alleging breach of the principles of legitimate expectations and equal treatment, nor the argument that the proposed publication would breach the principle set out in Article 28 of Regulation 1/2003, that information collected by the Commission is to be used only for the purpose for which it was acquired. In considering only whether the contested information was or was not confidential, the Hearing Officer improperly restricted the scope of the control he was to carry out pursuant to Article 8 of the Mandate. In the second part, Evonik Degussa maintained that the Hearing Officer had thereby also failed to respect the company's right to good administration. The General Court was not convinced by these arguments. Finding that the Hearing Officer was correct to decline competence in the present case, it noted that he and/or the Commission had nevertheless addressed all the issues in question during the course of the procedure leading up to the adoption of the contested decision. The General Court dismissed the first plea in law.[60]

By its second plea, Evonik Degussa had alleged failure to state sufficient reasons contrary to Article 296 TFEU, Article 41 of the Charter and Article 8 of the Mandate. In essence, the company claimed that it had not been given any explanation of why it was necessary to publish a new version of the PHP Decision.[61] To this the General Court responded that the obligation to state reasons must be assessed with regard not only to the wording of the decision, but also to its context and to all the legal rules governing the matter in question. When looking at the contested decision in the context that led to its adoption, it did include, implicitly but necessarily, the positions adopted by the Commission concerning the proposed publication. The General Court noted that Evonik Degussa had received letters from both DG COMP and the Hearing Officer explaining why the Commission

[59] Case T-341/12 *Evonik Degussa GmbH v European Commission*, EU:T:2015:51.
[60] Ibid para 51.
[61] Ibid para 52.

had decided to publish a longer and more complete version, and therefore also dismissed the second plea as unfounded.[62]

By its third plea, Evonik Degussa claimed that the Hearing Officer had disregarded the confidentiality of the information voluntarily communicated to the Commission, and that the contested decision therefore infringed both Article 339 TFEU and Article 8 ECHR. According to Evonik Degussa, such confidentiality resulted first of all from the fact that the information was derived from leniency statements, and that it formed part of the company's private activities, protected by Article 8 ECHR, independently even of their content. Moreover, Evonik Degussa referred to the Court's case law,[63] claiming that special protection should be afforded to information communicated voluntarily to the Commission on condition that it would not be disclosed. Evonik Degussa also considered the information to be covered by professional secrecy under Article 339 TFEU and Article 30 of Regulation 1/2003, alleging that it fulfilled the three conditions identified for that purpose in *Bank Austria*.[64]

Evonik Degussa further observed that parts of the contested information had not previously been made public, and that it revealed, in detail, not only the anticompetitive agreements and exchanges of information referred to in the PHP Decision, but also the way in which Evonik Degussa had participated in them. The information was accompanied by numerous citations taken from the documents produced by it under the leniency programme, along with aids to interpretation supplied by the Commission. Such publication, the company argued, must be assimilated to the direct publication of the leniency statements of such a kind as to cause serious harm to Evonik Degussa's reputation and to affect its position on the market. Evonik Degussa also maintained that it would be put in a worse position than its co-conspirators given that, in order to obtain immunity, it had been forced to acknowledge unreservedly its own participation in the infringement, and as far as possible, help the Commission shed light on the facts.[65] According to Evonik Degussa, information relating to the business relations of companies and to the prices of their products formed part of their commercial interests and was worthy of protection, even if it related to conduct recognised as unlawful. The proposed publication would expose the company to a greater risk of being ordered to pay damages in actions before the national courts, Evonik Degussa argued.[66] It further claimed that there was a general presumption of illegality attaching to the publication of information originating from leniency statements or documents voluntarily submitted during the course of the leniency procedure.

The General Court chose to divide the plea into three parts comprising breach of: (i) the applicant's business secrets or at least of the confidentiality of business

[62] Ibid para 67.
[63] Case 145/83, *Stanley George Adams v Commission of the European Communities*, EU:C:1985:448.
[64] *Bank Austria* (n 5).
[65] *Evonik Degussa* (n 59) para 71.
[66] Ibid para 72.

information relating to it, (ii) the confidentiality of information communicated to the Commission under the leniency programme, and (iii) the right to protection of private life. As for the first part, the General Court noted that the information at issue dated from more than five years previously, most of it even dating from more than 10 years previously. To the extent that the contested information had contained any business secrets or confidential business information, such information must therefore be considered historical, unless Evonik Degussa could demonstrate that it still constituted essential elements of its own commercial position or that of a third party.[67] As Evonik Degussa had not presented any specific arguments to rebut such presumption, the General Court found the information to be historical.

The General Court then addressed the claim that information communicated to the Commission under the leniency programme deserved protection for the sole reason that it had been submitted voluntarily with the aim of obtaining immunity from fines. The General Court noted that, according to Article 1 TEU, decisions within the EU shall be taken as openly as possible, and that this principle of openness is also reflected in Article 15 TFEU, which grants citizens the right of access to documents. Thus, the General Court continued, in accordance with that principle, and in the absence of provisions explicitly ordering or prohibiting publication, the power of the institutions to make acts that they adopt public is the rule, and protection from disclosure thus the exception. Neither Article 339 TFEU nor Article 28 of Regulation 1/2003 expressly indicates what information, apart from business secrets, is to be covered by the obligation of professional secrecy, the General Court observed. However, it could not be inferred from the latter article that all information acquired under the Regulation, with the exception of information publication of which was mandatory under Article 30 of the Regulation, should be covered by the notion of professional secrecy.

The General Court then noted that while it had previously acknowledged that in so far as the confidentiality of certain information is protected under Article 4 of the Transparency Regulation, such information must be considered to be covered by the obligation of professional secrecy in Article 28 of Regulation 1/2003, this no longer applied.[68] The change of stance was motivated by recent case law from the Court of Justice, which had now interpreted Article 4 of the Transparency Regulation as leaving it open to the institutions to base their decisions on general presumptions that apply to certain categories of documents.[69] If Article 4 of the Transparency Regulation were to prevent the Commission from publishing any information to which it would be entitled to refuse access in reliance on a general

[67] Ibid para 84.

[68] Ibid para 91, where the General Court referred to its rulings in *Bank Austria* (n 5) para 75 and *Pergan Hilfsstoffe* (n 15) para 64.

[69] *Evonik Degussa* (n 59) para 92, where the General Court referred to the ECJ's ruling in Case C-365/12 P, *European Commission v EnBW Energie Baden-Württemberg AG*, EU:C:2014:112.

presumption, Article 30 of Regulation 1/2003 would be rendered ineffective, the General Court concluded.[70] It also noted that such interpretation would have the effect, in practice, of reversing the burden of proof, which should be borne by the person requesting confidential treatment.[71]

These conclusions led the General Court to apply the principle established in *Bank Austria*.[72] Thus, in order for any information submitted under the leniency programme to fall within the ambit of professional secrecy, three cumulative criteria had to be fulfilled: (i) the information must be known only to a limited number of persons, (ii) its disclosure must be likely to cause serious harm, and (iii) the interests likely to be harmed must, objectively, be worthy of protection. As for the first criterion, the Commission had argued that it should not apply given that the information in question was part of the Commission's case file and thereby accessible to the other parties to the investigation. This argument was rejected by the General Court, which declared that a distinction had to be drawn between, on the one hand, information conveyed to those who had a right to be heard and, on the other, information conveyed to the general public. The General Court also considered the second criterion to be fulfilled, acknowledging that the contested information consisted essentially of the description of component elements of the infringement, and that the new version would permit an understanding of the significant role played by Evonik Degussa in the cartel. Furthermore, the publication of the new version was likely to facilitate matters for cartel victims and make it easier to establish the civil liability of the cartel members. The General Court thus concluded that the disclosure of the contested information would be of such kind as to cause Evonik Degussa serious harm.[73] There remained the third criterion. Here the General Court declared that the interest of a competition law offender in keeping the details of its offending conduct secret did not warrant any particular protection. As for the claim that the disclosure of the contested information would jeopardise the effectiveness of the public enforcement system, the General Court noted that any such balancing exercise must be carried out by the Commission when drafting the public version of an infringement decision.

The General Court then moved on to the third part of the plea, the claim that the publication would constitute a breach of Evonik Degussa's private life. It referred to the case law of the Strasbourg Court according to which a person cannot rely on Article 8 ECHR in order to complain of a loss of reputation that is a foreseeable consequence of its own illegal conduct.[74] Having established that

[70] Just as it had in both *AKZO* and *Pilkington*.

[71] *Evonik Degussa* (n 59) para 92.

[72] *Bank Austria* (n 5).

[73] *Evonik Degussa* (n 59) para 105.

[74] Ibid para 125. Reference is made to *Sidabras and Džiautas v Lithuania* App nos 55480/00 and 59330/00 (Judgment) (ECtHR, 27 July 2004) para 49; *Taliadorou and Stylianou v Cyprus* App nos 39627/05 and 39631/05 (Judgment) (ECtHR, 16 October 2008) para 56; and *Gillberg v Sweden* App no 41723/06 (Judgment) (ECtHR, 3 April 2012) para 67.

the protection of private life could not prevent the publication of the contested information, the General Court also dismissed the third plea.

By its fourth plea, Evonik Degussa had claimed that the publication of the contested information would constitute a breach of the principle of legitimate expectations. It had referred both to the Leniency Notice and to other statements made by the Commission, and argued that these had given it a legitimate expectation that no information voluntarily submitted during the course of the leniency procedure would be disclosed. The General Court did not accept these arguments. Reiterating its finding that the Commission had been motivated to publish a fuller and more detailed version of the PHP Decision, it declared that the existence of a certain practice did not mean that the Commission is prevented from changing such practice. Furthermore, as the contested information was not confidential in nature, the Commission had a wide discretion to decide whether or not to publish it. As previously established, Article 30 of Regulation 1/2003 could not be interpreted as preventing the Commission from publishing more information than strictly necessary, and this, the General Court continued, was even more essential where the publication could facilitate matters for cartel victims seeking to compensate their loss. Referring to both the 2002 and the 2006 Leniency Notices, acknowledging that the granting of immunity cannot protect a company from civil liability, the General Court rejected the fourth plea as unfounded.[75]

As for the fifth and final plea, alleging a breach of the 'purpose principle' enshrined in Article 28 of Regulation 1/2003, the General Court simply declared that the publication of an infringement decision is the final stage in the administrative procedure whereby the Commission finds infringements of Article 101 TFEU and brings them to an end. Thus, the publication of a non-confidential version of the infringement decision cannot be described as being outside the scope of the reason why the information was acquired. Rejecting the fifth plea as also unfounded, the General Court dismissed the action in its entirety.

B. The View of the ECJ

Evonik Degussa appealed the General Court's ruling, alleging an infringement of (i) the Hearing Officer's Mandate, (ii) Article 339 TFEU, Article 30 of Regulation 1/2003 and Article 4(2) of the Transparency Regulation, and (iii) the right to privacy as provided by Article 8 of the ECHR and Article 7 of the Charter. Moreover, it alleged an infringement of the principles of the protection of legitimate expectations and legal certainty. According to Evonik Degussa, the General Court had erred in law when holding that the contested information was neither confidential nor protected for reasons other than its confidential nature.

[75] *Evonik Degussa* (n 59) paras 158 and 165.

According to Evonik Degussa's first ground of appeal, the General Court had misconstrued the Mandate when declaring that the Hearing Officer lacked competence to examine arguments other than those relating to the confidential nature of the contested information. In a Grand Chamber ruling, the ECJ now declared that the aim of Article 8 of the Mandate is to provide, on a procedural level, for the protection required by EU law of information acquired by the European Commission during the course of an antitrust investigation. While Article 8 of the Mandate allows the Hearing Officer to find that information should not be disclosed if it constitutes a business secret or other confidential information, it shall not be read as preventing the Hearing Officer from paying regard to other grounds on which the interested person may rely in order to object to the proposed publication, the ECJ concluded. It would run counter to the aim of the Hearing Officer's Mandate if he could rely on only some of the grounds that may preclude the disclosure of a given piece of information. Finding that the Hearing Officer must examine any objection based on a ground – arising from rules or principles of EU law – relied on by the interested person in order to claim protection of the confidentiality of the contested information, the Court upheld the first ground of appeal.[76]

By its second ground of appeal, Evonik Degussa alleged an infringement of Article 339 TFEU, Article 30 of Regulation 1/2003, Article 4(2) of the Transparency Regulation, Article 8 ECHR and Article 7 of the Charter. First of all, the company argued against the General Court's view that the contested information had lost its confidential nature merely due to the passage of time. The Court did not accept this argument, declaring that information that was secret or confidential, but which was at least five years old, must as a rule be considered historical and therefore as having lost its secret or confidential nature, unless, exceptionally, the party relying on that nature was able to show that the information still constituted essential elements of its commercial position or that of interested third parties.[77] In the present case, Evonik Degussa had not put forward any specific argument to show that, in spite of its age, the information still constituted essential elements of its commercial position or that of a third party.[78] The Court saw no reason to reach a conclusion other than that of the General Court.[79]

As for Evonik Degussa's claim that the publication was contrary to the Transparency Regulation, the Court noted that the Regulation was not applicable in the present case, and that the case law deriving from the Regulation could not be transposed to the context of the publication of infringement decisions. Evonik Degussa had also argued that the publication of the contested information included information from the 'statements made by a leniency applicant', and

[76] *Evonik Degussa* (n 6) paras 55–57.

[77] Ibid para 64.

[78] All the contested information dated from more than five years previously, and some from more than 10 years previously.

[79] *Evonik Degussa* (n 6) para 67.

that such publication amounted to publishing verbatim quotations and extracts from those statements, which, Evonik Degussa claimed, could not be permitted.[80] To this the Court responded that the publication, in the form of verbatim quotations, of information from the documents provided by an undertaking to the Commission in support of a statement made in order to obtain leniency differed from the publication of verbatim quotations from that statement itself. Whereas the first type of publication should be authorised, subject to compliance with the protection owed, in particular, to business secrets, professional secrecy and other confidential information, the second type of publication was not permitted in any circumstances.[81]

As regards the Commission's treatment of the information submitted by leniency applicants, the Court acknowledged that the Commission, in point 29 of the 2002 Leniency Notice, was aware that that Notice would create legitimate expectations on which undertakings might rely when disclosing the existence of a cartel to it. In that regard, the Notice provides, first, in point 32, that normally, disclosure at any time of documents received in the context of that Notice would undermine the protection of the purpose of inspections and investigations within the meaning of Article 4(2) of the Transparency Regulation and, second, in point 33, that any written statement made vis-à-vis the Commission in relation to that Notice forms part of its file and may not be disclosed or used for any purpose other than the enforcement of Article 101 TFEU. The Commission had thereby imposed rules on itself as regards the written statements received by it in accordance with that Notice. However, the Court noted, those rules had neither the object nor the effect of prohibiting the Commission from publishing the information relating to the elements constituting the infringement of Article 101 TFEU submitted to it in the context of the leniency programme, which did not enjoy protection against publication on another ground.

Consequently, the only protection available to an undertaking that has cooperated with the Commission is the protection concerning (i) immunity from or reduction in the fine, and (ii) non-disclosure by the Commission of the documents and written statements received by it in accordance with the Leniency Notice. Based on these findings, the Court concluded that the publication, such as that envisaged, under Article 30 of Regulation 1/2003 in compliance with the protection of professional secrecy did not undermine the protection afforded by the Leniency Notice, since that protection could relate only to the determination of the fine and the treatment of the documents and statements specifically targeted by that Notice. The Court thus concluded that the General Court had not erred in law in the course of its analysis of the treatment to be given to information communicated by Evonik Degussa. The company's arguments in this respect were thus rejected.[82]

[80] Ibid para 80.
[81] Ibid para 87.
[82] Ibid para 99.

C. Comment on the Rulings

Through the Court's Grand Chamber ruling, a number of questions concerning the Commission's practices have now received clear answers.

First of all, the Court's clarification of the scope of the Hearing Officer's Mandate is welcomed. As has been shown in this chapter, the General Court has consistently upheld the Hearing Officer's narrow interpretation of his Mandate. While it is true that the wording of Article 8 calls for a narrow interpretation, the consequences of such interpretation are unacceptable, and do not reflect the role of the Hearing Officer, which is to guarantee that the Commission conducts its competition proceedings fairly, impartially and objectively while ensuring respect of the procedural rights of the parties concerned.

Furthermore, it is now clear that information that is more than five years old is presumed to have lost its confidential nature. As the Commission's investigations often take time, this means that by the time the Commission adopts its decision and publishes the infringement decisions, very little information will be considered confidential unless the addressees of the decisions manage to prove that it is still relevant. The Commission will thus be given considerable room for manoeuvre when drafting the non-confidential versions of the decisions, leaving it to the undertakings to go through the information and find arguments in support of any claims made.

Furthermore, in line with the Damages Directive, the Court has now established that although leniency statements deserve absolute protection from publication, nothing else relating to the leniency procedure does. This may lead to a more timely publication of detailed Commission decisions, which is welcome from a private enforcement perspective. However, and as will be discussed in more detail in section VII, the ruling highlights the fact that the Commission appears willing to risk any existing trust between the Commission and companies under investigation.

VI. The Court's Ruling in *AGC Glass* – The Role of the Hearing Officer

Like *Pilkington*, this case stems from the Commission's decision to impose fines on a number of companies found guilty of cartel participation in the car glass sector.[83] In March 2009, the Commission informed AGC Glass[84] of its intention to publish

[83] Commission Decision C (2008) 6815 final of 12 November 2008 relating to a proceeding under Article 81 [EC] and Article 53 of the EEA Agreement (COMP/39.125 – *Car glass*).

[84] The decision was addressed to the following companies within the AGC Glass group: AGC Glass Europe SA, AGC Automotive Europe SA, AGC France SAS, AGC Flat Glass Italia Srl, AGC Glass UK Ltd, and AGC Glass Germany GmbH. These companies are jointly referred to as AGC Glass.

a non-confidential version of the decision on its website, and asked the companies to identify any confidential information or information that constituted business secrets. After having considered the companies' requests for confidential treatment, the Commission adopted the non-confidential version of the *Car glass* decision to be published on its website. It is clear from the correspondence between the Commission and AGC Glass that the Commission had decided not to act on the companies' requests for redaction of information contained in 246 recitals of the *Car glass* decision and 122 footnotes thereto.

According to DG COMP, the information that AGC Glass sought to have redacted could be divided into three categories. The first category contained customer names, descriptions of the products concerned and any information that could enable an individual customer to be identified. The second category contained the number of parts supplied; the allocation of quotas to each car manufacturer; price agreements, pricing calculations and price changes; as well as the numbers or percentages involved in the allocation of customers between the cartel members. Lastly, the third category contained purely administrative information, consisting of references to documents in the file. AGC Glass later withdrew its application for confidential treatment regarding the third category.

The companies comprising AGC Glass then unsuccessfully turned to the Hearing Officer, who, on behalf of the Commission, rejected the requests for confidential treatment, declaring that the 2002 Leniency Notice did not give rise to a legitimate expectation preventing the Commission from publishing information other than that covered by professional secrecy. Furthermore, the Hearing Officer continued, the companies' interest in non-disclosure of such information did not warrant any particular protection. He also pointed out that he was not competent to decide (i) whether it was appropriate to publish non-confidential information or to take a position as regards any adverse effects that might have been brought about by the Commission's general policy, or (ii) on the extent of the intended publication in the light of the principle of equal treatment.

Furthermore, the Hearing Officer considered that the information in the first category, consisting of customer names and descriptions of the products concerned, was, by its very nature, 'historic'. Given the specific characteristics of the car glass market, the information was known outside the applicants and it referred to the very essence of the infringement. Moreover, the interests of the persons harmed required its disclosure. To the extent that the applicants had raised specific arguments seeking to establish that the information at issue was confidential notwithstanding its general characteristics, the Hearing Officer concluded that the information in the first category was not covered by the obligation of professional secrecy.[85] Lastly, the Hearing Officer granted the request in part, on the ground that the rules on the processing of personal data by the EU institutions and on the free movement of such data required certain information to be given

[85] Case T-465/12, *AGC Glass Europe SA and Others v European Commission*, EU:T:2015:505, para 12.

confidential treatment. The remainder of the request was dismissed and AGC Glass then turned to the General Court.

A. The View of the General Court

In its application, AGC Glass relied on a number of pleas, one of which was infringement of the provisions on the protection of professional secrecy. According to AGC Glass, the information on customer names and descriptions of the products concerned should be considered confidential, and the publication of such information would thus be contrary to the Commission's duty under Article 28 of Regulation 1/2003 not to publish information covered by professional secrecy. The General Court did not accept AGC Glass's arguments, declaring that the Hearing Officer had made no error in finding that the information could be published. The General Court noted that as AGC Glass had chosen to exchange this information with its competitors as part of the cartel arrangement, it could no longer be considered to be known only to a limited group of persons. In any event, as the glass installed in cars bears visible indication of trade origin, the car glass market was characterised by such a degree of transparency that the information in question could not be classified as confidential. Furthermore, the information in question was more than five years old and thus presumed to be historical. The General Court found that AGC Glass had presented no arguments capable of rebutting that presumption.[86] There had thus not been any infringement with regard to the protection of professional secrecy. Nor did the General Court consider that there had been an infringement of the Mandate, as, in any event, it was clear that the Hearing Officer had made an assessment not only of the confidential nature of the information concerned, but also of the applicant's arguments related to breach of the principles of legitimate expectations and equal treatment.[87]

As for the arguments concerning the principle of legitimate expectations, AGC Glass had claimed that the Leniency Notices of both 2002 and 2006 contained provisions that created legitimate expectations that information voluntarily provided would remain confidential even at the stage of publication of the Commission's decision. Again, the General Court did not agree. Instead it declared that the Notices contained no provision that supported AGC Glass's arguments, but that it was instead clear from their wording that they had been adopted with the sole aim to establish the conditions under which an undertaking may obtain either immunity from a fine or a reduction in the amount of the fine. The Notices did not provide for any other advantage an undertaking could claim in exchange for its cooperation. Furthermore, the General Court continued, the Notices expressly declared that the granting of leniency could not protect an undertaking

[86] Ibid para 40.
[87] Ibid para 60.

from the civil law consequences of its participation in an infringement of Article 101 TFEU.

The applicant had also argued that the intended publication of the identity of customers amounted to a departure from the Commission's established practice, and that this departure was both unexpected and arbitrary, thus constituting a breach of the principle of good administration. To this the General Court responded that the Commission was entitled to publish infringement decisions that were fuller than the minimum required in Article 30 of Regulation 1/2003. Furthermore, the General Court continued, the supervisory task conferred on the Commission included the duty not only to investigate and punish individual infringements, but also to pursue a general policy designed to apply, in competition matters, the principles laid down by the Treaty and to guide the conduct of undertakings in the light of these principles. Consequently, the General Court concluded, even if the contested decision might lead one to believe that there was a change in the Commission's approach as regards the degree of detail in the published version of the *Car glass* decision as compared with previous cases, that alone was not capable of affecting the lawfulness of the contested decision, from the perspective of the principle of good administration. The General Court dismissed the action in its entirety.

B. The View of the ECJ

The applicant then turned to the ECJ, which, after having heard the Advocate General, decided to proceed to judgment without an opinion. In its appeal, AGC Glass relied on three grounds: (i) infringement of Article 8 of the Hearing Officer's Mandate, (ii) breach of the principles of legitimate expectations and equal treatment, and (iii) breach of the obligation to state reasons.

As for the first ground of appeal, the Court referred to its recent ruling in *Evonik Degussa*, declaring that the Mandate must be framed in such a way as to safeguard the effective exercise of procedural rights throughout the proceedings before the Commission, in particular the right to be heard.[88] The aim of Article 8 of the Mandate, the Court continued, was to provide, on a procedural level, for the protection of information that has come to the Commission's knowledge in the context of proceedings applying the competition rules. That protection, the Court continued, must be understood as relating to any ground that could justify protecting the confidentiality of the information at issue,[89] as it would run counter to the aim of the Mandate if the Hearing Officer could rely on only some of the grounds that may preclude the disclosure of a given piece of information. Consequently,

[88] Case C-517/15 P, *AGC Glass Europe and Others v European Commission*, EU:C:2017:598, para 40 where the Court refers to *Evonik Degussa* (n 6) para 40.

[89] *AGC Glass* (n 88) para 51.

the General Court had erred in law when it held that the Hearing Officer had been correct to decline competence. However, the Court continued, the error of law was not of such a nature as to entail annulment of the judgment under appeal.[90] What was more, despite having declared that he lacked competence, the Court found that the Hearing Officer appeared to have taken the parties' argument into account when adopting his decision. The first ground of appeal was therefore rejected in its entirety as ineffective.

By its second ground of appeal, AGC Glass submitted that the General Court had erred in law when declaring that the decision at issue did not infringe the principles of protection of legitimate expectations and equal treatment. It submitted, in that respect, that the distinction made between the documents received in the context of the leniency programme, on the one hand, and the content of those documents, on the other, was both artificial and inappropriate.[91] To this the Court responded that it was apparent from paragraphs 3 to 7 of the 2002 Leniency Notice that the sole aim of that Notice was to lay down the conditions under which an undertaking may obtain either immunity from or a reduction in fines. This being said, the Court noted further that in points 29, 32 and 33 of the Notice, the Commission accepts that (i) it will create legitimate expectations on which undertakings may rely when disclosing the existence of a cartel, (ii) normally disclosure, at any time, of documents received in the context of that Notice would undermine the protection of the purpose of inspections and investigations within the meaning of Article 4(2) of the Transparency Regulation, and (iii) any written statement made vis-à-vis the Commission in relation to that Notice forms part of its file and may not be disclosed or used for any purpose other than the enforcement of Article 101 TFEU.

It was thus with the aim of protecting leniency statements that the Commission imposed these rules on itself. The rules, the Court continued, had neither the object nor the effect of prohibiting the Commission from publishing the information relating to the elements constituting the cartel infringement that had been submitted to the Commission in the context of the leniency programme, and which did not enjoy protection on any other ground. Reiterating what it had already established in *Evonik Degussa*, the Court then concluded that the only protection available to an undertaking that has cooperated with the Commission in the context of a proceeding under Article 101 TFEU is the protection concerning (i) the immunity from or reduction in the fine and (ii) the non-disclosure by the Commission of the documents and written statements received by it in accordance with the 2002 Leniency Notice. It was against this background that the Court then established that the General Court had not erred in law when it declared that there had been no infringement of AGC Glass's legitimate expectations. The appellant had also argued that the General Court had failed to pay due

[90] Ibid para 57.
[91] Ibid para 66.

regard to the fact that it was in a situation other than that of those companies that had not cooperated with the Commission, and that there had thus been a violation of the principle of equal treatment.[92] This argument was not accepted by the Court, which declared that the second ground of appeal should also be rejected as unfounded.[93]

The Court also rejected the third ground of appeal, declaring that the ruling of the General Court showed to the requisite legal standard why it considered that the Commission was entitled to publish the information at issue. Having rejected the third ground of appeal, the Court dismissed the appeal in its entirety.

C. Comment on the Rulings

The General Court's ruling in *AGC Glass* was delivered by the same judges as in *AKZO* and *Pilkington*, and on the same day as the ruling in *Pilkington*. The agents acting on behalf of the Commission were the same as in *Pilkington*. However, unlike *AKZO* and *Pilkington*, this case reached the ECJ. While the Court upheld the General Court's findings in most respects, leaving the Commission considerable room for manoeuvre when drafting the public versions of its infringement decisions, the ECJ nevertheless strikes down on the General Court's interpretation of the Mandate. Rightfully so. The Hearing Officer has the task of safeguarding the observance of the parties' procedural rights. This task cannot be properly accomplished if the Hearing Officer is only empowered to examine whether the information to be published is confidential.

VII. More Detailed Infringements Decisions – Concluding Remarks

The Damages Directive explicitly states that the full effectiveness of Articles 101 and 102 TFEU cannot be achieved without a well-functioning private enforcement system. This in turn requires that those who have suffered loss can gather the evidence necessary to substantiate their claims. The Commission is well aware of this, and while it has firmly closed the door on anyone trying to access evidence under the Transparency Regulation, it now opens the door to an alternative way of gathering relevant information; by publishing longer and more detailed infringement decisions.[94] Yet while the case law presented in this chapter shows that the

[92] Ibid para 85.

[93] Ibid para 89.

[94] That said, the Commission introduced a settlement procedure in 2008, and the increased recourse to cartel settlements has affected the possibilities for cartel victims to gain important information, as the Commission's decisions in these cases are often shorter than ordinary infringement decisions and

Court stands by the Commission and supports its endeavours to disclose more information in its decisions, it is also clear that these endeavours may not have the desired effect, as it often takes years – or even decades – before the Commission is able to publish these versions on its website. The publication of the PHP Decision can be used to illustrate this.

The PHP Decision was adopted in May 2006, and the first non-confidential version was published the following year. In March 2009, CDC, acting on behalf of 32 hydrogen peroxide purchasers, filed an action for damages against six members of the hydrogen peroxide cartel before the Regional Court of Dortmund, Germany.[95] In its action for damages, CDC sought to recover €430 million in damages and €200 million in interest. As discussed in chapter 6, CDC had previously requested full access to the statement of contents of the Commission's case-file in the PHP case. This request had been rejected by the Commission, which considered that the granting of access would jeopardise its leniency system as it would deter companies from cooperating with the Commission in the future.[96] The decision to reject the request was challenged before the General Court, which upheld the application and annulled the Commission's decision.[97] Since then, CDC has reached out-of-court settlements with four of the defendants, and has subsequently withdrawn the action against those companies. The case continues against the remaining defendants.[98] In April 2011, CDC filed a legal action for damages before the District Court of Helsinki against the Finnish cartel member Kemira Oyj. It later reached an out-of-court settlement with Kemira, which is reported to have agreed to pay €12.7 million in compensation for its role in the hydrogen peroxide cartel.[99] However, while the Commission adopted the infringement decision against the hydrogen peroxide producers in May 2006, it was not until April 2017, almost 11 years after its adoption, that a full version was published on the Commission's website. By then, CDC and a number of the cartel members had already reached out-of-court settlements, and the publication had thus already lost much of its intended value.

When challenging the Commission's deciding to publish a more detailed infringement decision, the applicants often seek interim measures in order to postpone such publication until the underlying case has been adjudicated by the EU Courts. Pilkington is one of these companies. When it applied for interim

are seldom challenged before the EU Courts. More detailed infringement decisions may potentially make companies more inclined to settle with the Commission, in which case the publication of more detailed decisions would have the opposite effect leading to more succinct decisions.

[95] Including both Akzo Nobel and Evonik Degussa.

[96] Case T-437/08, *CDC Hydrogene Peroxide Cartel Damage Claims v European Commission*, EU:T:2011:752, para 31.

[97] Ibid.

[98] Available at www.carteldamageclaims.com/competition-law-damage-claims/hydrogen-peroxide-cartel/.

[99] See at https://globalcompetitionreview.com/article/1149070/cdc-settles-hydrogen-peroxide-damages-claim.

measures, the Commission objected and argued that a postponed publication would be detrimental to potential cartel victims who need the information to make their cases against the cartel members. To this the President of the General Court simply responded that there was nothing to prevent them from bringing their actions for damages in due time whilst obtaining a stay of national proceedings until judgment was given in the main action.[100]

While the President's statement is correct, such an order requires a more speedy procedure before the EU Courts. If the publication of more detailed infringement decisions is intended to serve the aim of facilitating damages actions, it should not take 11 years before the full version of the decision is published on the Commission's website. By the time any damages are awarded, decades may have passed since the victims were hurt by the cartel activity, and some victims may even have ceased to exist. Furthermore, the length of these proceedings may have a huge impact on the sum that the cartel members will eventually have to pay to the victims. Article 3 of the Damages Directive mirrors the Court's ruling in *Manfredi* and declares that cartel victims shall receive full compensation for their loss.[101] Such compensation shall cover the right to compensation for actual loss, loss of profit plus the payment of interest. Recital 12 of the Damages Directive acknowledges that payment of interest should be due from the time when the harm occurred until the time when compensation is paid. The potential effects of this can be illustrated by the claims made following the gas insulated switchgear cartel case in the UK, which were allegedly divided as follows: damages, £85 million; interest, £185 million.[102]

The current order can thus not be considered satisfactory from either a claimant's or a defendant's perspective, and is also likely to impact the effectiveness of the leniency programme. As is discussed in chapter 9, any incentives to apply for leniency are by necessity affected by the risk of having to pay damages. Although the current order – where the Commission is allowed to refuse access to its case file, but is given ample room for manoeuvre when deciding what information to include in its cartel decisions – must be preferable from the cartelists' perspective than if the Commission were to be forced to hand over its case file to potential cartel victims, it may still deter companies from cooperating with the Commission.[103]

[100] *Pilkington* (n 5) para 36.

[101] Case C-295/04, *Vincenzo Manfredi v Lloyd Adriatico Assicurazioni SpA*, EU:C:2006:461.

[102] Strategic Considerations in Cartel Follow-On litigation, Workshop organised by Concurrences in Brussels, June 2016, available at file://storage/home/hean/Downloads/concurrences_transcript_strategic_considerations_in_cartel_follow-on_litigation_02062016.pdf.

[103] In the cases of *Bank Austria* and *Pergan Hilfsstoffe*, the General Court had established that information that is covered by the exceptions in Art 4 of the Transparency Regulation should automatically be considered to be covered by the obligation of professional secrecy in Art 28 of Regulation 1/2003. However, this door was shut when the ECJ delivered its ruling in *EnBW*, allowing the Commission to rely on a general presumption that the exceptions in Art 4 of the Transparency Regulation covered the entire case file. This turn of events undoubtedly puts the Commission in the driver's seat, allowing it to control which information should be shared with the public.

While the Leniency Notice acknowledges the potential tension between the leniency programme and the private enforcement system, this is not necessarily reflected in the Commission's recent practices. Judging from the rulings examined in this chapter, there is not much that is safe from publication. While your leniency statement may not be disclosed, and while the Commission may not use verbatim quotations from such statements in the non-confidential versions of its decisions, the information provided is not protected unless it contains business secrets or is covered by professional secrecy. Thus, the information submitted in the leniency statement may later be published on the Commission's website – although not framed in your own words – and this will definitely be a factor influencing the decision to apply for leniency. In fact, this is acknowledged by the Court in the cases concerning the application of the Transparency Regulation, In *EnBW*, the Court declared that the Commission's investigative powers, which mostly rely on the information provided by companies, would be undermined by the lack of a guarantee that the documents submitted (voluntarily or not) by investigated companies would be treated with the highest degree of confidentiality. While you may resort to semantics and distinguish between document and information, the fact remains that companies have cooperated with the Commission believing that it was the information that was protected and not the physical documents.

As for information that is protected from publication due to its confidential character, the EU Courts have established the following. First of all, information that is more than five years old is deemed to have lost its confidential character, and it is then up to the cartel member to prove that it is still valuable and should thus remain confidential, provided of course that it meets the criteria in *Bank Austria*. Second, a company that shares confidential information with its competitors is deemed by the General Court to have renounced the confidentiality of such information. Third, the information shared during the course of the cartel constitutes the very essence of the infringement, and should thus be part of the public version of the infringement decision. While there is nothing in principle to say against these findings of the EU Courts, they will, by necessity affect the functioning of the Commission's leniency programme. Eventually, and as noted by the General Court, it will be up to the Commission to decide how detailed the public versions of the infringement decisions should be to maintain the attractiveness of both the leniency system and the private enforcement system. At this stage, however, the publication of more detailed infringement decisions does not appear to be the way forward, at least not if it takes the Commission more than a decade to publish those versions on its website.

While it may be wise of the Commission to publish longer and more detailed infringement decisions, and while it may be in the best interest of both the Commission and the addressees of the infringement decisions that the Commission controls which information should be dispersed to the public, the Commission's actions can still be questioned, as they have undoubtedly impacted companies' trust in the Commission and may affect companies' willingness not only to apply for leniency but also to cooperate in general.

The Leniency Notice does not only acknowledge that leniency applicants might be dissuaded from cooperating with the Commission under the Notice if this might impair their position in civil proceedings – as compared to companies who do not cooperate. It also states that such undesirable effect would significantly harm the public interest in ensuring effective public enforcement of Article 101 TFEU in cartel cases and thus its subsequent or parallel effective private enforcement. Furthermore, the Commission acknowledges that the Notice will create legitimate expectations and that, normally, the public disclosure of documents and written or recorded statements received in the context of the Notice would undermine certain public or private interests, for example the protection of the purpose of inspections and investigations, within the meaning of Article 4 of the Transparency Regulation.[104] It is true that the Court's case law in cases such as *Pfleiderer* and *Donau Chemie* is moving in another direction,[105] but the fact remains that the Commission has maintained the wording in its Leniency Notice, and although the Court may consider that the Commission does nothing wrong when publishing the information contained in the corporate statements – as long as there are no verbatim quotations – any trust in the Commission is definitely in the balance.

Both the *AKZO* and *Degussa* cases concern the Commission's decision to publish information submitted under the leniency programme, and it is clear from those cases that the applicants had presumed that such information would be kept secret. It is fair to assume that this presumption played a part in the process leading up to the decision to file a leniency application. In *AKZO*, the applicants claimed that the confidential treatment of information voluntarily submitted within the frame of a leniency application is essential to the proper functioning of the Commission's leniency programme and, accordingly, for the effectiveness of EU law on cartels.[106] This is also what the Commission argues when it refuses to grant access to its cartel files, even when the request does not cover the entire file but only the statement of contents. While there may be reasons justifying the differences in the Commission's approach, and while the Commission needs to find a way to promote both private and public enforcement, it is balancing on a fine wire. Either the information submitted by the companies must be protected in order to ensure the attractiveness of the leniency programme and the companies' willingness to cooperate, or it must not.

To conclude, the Court's recent case law gives the Commission better control over the information to be shared with the public by allowing it (i) to rely on a general presumption of confidentiality when receiving requests for access under the Transparency Regulation, and (ii) a broad margin of discretion when determining what information to publish in its infringement decisions. However, as

[104] The Commission's Leniency Notice, 40.
[105] Case C-360/09, *Pfleiderer AG v Bundeskartellamt*, EU:C:2011:389; and Case C-536/11, *Bundeswettbewerbsbehörde v Donau Chemie AG and Others*, EU:C:2013:366.
[106] *AKZO* (n 28) para 48.

has been discussed in this concluding section, better control does not equal less tension between the public and the private enforcement systems. The following chapter will examine the leniency system and whether the best way to ease this tension is to expand the categories of documents to be protected from disclosure to cover all documents submitted by the leniency applicants and not only the leniency statements, or to extend leniency into the field of private enforcement, allowing the companies that receive immunity from fines to also receive immunity from civil liability.

9

The Survival of the Leniency System

> The challenge in attacking hard-core cartels is to penetrate their cloak of secrecy. To encourage a member of a cartel to confess and implicate its co-conspirators with first-hand, direct 'insider' evidence about their clandestine meetings and communications, an enforcement agency may promise a smaller fine, shorter sentence, less restrictive order, or complete amnesty.[1]

The Commission's desire to preserve the effectiveness of its leniency programme runs like a connecting thread through this work. Any unwillingness on the Commission's side to part with information is to a lesser or greater extent motivated by concern for the well-being of the leniency programme. This chapter examines the merits of any such concern, and whether any changes to the leniency system could make its effectiveness less dependent on whether or not the Commission discloses evidence from its case files. Furthermore, it examines whether there are other methods that could complement or replace the leniency system in order to ease any tension between private and public enforcement of the EU competition rules.

In principle, the combination of private and public enforcement should increase the deterrent effect of the competition rules. If companies engaging in cartel activity risk not only having to pay a hefty fine but also having to compensate the victims of the cartel, this should make them think twice before colluding with their competitors. As noted by Balsaningham, private actions may serve as an additional financial burden on top of the fines imposed within the public enforcement scheme, and therefore increase deterrence.[2] This was also the view reflected in the Green Paper preceding the Damages Directive, which stated that Articles 101 and 102 TFEU are enforced by both public and private enforcement, and that the two forms are part of a common enforcement system and serve the same aims: to deter anti-competitive practices forbidden by antitrust law; and to protect firms and consumers from these practices and any damage caused by them.[3] Both private and

[1] OECD Report, *Fighting Hard Core Cartels: Harm, Effective Sanctions and Leniency Programmes* (OECD 2002).

[2] B Balsaningham, *The EU Leniency Policy; Reconciling Effectiveness and Fairness* (Alphen aan den Rijn, Wolters Kluwer, 2017) 151.

[3] Thus indicating that the private enforcement rules pursue a twofold aim: (i) to deter companies from engaging in cartel activities, and (ii) to ensure corrective justice by compensating those who

public enforcement are important tools to create and sustain a competitive economy, the Commission declared.[4] This view is also reflected in the preamble to the Damages Directive, according to which full effectiveness of Articles 101 and 102 TFEU cannot be achieved unless anyone can claim compensation before national courts for the harm caused to them. However, recent developments suggest that the public and private enforcement pillars, as they are now framed, do not necessarily ensure the required stability to the EU antitrust enforcement system. As noted by Wardhaugh, effective cartel enforcement does not stand on two but three limbs: public and private enforcement procedures, and leniency programmes. An effective anti-cartel scheme will appropriately balance these components, ensuring that one will not hinder the efficacy of another.[5]

In the EU, the third limb, or pillar, was introduced in 1996 through the adoption of the Commission's Leniency Notice.[6] Since then, the Commission has come to rely heavily on its leniency programme, under which the colluding companies themselves inform the Commission of the cartel, provide the evidence required for the Commission to carry out surprise inspections and cooperate fully throughout the investigation. In exchange, they receive immunity from or a reduction in fines.[7] As noted by Beaton-Wells, the use of leniency policies is justified by the authorities generally on the grounds that it is the most effective and least costly mechanism for detecting and prosecuting activity that is systematic, deliberate and covert. It is also seen as contributing to the deterrence of cartel conduct.[8]

However, as noted by Jaspers, leniency policies do not operate in a vacuum; they interact with other legislation and enforcement, such as criminal liability and private damages actions.[9] This may be the reason why, despite the initial success

have suffered harm. This was confirmed by the Commission in the subsequent White Paper, where it declared that 'Effective remedies for private parties also increase the likelihood that a greater number of illegal restrictions of competition will be detected and that the infringers will be held liable. Improving compensatory justice would therefore inherently also produce beneficial effects in terms of deterrence of future infringements and greater compliance with EC antitrust rules.' White Paper on Damages Actions for Breach of the EC Antitrust Rules, COM(2008) 165 final. This stance has been confirmed by the Court on numerous occasions, most recently in Case C-435/18, *Otis GmbH and Others v Land Oberösterreich and Others*, EU:C:2019:1069, para 24.

[4] Green Paper on Damages for Breach of the EC Antitrust rules, COM(2005) 672 final, 1.1.

[5] B Wardhaugh, 'Cartel Leniency and Effective Compensation in Europe: The Aftermath of Pfleiderer' (2013) 19(3) *Web JCLI*.

[6] At the time, the private enforcement pillar was much weaker than its public equivalent, and it may be questioned whether the EU system was actually standing on three limbs when the leniency programme was introduced.

[7] According to Forrester and Berghe, save for two decisions, all cartel decisions adopted since 2000 (and at least up until the publication of their paper) appear to have involved at least one leniency applicant. See I Forrester and P Berghe, 'Leniency: The Poisoned Chalice or the Pot at the End of the Rainbow?' in C Beaton-Wells and C Tran (eds), *Anti-cartel Enforcement in a Contemporary Age: Leniency Religion* (Oxford, Hart Publishing, 2015) 159, 160.

[8] C Beaton-Wells, 'Leniency Policies: Revolution or Religion?' in Beaton-Wells and Tran (eds), *Anti-cartel Enforcement* (n 7) 3, 3.

[9] JD Jaspers, 'Leniency in Exchange for Cartel Confessions' (2020) 17(1) *European Journal of Criminology* 106, 111.

of the leniency programme, there are indications that the balance has been tilted, and that companies are becoming less inclined to apply for immunity.[10] As will be further discussed in this chapter, there may be a number of reasons for this, but one of them is most likely the ever-growing risk of having to compensate cartel victims. Companies apply for immunity in order to escape sanctions. If, by drawing the Commission's attention to a cartel, the company escapes a fine but instead has to pay damages that cannot be calculated beforehand but that may well meet or even exceed the potential fine, it may choose to keep the cartel from the eyes of the Commission.[11]

Relevant to this study is the fact that any changes in the Commission's policies as regards either the information to be disclosed in its cartel decisions, or the granting of access to third parties or NCAs may have a direct impact on undertakings' willingness to report their illegal behaviour to the Commission. As noted by the General Court in *AKZO* and *Evonik Degussa*, it is for the Commission to balance the interests of maintaining the attractiveness of the leniency system against those of cartel victims when drafting the non-confidential versions of its infringement decisions.[12] That said, despite the absence of a *de jure* hierarchy between public and private enforcement, Balsaningham argues, referring to the Opinion of Advocate General Mázak in *Pfleiderer*, that public enforcement is currently of greater importance than private enforcement, pointing to the fact that the issuance of public infringement decisions, on the back of which the vast majority of private actions are brought, is undoubtedly dependent on an effective leniency programme.[13] Yet, according to Ysewyn and Kahmann, the number of leniency applications received by the Commission has reduced by almost 50 per cent over the last few years. In their article, the authors also refer to a survey among a number of practitioners with allegedly extensive leniency experience, declaring that an overwhelming majority of the participants had sensed a decrease in interest from their clients to apply for leniency in recent years.[14] The increased exposure to civil damages claims was the factor most frequently mentioned in the survey.[15]

[10] See eg J Ysewyn and S Kahmann, 'The Decline and Fall of the Leniency Programme in Europe' (2018) 1 *Concurrences* 44, 44; and R Polley, 'Is the Continued Success of Leniency in Cartel Cases in Danger? Some Comments from a Private Practitioner's Perspective' *CPI Antitrust Chronicle* September 2015(1).

[11] Yet, as noted by Balsaningham, while the threat of private actions may reduce the incentives to defect, the risk of damages if the cartel member does not defect and the cartel is later detected diminishes the incentives to continue participating in a cartel. Balsaningham, *The EU Leniency Policy* (n 2) 165.

[12] Case T-345/12, *AKZO Nobel NV and Others v European Commission*, EU:T:2015:50; and Case T-341/12 *Evonik Degussa GmbH v European Commission*, EU:T:2015:51.

[13] Balsaningham, *The EU Leniency Policy* (n 2) 175. Reference is made to the Opinion of AG Mázak in Case C-360/09, *Pfleiderer AG v Bundeskartellamt*, EU:C:2010:782, paras 40–41.

[14] 30 practitioners, of whom 83% considered the risk of damages claims to be the major deterrent.

[15] Ysewyn and Kahmann, 'Decline and Fall' (n 10) 45. The authors refer to *Global Competition Review, Rating Enforcement*. The survey referred to was prepared by Brussels Matters for its meeting 'The European antitrust leniency calculus c. 2016: still worth it?' (Brussels 16 June 2016), referred to in WPJ Wils, 'Private Enforcement of EU Antitrust Law and its Relationship with Public Enforcement: Past, Present and Future' (2017) 40(1) *World Competition Law and Economics Review* 3, 41. The issue

This chapter examines the merits of these claims and whether any decline in leniency applications is primarily motivated by the fear of having to compensate cartel victims. Finding that the increased focus on private enforcement is indeed one of the main reasons behind any such decline, the chapter continues with a discussion of how to best avoid any threats to the leniency system. It is suggested that there are at least three possible ways to tackle the problem. The first option is to ban third party disclosure of all evidence submitted by the leniency applicant. Second, the stakes may be raised through increased corporate fines and the possibility to impose fines or other sanctions on natural persons. The third possibility is to extend the leniency system to also cover immunity from damages claims.[16] It is suggested that bans on disclosure or other attempts to keep evidence from cartel victims may not be the most appropriate or effective tool. While more severe public sanctions may have an effect on the attractiveness of the leniency system, it is nevertheless proposed that the first leniency applicant should be granted immunity not only from fines but also from any liability to compensate the cartel victims. This in return for an obligation to provide cartel victims with the evidence at the leniency applicant's disposal. The extension of the leniency system to also cover immunity from civil liability would not only help restore the attractiveness of the leniency programme, but also ensure that cartel victims access the evidence required to prove their loss, thereby reinforcing the private enforcement regime.

I. The EU Leniency System

In July 1994, the Commission adopted its decision in the *Cartonboard* case, imposing fines on a number of companies for involvement in a complex and long-lasting cartel. In its decision, the Commission noted that 'By its very nature, the cartel was a clandestine activity. Considerable efforts were made to conceal its existence and to ensure (not always successfully, however) that incriminating evidence was not kept.'[17] Although the statement relates to the specific circumstances of the case at hand, its essence would probably be applicable to most cartels. Cartel activity is clandestine, and cartel members make considerable efforts to conceal or destroy any incriminating evidence. As noted by the Court in *Aalborg Portland*, since the prohibition on restrictive practices and the penalties infringers may

was also addressed by a Working Party of the OECD as recently as in June 2018. In his report to the Working Party meeting, Snyder takes note of the fact that some competition enforcers have expressed concern that the number of leniency applications, particularly relating to international cartels, has been declining. See B Snyder, 'Challenges to Leniency Posed by the Proliferation of Leniency Programs and Private Enforcement', Paper submitted as background material for Item 3 at the 127th Meeting of the OECD Working Party No 3 on Cooperation and Enforcement of 5 June 2018.

[16] C Caufmann, 'The Interaction of Leniency Programmes and Actions for Damages' (2011) 7(2) *The Competition Law Review* 181.

[17] *Cartonboard* (Case IV/C/33.833) Commission Decision 94/601/EC [1994] OJ L243/1, para 116.

incur are well known, the activities involved in those practices and agreements often take place in a clandestine fashion; it is common for meetings to be held in secret, frequently in a non-member country, and for the associated documentation to be reduced to a minimum.[18] Yet despite the secretive nature of cartels and the efforts made not to leave any paper trails, the Commission is known as an aggressive and diligent enforcer of the EU competition rules. During the period January 2010 to September 2019, 57 cartel cases were decided by the Commission, and fines of more than €18 billion were imposed.[19] The Commission's leniency policy is one reason behind these figures.

Looking back, the Commission has not always been considered an aggressive enforcer. Articles 101 and 102 TFEU have formed part of the legal framework ever since the Treaty of Rome, and already at the outset it was recognised that price-fixing cartels should be the Commission's primary target. The reality was otherwise. While there were a few landmark cases where the Court was allowed the chance to give life and structure to the rules governing cartels, the Commission did not deal with many such cases in the early years. Instead, and rightly so, it focused its resources on finding a correct approach to dealing with often complex and difficult antitrust issues in the course of notification procedures. In the majority of these cases, the procedure resulted in the publication of worked-out and detailed exemption decisions, providing guidance on the Commission's competition policy for a particular sector or business practice.[20] In fact, it was only after more than 30 years of dealing mainly with notification procedures, and having witnessed the positive results from the introduction of sentencing guidelines and leniency programmes in the United States, that the Commission decided that the time was ripe to change its enforcement strategies and focus its resources on pursuing cartels and other hard-core infringements of the EU competition rules.

In 1996, the Commission launched its own leniency programme, adopting a notice designed to destabilise cartels and divide cartel infringers by giving companies incentive to cheat on the other cartel members and incriminate themselves.[21] The adoption of the Leniency Notice led to a sharp increase in the number of detected cartels.[22] Following a review of its application, the Commission decided

[18] Joined Cases C-204/00 P, C-205/00 P, C-211/00 P, C-213/00 P, C-217/00 P and C-219/00 P, *Aalborg Portland A/S and Others v Commission of the European Communities*, EU:C:2004:6.

[19] http://ec.europa.eu/competition/cartels/statistics/statistics.pdf.

[20] A Riley, *The Modernisation of EU Anti-Cartel Enforcement: Will the Commission Grasp the Opportunity?*, CEPS Special Report (January 2010) 11.

[21] In its 1996 Notice, the Commission acknowledges that companies engaging in cartel activity may want to terminate their infringement and report it to the Commission but are deterred from doing so by the risk of incurring large fines. It is further stated that it is in the Community interest to grant favourable treatment to leniency applicants, and that the interest of consumers and citizens in ensuring that such practices are detected and prohibited outweigh the interest of fining those companies that cooperate, thereby enabling the Commission to detect and prohibit cartels.

[22] J Ratliff, *EC Cartel Leniency Programme*, available at www.wilmerhale.com/files/Publication/515f785c-9663-44d7-bf82-45c19f099fd9/Presentation/PublicationAttachment/465fc5e4-addb-4a49-

to adopt a new and revised Notice in 2002, in which a lower evidence standard was applied and immunity was extended to undertakings already under investigation. As a result of the Commission's efforts, leniency now plays a prominent role in EU cartel enforcement.[23] According to Wils, as many as 91 per cent of the cartel decisions adopted by the Commission during the period 2011–15 involved immunity.[24]

The EU leniency system sets out a framework for rewarding cooperation by companies that have participated or are participating in secret cartels. The current Notice, adopted in 2006, establishes two kinds of immunities: total and partial immunity. In order to obtain total immunity, the self-reporting company must be the first one to inform the Commission of an undetected cartel by providing sufficient information to allow the Commission to carry out dawn raids at the premises of the companies allegedly participating in the cartel. If the Commission is already in possession of enough information to launch an inspection, or has already undertaken one, the company must provide evidence that enables the Commission to prove the cartel infringement. In all cases, the company must also fully cooperate with the Commission throughout its procedure, provide it with all evidence in its possession, and put an end to the infringement immediately. Leniency is not granted to companies that have taken steps to coerce others to join or stay in the cartel.[25] Companies that do not qualify for total immunity may still benefit from partial immunity, or a reduction in fines, if they provide evidence that represents 'significant added value' to that already in the Commission's possession and have terminated their participation in the cartel. Evidence is considered to be of a 'significant added value' when it reinforces the Commission's ability to prove the infringement.[26] The first company to meet these conditions is granted a 30 to 50 per cent reduction, the second 20 to 30 per cent and subsequent companies up to 20 per cent.

In order for a company to be granted immunity, it must provide the Commission with a corporate statement.[27] The statement may be either written or oral and must include, in so far as it is known to the company, (i) a detailed description of the alleged cartel arrangement, (ii) names and contact details of the companies and individuals involved in the conspiracy, and (iii) information on which other competition authorities have been approached or are intended to be approached by the company. As for oral corporate statements, they should be

8bd7-4c4c179962cb/ECLENIENCY_Ratliff_Nov2004.pdf; and WPJ Wils, 'The Use of Leniency in EU Cartel Enforcement: An Assessment after Twenty Years' (2016) 39(3) *World Competition: Law and Economics Review* 327.

[23] Wils, 'The Use of Leniency' (n 22). In 2006, the Commission adopted a new Notice on leniency that still applies.

[24] Wils, 'The Use of Leniency' (n 22).

[25] The Leniency Notice, 13.

[26] Ibid 25.

[27] Ibid 9.

clear, factual and to the point, with precise and sufficiently detailed information. In addition to the corporate statement, the company is required to submit any pre-existing evidence relating to the alleged cartel that is in its possession or available to it at the time of the submission, including in particular any evidence contemporaneous to the infringement.

While the leniency applicant may receive conditional immunity from fines in the early stages of the investigation, the final decision is not made until the end of the administrative procedure. The decision to grant immunity or a reduction in fines is made by the Commissioners simultaneously with the infringement decision.

II. Necessary Features in a Successful Leniency Programme

The Commission adopted its leniency programme in 1996, but it was not until the programme was revised in 2002 that the number of applications really took off. This is an experience shared with the US authorities. As will be discussed further in section VII, the US Antitrust Division has maintained a leniency programme since 1978, but it was only following a substantial revision of the programme in 1993 that the Division started receiving leniency applications. Designing and maintaining an effective leniency programme thus requires careful consideration.[28] Whilst leniency programmes may raise the probability of detection, poorly designed programmes may actually reduce the deterrent impact of fines.[29] For example, and as noted by Marvão and Spagnalo, a generous leniency policy combined with mild sanctions is likely to maintain or increase the deadweight losses from administration, prosecution and litigation costs, with no balancing benefits for the taxpayer.[30] Given this, the following section presents some of the features that are generally considered necessary to achieve and maintain a successful leniency programme.

[28] In its Communication to the European Parliament and the Council preceding the proposal for the ECN+ Directive, the Commission acknowledges that a well-designed leniency programme is an essential tool for enhancing enforcement against the most serious infringements, in particular secret price-fixing and market-sharing cartels. Communication from the European Commission to the European Parliament and the Council, Ten Years of Antitrust Enforcement under Regulation 1/2003: Achievements and Future Perspectives.

[29] Office of Fair Trading, *An Assessment of Discretionary Penalties Regimes*, Final Report prepared by London Economic (October 2009). This may be the case, for example, if leniency is administered too generously.

[30] C Marvão and G Spagnolo, 'What Do We Know about the Effectiveness of Leniency Policies? A Survey of the Empirical and Experimental Evidence' in Beaton-Wells and Tran (eds) (n 7) *Anti-cartel Enforcement* 57, 79

A. Visible Enforcement Activity and Severe Penalties

One important aspect – that is related not so much to the framing of the leniency programme as to the activities of the public enforcers – concerns the need for competition agencies to be sufficiently active for cartel members to consider that there is a significant risk of being detected and punished if they do not apply for leniency. As Wils points out, 'In the case of a cartel or other collective violation, leniency will work only if one cartel member either believes that the cartel risks being detected and punished without leniency or fears that at least one cartel member may hold such belief.'[31]

The offer of immunity is only as strong as the size of the potential threat of detection and the sanction otherwise incurred. The issue of how to create deterrence, and thereby also the incentive to apply for leniency, has been addressed by many writers. One of them is Baker, who points out that consistency and comprehensiveness in enforcement are very important and that 'enforcement must be frequent and highly visible'.[32] Effective deterrence requires that those who might be tempted to take illegal action not only believe that there is some reasonable probability of their being caught, but that, if this happens, the consequences are likely to be grave.[33] According to Parker and Lehamnn Nielsen, many business managers do not make, or act on, cost–benefit calculations about compliance until something – like a regulatory enforcement action or publicly reported breach or accident – brings the risks of non-compliance to their attention.[34] On a similar note, Barnett declares that deterrence only works when the consequences are real. To deter cartels effectively, antitrust enforcers must aggressively and predictably prosecute cartelists and use the full range of weapons in the enforcement arsenal.[35] As Scordamaglia-Tousis puts it, the goal of effective deterrence depends on two components: the level of the fines and the likelihood of being caught.[36] The deterrent effects of any antitrust enforcement scheme thus depend upon whether companies actually believe that they may be caught.[37]

[31] WPJ Wils, *Efficiency and Justice in European Antitrust Enforcement* (Oxford, Hart Publishing, 2008) 419–20.

[32] D Baker, 'Punishment for Cartel Participation in the US: A Special Model?' in C Beaton-Wells and A Ezrachi (eds), *Criminalising Cartels – Critical Studies of an International Movement* (Oxford, Hart Publishing, 2011) 35.

[33] Ibid.

[34] C Parker and V Lehmann Nielsen, 'Deterrence and the Impact of Calculative Thinking on Business Compliance with Competition and Consumer Regulation' (2011) 56(2) *The Antitrust Bulletin* 377, 386.

[35] *Seven Steps to Better Cartel Enforcement*, speech made by TO Barnett, Assistant Attorney General of the Antitrust Division of the US Department of Justice, at the 11th Annual Competition Law & Policy Workshop, European Union Institute in Florence Italy (2 June 2006), available at www.justice.gov/atr/speech/seven-steps-better-cartel-enforcement#N_7_.

[36] A Scordamaglia-Tousis, *EU Cartel Enforcement – Reconciling Effective Public Enforcement with Fundamental Rights* (Alphen aan den Rijn, Wolters Kluwer, 2013) 12.

[37] JB Baker, 'The Case for Antitrust Enforcement' (2003) 17(4) *Journal of Economic Perspectives* 27, 40. See also Parker and Lehmann Nielsen (n 34), where the authors argue that enforcement probability is more important than sanction severity.

Not only do the authorities need to be perceived as aggressive enforcers, Harrington and Chang argue that competition authorities must also continue to actively pursue non-leniency cases after the implementation of a leniency programme. This can be challenging to a competition authority that receives a significant number of leniency applications, but according to the authors it is necessary in order to maintain the attractiveness of the leniency programme. If resources are used to handle leniency cases then fewer resources are available to pursue non-leniency cases effectively. However, according to Harrington and Chang, a change in the likelihood of being sanctioned for a non-leniency case has implications for the leniency process itself. A cartel member will apply for leniency only if it believes that doing so is better than running the risk of being caught and paying full penalties, they argue. Thus, according to the authors, it is not only necessary that the competition authority is perceived as an aggressive enforcer; part of 'the aggressiveness' must also derive from non-leniency cases after the adoption of a leniency programme.[38]

If penalties are too weak or applied too infrequently then firms may disregard an offer to relax them. This, on the other hand, means that the incentives may increase if the competition authority raises the size of the fines and increases the number of completed cases, and where such action is well publicised.[39] An enforcement agency may see few results from a leniency programme before it has succeeded in imposing a significant penalty on a cartel. The Commission has embraced this stance, and combined the leniency programme with fining guidelines adopted with the express view of increasing the deterrent effect of the competition rules. When the guidelines now in force were adopted in 2006, Kroes, Commissioner at the time, declared:

> These revised Guidelines will better reflect the overall economic significance of the infringement as well as the share of each company involved. The three main changes – the new entry fee, the link between the fine and the duration of the infringement, and the increase for repeat offenders – send three clear signals to companies. Don't break the anti-trust rules; if you do, stop it as quickly as possible, and once you've stopped, don't do it again. Of course, if the Commission's leniency policy applies, companies should also report the infringement without delay. If companies do not pay attention to these signals, they will pay a very high price.[40]

The same year as the revised guidelines were adopted, the Commission issued three decisions in which the undertakings with the highest fines were sentenced to penalties in the three-digit millions. In the *Bleaching chemicals* cartel,

[38] JE Harrington Jr and MH Chang, 'When Can We Expect a Corporate Leniency Program to Result in Fewer Cartels?' (2015) 58(2) *The Journal of Law & Economics* 417, 443.

[39] A Stephan and A Nikpay, 'Leniency Decision-Making from a Corporate Perspective: Complex Realities' in Beaton-Wells and Tran (eds), *Anti-cartel Enforcement* (n 7) 139, 141.

[40] Ibid.

Solvay was fined €167 million;[41] in the *Methacrylates case*, Arkema was fined €219.1 million;[42] and in the *Synthetic rubber case*, Eni received a fine of €272.3 million.[43] This, however, was only the starting point. Since then, the fines imposed by the Commission have increased further. Today, the record fine imposed on a single undertaking is €4.34 billion, imposed on Google for breach of Article 102 TFEU.[44] Yet, and as will be discussed in section III.D, in the study carried out by Jaspers, respondents indicated that civil litigation could lead to corporate liability for damages up to four or five times the amount of (public) financial penalties imposed by the competition authority.[45]

While a risk of detection coupled with high fines is generally considered to be a necessary ingredient of an effective leniency system, it should be noted that a recent study by Bignoni et al suggests that the risk of detection is not necessarily a key element. Instead they argue that with leniency policies offering immunity to the first reporting party, a high fine is the main determinant of deterrence, having a strong effect even when the probability of exogenous detection is zero.[46] Thus, the leniency system itself guarantees a risk of detection if the sanctions are severe, and deterrence appears to be mainly driven by 'distrust', that is the fear of partners' deviating and reporting. Absent leniency, the probability of detection and the expected fine matter more, and low fines are exploited to punish defections.[47] In 2014, Marvão and Spagnolo carried out a survey of existing studies on the effectiveness of leniency, which supported this theory. According to their survey, most experiments suggested that cartel deterrence effects of well-designed and well-administered leniency policies tend to be positive but rather modest, unless sanctions for non-applicants are really severe or monetary rewards are introduced. Furthermore, they noted, most recent experiments suggested that severe sanctions were the crucial precondition for the effectiveness of a leniency policy, allowing it to produce substantial cartel deterrence effects even when the probability of a cartel's being detected without reports was zero.[48] Thus, while visible

[41] *Hydrogen peroxide* (Case COMP/F/38.620) Commission Decision 2006/903/EC [2006] OJ L353/54.

[42] *Methacrylates* (Case COMP/F/38.645) Commission Decision C(2006) 2098 final [2006] OJ L322/20.

[43] *Synthetic rubber* (Case COMP/38.628) Commission Decision 2009/C 86/06 [2006] OJ C86/7.

[44] Imposed on Google for illegal practices regarding Android mobile devices. The decision to impose a fine, which has been appealed, came less than a year after the Commission had fined the company €2.42 billion for abusing its dominant position by giving illegal advantage to its own comparison shopping service Google Shopping. The record fine imposed on a single company engaged in cartel activity amounts to €1.01 billion, a fine imposed on Daimler for participation in a price-fixing cartel among truck producers (the total fines imposed on the cartel members amounted to €3.81 billion). See at http://ec.europa.eu/competition/cartels/statistics/statistics.pdf.

[45] Jaspers, 'Leniency' (n 9) 120.

[46] This is also argued by Balsaningham, *The EU Leniency Policy* (n 2) 164: 'By increasing the fine, it is possible to enhance the deterrence of the leniency programme, even if the likelihood of detection remains unchanged.'

[47] M Bignoni et al, *Trust, Leniency and Deterrence*, available at www.konkurrensverket.se/globalassets/publikationer/workingpaper/working_paper_2014-2.pdf.

[48] Marvão and Spagnolo, 'What Do We Know' (n 30) 80.

and aggressive enforcement of the competition rules increases the attractiveness of the leniency programme, severe sanctions appear to be a precondition for its effectiveness.

B. Transparency and Predictability

It can be assumed that a fair number of potential leniency applicants will decide to come forward and self-report only if they can be certain that their position, having revealed the cartel conduct, is at least going to be no worse than the expected outcome in the absence of the leniency application. In order to attract leniency applicants and destabilise cartels, the leniency programme should be sufficiently transparent and predictable to enable potential applicants to predict how they will be treated should they decide to apply for leniency. Clarity, certainty and priority are critical, as firms may be more likely to come forward if the conditions and the likely benefits of doing so are clear.[49] To maximise the incentives for defection and encourage cartels to break down more quickly, it is important not only that the first one to confess receives the 'best deal', but also that the terms of the deal be as clear as possible at the outset.

A general offer to reduce penalties in exchange for information may thus not be enough to encourage firms to come forward. The benefits of remaining with the cartel may then appear larger and more certain than the unknown reward that would result from confessing. The original US leniency programme, which made only a relatively general offer, produced only about one case per year. One of the key changes in 1993 that made the US programme more effective was to make complete amnesty automatic for the first applicant if certain clearly specified conditions were met.[50] As noted by Forrester and Berghe, any aspect of a leniency system that dilutes immunity from fines for the first applicant significantly reduces the incentives to come forward. Leniency is replacing the trust among cartel participants with the trust in public authorities.[51]

However, it is important to distinguish between the possibility to foresee the effects of the leniency application – if I am the first to self-report, cooperate with the Commission and can show that I did not force my co-conspirators to join the cartel, I will receive immunity – and the possibility to calculate the possible fine should I decide not to apply for leniency. Whereas most scholars seem to agree

[49] See eg OFT, *An Assessment of Discretionary Penalties Regimes* (n 29) 22. Furthermore, the US Department of Justice has declared that prospective leniency applicants will come forward in direct proportion to the predictability and certainty of whether they will be accepted into the programme. A O'Brien, 'Leadership of Leniency' in Beaton-Wells and Tran (eds), *Anti-cartel Enforcement* (n 7) 17, 25, where reference is made to SD Hammond, *Detecting and Deterring Cartel Activity through an Effective Leniency Program* (International Workshop on Cartels, Brighton, 21–22 November 2000), available at www.justice.gov/atr/speech/detecting-and-deterring-cartel-activity-through-effective-leniency-program.

[50] OECD Report, *Fighting Hard Core Cartels* (n 1) 8.

[51] Forrester and Berghe, 'Leniency' (n 7) 169.

that leniency programmes should provide for certainty and predictability as to the conditions for immunity, the views appear to diverge as to whether potential leniency applicants should also be able to predict the possible fines, and thus also to calculate the risk of not self-reporting.

Stephan and Nikpay consider the requirement of transparency and predictability to encompass not only predictability concerning the reduction in the sanction, but also the possibility for the potential leniency applicant to assess the amount of the fine or the severity of the sanction, should it decide not to apply for leniency but take the risk of being caught and sanctioned. They are therefore critical of what they view as the Commission's deliberate policy of uncertainty when it comes to the calculation of fines. They refer to a statement made by Kroes, where she declared that she could not 'see how allowing potential infringers to calculate the likely cost/benefit ratio of a certain cartel in advance will somehow contribute to a sustained policy of deterrence and zero tolerance'.[52] Kroes's view on predictability is also in line with the view of the General Court, which in the case of *BPB plc v Commission* made the following statement:

> Moreover, it is important to ensure that fines are not easily foreseeable by economic operators. If the Commission were required to indicate in its decision the figures relating to the method of calculating the amount of fines, the deterrent effect of those fines would be undermined. If the amount of the fine were the result of a calculation which followed a simple arithmetical formula, undertakings would be able to predict the possible penalty and to compare it with the profit that they would derive from the infringement of the competition rules.[53]

Furthermore, and as noted by the Court in *Chalkor*,[54] the fining guidelines, which form rules of practice from which the administration may not depart in an individual case without giving reasons, merely describe the method used by the Commission to examine infringements and the criteria that it requires to be taken into account in setting the amount of a fine. This leaves the Commission with a margin of discretion, both as regards the choice of factors taken into account in the application of the criteria mentioned in the guidelines and as regards the assessment of those factors. Thus, the Court concluded, while the Commission has issued fining guidelines in order to ensure the transparency and impartiality of its decisions, they are not intended to allow the companies to actually calculate the possible fine.[55]

[52] Stephan and Nikpay, 'Leniency Decision-Making' (n 39) 143. Reference is made to N Kroes, 'The First Hundred Days, 40th Anniversary of the Studienvereinigung Kartellrecht 1965–2005', International Forum on European Competition Law, Brussels (7 April 2005), available at http://europa.eu/rapid/press-release_SPEECH-05-205_en.htm.

[53] Case T-53/03, *BPB plc v Commission of the European Communities*, EU:T:2008:254, para 336.

[54] Case 386/10 P, *Chalkor AP Expergasias Metallon v European Commission*, EU:C:2011:815.

[55] Ibid paras 60–62. It should be noted, however, that, according to Wils, one of the reasons for introducing the fining guidelines was the desire to offer potential leniency applicants a somewhat higher degree of predictability as to the amount of the fines normally imposed: see Wils, 'The Use of Leniency' (n 22) 330.

Wils shares this view, declaring, inter alia, that 'because the marginal hurtfulness of fines increases with their amount ... undertakings tend to be risk averters. This implies that a more indeterminate structure for setting fines generates more deterrence.'[56] Connor pursues a similar line and lists the main economic arguments in favour of uncertainty about expected fines as (i) a range of possible fines will discourage risk-averse firms from violations because they will focus on the high end of the range, and (ii) cartel formation is less likely if diverse firms try to collude, including firms with inconsistent conjectures about the costs of being caught.[57]

To conclude, whereas the views diverge on the benefits of allowing potential leniency applicants to assess the size of the potential fines, there appears to be consensus as regards the benefits of maintaining a leniency programme with clear rules as regards the conditions for obtaining total or partial immunity.

C. Total Immunity from Fines

A general offer to reduce penalties in exchange for information may not be enough to encourage firms to come forward. The benefits of remaining with the cartel may appear larger and more certain than the unknown reward that would result from confessing. One of the critical 1993 changes that made the US leniency programme more effective was to make complete amnesty automatic for the first applicant if certain clearly specified conditions are met.[58] This is in line with the reasoning pursued by Connor and Miller, who consider the idea of granting a successful leniency applicant total immunity to be well accepted. They refer to game-theory models of the Prisoner's Dilemma, which show that, under a wide array of conditions, full leniency reduces cartel stability; it induces members of functioning cartels to defect by confessing to antitrust authorities.[59] However, a successful leniency programme not only requires that the first applicant is granted total or near total immunity. Any penalty imposed on the first applicant should be much less than that imposed on later applicants. While the first applicant may well be relieved from the duty of having to pay fines, the one next in line should not also be able to receive total or near total immunity, as this would not achieve the desired aim of sparking a race to the competition authority.[60]

[56] WPJ Wils, 'The European Commission's 2006 Guidelines on Antitrust Fines: A Legal and Economic Analysis' (2007) 30(2) *World Competition: Law and Economics Review* 197, 210.

[57] JM Connor and DJ Miller, 'Determinants of EC Antitrust Fines for Members of Global Cartels', Presentation at the 3rd LEAR Conference on the Economics of Competition Law, available at www.learlab.com/conference2009/documents/Predicting%20EC%20Fines%20for%20Members%20of%20Global%20Cartels%209-11-09.pdf.

[58] OECD Report, *Fighting Hard Core Cartels* (n 1) 8.

[59] Connor and Miller, 'Determinants of EC Antitrust Fines' (n 57).

[60] See eg Stephan and Nikpay, 'Leniency Decision-Making' (n 39) 152.

D. Immunity from Individual Sanctions

As noted by Stephan and Nikpay, cartels are organised by individuals, not firms. This means that the threat underpinning most leniency policies – administrative fines against the company in question – does not constitute an immediate threat to the individual decision-makers. By the time the cartel is caught, fines are imposed and subsequent appeals are held, these persons may well no longer work for the firm.[61] An increasing number of jurisdictions have therefore introduced individual sanctions, such as imprisonment or director disqualification. This in turn means that the incentives to apply for corporate leniency may diminish when those administering the cartel have a personal interest in keeping it secret in order to avoid individual sanctions. When the US leniency programme was revised during the mid-1990s, a leniency policy was also introduced for individuals. If an individual is the first to self-report illegal market conduct, he or she can be granted immunity from any criminal sanction that would otherwise have been levied. The programme also encompasses the possibility of considering statutory or informal immunity from criminal sanctions, this being decided on a case-by-case basis.

It would seem safe as a matter of logic to argue that the possibility also to grant leniency to individuals will affect the number of corporate leniency applications received by the competition authorities, at least in those jurisdictions where individual sanctions not only exist on paper but are actually imposed on managers and employees engaging in cartel activities. Few managers would take the decision to let the company self-report if that would entail that they themselves were sent to prison. An effective leniency policy thus requires not only corporate but also individual leniency.

E. Protection of Information Provided

A question that is not only key to ensuring an effective leniency system but also of crucial importance to this work, is how to ensure a balance between the leniency applicant's interest in protecting the information provided during the course of the investigation and at the same time promoting the interests of a transparent administration and an effective private enforcement system. The recitals to the Leniency Notice acknowledge that, in addition to submitting pre-existing documents, undertakings may provide the Commission with voluntary presentations of their knowledge of the cartel and their role therein prepared specifically for submission under the leniency programme. According to the recitals, these corporate statements have proved to be useful for the effective investigation and termination of cartel infringements, and the Commission declares that applicants should not be discouraged by disclosure orders in civil litigation. It is noted

[61] Ibid 144.

that potential leniency applicants may be dissuaded from cooperating with the Commission under the Notice if this might impair their position in civil proceedings as compared to companies who do not cooperate. Such undesirable effect would significantly harm the public interest in ensuring effective public enforcement of Article 101 TFEU in cartel cases, and thus its subsequent or parallel effective private enforcement, the recitals conclude.

However, it can be assumed that the possible disclosure of pre-existing documents also may discourage companies from applying for leniency. From a leniency perspective, an effective leniency system can be secured either through a commitment not to disclose any of the information or evidence provided, or, as will be discussed further in section III.D, by also granting immunity from damages (as well as individual sanctions).

III. Why Decide against Filing a Leniency Application?

A company seeking to end its involvement in a cartel will most probably consider the option of applying for leniency. Any such decision will be based on a number of factors. The most obvious one speaking in favour of an application is the possibility of no longer having to fear the 'betrayal' of the co-conspirators but instead be the one that files for immunity in the hope of escaping a fine. However, this section will focus not on the possible upside of a leniency application but on the reasons a company may have not to turn to the Commission. The factors discussed in the previous section may of course speak both in favour of and against an application. If the competition rules are not enforced properly, or if the sanctions imposed are low, this may make cartelists decide against filing an application. However, there are other factors that may also discourage companies from filing for leniency. This section presents some of these.

A. The Notion of 'Secret Cartel' Hard to Define

In its Leniency Notice, the Commission declares that the Notice sets out a framework for rewarding cooperation in its investigations by companies that are or have been members of a secret cartel. The Commission defines cartels as agreements and/or concerted practices between two or more competitors aimed at coordinating their competitive behaviour on the market and/or influencing the relevant parameters of competition through practices such as the fixing of purchase or selling prices or other trading conditions, the allocation of production or sales quotas, the sharing of markets including bid-rigging, restrictions of imports or exports and/or anti-competitive actions against other competitors.[62]

[62] Commission Notice on Immunity from Fines and Reduction of Fines in Cartel Cases (2006/C 298/11) 1.

As noted by Laserre, it is self-evident that leniency programmes apply to 'secret' cartels, as the aim of such programmes is precisely to uncover otherwise concealed practices.[63] However, the explanatory notes to the ECN Model Leniency Programme declare that the secrecy requirement does not imply that all aspects of the conduct should be secret, even though particular elements that make the full extent of the conduct and the fact that it constitutes a cartel more difficult to detect are not known to the public or the customers/suppliers.[64] Furthermore, while the programme does not apply to vertical restrictions, it is not excluded that a cartel that includes vertical elements may be covered by the leniency programme, as would be the case in a 'hub-and-spoke' cartel.[65] Thus, while a classic, purely horizontal, price-fixing cartel is clearly covered by the Notice, companies may be engaging in other forms of cooperation where only part of the illegal conduct would qualify as a secret cartel, creating uncertainties as to whether any immunity will cover the cooperation in its entirety.

B. Uncertainties around the Size and Scope of the Cartel

Cartels often grow when the competition authorities start investigating. Even the leniency applicant does not always know the whole scope of the cartel. Perhaps the leniency applicant only knew of and filed for leniency regarding a national cartel for one product, while it tuns out later that the applicant was part of a national branch of a global multi-product cartel. It seems clear that some cartels have different levels with different participants, that is separate national, regional and even global levels, which are all interconnected but where only a few firms actually know about the full magnitude of the cartel. A cartel can thus look very different when comparing the initial leniency application to what the Commission finally decides to fine. Indeed, there may be several members of national cartels that only knew about the national dimension of the cartel, while in fact they were part of an EU-wide multiproduct cartel. If such company files a leniency application with the NCA, there is thus a risk that the case will later end up in the hands of the Commission, or be dealt with by a number of NCAs.

C. The Costs of Applying for Leniency

As noted by Snyder, enforcers should be mindful of the costs to leniency applicants, which could prove to be a disincentive to seeking immunity from fines. A leniency applicant in any cartel investigation incurs unavoidable costs: an internal

[63] B Laserre, 'Several Strokes of Black and a Palette of Grays' in B Hawk (ed), *International Antitrust Law & Policy: Fordham Competition Law 2013* (Huntington, Juris Publishing, 2014) 49, 50.

[64] ECN Model Leniency Programme, Explanatory Notes, point 11.

[65] Ibid point 14.

investigation by legal counsel, demands for documents, witness interviews and, possibly, trial testimony. The costs include both monetary expenditure and the cost of disruption to business operations.[66] According to Jaspers, the high costs of legal consultation and of internal data collection to prepare a leniency report, plus the management time of highly-paid executives, could put a brake on business activities for months or years; and more importantly, he notes, these are certain and short-term costs that the firm is confronted with, in contrast to the highly uncertain long-term consequences of an administrative fine.[67] When it comes to international cartels, multiple applications will be necessary, which will lead to an exponential increase in these costs. As the number of jurisdictions adopting both competition laws and leniency programmes has increased dramatically over the years, so have the different procedural, substantive and enforcement practice requirements that leniency applicants must satisfy to obtain leniency. It is not only the costs associated with a leniency application that are affected by the fact that competition law has gone global; the risks associated with an application have also increased. As noted by Forrester and Berghe, the multiplication of competition laws around the world and the ensuing proliferation of leniency policies makes it difficult – if not impossible – to be the first leniency applicant in all jurisdictions.[68] On this note, Ritz and Marx illustrate these risks with a few examples. According to them, truck manufacturer MAN apparently saved €1.2 billion by submitting a leniency application to the Commission, thereby uncovering the so-called truck cartel.[69] They also noted that DHL Express was not so lucky; due to unfortunate circumstances and lack of harmonisation among European leniency programmes, the company was fined €6.6 million by the Italian competition authority, despite benefitting from full immunity from fines at the Commission level.[70]

D. The Risk of Civil Liability

> I will not be quick to advise leniency anymore, especially because of these follow-on damages claims. That is a classic 'The operation was successful, but the client died'. So leniency no longer means closure, today it is only the beginning.[71]

This was one of the responses received by Jaspers when he carried out a study among lawyers and cartelists on the functioning of leniency programmes in the Netherlands. According to his study, the threat of follow-on damages claims

[66] Snyder, 'Challenges to Leniency' (n 15) 3.
[67] Jaspers, 'Leniency' (n 9) 118.
[68] Forrester and Berghe, 'Leniency' (n 7) 160.
[69] That is assuming that the cartel was discovered by the Commission. See C Ritz and L Marx, 'Leniency Carrots and Cartel Sticks – A Practitioners' View on Recent Trends and Challenges Presented by the EU Leniency Program' *CPI Antitrust Chronicle* (January 2019).
[70] Ibid.
[71] Jaspers, 'Leniency' (n 9) 120.

constitutes an important disincentive to come forward as a leniency applicant. Respondents indicated that civil litigation could lead to corporate liability for damages up to four or five times the amount of any fines imposed by the competition authority.[72]

In the preceding section, a number of factors necessary for a successful leniency scheme were listed. It was stated that (i) the fines should be severe, (ii) the system should be transparent and allow leniency applicants to predict the consequences of filing a leniency application, and (iii) the first leniency applicant should receive immunity from fines. If a private enforcement system is put in place alongside the public one, there is an obvious risk that these requirements cannot be fulfilled. First of all, it is now impossible for the leniency applicant to predict the consequences of its leniency application. While the company may be certain that it will escape a fine, the risk of having to pay damages remains and causes a significant degree of uncertainty. The number and size of any damages claims are hard to foresee and may spread as ripples on water. To give an example, on its website, Cartel Damages Claims reports on the first Spanish rulings in the trucks cartel follow-on actions. According to the report, the Commission's infringement decision has provoked a flood of individual claims all over Spain.[73] In Germany, Financialright Claims is allegedly seeking damages of €600 million plus interest on behalf of 3,200 potentially injured parties from around 20 EU Member States. The claims are said to represent more than 84,000 individual truck acquisitions.[74] In the UK, there are a number of ongoing cases against the truck manufacturers. And so it goes. Second, the introduction of a private enforcement system implies that a leniency application will no longer lead to total immunity. While the company may be able to receive total immunity from fines, it may have to pay the same or a larger amount in damages. Third, while the fines imposed by the Commission may be substantial, they do not match the potential damages. According to the study carried out by Jaspers, the damages may be four or five times as high as any fines imposed.

The fact that leniency applicants risk civil suits highlights the need for significant penalties in the law. If the civil liability looks bigger than the fine then the net incentive might be not to cooperate.[75] If leniency is to remain an attractive option despite the risk of exposure to massive damages claims, the fines thus need to be significant, preferably combined with the possibility to impose prison sentences or substantial fines on company representatives or employees too. The risk of personal liability could be a powerful motivator. However, this is not enough. The risk of having to pay hefty fines or being sent to prison needs to be considered as real. If no prison sentences are passed or the fines imposed are moderate, the deterrent effect will be negligible. The seriousness of the possible penalties, and

[72] Ibid.

[73] See at www.carteldamageclaims.com/first-spanish-judgments-in-trucks-cartel-follow-on-actions/.

[74] See at www.parr-global.com/munich-trucks-cartel-validity-claims-vehicle-mulled-giant-damages-action.

[75] OECD Report, *Fighting Hard Core Cartels* (n 1) 21.

thus the significance of relief that leniency can promise, is an important factor. If penalties are too weak or are applied too infrequently, firms may disregard an offer to relax them.

Another factor speaking against a leniency application is the fact that the applicant will most likely not only be the most obvious but also the first target of any damages claims. Companies cooperating with the Commission are likely to be attractive targets for any follow-on claims, as they may face such claims sooner than companies that have not cooperated. First, seeking immunity by definition involves an admission of guilt. While a leniency applicant may attempt to submit factual evidence only, avoiding any statements qualifying or explaining those facts, the Commission will be unwilling to grant immunity unless the company contributes to the investigation in a more substantial way. Second, a leniency applicant is likely to have collected and processed the evidence before filing for immunity, and is thus likely to have collated evidence. This makes it an easier target for discovery, allowing claimants to quickly access important evidence, which in turn allows them to build their case against the leniency applicant and the other companies involved in the cartel. If the Commission takes enforcement action, its decision will identify the leniency recipient as an infringer of Article 101 TFEU, and will describe in full the part it played in the cartel. The company's cooperation with the Commission will also be described to explain why the fine was reduced. The Commission is required to disclose details and explain the motivation for the lenient treatment.[76] Appeals against the Commission's fining decisions are generally waived by leniency applicants, at least as far as the existence of the cartel is concerned. Usually, cartel proceedings against the leniency applicant are therefore the first to be launched and concluded. Additionally, since the national courts are bound by the Commission's findings, the question raised in these proceedings is usually the exact amount of the damage, rather than whether the damage has occurred in the first place.[77] Thus, while the Damages Directive attempts to reduce this effect by limiting the liability of leniency recipients, they are still more exposed than others.[78]

Given the above, potential leniency applicants may decide that accepting the risk of detection if they refrain from seeking leniency is preferable to the near certainty of being party to a civil damages action if they do apply for leniency.[79] To use the words of Guttuso, the probability of exposure to private damages not only in the jurisdiction where leniency was obtained but also in other jurisdictions has been cited as a key factor inhibiting potential leniency applicants from self-reporting.[80]

[76] OECD Report, *Fighting Hard Core Cartels* (n 1) 20.

[77] Ritz and Marx, Leniency Carrots and Cartel Sticks' (n 69).

[78] According to Art 11 of the Damages Directive, immunity recipients are only exceptionally liable for the damage caused by the other members of the cartel.

[79] Snyder, 'Challenges to Leniency' (n 15) 3.

[80] L Guttuso, 'Leniency and the Two Faces of Janus' in Beaton-Wells and Tran (eds), *Anti-cartel Enforcement* (n 7) 273, 279.

IV. Are We Really Witnessing the Decline and Fall of the EU Leniency Programme?

In their article 'the Decline and Fall of the Leniency Programme in Europe', Ysewyn and Kahmann declare that behind its provocative title hides a worrying reality for anti-cartel enforcement,[81] and indeed there appears to be some cause for concern among the proponents of effective leniency systems. In February 2018, Villarejo, Deputy Director General at DG COMP, was asked about the trend in leniency applications over the last two years. The answer was, 'it is not going up'.[82] In June the same year, the OECD arranged a round table to discuss the challenges to which leniency programmes are exposed and proposals for improvements. In its report to the round table, the Commission acknowledged that it shares several of the challenges faced by other competition agencies worldwide, stating that, over the years, its rules and practices regarding leniency have been adapted to face some of the challenges linked to the greater probability of follow-on actions for private damages, the globalisation of cartels and the increasing risk of sanctions imposed on individuals for cartel behaviour. The question is of course whether these efforts are adequate. Ritz and Marx report on the recent decline in leniency applications, and refer to a statement made by DG COMP's director of the cartel enforcement unit, who has allegedly stated that competition authorities need to send the message that leniency carrots are sweet and cartel sticks are heavy, if they want the success of the leniency programmes to prevail.[83]

Snyder declares that although it can fairly and accurately be said that the costs of leniency and civil damages exposure are the necessary consequences and deterrents of secret cartels, and that a company that is granted immunity still comes out far ahead of its co-cartelists, it would be a mistake for competition law enforcers to turn a deaf ear to concerns among practitioners about the high costs of leniency.[84] However, there are also those who question any significant decline in the number of applications filed with the Commission. Guttoso acknowledges that both public enforcers and academics alike have continuously emphasised the detrimental effect of private actions and document disclosures on leniency incentives. Yet she finds surprisingly little in the way of a conclusive body of evidence substantiating this.[85] While she may be right, her paper was published in 2015, one year before the Damages Directive was to be transposed into national legislation, and it may

[81] Ysewyn and Kahmann, 'Decline and Fall' (n 10).

[82] P Guniganti, 'Leniency Applications Are 'Not Going Up' says DG Comp Official' (2018), available at https://globalcompetitionreview.com/article/1159219/leniency-applications-are-%E2%80%9Cnot-going-up%E2%80%9D-says-dg-comp-official.

[83] Ritz and Marx, 'Leniency Carrots and Cartel Sticks' (n 69).

[84] Snyder, 'Challenges to Leniency' (n 15) 3.

[85] Guttuso, 'Leniency and the Two Faces of Janus' (n 80) 279.

therefore be that the full effects of the EU's private enforcement policy had not yet materialised. To conclude, while we may not necessarily be witnessing the fall of the Commission's leniency programme, much indicates that we are witnessing a decline in the number of leniency applications.

V. Is Leniency the Only Option?

This book focuses on issues of access to the Commission's cartel case files. It has become evident during the course of this work that the Commission's actions in these cases are all to some extent motivated by its concern for the well-being of the leniency programme. For this reason, the current section will discuss the possibility of replacing or complementing the current leniency regime with other methods of detection as a means to ease any tension between the diverging interests of securing effective public and private enforcement and transparent EU administration. However, as the issue is not core to this research, there will be no in-depth analysis of other available options but instead a more general discussion of the necessity of maintaining the attractiveness of the leniency programme, and possible alternative or complementary methods of detecting cartels.

A. Possible Sources of Information

According to Wils, competition authorities can try to obtain the information and intelligence necessary to prove a competition law infringement from three possible sources.[86] First, they can monitor markets, observing publicly available information and data, and possibly use economic analysis of these data to try to detect and prove an infringement. However, Wils does not consider this method to be very useful in practice, as economic evidence is generally insufficient in court to establish collusion. Second, Wils points to the possibility for competition authorities to rely on information from third parties, such as consumers and competitors affected by the anticompetitive practice. The third and, as noted by Wils, often the most valuable source of information is the companies and individuals that have participated in the cartel.[87] For secret cartels, they may be the only ones holding the information the authorities need to detect and punish the cartel. As further noted by Wils, competition authorities may only apply their investigatory tools when they have reason to suspect a company of wrongdoing. As a consequence, the leniency programme significantly reduces the difficulty, time and administrative cost of collecting intelligence and evidence of cartel infringements. This, Wils

[86] Wils, 'The Use of Leniency' (n 22) 335.
[87] Ibid 336.

notes, allows the Commission to detect and punish more cartels, while keeping the resources spent on cartel enforcement constant.[88]

Stephan and Nikpay pursue the same line of argumentation when they declare that uncovering cartels is very difficult and resource-intensive. Since investigations can be triggered not only by leniency applications but also by complaints from buyers or from media attention, the fact that secret cartel activity can potentially occur in any given market or industry means that policing markets for infringements and uncovering sufficient evidence to prove wrongdoing can prove extremely difficult without any aid 'from the inside'. They further note that this detection problem can be compounded by the fact that many cartels are in upstream industries, with any resulting higher prices often passed down several times before they are borne by end consumers.[89] The provision of information and evidence results in significant savings for enforcement authorities, especially in building up a body of evidence, preparing the decision and defending against appeals.[90] This is also in line with the findings in the OECD Report on the fight against hard-core cartels, which declares that leniency programmes uncover cartels that would otherwise go undetected, and also make the ensuing investigations more efficient and effective. Experience shows that the programmes work, the Report notes.[91] A further advantage noted by Hammond is that the competition authority gets access to documents regardless of their geographic location, and to witnesses regardless of their nationality.[92] When they work, leniency programmes thus have several advantages. Not only do they help uncover cartels and possibly also deter companies from engaging in cartel activity, they also make the ensuing cartel investigations more efficient and less costly and time-consuming.

B. Any Risk of Relying too Heavily on Leniency?

While there appears to be consensus among enforcers and academics that well-functioning leniency systems lead to more effective and efficient cartel enforcement, this does not mean that there are no voices raised against leniency policies or that leniency is considered to be the only solution in the fight against cartels. One objection sometimes raised is that law enforcement agencies should

[88] Ibid. There is of course also the option to use the three methods simultaneously, by monitoring markets and launching a sector inquiry when the requirements in Art 17 of Regulation 1/2003 are met. The results from the sector inquiry may allow the Commission to open up investigations against individual firms suspected of wrongdoing. One example of this is the Pharma sector inquiry, launched by the Commission in 2008 as a response to indications that competition in Europe's pharmaceutical markets was not working well, as fewer new medicines were being brought to market and the entry of generic medicines sometimes seemed to be delayed. The inquiry would look at the reasons for this.

[89] Stephan and Nikpay, 'Leniency Decision-Making (n 39) 140.

[90] Ibid.

[91] OECD Report, *Fighting Hard Core Cartels* (n 1) 7.

[92] SD Hammond, 'Cracking Cartels with Leniency Programs', OECD Competition Committee, Paris France, October 2005, available at www.justice.gov/atr/speech/cracking-cartels-leniency-programs.

always take vigorous action against violations. That said, some prioritising and balancing of costs and benefits in the enforcement process is inevitable in all legal systems. According to the OECD, overall enforcement effectiveness and compliance is likely to improve, as leniency for a few participants makes it possible to apply the law more thoroughly to others. Permitting a violator to avoid the consequences of its action by confessing and shifting the burden to others may appear unjust, but for violations like cartels, where there will be several parties, considerations of enforcement effectiveness may outweigh that concern.[93] When the US Antitrust Division revised its leniency policy in the 1990s, granting full immunity to the first applicant, it met with steep resistance from a number of stakeholders. As noted by O'Brien, giving up prosecution of the first company to 'rat out' its co-conspirators was initially considered unsettling, even by many prosecutors. In the end, they were convinced by the argument that leniency policies disclose highly secretive cartels that would otherwise go undetected and unpunished. Furthermore, as cartels by definition involve more than one company, leniency policies provide the valuable information necessary to pursue a case against the co-conspirators.[94]

In the impact assessment report accompanying the Commission's proposal to the Damages Directive, the Commission declared that it would not be possible to offset the negative effects of impaired leniency programmes by increased ex officio investigations into suspected infringements. Such an attempt would not only be more costly for both public enforcers and undertakings alike, but it would not enable public enforcers to uncover comparably useful evidence with a view to proving infringements, the Commission declared. On the one hand, leniency programmes allow the Commission and NCAs to pursue targeted enforcement of conduct where the likelihood of finding an infringement is much higher, and thereby free resources for the pursuit of ex officio cases while maintaining an adequate degree of deterrence. On the other hand, diverting resources from leniency cases in order to pursue more ex officio cases would impose a significant administrative burden on businesses, as there would be a higher risk of their being subject to an investigation even though no infringement is later found. Moreover, because of the higher costs and administrative burdens of ex officio cases, in the absence of cooperation from leniency applicants and of the targeted evidence they provide, the number of secret cartels uncovered would be significantly lower.[95]

The Commission's arguments do not appear to be fully embraced by all. While Stephan and Nikpay accept the difficulties associated with uncovering cartels without help from the inside, they are not altogether convinced that leniency programmes are the perfect solution to all problems. According to them,

[93] OECD Report, *Fighting Hard Core Cartels* (n 1) 10.
[94] O'Brien, 'Leadership of Leniency' (n 49) 20.
[95] Impact Assessment Report: Damages Actions For Breach of the EU Antitrust Rules, Accompanying the Proposal for a Directive of the European Parliament and of the Council, COM(2013) 404 final, para 35.

many cartels are born out of market downturns and are often operated by a small number of rogue employees. Furthermore, they argue that many leniency applications concern cartels that have already ceased to exist. Thus, while acknowledging that the leniency system is likely to continue to play an important role, they argue that enforcement agencies should refocus their attention to a greater extent than currently on increasing their ability to uncover cartels through their own investigative efforts.[96]

Stephan and Nikpay are not the only ones pointing to the risks associated with competition authorities relying too heavily on the leniency programmes. In a speech given in 2005, Hammond declared that the cooperation from leniency applicants had allowed the Department of Justice to crack more cartels than all the other tools at the Department's disposal combined. However, he also noted that the fear of detection constituted a precondition to an effective leniency policy, and that cultivating such fear requires a demonstrated track record of cracking cartels.[97] On a similar note, Harrington and Chang argue that the introduction of a leniency programme may actually raise the cartel rate if the competition authority does not make sure to continue pursuing non-leniency cases. If the introduction of a leniency programme takes too many resources from the handling of non-leniency cases, this may eventually have as a result that the authority is no longer perceived as an aggressive enforcer, and that companies no longer fear that their unlawful behaviour will come to the authority's attention. The destabilising effect of the leniency programme is then diminished, Harrington and Chang argue.[98]

While the Commission values its leniency programme, it appears to acknowledge that leniency needs to be complemented by other tools of detection. During an American Bar Association webcast in April 2020, Tierno Centella, deputy head of unit in the cartels section of DG COMP, was reported to have declared that over 25 per cent of the Directorate General's open cartel investigations had started ex officio, and that 'the success of these own-initiative investigations, helped by a new data analysis unit and whistleblower tool, was not yet obvious in the [public] record'. She is further reported to have said that DG COMP 'was taking care not to be too reliant on companies themselves blowing the whistle on cartels and applying for leniency – with an apparent decline in such applications over recent years'.[99]

While voices are thus sometimes raised against leniency programmes, questioning their effectiveness or appropriateness, the general view appears to be that

[96] A Stephan and A Nikpay 'Leniency Decision-Making' (n 39) at 140. On a similar note, Guttoso argues that leniency policies display a bias towards uncovering collusive conduct close to the breaking point, and that this seems to signal that leniency policies may be least efficient at dismantling cartels when they are at their most detrimental. See Guttuso, 'Leniency and the Two Faces of Janus' (n 80) 282.

[97] Hammond, 'Cracking Cartels' (n 91).

[98] Harrington Jr and Chang, 'When Can We Expect Fewer Cartels?' (n 38).

[99] M Acton and N Hirst, 'EU Cartel Enforcement Involves Healthy Proportion of Own-Initiative Probes, Official Says' *MLEx Editorial* (21 April 2020).

while it may be complemented by other means of detection, a neatly designed and well-functioning leniency programme increases the likelihood of detection without requiring too much of the competition authorities, and makes the ensuing investigations more effective and less costly than ex officio investigations. The question is whether there are other tools for detection that may substitute for or complement the leniency programme.

C. Private Enforcement as an Alternative Solution?

While leniency programmes are considered a valuable means to crack existing cartels, the ultimate goal is of course that these programmes, together with other measures, will have a deterrent effect and prevent cartels from being formed in the first place. As noted by Parker and Lehmann Nielsen,[100] it is not only the deterrence of formal legal sanctions that can provide calculative motivations for compliance. Informal economic and social sanctions applied by various third parties in the case of breach, such as stock price declines and social embarrassment among family and peers, may be even more effective at influencing compliance behaviour. Indeed, they note, in an age when much of business is about managing brand value and reputation, they expect that the financial and moral costs of bad publicity from non-compliance would loom particularly large in businesses' thinking about the costs and gains of compliance and non-compliance.[101] According to this line of reasoning, the attachment of a moral stigma to cartel behaviour could therefore, at least in the long run, make companies more eager to comply with the competition rules. It is then also fair to assume that the recent focus on private enforcement could help achieve such a goal. The press coverage of the antitrust damages cases will draw the public's attention to the fact that the gains made by cartels are achieved at the expense of customers and ultimately the consumers.

This spurs the question whether the private enforcement regime can act as an alternative option or complement the leniency programme. At the moment we do not know if all the ongoing damages cases will have the desired effect and actually ensure that cartel victims are compensated for the loss suffered. However, should that prove to be the case, the threat of civil liability may act as a deterrent to anyone contemplating cartel participation, and may also motivate direct and indirect purchasers to come forward and report on suspected cartel activity to the Commission or the NCAs in the hope that they will open an investigation against the companies in question. As discussed in chapter 5, third parties may be incentivised to report on cartels if, by doing so, this increases their chances of being compensated for any loss suffered. Thus, the number of complaints may increase if the private enforcement regime proves to be a success. In the recent ruling in

[100] Parker and Lehmann Nielsen, 'Deterrence and the Impact of Calculative Thinking' (n 34).
[101] Ibid 382.

Otis, the Court once again confirmed its stance that the right of any individual to claim compensation for loss suffered due to a competition law infringement actually strengthens the working of the EU competition rules, since it discourages frequently covert agreements, which are liable to restrict or distort competition, thereby making a significant contribution to the maintenance of effective competition in the EU.[102]

While the ongoing proceedings may discourage companies from engaging in cartel activity and may increase the number of complaints, the private enforcement regime is heavily dependent on a well-functioning public enforcement regime, as most damages cases are follow-on actions. Any deterrent effect is thus likely to be only temporary if the public enforcement system is weakened through a decline in the number of leniency applications. The private enforcement regime now in place should thus only be considered an alternative option if an increase in the number of complaints can help keep the public enforcement pillar strong. Guttuso holds such a belief, as she argues that the private enforcement pillar could complement, and even reinforce the Commission's leniency programme.[103] If private parties are now encouraged to report on suspected cartels and initiate stand-alone actions, this will increase the likelihood of detection, which will in turn help destabilise cartels and provide an incentive for cartel members to come forward and apply for leniency, Guttuso argues.[104]

D. Can Whistleblowers Fill the Shoes of the Leniency Programme?

In March 2017, the Commission introduced a new tool aimed at detecting cartels and other forms of anticompetitive practices. Through the introduction of an anonymous whistleblower tool, individuals are now encouraged to disclose anti-competitive conduct on an anonymous basis. In its press release,[105] the Commission declared that the new system would increase the likelihood of detection and prosecution, and so stood to further deter businesses from entering or remaining in cartels or carrying out other types of illegal anticompetitive behaviour. It would therefore complement and reinforce the effectiveness of the Commission's leniency programme. As the leniency programme only grants full immunity in those cases where the Commission is not yet in possession of sufficient information to carry out an unannounced inspection, the whistleblower tool aims to put pressure

[102] Case C-435/18, *Otis GmbH and Others v Land Oberösterreich and Others*, EU:C:2019:1069, at para 24.
[103] Guttuso, 'Leniency and the Two Faces of Janus' (n 80) 285.
[104] Ibid 286.
[105] Antitrust: Commission introduces new anonymous whistleblower tool, available at https://ec.europa.eu/commission/presscorner/detail/en/IP_17_591.

on cartel members to act before their own employees do. For the same reason, the new tool could also help to address any criticism that the leniency programme mainly catches dying cartels or cartels that have already passed. Acknowledging the risks involved in whistleblowing, the European Parliament and the Council have recently adopted a Directive aimed at protecting persons who report breaches of EU law ('the Whistleblower Directive').[106] The Directive is to be transposed into the Member States' laws by 17 December 2021.[107]

Thus, at EU level, individuals are now able to report anonymously, and the legislator has also made sure that they will be protected from any repercussions should their identity be revealed or should they decide to blow the whistle without hiding their identity. It is hoped that this will make individuals come forward and provide the Commission with information on anticompetitive practices to a greater extent than previously. As mentioned in section V.C, DG COMP is now pursuing a number of own-initiative investigations, and this partly thanks to its whistleblower tool.[108] However, should the envisaged result not materialise, the Commission has one further means to increase the attractiveness of the whistleblower tool, and that is by rewarding those who report cartels. Both Stucke and Stephan discuss the possibilities for competition authorities to rely on whistleblowers to a greater extent than is done at the moment. Stephan mentions the infamous FBI informant Mark Whitacre, who revealed the ADM price-fixing cartel, as well as Sharon Watkins and Cynthia Cooper, who were instrumental in uncovering large-scale fraud at Enron and Worldcom.[109] Yet, Stephan notes, despite the potential value of corporate whistleblowers, they have generally received no reward from the authorities. Nor, Stephan argues, have they enjoyed adequate protection from the retaliatory actions of their employers or the wider consequences for their careers and personal lives.[110]

There are jurisdictions that offer carrots to informants. As noted by Stucke, several competition authorities offer monetary rewards to foster a race to their doors. In Korea, the competition authority has had an Informant Reward Programme in place since 2002, allowing it to provide monetary rewards to those who report or provide information on certain violations of competition law with supporting evidence.[111] Stucke also mentions a number of other countries where

[106] Directive (EU) 1937/2019 of the European Parliament and of the Council of 23 October 2019 on the protection of persons who report breaches of Union law [2019] OJ L305/17.

[107] According to Art 2(c), the Directive protects persons reporting breaches of the EU competition rules.

[108] Acton and Hirst, 'EU Cartel Enforcement' (n 98).

[109] A Stephan, 'Is the Korean Innovation of Individual Informant Rewards a Viable Cartel Detection Tool?', *CCP Working Paper 14-3*, available at http://competitionpolicy.ac.uk/documents/8158338/8199490/CCP+Working+Paper+14-3.pdf/7a9c1d06-d790-4e83-86bf-d43c68c83d0d.

[110] Ibid.

[111] ME Stucke, 'Leniency, Whistle-Blowing and the Individual: Should we Create Another Race to the Competition Agency?' in Beaton-Wells and Tran (eds), *Anti-cartel Enforcement* (n 7) 209, 216.

the competition authorities can reward informants.[112] While the number of jurisdictions offering rewards is limited, the OECD acknowledges that they fill a function similar to leniency systems, as the strategy works by driving or expanding a wedge between the individual's incentives and the employer's incentives. However, unlike the leniency system, which relieves the company from a fine, all companies engaging in the cartel will now be sanctioned. Furthermore, and as noted by both Stucke and Stephan, a whistleblower system can sow distrust among the cartel members, who must now fear any current or former employee, or other person likely to be privy to damaging information, racing to the competition authority.[113] Stephan concludes by observing that rewards could increase the detection rate of cartels, but that this is unlikely to happen unless they reflect the very significant cost and risk faced by individuals who are willing to come forward and inform on the actions of others within their firm or industry.[114] As an employee, you risk your career if you turn on your employer.

The UK is one of the countries to offer rewards to informants. In April 2019, *Financial Times* reported on the application of the whistleblower tool, declaring that the number of whistleblowing reports to the UK's competition regulator had risen to its highest ever level in 2018, indicating that new protections – and financial rewards for cooperation – were driving people to call out wrongdoing. According to the article, calls to the Competition and Markets Authority's (CMA's) cartels hotline rose 18 per cent in 2018 to 556, up from 471 the previous year. In the UK, *Financial Times* reports, whistleblowers can be rewarded up to £100,000 for reporting cartels, with any payment being dependent on the value of the information and the harm done to consumers by the cartel's existence. However, despite the rise in numbers, relatively few whistleblower reports were said to lead to a formal investigation. In the 2017–18 financial year, only 15 prompted 'further investigation', according to CMA statistics.[115] While there may be several reasons behind this, one can assume that the information provided by a whistleblower is seldom as comprehensive or valuable as that provided by a leniency applicant. It is unlikely that the employee or other individual blowing the whistle is in possession of as much or as detailed information about the cartel as a company filing for leniency. Thus, while the whistleblower tool may complement and even reinforce the leniency programme, it is not likely to become a substitute for leniency. As the risk of damages actions will not likely affect an employee's decision to blow the whistle, companies fearing that their employees will turn on them and report them to the Commission may thus decide to file for leniency despite the risk of civil action.

[112] Hungary, Pakistan, Singapore and the UK are the countries mentioned.

[113] Stucke, 'Leniency, Whistle-Blowing and the Individual' (n 110) 219. Stucke makes reference to Stephan, *CCP Working Paper 14-3* (n 108).

[114] Stephan, *CCP Working Paper 14-3* (n 108).

[115] B Thompson, 'Number of Whistleblowing Reports on UK Cartels Up 18% Last Year' *Financial Times* (28 May 2019).

E. Responsive Regulation an Alternative to the Current Enforcement System?

Voss is another academic who discusses alternative options of enforcing the EU competition rules. In her work, she presents a potential design of a case resolution system based on the theory of responsive regulation. Instead of choosing a case resolution mechanism on a case-by-case basis, Voss presents a prescriptive system. According to her proposal, infringement history and the cooperation offered by the undertaking would determine what case resolution mechanism to employ. The aim of such system would be to reduce the focus on fines. Instead, the focus would be on cooperation as a means of bringing infringements to an end and preventing infringements by way of corporate compliance programmes. As a general rule, no fines would be imposed on first time 'offenders'. This would also have the effect that the leniency system would lose its value.[116]

F. Concluding Remarks

Judging from the foregoing, there appear to be some but still relatively few ideas on how to achieve an equally effective and efficient enforcement system without a well-functioning leniency programme in place. Thus, while there may be other ways to achieve deterrence, compliance and detection, thereby securing effective cartel enforcement, there does not appear to be an alternative solution readily available that can both achieve those aims and keep the administrative costs down. A whistleblowing system may complement and reinforce the leniency system, but the question is whether it should be allowed to substitute for the Commission's leniency policy. The whistleblower tool could complement the leniency programme in several ways. First, unlike leniency applicants, whistleblowers' incentives to report on cartels are unlikely to be affected by the presence of a private enforcement regime. Second, whistleblowers may put additional pressure on companies to self-report and apply for leniency. If a company fears that not only its co-conspirators but also its employees will report on the cartel, it may seem sensible to apply for leniency, also given the risk of any damages claims. This especially since immunity is no longer available should the whistleblower be the first to report on the cartel and provide the Commission with enough evidence to carry out a dawn raid. However, it is unlikely that an employee or other individual blowing the whistle on a cartel will be in possession of as much or as detailed

[116] K Voss, *Between Enforcement and Regulation: A Study of the System of Case Resolution Mechanisms Used by the European Commission in the Enforcement of Articles 101 and 102 TFEU* (Stockholm, Stockholm University, 2019). Also Guttuso touches upon the issue of responsive regulation and the linking of private action to regulatory compliance. See Guttuso, 'Leniency and the 'Two Faces of Janus' (n 80) 287.

information about the cartel as a company filing for leniency. While whistleblowers may draw the Commission's attention to unlawful practices and put pressure on companies to self-report, the Commission will still have to invest a significant number of resources in order to investigate these cases. To conclude, as long as there are no other alternative and equally efficient options, it seems sensible to try to maintain the attractiveness of the leniency programme.

VI. Keeping the Leniency Programme Attractive

Under the current regime, the Damages Directive offers leniency recipients two forms of protection. First, Article 6(6) prevents national courts from ordering the disclosure of leniency statements. Secondly, immunity recipients escape joint liability. Article 11(5) stipulates that the amount of contribution of an infringer that has been granted immunity from fines under a leniency programme shall not exceed the amount of the harm it caused to its own direct or indirect purchasers or providers.

In section II.B predictability was identified as key to achieving an attractive leniency system. It was acknowledged that a general offer to reduce penalties in exchange for information may not be enough to encourage firms to come forward. The benefits of remaining with the cartel may then appear greater and more certain than the unknown reward that would result from confessing. However, as noted by Jaspers, a leniency programme does not operate in a vacuum, and the current EU system does not appear to offer the required predictability.[117] While a leniency applicant may be reasonably confident that it will escape a fine if it follows the order prescribed in the Leniency Notice, it is impossible to predict the likelihood and outcome of any ensuing damages proceedings. Furthermore, as discussed in chapter 8, while the Damages Directive protects leniency statements, it does not protect the information contained therein. Add to that the fact that any limitation of liability applies only as long as the cartel victims receive compensation from the other cartel participants. The discussion in section IV made it clear that the current system does not offer the predictability required to maintain the attractiveness of the leniency system. Extending protection to pre-existing documents will not necessarily restore confidence in the system.

It can be assumed that a fair number of potential leniency applicants will decide to come forward and self-report only if they believe that their position, having revealed the cartel conduct, is at least no worse than the expected outcome in the absence of the leniency application. At the present time, potential leniency applicants do not appear convinced that this is the case under the current EU regime, and the survival of the leniency system therefore requires some form of

[117] Jaspers, 'Leniency' (n 9) 111.

action from the legislator. There are at least two possible ways to try to remedy this problem. The first option is to raise the stakes for those participating in cartels by imposing higher fines and introducing individual sanctions. The other is to extend the leniency system to cover immunity from damages.

As to the first option, there are other areas of EU law where the legislator has introduced far tougher sanctions than those available under the EU competition rules. The rules governing financial markets is one example. The financial crisis of 2008 pushed the world's financial system towards the edge of collapse, and exposed weaknesses in both the functioning and the transparency of financial markets around the world. The crisis triggered a number of forceful regulative responses from the EU legislator. One was the adoption of the MAR in 2014.[118] The MAR pushes for greater transparency in financial markets and aims at fighting market manipulation and insider trading. Violations of the prohibitions laid down in the Regulation may result not only in the withdrawal or suspension of the authorisation, but also in imprisonment and substantial administrative fines. For natural persons, the maximum fine is €5,000,000, and for legal persons €15,000,000 or 15 per cent of the annual turnover. The accompanying Directive requires Member States to criminalise market abuse and to ensure that the offences are punishable by certain terms of imprisonment.[119] Closely connected to the MAR is the Directive on markets in financial instruments, MiFID II, which also provides for substantial fines. For natural persons, the maximum fine is €5,000,000, and for legal persons €5,000,000 or 10 per cent of the annual turnover. The Directive contains an additional feature of interest to this study. These thresholds may be pushed upwards, as the maximum fines should be at least twice the amount of the benefit derived from the infringement, where this can be determined.[120]

In order for this option to be effective, it is not sufficient to adopt rules allowing for tougher sanctions and individual sanctions. The enforcers are required to apply the rules and make sure that the public knows that the threats are real. According to Parker and Lehamnn Nielsen, many business managers do not make, or act on, cost–benefit calculations about compliance until something – like a regulatory enforcement action or publicly reported breach or accident – brings the risks of non-compliance to their attention.[121] That said, and as discussed in section II.A, a study by Bignoni et al suggests that the actual risk of detection is not necessarily a key element in ensuring deterrence.[122] Instead the authors argue that with leniency policies offering immunity to the first reporting party, a high fine is the

[118] Regulation (EU) No 596/2014 of the European Parliament and of the Council of 16 April 2014 on market abuse [2014] OJ L173/1.
[119] Directive (EU) No 57/2014 of the European Parliament and of the Council of 16 April 2014 on criminal sanctions for market abuse [2014] OJ L173/179.
[120] Art 70 of Directive (EU) No 65/2014 of the European Parliament and of the Council of 15 May 2014 on markets in financial instruments and amending Directive 2002/92/EC and Directive 2011/61/EU [2014] OJ L173/349.
[121] Parker and Lehmann Nielsen, 'Deterrence and the Impact of Calculative Thinking' (n 34) 386.
[122] Bignoni et al, *Trust, Leniency and Deterrence* (n 47).

main determinant of deterrence, having a strong effect even when the probability of exogenous detection is zero.[123] Thus the leniency system itself guarantees a risk of detection if the sanctions are severe, and deterrence appears to be mainly driven by 'distrust', that is, the fear of partners' deviating and reporting.

However, while the first option may help restore the attractiveness of the leniency system, it will not make cartel members or the Commission more willing to depart with evidence of the cartel activity. Thus, for the sake of this study, and also in the interest of ensuring a competition law enforcement system in which the two public and private enforcement pillars may co-exist and even reinforce each other, the first option is not the best, at least not unless it is introduced together with option number two.

The second option, to extend the leniency system into the area of private enforcement, appears tempting from an effectiveness perspective. Indeed, if companies are assured not only immunity from fines, but also immunity from civil liability, this would most probably lead to an upsurge in the number of leniency applications. In 2008, Green and McCall, anticipating the introduction of EU legislation on private enforcement, examined whether the leniency system should be extended also to cover civil claims.[124] They found that, given the general success of leniency programmes in encouraging disclosure of cartels, it is important not to undermine them with any changes that might increase the likelihood of companies' facing private action claims. In principle, they declared, if leniency is not extended to civil liabilities, the incentive for first movers to come forward would be reduced. However, they also declared that, based on the evidence from the US, it was not certain that an extension to civil action would have a significant effect if fines were increasing at the same time. Nonetheless, they concluded, maintaining the strength of the incentive for first movers to disclose would be an important element of the work the Commission is carrying out to encourage civil actions.[125] Harrington pursues the same line of argument, but takes it even further. He suggests that in most cases it is best to waive all the penalties against the first firm to come forward, and raises the question whether it would be optimal to offer positive rewards, rather than just the absence of penalties.[126]

While there are proponents of an extension, there are likely to be as many opponents. Unlike the public enforcement system, which aims at deterring and punishing violations of the competition rules, the main aim of the private enforcement system is to compensate victims and ensure that those who have suffered loss receive compensation in full. It may therefore seem immoral or unjust to let

[123] This is also argued by Balsaningham, *The EU Leniency Policy* (n 2) 164: 'By increasing the fine, it is possible to enhance the deterrence of the leniency programme, even if the likelihood of detection remains unchanged.'

[124] J Green and I McCall, 'Leniency and Civil Claims; Should Leniency Programmes Extend to Private Actions?' *Competition Law Insight* (July 2009) 5.

[125] Ibid.

[126] Harrington Jr and Chang, 'When Can We Expect Fewer Cartels?' (n 38) 237.

cartel offenders off the hook. In the EU, the Damages Directive has already introduced different levels of liability as it relieves immunity recipients from joint and several liability for the damage caused. However, and perhaps more importantly, one must not forget that the private enforcement system is heavily dependent on a well-functioning public enforcement system, as most damages cases are follow-on actions. By restoring the attractiveness of the leniency system, the public enforcement system may remain effective, thereby also allowing the private enforcement system to prosper. Furthermore, immunity should only be granted to one company, allowing victims to seek compensation from the other cartel participants. If only one firm can escape liability, that would not only destabilise cartels but would also allow cartel victims to be compensated for the harm caused to them. Finally, and as will be discussed in section VII on the US experience, the immunity recipient can be required to cooperate with cartel victims and provide them with the evidence in its possession. Receiving all the evidence held by one of the cartel participants would most likely increase aggregate recoveries.

VII. The US Experience

As discussed previously in this chapter, it was partly the success of the US leniency system that inspired the Commission to draft and adopt its own leniency programme in the mid-1990s. The Department of Justice has maintained a leniency programme since 1978, but the programme was initially little used and ineffective. Following a revision to make the scope of amnesty clearer and somewhat broader, the number of leniency applications soon picked up.[127] Under the current programme, the leniency applicant may receive amnesty from criminal prosecution in exchange for its full cooperation in the investigation and prosecution of the remaining cartel members. This provides the leniency applicant with complete immunity from corporate fines, as well as from the incarceration of the directors, officers and employees covered by the grant. The Antitrust Division grants two types of leniency – Type A and Type B. Type A leniency is granted for applicants reporting illegal antitrust activity before the Antitrust Division has received information about the activity from any other source, and before an investigation has begun. Type B leniency is available for applicants reporting illegal antitrust activity after the Antitrust Division has received information about the activity.[128] Up until 2004, leniency applicants still faced a disincentive for cooperating with the investigators: in any related civil litigation, a leniency applicant, like any other cartelist,

[127] United States Government Accountability Office, Report to Congressional Committees, *Criminal Cartel Enforcement; Stakeholders Views on Impact of 2004 Antitrust Reform Are Mixed But Support Whistleblower Protection*, July 2011, GAO-11-619, OECD Report (GAO Report) 7; and Snyder, 'Challenges to Leniency' (n 15).

[128] The GAO Report (n 126) 7.

would remain jointly and severally liable for treble damages resulting from the cartel.

This changed in 2004 when the Antitrust Criminal Penalty Enforcement and Reform Act (ACPERA) was adopted. ACPERA brought about a number of major changes to the US antitrust world – from both criminal and civil perspectives. From a criminal standpoint, the statute increased the maximum fine for corporations from $10 million to $100 million, increased the maximum prison sentence from three years to 10 years, and increased the maximum individual fines from $350,000 to $1 million. The statute also created a significant civil benefit for amnesty applicants. An amnesty applicant may now reduce its damages from treble to single damages, and avoid joint and several liability as long as it can demonstrate that it has rendered 'satisfactory cooperation' to plaintiffs. It is clear from the GAO Report that ACPERA was intended to increase the number of companies and individuals self-reporting anticompetitive behaviour, as well as to benefit consumers by encouraging leniency applicants to cooperate with cartel victims in their civil cases.[129]

As mentioned, in order to qualify for protection, ACPERA requires the leniency applicant to provide 'satisfactory cooperation' to the plaintiffs. It is the court hearing the civil case that determines whether or not cooperation is satisfactory. According to ACPERA's provisions, 'satisfactory cooperation' includes, among other things:

- providing a full account to the plaintiffs of all facts known to the applicant that are potentially relevant to the civil action;
- furnishing all documents or other items potentially relevant to the civil action; and
- making cooperating individuals available for interviews, depositions or testimony.

Thus, unlike the EU system, which strives to keep leniency statements from the cartel victims, ACPERA requires the leniency applicant to cooperate fully and to provide the cartel victims with all the evidence in its possession.

According to the GAO Report, analysis of Antitrust Division data indicated that after ACPERA's enactment there was little change in the number of leniency applications submitted by individuals and companies – the most relevant indicator of ACPERA's impact. However, there was a shift in the type of successful applications, with nearly twice as many applicants successfully applying for Type A leniency after ACPERA's enactment. The Division values this type of leniency application the most because these applicants are reporting criminal cartel activity about which the Division had no prior knowledge. Interviews with defence attorneys representing 18 leniency applicants who came forward to the Antitrust Division both before and after ACPERA indicated that ACPERA's offer of relief

[129] Ibid 13.

from civil damages had a slight positive effect on leniency applicants' decisions to apply for leniency, though the threat of imprisonment and corporate fines were the most motivating factors both before and after ACPERA's enactment.[130] Furthermore, and as noted by Crane, the mandatory cooperation requirement has led leniency applicants to provide information that has been valuable in pursuing damages cases against other members of the cartel, thus potentially increasing aggregate recoveries.[131] The EU has imported parts of the US leniency system into its legislative framework. Perhaps it is appropriate now also to import this part of the system to help restore the balance between public and private enforcement.[132]

VIII. The Survival of the Leniency System – Concluding Remarks

This chapter has discussed the decline in the number of leniency applications filed with the Commission and the possible reasons for this. It is clear from the foregoing that one of the main reasons is the introduction of rules on private enforcement and the risk of having to compensate cartel victims. As one practitioner puts it, '[l]eniency no longer means closure, today it is only the beginning'.[133] While the public and private enforcement systems should in theory reinforce each other and strengthen EU competition law enforcement, the reality is otherwise. Absent other equally effective and efficient methods of detecting cartels, there is an apparent risk that a weakened leniency system will lead to fewer cartel investigations. This, in turn, will have a negative impact on the private enforcement system, as most damages actions are follow-on actions.

[130] Ibid 15.

[131] DA Crane, 'Why Leniency Does not Undermine Compensation' in Beaton-Wells and Tran (eds), *Anti-cartel Enforcement* (n 7) 263, 267.

[132] In April 2019, the Department of Justice held a public round table discussion on ACPERA, which was due to sunset in June 2020. A series of panel discussions allowed judges, lawyers, economists, academics and other stakeholders to weigh in on how the law can be improved. The Department was particularly interested in the public's views on whether ACPERA has properly incentivised the self-reporting of criminal conduct, and whether there are issues that have impeded the law's intended effect. Apparently the Department is also experiencing a decline in the number of leniency applications. See at www.justice.gov/atr/events/public-roundtable-antitrust-criminal-penalty-enhancement-reform-act-acpera. See also DH Ginsburg and C Cheng, 'The Decline in US Criminal Antitrust Cases: ACPERA and Leniency in an International Context' (forthcoming 2020) in N Charbit et al (eds), *Albert A Foer, Liber Amicorum*, *George Mason Law & Economics Research Paper No 19–31*, available at SSRN at https://ssrn.com/abstract=3460091 or http://dx.doi.org/10.2139/ssrn.3460091. Despite efforts, legislators could not gather enough support to renew the law before its 22 June expiration date, which has now come and gone, changing the cartel enforcement landscape in the United States. While Congress may later decide to reauthorise or reform the law, including extending benefits retroactively, there is currently no possibility for immunity recipients to receive a de-trebling of any civil liability.

[133] Jaspers, 'Leniency' (n 9) 120.

At present, there are no other methods that allow the Commission to detect cartels and receive much of the evidence required from the cartel members themselves without having to utilise considerable resources. It is therefore suggested that, absent equally effective methods, efforts should be made to restore the attractiveness of the EU leniency system.

Today, national courts are prevented from ordering disclosure of leniency statements. Extending protection to pre-existing documents will not necessarily restore confidence in the system. While the evidence provided by the leniency applicant will then be safe from disclosure, the information contained therein is not necessarily protected, and cartel victims may access pre-existing documents from other sources. Furthermore, while the whistleblower tool discussed in section V.D may not be a substitute for the leniency programme, as employees are unlikely to provide the Commission with as much evidence as a leniency applicant, it may still complement and help reinforce the Commission's leniency programme. This given that whistleblowers are not as concerned with the risk of private enforcement as leniency applicants are. They may therefore put pressure on companies to self-report, even considering the risk of damages actions.

Two further options are presented in this chapter. The first concerns the sanctions available. The study carried out by Jaspers reveal that cartelists fear that any damages may well meet or even exceed the size of any fines imposed by the Commission. If the cap on fines is increased drastically, and if, like the MAR, the Antitrust Regulations were to allow the Commission to impose significant fines on individuals too, this might increase the attractiveness of the leniency system. However, such an option would not necessarily ease the tension addressed in this work, as the cartel members would remain reluctant to allow third parties access to any evidence of the cartel, and would fight any such measures taken by the Commission or the national courts. There is also a risk that higher fines coupled with a well-functioning private enforcement system may force companies to exit the market.

The second option is to extend leniency into the area of private enforcement and to let the first leniency applicant receive immunity not only from fines, but also from damages. This would most likely help restore the attractiveness of the leniency system and thus allow the Commission to detect and punish more cartels, while still keeping the resources spent on public cartel enforcement constant.[134] This is because the leniency programme significantly reduces the difficulty, time and administrative cost of collecting intelligence and evidence of cartel infringements. By maintaining the effectiveness of the public enforcement system, the private enforcement system would also be allowed to prosper, as most damages cases are follow-on actions and thus dependent on effective public enforcement.

[134] Ibid. There is of course also the option to use the three methods simultaneously, by monitoring markets and launching sector inquiries when the requirements in Art 17 of Regulation 1/2003 are met. The results from the sector inquiry may allow the Commission to open up investigations against individual firms suspected of wrongdoing.

Furthermore, it is suggested that immunity or leniency from civil liability should only be granted to one company, allowing victims to seek compensation from the other cartel participants. If only one firm can escape liability, that would not only destabilise cartels but would also allow cartel victims to be compensated for the harm caused to them. Finally, the EU system could, like its US equivalent, require immunity recipients to cooperate closely with cartel victims and provide them with the evidence in their possession. This would definitely ease any tension identified in this work.

However, while the current leniency system was put in place by the Commission itself, any rules on immunity from damages claims would have to be adopted by the EU legislator. It is therefore unlikely that we shall see such change in the near future.

PART V

Summing Up

10

Joining the Dots

As stated in the outset, this book examines the legislative patchwork surrounding access to the Commission's cartel case files and seeks to establish how best to ensure a proper balance between the often diverging – but legitimate – interests of the parties, of third parties and of national competition authorities. Having reached the final chapter it may be concluded that, indeed, the rules surrounding access constitute a patchwork as they have been adopted at different stages and pursue different objectives. The Antitrust Regulations serve the aim of ensuring effective competition law enforcement and are framed to further effectiveness and efficiency rather than transparency and accessibility. The Transparency Regulation, on the other hand, aims at ensuring the fullest possible access to documents held by the EU institutions. The Commission is undoubtedly caught between a rock and a hard place, charged with the task of ensuring both public and private enforcement while at the same time respecting the fundamental rights of parties and third parties. It is evident from the foregoing that, when forced to prioritise, the measures taken by the Commission are all, to a lesser or greater extent, motivated by its desire to ensure a well-functioning leniency programme and thereby also effective and efficient public enforcement of the EU competition rules. In the following, the conclusions drawn throughout the book are summarised, followed by a discussion of the way forward. It is suggested that any tension is best eased by extending the leniency programme into the area of private enforcement.

I. Information Exchange between Competition Authorities

In recent years, we have witnessed a globalisation of competition law alongside an increase in international trade. At EU level, the application of the competition rules has been decentralised and much of their enforcement is handled by the NCAs. With competition rules in place in many countries around the world and an increasing number of international cartels, competition authorities seek ways to cooperate. Case-specific information exchange may constitute one component in such cooperation. However, while being valuable, it is not unproblematic. Not only is there a risk that the rights of targeted undertakings are not adequately safeguarded, there is also a risk that leniency systems are negatively affected if information submitted as part of a leniency application is later transmitted to other authorities pursuing parallel proceedings under their domestic laws.

There is a clear dividing line between the cooperation that takes place within the ECN and cooperation with third country authorities. The EU enforcement regime is based on parallel powers and decentralisation. This requires close cooperation between the competition authorities of the EU, which all apply the same set of rules: Articles 101 and 102 TFEU. Article 12 of Regulation 1/2003 explicitly allows for information exchange between competition authorities, but requires the recipients of transmitted information to use it for the purpose of applying the two treaty articles and in respect of the subject matter for which it was collected by the transmitting authority. The article can thus be seen as a necessary extension of Article 28, and while certain elements in the information exchange within the ECN may raise concerns, the exchange as such is rather uncontroversial. However, information exchange with third country authorities is not necessarily equally uncontroversial.

According to Article 28 of Regulation 1/2003, information collected during an investigation shall be used only for the purpose for which it was acquired. The underlying rationale behind this provision is to safeguard targeted companies' defence rights. While the Commission and a third country competition authority may investigate the same factual circumstances, the infringement investigated by the third country authority will by necessity concern competition restrictions outside the remits of the EU and rules other than Article 101 or 102 TFEU. As the Commission's powers are limited to enforcing the EU competition rules, any inspection decision or request for information should be limited in scope to infringements of these rules and to examining the effects of any anticompetitive behaviour in the EU.[1] This in turn means that information transmitted to and used by third country authorities should be considered used for a purpose other than that for which it was acquired.

The wording of Article 28 prompts two further reflections. First, it is the information collected that is protected. This means that it is not only the physical documents collected that are protected from being used for another purpose, but also their contents. Second, there is no limitation to 'confidential' information. Thus, a bilateral agreement that only prohibits exchange of confidential information, requiring the source of the information to consent to such transfer, does not satisfy the requirements in Article 28. The agreement with the US explicitly prohibits the Commission from transmitting information gathered during the course of its investigations, but other bilateral agreements, such as the one with Canada, do not restrict the Commission's actions in a similar way. It is likely that some information gathered during the course of a cartel investigation, while not being in the public domain, is still not considered confidential. The question is

[1] Art 4 of Regulation 1/2003.

then whether the Commission should be allowed to transfer case-specific information. An international agreement may trump a regulation, but it does not prevail over the Charter or the general principles of EU law. As the requirement in Article 28 serves to protect targeted companies' defence rights, it is argued that the Commission should be prevented from transmitting any information from its case files to third country authorities, at least unless such transmission was already foreseen in the request for information or the inspection decision. The targeted companies should already have been informed of this possibility at the time the information was gathered, and had the chance of challenging the inspection decision or such transmission without the fear of repercussions.

As for the agreement with Switzerland, which allows for the exchange of confidential information gathered during the course of an investigation, the Commission has not yet availed itself of this right. However, it has pointed to the fact that the cooperation agreement does not require a decision, nor define the formality of the transfer itself any more closely, indicating that it would be willing to transfer such information without adopting a formal decision or receiving prior consent from the owner of the information.[2] This should be questioned from a due process perspective, especially if there is no mention of a possible exchange of information in the inspection decision or the decision to request information. If companies are required, under the penalty of a fine, to cooperate and submit information – which may be both incriminating and commercially sensitive – to the Commission, and such information is informally transmitted to third country authorities without the consent of the company, and without any possibility for either the Commission or the owner to control the subsequent use of the information, this would not only violate targeted companies' defence rights, it could also constitute a violation of Article 7 of the Charter and the right to privacy enshrined therein.

A final finding concerns the actual value of exchanging case-specific information. In 2014, the ICN and OECD presented the findings from a joint survey on the challenges of international cooperation. The report shows that cooperation may be useful even without the exchange of confidential information, and that – perhaps partly given the strict procedural safeguards surrounding such exchange – those authorities that were empowered to exchange confidential information with one or several agencies, rarely availed themselves of this possibility. Instead, the report shows that what the agencies considered to be the most useful form of cooperation was informal case cooperation. Such cooperation may never involve the exchange of confidential information, as this would infringe targeted companies' defence rights. Thus, while it may be desirable in theory, the exchange of confidential information may in practice not be the most valuable or useful form of cooperation between competition authorities.

[2] This according to the International Team of DG COMP in an e-mail dated 21 January 2020.

II. Party Access

Already in the early cartel cases, the Court recognised that companies enjoyed a right of the defence during the investigatory phase and that the Commission was prevented from adopting infringement decisions without first having allowed the parties to present their observations on the Commission's objections. This meant that they were to be informed of the facts upon which the complaints were based. However, the Court was also clear that this did not mean that they had a right of access to the file. Instead, it was the Commission that committed to granting such access in the early 1980s, and that was later forced to stick by its words.

Today, Article 41 of the Charter protects the right to good administration, and includes the right of every person to have access to the file. Article 27(2) of Regulation 1/2003 mirrors this obligation and grants parties a right to access their file. In competition cases, the right belongs to addressees of the statement of objections. They will be given the opportunity to access the file on one occasion, after the statement of objections has been issued but before the oral hearing is held. There is no general right to access other parties' replies to the statement of objections, but as the Commission is prevented from relying on evidence to which the parties have not had access, it will inform them of any incriminating evidence contained in or attached to such statements. The Commission is also required to inform the parties of any exculpatory evidence. While the division between evidence received before and after the adoption of the statement of objections may be acceptable from an ECHR point of view – provided that access is also granted to both inculpatory and exculpatory evidence received during the adversarial stage – one may question whether it is appropriate to maintain this to some extent artificial division, and whether it should be up to the Commission to then determine if a certain piece of information may or may not be useful for the targeted company's defence. This especially given that the Court has established that this should not be for the Commission to decide concerning evidence collected during the investigatory stge.

Failure to grant access may have several consequences. First, Article 27 of Regulation 1/2003 requires the Commission to base its decisions solely on objections on which the parties concerned have been able to comment. The Commission may not rely on evidence to which they have not been granted access, and such evidence will therefore be struck.[3] Furthermore, the infringement decision may be annulled, but this requires that the parties' defence rights have been infringed, reflecting the EU Courts' view that access to the file is not an end in itself but intended to protect the rights of the defence.[4] As for incriminating evidence, the

[3] Parties may be required to request such access both under the EU rules and the ECHR.

[4] Joined Cases T-25/95, T-26/95, T-30/95 to T-32/95, T-34/95 to T-39/95, T-42/95 to T-46/95, T-48/95, T-50/95 to T-65/95, T-68/95 to T-71/95, T-87/95, T-88/95, T-103/95 and T-104/95, *Cimenteries CBR and Others v Commission of the European Communities*, EU:T:2000:77, para 156.

Commission must have relied on the evidence in question, and the company must also show that absent that document, the Commission would not have been able to substantiate its objection. The failure to grant access to exculpatory evidence may constitute a breach of the company's defence rights. The company will then not have to show that the evidence in question would have let it off the hook, only that it would have been able to use it for its defence. The threshold for annulling a decision is set quite high, and rightly so. Annulling a decision for the sole reason that the Commission has failed to communicate one document, which together with a number of others formed the basis for the Commission's objections, would have negative consequences far outweighing the rights and interests of the company in question. However, while the rules now in place should guarantee adequate protection, there is always the risk that the Commission fails to communicate potentially exculpatory evidence received from the other parties during the adversarial stage, and it is then likely that such failure would not come to the attention of the company in question. The Commission is walking a fine line between the interests of efficiency and objectivity.

III. Third Parties and Regulation 1/2003

As discussed in chapter 5, there are certain circumstances in which third parties may have a right to access documents from the Commission's case file under Regulation 1/2003. That is where they have a right to be heard, either because they are complainants or because the Commission considers that they have a sufficient interest in or can contribute to the investigation. Recently, third parties have also sought leave to intervene in annulment actions before the General Court with a view to accessing the evidence relied on by the Commission. While parties' right to access the file is motivated by a need to protect their right of the defence, the Court's reasoning in these cases suggests that it is the interest of ensuring a proper and efficient conduct of the investigation that mandates a disclosure of documents.

A further observation concerns the complainants' use of any information received from the Commission. This was already a question for the Court in *AKZO*, where the applicant argued that the Commission had acted unlawfully when transmitting information to AKZO's competitor ECS, and authorising ECS to use the information in damages proceedings before the UK courts.[5] Finding that the decision to transmit the information was unlawful on other grounds, the Court dismissed the applicant's plea. However, the question raised by *AKZO* is of

[5] This despite the fact that the Commission had imposed an obligation on ECS only to use the transmitted documents for the purposes of the Commission's proceedings; see Case 53/85, *AKZO Chemie BV and AKZO Chemie UK Ltd v Commission of the European Communities*, EU:C:1986:256, para 6.

relevance, especially following the adoption of the Damages Directive. According to Article 16a of the Procedural Regulation, any documents obtained pursuant to the Regulation may be used only for the purposes of judicial or administrative proceedings for the application of Articles 101 and 102 TFEU. Should this be considered to include cartel damages proceedings before national courts, customers or competitors suspecting cartel behaviour may nowadays have greater incentives to bring the Commission's attention to any signs of unlawful conduct. Following the adoption of the Damages Directive, the Procedural Regulation has been aligned with the provisions of the Directive, and it is clear from these amendments that documents received pursuant to the Regulation may be used in cartel damages proceedings. Mirroring Article 6(5) of the Damages Directive, Article 16(a)(2) of the Regulation imposes further restrictions on the use of certain information, declaring that certain categories of information may not be used in proceedings before national courts until the Commission has closed its proceedings against all parties under investigation or otherwise terminated its proceedings.[6] Thus, judging from this limitation, other information received pursuant to the Procedural Regulation may be used already prior to the termination of the Commission's proceedings.

Filing a formal complaint is not without risk – the complainant becomes part of the procedure and its status as complainant is disclosed to the defending parties. That said, if cartel victims are able to access important evidence at an early stage of the cartel case, this will of course increase their incentives to bring any unlawful behaviour to the Commission's attention. Provided that they can prove a legitimate interest or in some way assist the Commission in the investigation, cartel victims can now access valuable information following the adoption of the statement of objections. Paradoxically, this could in turn increase the attractiveness of the leniency programme, as cartelists would then have to fear not only the betrayal of their co-conspirators but also complaints from cartel victims. Indeed, it is better to have to pay only damages than damages alongside a hefty fine.

IV. Third Parties and the Transparency Regulation

The Commission has been consistent in its attitude towards third parties seeking access to its case files, rejecting requests no matter if they concern one document or the entire case file. In *VKI* the main argument for such refusal was that an individual examination would require too much work, and in the case of *EnBW* the Commission also argued that the review of the documents requested would take

[6] That is information that was prepared by other natural or legal persons specifically for the proceedings of the Commission, and information that the Commission has drawn up and sent to the parties in the course of its proceedings.

a disproportionate amount of time.[7] However, this does not appear to be the only or perhaps not even the main reason behind its stance. Instead, it is concern for the leniency programme and the effectiveness of its enforcement activities that appears to be the principal reason behind the Commission's consistent refusals.

While the Commission is consistent in its attitude, the case law of the EU Courts has developed over the years. Today, and following a number of rulings in areas such as state aid and merger control, the Commission can 'respond to a global application in a global way'. As long as the request concerns a 'set of documents', there is no need to investigate all other conceivable options, as the exceptions in Article 4 of the Transparency Regulation are presumed to apply to the documents in the Commission's file. In fact, the Court's reasoning in *Technische Glaswereke Ilmenau* would allow for an even more restrictive approach towards access requests. Presumably, these findings are also the result of a proportionality analysis. However, the weights put in the balance are not the same as those in *VKI*. First, since the ruling in *VKI*, the ECJ has acknowledged that the Commission's administrative practice does not require such extensive access as is required by the legislative activity of the EU institutions.[8] Second, it is now established that the Transparency Regulation cannot be seen or applied in isolation but should be interpreted in harmony with the Antitrust Regulations, in order to secure coherence and consistency in the EU legal system.

The Court is right in acknowledging that the Transparency Regulation cannot be seen in isolation. The Antitrust Regulations were adopted after the Transparency Regulation had entered into force, and are built not on the principle of transparency, but rather on principles of efficiency, effectiveness and confidentiality. Partly due to targeted companies' duty to cooperate and submit information to the Commission, access to the file is only granted to the parties and to those who are given the status of complainants. If third parties could circumvent these rules and access the case file through the Transparency Regulation, this would undoubtedly upset the order established by the Antitrust Regulations. Furthermore, as Article 4 of the Transparency Regulation is framed – acknowledging the interest of protecting commercial interests, inspections and investigations – such interpretation would not go against the wording of the Regulation. That said, it can of course be questioned whether the system put in place by the Antitrust Regulations is optimal, and whether the limited access to the Commission's case files is necessary to ensure effective competition law enforcement. Furthermore, harmonious interpretation does not mean that one regulation shall at all times give way to the other. While it may be reasonable to let the Commission rely on a general presumption when it receives a request for a large number of documents, it is not

[7] Case T-344/08, *EnBW Energie Baden-Württemberg AG v European Commission*, EU:T:2012:242, para 65.

[8] Case C-365/12 P, *European Commission v. EnBW Energie Baden-Württemberg AG*, EU:C:2014:112, para 91, and Case C-139/07 P, *European Commission v Technische Glaswerke Ilmenau GmbH*, EU:C:2010:376, para 60.

necessarily equally appropriate to let it rely on such presumption when the request concerns only a limited number of documents. It could then be argued that it should review the documents requested and assess whether they are actually to be kept confidential.

Important to note is that the Court's case law does not formally force the Transparency Regulation to give way to the Antitrust Regulations. This merits a couple of comments. First of all, the Court does not consider the interest of avoiding damages actions to constitute a commercial interest within the meaning of Article 4 of the Transparency Regulation. On the other hand, it seems to accept the view that the leniency programme should be protected, and that any refusal to grant access to documents submitted by the parties will therefore be covered by the exception in the third indent of Article 4(2), that is, the protection of the Commission's investigations and inspections. Thus, while the Court may have a hard time accepting that the interest in avoiding damages claims should constitute a legitimate commercial interest, the end result is, at least in most cases, the same. Furthermore, the general presumption that one or more of the exceptions in Article 4 of the Transparency Regulation applies makes it more or less impossible for third parties to gain access to the Commission's case files. Thus, while the Transparency Regulation establishes an order that in theory should ensure the fullest possible access to the documents held by the EU institutions, and where any limitations to this obligation should be narrowly construed,[9] the reality is different. While the Court's case law may be in line with applicable legislation, it nevertheless endorses an order where the interests of preserving a well-functioning public enforcement system are allowed to prevail over the interests of transparency and a well-functioning private enforcement system. It is therefore important that these interests are secured in some other way.

V. Seeking Access Through National Courts

Article 4(3) TEU requires the Commission to assist national courts in their application of EU legislation. In competition matters, this obligation is further reinforced by Article 15 of Regulation 1/2003, which allows national courts to ask the Commission to transmit to them information in its possession or its opinion on questions concerning the application of the EU competition rules. Over the years, the Commission has taken this obligation seriously and cooperated with national courts. The *Alstom* case, discussed in chapter 7, shows that it has even been willing to hand over documents to which not even the parties normally have access, and which the Commission would not disclose under the Transparency Regulation. When challenging the Commission's decision, Alstom had argued

[9] Art 4(2) and (3).

that the information was protected by professional secrecy and contained material submitted under the leniency programme. As for the argument concerning professional secrecy, Article 4(3) TEU requires the Commission also to transmit confidential information. However, in order to ensure that the obligation is protected, the Commission's cooperation is conditioned upon the national court's assurance to safeguard the confidentiality of any information received.

The Damages Directive can be seen as something of a game changer in this area, limiting the possibilities for national courts to seek the Commission's assistance. Not only are national courts prevented from requesting documents from the Commission if the documents can reasonably be accessed elsewhere, they may never order or request disclosure of leniency statements or settlement submissions. Other types of evidence, such as information drawn up by a competition authority and sent to the parties in the course of its proceedings, may only be disclosed once the case is closed. Furthermore, the Commission does not consider broad disclosure orders encompassing a large number of documents from its case files to be compatible with the provisions of the Damages Directive. In 2015, the Commission amended its Notice on cooperation with national courts,[10] which now explicitly acknowledges that disclosure must not unduly affect the effectiveness of the Commission's enforcement of the competition rules, in particular so as not to interfere with pending investigations nor with the functioning of the leniency programme or the settlement procedure. This means that the Commission will at no time transmit leniency statements or settlement submissions. It can thus be concluded that the Commission's practices have changed following the adoption of the Damages Directive, and that the concern for the leniency programme is affecting its cooperation with national courts, bringing its practices closer to its stance in other areas, such as the application of the Transparency Regulation. It is to be hoped the Damages Directive will make it easier for cartel victims to access evidence elsewhere.

VI. More Detailed Infringement Decisions

The Commission is unwilling to grant public access and the Damages Directive has limited the possibilities for national courts to ask the Commission to transmit evidence from its case files. Furthermore, the Commission's settlement procedure has resulted in a larger number of shorter and less detailed infringement decisions. However, in those cases where the parties do not settle, the Commission is now endeavouring to publish longer and more detailed versions of its infringement decisions. These attempts have not run smoothly, as the Commission's publication of longer decisions is being challenged by the addressees of those decisions. As a

[10] Commission Notice on the Cooperation between the Commission and the Courts of the EU Member States in the Application of Articles 81 and 82 EC [2004] OJ C101/54.

result, the publication is postponed by years, or even decades. Furthermore, the length of these proceedings may have a huge impact on the sum that the cartel members will eventually have to pay to the victims. According to Article 3 of the Damages Directive, cartel victims shall receive full compensation for their loss; that is actual loss, loss of profit plus interest.[11] Recital 12 of the Damages Directive acknowledges that payment of interest should be due from the time when the harm occurred until the time when compensation is paid. By the time any damages are awarded, the interest may far outweigh the loss.

Furthermore, and as has been acknowledged by the Court, allowing the Commission to publish information received from the leniency applicants is not unproblematic. The Commission has a duty to publish the details of the infringement, and some information provided by leniency applicants will thus have to be made known to the public. However, not only does the Leniency Notice state that the Commission considers that the public disclosure of documents and statements received under the Notice would undermine certain public or private interests, such as the protection of the purpose of investigations, it also acknowledges that the Notice will create legitimate expectations.[12] While you may resort to semantics and distinguish between document and information, the fact remains that companies have cooperated with Commission believing that the information provided was protected.

What seemed to be a viable route in theory has thus proved to be of little practical use. It is to be hoped that the Court's case law on how decisions may be framed will eventually make them less challengeable, but at the moment they are of little or no use to cartel victims. Nor will the Commission's endeavours have any positive effects on companies' willingness to apply for leniency. Important to note, however, is that the Court stands by the Commission and allows it to decide how to balance the well-being of the leniency system against the interests of transparency.

VII. The Leniency System – Worthy of Protection?

The Commission's concern for its leniency system runs like a connecting thread through the chapters of this work. The Commission appears to be witnessing a decline in the number of leniency applications, and one of the reasons for this is the strengthening of the private enforcement system. As one practitioner puts it, '[l]eniency no longer means closure, today it is only the beginning'.[13] While the public and private enforcement regimes should in theory reinforce each other

[11] Case C-295/04, *Vincenzo Manfredi v Lloyd Adriatico Assicurazioni SpA*, EU:C:2006:461.

[12] Points 38 and 40.

[13] JD Jaspers, 'Leniency in Exchange for Cartel Confessions' (2020) 17(1) *European Journal of Criminology* 106, 120.

and strengthen EU competition law enforcement, the reality thus appears to be otherwise. Absent other equally effective and efficient methods of detecting cartels, there is an apparent risk that a weakened leniency system will lead to fewer cartel investigations. This, in turn, will affect the private enforcement system, as most damages actions are follow-on actions. At present, there are no substitutes available to the leniency programme. While the whistleblower tool recently introduced appears to be generating new cases, it is unlikely that employees blowing the whistle will be able to provide as much and as detailed information as a company filing a leniency application and cooperating with the Commission throughout the investigation. Thus while it may complement and to some extent even reinforce the leniency system, it does not appear to be a substitute. It is therefore suggested that, absent equally effective methods, efforts should be made to restore the attractiveness of the EU leniency system.

Today, national courts are prevented from ordering disclosure of leniency statements during the course of damages proceedings. Extending protection to pre-existing documents will not necessarily restore confidence in the system. While the evidence provided will then be safe from disclosure, the information contained therein is not necessarily protected, and cartel victims may access pre-existing documents from other sources. Two further options are discussed in this work. The first concerns the sanctions available. Cartelists often fear that any damages may meet or even exceed the size of any fines imposed by the Commission. If the cap on fines is increased drastically, and if, like the MAR, the Antitrust Regulations would allow the Commission to impose significant fines on individuals too, this may increase the incentives to apply for leniency. However, such option would not necessarily ease the tension addressed in this work, as cartel members would remain reluctant to allow third parties access to any evidence in their possession, and would fight any such measures taken by the Commission or the national courts. There is also a risk that higher fines coupled with a well-functioning private enforcement system may force companies to exit the market.

The second option is to extend leniency into the area of private enforcement and to let the first leniency applicant also receive immunity from damages. This may help restore the attractiveness of the leniency system, and thus allow the Commission to detect and punish more cartels, while still keeping the resources spent on public cartel enforcement constant. By maintaining the effectiveness of the public enforcement system, the private enforcement system would be allowed to prosper, as most damages cases are follow-on actions. Furthermore, it is suggested that immunity or leniency from civil liability should only be granted to one company, allowing victims to seek full compensation from the other cartel participants. If only one firm can escape liability, that would not only destabilise cartels but also allow victims to be compensated for the harm caused. Finally, the EU system could, like its US equivalent, require immunity recipients to cooperate closely with cartel victims and provide them with the evidence in their possession. This would definitely ease any tension identified in this work. Not only may the balance between public and private enforcement be restored, cartel victims would get valuable evidence directly from the hands of the cartel members, allowing any requests for public access to be both narrow in scope and with a high degree of specificity. However, while the current leniency system was put in place by the Commission itself, any rules on immunity from damages would have to be adopted by the EU legislator. It is therefore unlikely that we shall see such change in the near future.

VIII. The Way Forward

This work has examined access from three different perspectives: those of national competition authorities, parties and third parties. As for the two first perspectives, the tension lies mainly between the interests of efficiency and effectiveness, on the one hand, and the defence rights of targeted companies, on the other. Information exchange between competition authorities may be extremely valuable from an enforcement perspective, especially if such exchange covers information gathered during the course of cartel investigations. However, absent adequate procedural safeguards, such exchange may violate the parties' defence rights as well as their right to privacy. The safeguards required are high, and if they are to be fully respected any exchange may lose much of its value. It is therefore suggested that competition authorities continue to strengthen their relationships without necessarily exchanging information gathered during the course of their investigations.[14] As for the second perspective, the Commission will have to make sure that the parties' defence rights are protected, and that they are given access to the information in the Commission's file. While the Commission's division between documents received before or after the adoption of the statement of objections may increase the risk that some exculpatory evidence is not brought to the attention of the parties, the procedures are in all other respects acceptable from a due process point of view.

There remains the third perspective: that of third parties. It is clear from the foregoing that the Commission's concern for its leniency programme constitutes a road block, and unless it is removed, there is no straight way forward. Admittedly, it was the Court that put the private enforcement train in motion but, given its role, the Commission soon had to place itself in the driver's seat and promote the introduction of a private enforcement regime in the EU. While the legislator has attempted to adjust the regime to fit the European legal tradition(s), it is certainly not an easy task to make it interact with the rules already in place. It is becoming increasingly evident that the Commission struggles to reconcile the needs to ensure due process, transparency and effectiveness, while at the same time promoting both public and private enforcement of the EU competition rules.

[14] Save for the cooperation within the ECN.

The private enforcement system is heavily dependent on a well-functioning public enforcement system as most damages actions are follow-on actions. At the same time, the fear of having to pay damages appears to weaken the incentives for cartelists to self-report, threatening the effectiveness of the public enforcement system, and thus potentially creating a downward spiral. Absent any readily available substitutes to the leniency programme, the Commission has had to rely on the only remaining option – to protect the documents in its case files. As a result, the application of the Transparency Regulation may not necessarily go against the wording of its provisions, but it is certainly not in line with its spirit. What is more, there is an inconsistency in the Commission's view on the confidentiality of the information in its files; it may treat a certain piece of information as confidential under the Transparency Regulation, while deciding to disclose it in the public versions of its infringement decisions. Just to give an example, in cases concerning the publication of infringement decisions, the Court allows the Commission to presume that information that is more than five years old has lost its commercial value, but in cases on public access, it may presume that the same information should be protected for up to 30 years.

That said, it is perfectly understandable that the Commission prefers to choose which information is to be relayed to the public. When the Commission drafts its infringement decisions it can choose what information to disclose, focusing on the infringement and on what is of relevance to describe the unlawful actions, leaving irrelevant information aside and balancing the interests of the parties involved against each other. It is undoubtedly easier to carry out a balancing exercise when drafting an infringement decision than when reviewing thousands of documents covered by an application for access. There is thus a greater risk that the disclosure of information under the Transparency Regulation jeopardises the Commission's enforcement practices, and thus also a greater need to put a brake on disclosure. Furthermore, the Transparency Regulation cannot be seen in isolation but needs to be reconciled with the Antitrust Regulations. The latter are built not on the principle of transparency, but rather on principles of effectiveness, efficiency and confidentiality. This is partly due to the fact that companies are forced to submit large amounts of commercially sensitive information and otherwise cooperate with the Commission, and that failure to do so will not go unpunished. Thus, while not promoting the spirit of the Transparency Regulation, the Commission's refusals to grant access may, at least when the requests cover a large part of the documents in the file, still be justified by the need to ensure an effective public enforcement system and to protect the commercial interests of targeted companies.

However, the Commission cannot turn a blind eye to the needs of cartel victims, and it has therefore tried to find other ways to promote and facilitate private enforcement. The most obvious measure taken was of course the proposal for the Damages Directive. While the Directive includes a chapter on disclosure, aiming at facilitating access to evidence, it does not necessarily create the level playing field envisaged in the Directive's preambles, as the requirements that need to be fulfilled in order to obtain disclosure are set high, higher than in the Commission's initial proposal. Another route chosen by the Commission is to publish more detailed infringement decisions. However, as has been discussed previously, these attempts are being challenged by the addressees of the decisions, and by the time they are finally published, the information contained therein may be of little or no use to the cartel victims. It is hoped that these court cases will provide guidance on what information may be published, making future decisions less challengeable. However, at present, these attempts by the Commission not only lead to inconsistencies in its handling of information, they also violate the legitimate expectations of the leniency recipients without necessarily promoting or facilitating private enforcement of the EU competition rules.

Furthermore, no matter how the Commission's practices in these cases are fine-tuned in order to achieve greater coherence and consistency, the fact remains that it is the risk of civil liability per se that causes the road block. As long as it is there, companies engaging in cartel activity will think twice before self-reporting, and will fight any attempts by the Commission to part with evidence or details of the unlawful behaviour. As noted by Jaspers, leniency no longer means closure, today it is only the beginning.[15] The increased focus on private enforcement has tilted the balance, as cartelists are now more hesitant to file a leniency application than they used to be. That said, while the number of damages proceedings is increasing exponentially, we have not yet seen how these cases work out in court. If cartel victims are successful, we shall most likely witness a continued drop in the number of leniency applications. If, on the other hand, no or low damages are awarded, the leniency programme may regain its attractiveness. However, the private enforcement system is in place, and its aim is to achieve a system where victims of competition law infringements are fully compensated. One should therefore not wait and 'hope for' a weak private enforcement system.

It is therefore suggested that, absent readily available and equally efficient methods of detection, ways should be sought to restore the attractiveness of the leniency system, thereby easing the tension between the diverging interests presented in this work. Finding that increased sanctions or the introduction of individual sanctions may make leniency appear a more interesting option, it would not make cartelists more inclined to disclose information to cartel victims or other third parties. Quite the opposite. The tension would thus still remain. It is therefore suggested that the leniency programme is extended to also cover liability for damages. Any moral concern that cartelists should not escape liability must be balanced against the fact that absent a well-functioning leniency system, few cartels will be discovered. This in turn will have as a consequence not only that many consumers will suffer loss for a longer period than they would have with a well-functioning leniency system in place, but also that they may not be compensated for such loss if the cartel escapes the eyes of the Commission. If, on the other hand, the leniency system is later replaced by other means of detection, this will have positive effects on the private enforcement system.

[15] Jaspers, 'Leniency in Exchange' (n 13) 120.

Requiring the immunity recipient to assist cartel victims and actively provide them with the evidence in its possession will allow the victims to access evidence at an early stage. This in turn may make cartel victims less inclined to request access from the Commission's case files, and any requests for public access or disclosure orders in national courts will then be more specific and circumscribed. Furthermore, if the attractiveness of the leniency programme is restored or is not affected by disclosure, requests made under the Transparency Regulation may not be quite as problematic as they currently are, as the Commission will no longer have to seek to protect leniency recipients to the same extent. However, unlike the leniency programme now in place, which is a product of the Commission, extending the leniency programme to also cover immunity from damages claims will have to be a matter for the EU legislator, and thus a matter for the future. One can only hope that the question is brought to the table within a foreseeable future, as the EU competition law enforcement system would otherwise risk losing much of its effectiveness.

BIBLIOGRAPHY

Books

Andersson, H, *Dawn Raids Under Challenge – Due Process Aspects on the European Commission's Dawn Raid Practices* (Oxford, Hart Publishing, 2018)

Ashton, D, *Competition Damages Actions in the EU – Law and Practice*, 2nd edn (Cheltenham, Edward Elgar, 2018)

Balsaningham, B, *The EU Leniency Policy; Reconciling Effectiveness and Fairness* (Alphen aan den Rijn, Wolters Kluwer, 2017)

Beaton-Wells, C and Ezrachi, A (eds), *Criminalising Cartels – Critical Studies of an International Movement* (Oxford, Hart Publishing, 2011)

—— and Tran, C (eds), *Anti-cartel Enforcement in a Contemporary Age: Leniency Religion* (Oxford, Hart Publishing, 2015)

Bernitz, U, Nergelius, J and Cardner, C (eds), *General Principles of EC Law in a Process of Development* (Alphen aan den Rijn, Kluwer Law International, 2008)

Blanco, LO (ed), *EU Competition Procedure*, 3rd edn (Oxford, Oxford University Press 2013)

Craig, P, *EU Administrative Law*, 2nd edn (Oxford, Oxford University Press, 2012)

—— and de Búrca, G, *The Evolution of EU Law*, 2nd edn (Oxford, Oxford University Press 2011)

Cremona, M and Scott, J (eds), *EU Law Beyond Borders: The Extraterritorial Reach of EU Law* (Oxford, Oxford University Press, 2019)

Demedts, V, *The Future of International Competition Law Enforcement* (Leiden, Brill Nijhoff, 2018)

Di Federico, G (ed), *The EU Charter of Fundamental Rights: From Declaration to Binding Instrument* (Dordrecht, Springer, 2011)

Harris, DJ, O'Boyle, M, Bates, EP and Buckley, CM, *Harris, O'Boyle and Warbrick: Law of the European Convention on Human Rights*, 4th edn (Oxford, Oxford University Press, 2018)

Horna, P, *Fighting Cross-Border Cartels – The Perspective of the Young and Small Competition Authorities* (Oxford, Hart Publishing, 2020)

Kerse, C and Khan, N, *EU Antitrust Procedure*, 6th edn (London, Sweet & Maxwell, 2012)

Micklitz, HW and Wechsler, A (eds), *The Transformation of Enforcement – European Economic Law in a Global Perspective* (Oxford, Hart Publishing, 2016)

Nehl, HP, *Principles of Administrative Procedure in EC Law* (Oxford, Hart Publishing, 1999)

Nergelius, J and Kristoffersson, E (eds), *Human Rights in Contemporary European Law* (Oxford, Hart Publishing, 2015)

Papadopoulos, AS, *The International Dimension of EU Competition Law and Policy* (Cambridge, Cambridge University Press, 2010)

Peers, S et al (eds), *The EU Charter of Fundamental Rights; A Commentary* (Oxford, Hart Publishing, 2014)

Rossi, L and Vinagre e Silva, P, *Public Access to Documents in the EU* (Oxford, Hart Publishing, 2017)

Scordamaglia-Tousis, A, *EU Cartel Enforcement – Reconciling Effective Public Enforcement with Fundamental Rights* (Alphen aan den Rijn, Wolters Kluwer, 2013)

Sokol, D and Guzman, A, *Antitrust Procedural Fairness* (Oxford, Oxford University Press, 2019)

Treschel, S, *Human Rights in Criminal Proceedings* (Oxford, Oxford University Press, 2006)

Van Bael, I, *Due Process in EU Competition Proceedings* (Alphen aan den Rijn. Wolters Kluwer, 2011)

Voss, K, *Between Enforcement and Regulation: A Study of the System of Case Resolution Mechanisms Used by the European Commission in the Enforcement of Articles 101 and 102 TFEU* (Stockholm, Stockholm University, 2019)

Wils, WPJ, *Efficiency and Justice in European Antitrust Enforcement* (Oxford, Hart Publishing, 2008)

Chapters in Edited Books

Baker, D, 'Punishment for Cartel Participation in the US: A Special Model?' in C Beaton-Wells and A Ezrachi (eds), *Criminalising Cartels – Critical Studies of an International Movement* (Oxford, Hart Publishing, 2011) 29

Beaton-Wells, C, 'Leniency Policies: Revolution or Religion?' in C Beaton-Wells and C Tran (eds), *Anti-cartel Enforcement in a Contemporary Age: Leniency Religion* (Oxford, Hart Publishing, 2015) 3

Craig, P, 'Article 41; Right to Good Administration' in S Peers et al (eds), *The EU Charter of Fundamental Rights; A Commentary* (Oxford, Hart Publishing, 2014) 1069

Crane, DA, 'Why Leniency Does not Undermine Compensation' in C Beaton-Wells and C Tran (eds), *Anti-cartel Enforcement in a Contemporary Age: Leniency Religion* (Oxford, Hart Publishing, 2015) 263

Drexl, J, 'The Interaction Between Private and Public Enforcement in European Competition Law' in HW Micklitz and A Wechsler (eds), *The Transformation of Enforcement – European Economic Law in a Global Perspective* (Oxford, Hart Publishing, 2016) 135

Di Federico, G, 'Fundamental Rights in the EU: Legal Pluralism and Multi-Level Protection After the Lisbon Treaty' in G Di Federico (ed), *The EU Charter of Fundamental Rights: From Declaration to Binding Instrument* (Dordrecht, Springer, 2011) 15

Forrester, I and Berghe, P, 'Leniency: The Poisoned Chalice or the Pot at the end of the Rainbow?' in C Beaton-Wells and C Tran (eds), *Anti-cartel Enforcement in a Contemporary Age: Leniency Religion* (Oxford, Hart Publishing, 2015) 159

Groussot, X and Stavefeldt, E, 'Accession of the EU to the ECHR: A Legally Complex Situation' in J Nergelius and E Kristoffersson (eds), *Human Rights in Contemporary European Law* (Oxford, Hart Publishing, 2015) 7

Guttuso, L, 'Leniency and the Two Faces of Janus' in C Beaton-Wells and C Tran (eds), *Anti-cartel Enforcement in a Contemporary Age: Leniency Religion* (Oxford, Hart Publishing, 2015) 273

Kellerbauer, M et al, 'Procedures to Establish the Existence of an Infringement' in L Ortiz Blanco (ed), *EU Competition Procedure*, 3rd edn (Oxford, Oxford University Press, 2013) 393

Laserre, B, 'Several Strokes of Black and a Palette of Grays' in B Hawk (ed), *International Antitrust Law & Policy: Fordham Competition Law 2013* (Huntington, Juris Publishing, 2014) 49

Martyniszyn, M, 'Due Process in EU Competition Proceedings' in D Sokol and A Guzman (eds), *Antitrust Procedural Fairness* (Oxford, Oxford University Press, 2019) 48

Marvão, C and Spagnolo, G, 'What Do We Know about the Effectiveness of Leniency Policies? A Survey of the Empirical and Experimental Evidence' in C Beaton-Wells and C Tran (eds), *Anti-cartel Enforcement in a Contemporary Age: Leniency Religion* (Oxford, Hart Publishing, 2015) 57

Monti, G, 'The Global Reach of EU Competition Law' in M Cremona and J Scott (eds), *EU Law Beyond Borders: The Extraterritorial Reach of EU Law* (Oxford, Oxford University Press 2019) 174

Nehl, HP, 'Article 48 Presumption of Innocence and Right of Defence (Administrative Law)' in S Peers et al (eds), *The EU Charter of Fundamental Rights; A Commentary* (Oxford, Hart Publishing, 2014) 1277

O'Brien, A, 'Leadership of Leniency' in C Beaton-Wells and C Tran (eds), *Anti-cartel Enforcement in a Contemporary Age: Leniency Religion* (Oxford, Hart Publishing, 2015) 17

Prechal, S and de Leeuw, M, 'Transparency: A General Principle of EU Law?' in U Bernitz, J Nergelius and C Cardner (eds), *General Principles of EC Law in a Process of Development* (Alphen aan den Rijn, Kluwer Law International, 2008) 201

Renda, A, 'Private Antitrust Damages Actions in the EU: Chronicle of an Attempted Golpe' in HW Micklitz and A Wechsler (eds), *The Transformation of Enforcement – European Economic Law in Global Perspective* (Oxford, Hart Publishing, 2016) 273

Stephan, A and Nikpay, A, 'Leniency Decision-Making from a Corporate Perspective: Complex Realities' in C Beaton-Wells and C Tran (eds), *Anti-cartel Enforcement in a Contemporary Age: Leniency Religion* (Oxford, Hart Publishing, 2015) 139

Stucke, ME, 'Leniency, Whistle-Blowing and the Individual: Should we Create Another Race to the Competition Agency?' in C Beaton-Wells and C Tran (eds), *Anti-cartel Enforcement in a Contemporary Age: Leniency Religion* (Oxford, Hart Publishing, 2015) 209

Zetterqvist, O, 'The Charter of Fundamental Rights and the European Res Publica' in G Di Federico (ed), *The EU Charter of Fundamental Rights: From Declaration to Binding Instrument* (Dordrecht, Springer, 2011) 3

Articles

Anderson, D and Murphy, CC, 'The Charter of Fundamental Rights: History and Prospects in Post-Lisbon Europe', *EUI Working Paper Law, 2011/08*

Baker, JB, 'The Case for Antitrust Enforcement' (2003) 17(4) *Journal of Economic Perspectives* 27–50

Bignami, F, 'Three Generations of Participation Rights Before the European Commission' (2004) 68(1) *Law and Contemporary Problems* 61–83

Bignoni, M et al, 'Trust, Leniency and Deterrence' available at www.konkurrensverket.se/globalassets/publikationer/workingpaper/working_paper_2014-2.pdf

Buijze, A, 'The Six Faces of Transparency' (2013) 9(3) *Utrecht Law Review* 3–25

Caufmann, C, 'The Interaction of Leniency Programmes and Actions for Damages' (2011) 7(2) *The Competition Law Review*181–220

Connor, JM, 'Twilight of Prosecutions of the Global Auto-Parts Cartel' (9 July 2019) available at SSRN at https://ssrn.com/abstract=3456279 or http://dx.doi.org/10.2139/ssrn.3456279

—— and Lande, R, 'Cartel Overcharges and Optimal Cartel Fines' in *3 Issues in Competition Law and Policy* (ABA Section of Antitrust Law, 2008) ch 88 2203–18

—— and ——, 'How High Do Cartels Raise Prices? Implications for Reform of the Antitrust Sentencing Guidelines' (2005) 80 *Tulane Law Review* 513–70

—— and ——, 'Cartels as Rational Business Strategy: Crime Pays' (2012) 34 *Cardozo Law Review* 427–90

Douglas-Scott, S, 'The European Union and Human Rights After the Treaty of Lisbon' (2011) 11(4) *Human Rights Law Review* 645–82

Durande, S and Williams, K, 'The practical impact of the exercise of the right to be heard: A special focus on the effect of Oral Hearings and the role of the Hearing Officers' *Competition Policy Newsletter* (Summer 2005) 22–28

Føllesdal, A, 'Legitimacy Theories of the European Union', *Centre for European Studies, University of Oslo, Arena Working Papers WP 04/15*

Fox, EM, 'Extraterritorial Jurisdiction, Antitrust, and the EU Intel Case: Implementation, Qualified Effects, and the Third Kind' (2019) 42(3) *Fordham International Law Journal* 981–97

Ginsburg, DH and Cheng, C, 'The Decline in US Criminal Antitrust Cases: ACPERA and Leniency in an International Context' (forthcoming 2020) in N Charbit et al (eds) *Albert A Foer, Liber Amicorum, George Mason Law & Economics Research Paper No 19-31*, available at SSRN at https://ssrn.com/abstract=3460091 or http://dx.doi.org/10.2139/ssrn.3460091

Green, J and McCall, I, 'Leniency and Civil Claims; Should Leniency Programmes Extend to Private Actions?' *Competition Law Insight* (July 2009) 3–5

Harrington, JE, Jr, 'Optimal Corporate Leniency Programs' (2008) 56(2) *Journal of Industrial Economics* 215–46

—— and Chang, MH, 'When Can We Expect a Corporate Leniency Program to Result in Fewer Cartels?' (2015) 58(2) *The Journal of Law & Economics* 417–49

Jaspers, JD, 'Leniency in Exchange for Cartel Confessions' (2020) 17(1) *European Journal of Criminology* 106–24

Kokott, J and Sobotta, C, 'Constitutional Core Values and International Law – Finding the Balance?' (2012) 23(4) *The European Journal of International Law* 115–24

Kratochvíl, P and Sychra, Z, 'The End of Democracy in the EU? The Eurozone Crisis and the EU's Democratic Deficit' (2019) 41(2) *Journal of European Integration* 169–85

Laborde, JF, 'Cartel Damages Claims in Europe: How Courts Have Assessed Overcharges' (2017) 1 *Concurrences* 36–42

Leino, P, 'Efficiency, Citizens and Administrative Culture. The Politics of Good Administration in the EU' (2014) 20(4) *European Public Law* 681–710

Lenaerts, K, 'The Principle of Democracy in the Case Law of the European Court of Justice' (2013) 62(2) *International and Comparative Law Quarterly* 271–315

—— and Gutiérrez-Fons, J, ,To Say What the Law of the EU Is: Methods of Interpretation and the European Court of Justice', *EUI Working Papers, AEL 2013/9*

McCrudden, C, 'The Future of the EU Charter of Fundamental Rights', available at SSRN at https://ssrn.com/abstract=299639 or http://dx.doi.org/10.2139/ssrn.299639

Miller, V, 'Human Rights in the EU: The Charter of Fundamental Rights', *Research Paper 00/32*, House of Commons Library

Monti, M, 'International Cooperation in Antirust: US/EU and Beyond' (2001) 69(1) *Antitrust Law Journal* 361–66

Moravcsik, A, 'In Defence of 'the Democratic Deficit': Reassessing Legitimacy in the European Union' (2002) 40(4) *Journal of Common Market Studies* 603–24

Parker, C and Lehmann Nielsen, V, 'Deterrence and the Impact of Calculative Thinking on Business Compliance with Competition and Consumer Regulation' (2011) 56(2) *The Antitrust Bulletin* 377–426

Peyer, S, 'Access to Competition Authorities' Files in Private Antitrust Legislation' (2015) 3(1) *Journal of Antitrust Enforcement* 58–86

Polley, R, 'Is the Continued Success of Leniency in Cartel Cases in Danger? Some Comments from a Private Practitioner's Perspective' *CPI Antitrust Chronicle* (September 2015(1))

Ratliff, J, 'EC Cartel Leniency Programme' available at www.wilmerhale.com/files/Publication/515f785c-9663-44d7-bf82-45c19f099fd9/Presentation/PublicationAttachment/465fc5e4-addb-4a49-8bd7-4c4c179962cb/ECLENIENCY_Ratliff_Nov2004.pdf

Riley, A, 'The Modernisation of EU Anti-Cartel Enforcement: Will the Commission Grasp the Opportunity?' *CEPS Special Report* (January 2010)

Ritz, C and Marx, L, 'Leniency Carrots and Cartel Sticks – A Practitioners' View on Recent Trends and Challenges Presented by the EU Leniency Program' *CPI Antitrust Chronicle* (January 2019)

Snyder, B, 'Challenges to Leniency Posed by the Proliferation of Leniency Programs and Private Enforcement', paper submitted as background material for Item 3 at the 127th Meeting of the OECD Working Party No 3 on Cooperation and Enforcement of 5 June 2018

Spahiu, I, 'Courts: An Effective Venue to Promote Government Transparency? The Case of the Court of Justice of the European Union' (2015) 31(80) *Utrecht Journal of International and European Law* 5–24

Stephan, A, 'Is the Korean Innovation of Individual Informant Rewards a Viable Cartel Detection Tool?' *CCP Working Paper 14-3*, available at http://competitionpolicy.ac.uk/documents/8158338/8199490/CCP+Working+Paper+14-3.pdf/7a9c1d06-d790-4e83-86bf-d43c68c83d0d

Stiglitz, JE, 'Information and the Change in Paradigm in Economics' (2002) 92(3) *The American Economic Review* 460–501
Tomkins, A, 'Responsibility and Resignation in the European Commission' (1999) 62(5) *The Modern Law Review* 744–65
Vajda, C, 'The Application of the EU Charter of Fundamental Rights; Neither Reckless Nor Timid?' *Edinburgh School of Law Research Paper, 2014/47, Europa Working Paper No 2014/99* (November 2014)
Van Barlingen, B and Barennes, M, 'The European Commission's 2002 Leniency Notice in Practice' (2005) 3 *EC Competition Policy Newsletter* 6–16
Wardhaugh, B, 'Cartel Leniency and Effective Compensation in Europe: The Aftermath of Pfleiderer' (2013) 19(3) *Web JCLI*
Weiss, W, 'Human Rights in the EU: Rethinking the Role of the European Convention on Human Rights After Lisbon' (2011) 7(1) *European Constitutional Law Review* 64–95
Wils, WPJ, 'The European Commission's 2006 Guidelines on Antitrust Fines: A Legal and Economic Analysis' (2007) 30(2) *World Competition: Law and Economics Review* 197–230
——, *The Use of Leniency in EU Cartel Enforcement: An Assessment after Twenty Years,* (2016) 39(3) *World Competition: Law and Economics Review* 327–88
—— 'Private Enforcement of EU Antitrust Law and its Relationship with Public Enforcement: Past, Present and the Future' (2017) 40(1) *World Competition: Law and Economics Review* 3–46
Ysewyn, J and Kahmann, S, 'The Decline and Fall of the Leniency Programme in Europe' (2018) 1 *Concurrences* 44–59

Speeches

Barnett, TO, 'Seven Steps to Better Cartel Enforcement' (11th Annual Competition Law & Policy Workshop, European Union Institute in Florence Italy, 2 June 2006), available at www.justice.gov/atr/speech/seven-steps-better-cartel-enforcement#N_7_
Connor, JM and Miller, DJ, 'Determinants of EC Antitrust Fines for Members of Global Cartels' (3rd LEAR Conference on the Economics of Competition Law), available at www.learlab.com/conference2009/documents/Predicting%20EC%20Fines%20for%20Members%20of%20Global%20Cartels%209-11-09.pdf
Hammond, SD, 'Detecting and Deterring Cartel Activity through an Effective Leniency Program' (International Workshop on Cartels, Brighton, 21–22 November 2000), available at www.justice.gov/atr/speech/detecting-and-deterring-cartel-activity-through-effective-leniency-program
——, 'Cracking Cartels with Leniency Programs', OECD Competition Committee, Paris France, October 2005, available at www.justice.gov/atr/speech/cracking-cartels-leniency-programs
Jenny, F, 'International Cooperation on Competition: Myth, Reality and Perspective', The University of Minnesota Law School Conference on Global Antitrust Law and Policy, Minneapolis, 20–21 September 2002, available at www.iilj.org/wp-content/uploads/2017/02/Jenny-International-Cooperation-on-Competition-2002.pdf
Kiriazis, G, 'Jurisdiction and Cooperation Issues in the Investigation of International Cartels' Speech made in June 2001, available at https://ec.europa.eu/competition/speeches/index_2001.html
Kroes, N, 'The First Hundred Days, 40th Anniversary of the Studienvereinigung Kartellrecht 1965–2005', International Forum on European Competition Law, Brussels, 7 April 2005, available at http://europa.eu/rapid/press-release_SPEECH-05-205_en.htm
Laitenberger, J, 'Developments in EU competition control in the global and digital age', Speech made at the Fordham Antitrust Law and Policy Conference, New York, September 2018

Other

Antitrust Manual of Procedures, Internal DG Competition Working Documents on Procedures for the Application of Articles 101 and 102 TFEU, November 2019

Ashurst, *Study on the Conditions of Claim for Damages in Case of Infringement of EC Competition Rules*, Comparative Report, August 2004, prepared by D Waelbroeck, D Slater and G Even-Shoshan for the Commission

Commission of the European Communities, *Eleventh Report on Competition Policy* (1981)

Commission of the European Communities, *Twelfth Report on Competition Policy* (1982)

Commission Notice on the handling of complaints by the Commission under Articles 81 and 82 of the EC Treaty [2004] OJ C101/65

Commission Notice on cooperation within the Network of Competition Authorities [2004] OJ C101/43

Commission Notice on the Cooperation between the Commission and the Courts of the EU Member States in the Application of Articles 81 and 82 EC [2004] OJ C101/54

Commission Notice on Best Practices for the Conduct of Proceedings Concerning Articles 101 and 102 TFEU [2011] OJ C308/06

Commission Notice on Immunity from Fines and Reduction of Fines in Cartel Cases [2006] OJ C298/17

Commission Notice on the rules for access to the Commission file in cases pursuant to Articles 81 and 82 of the EC Treaty, Articles 53, 54 and 57 of the EEA Agreement and Council Regulation (EC) No 139/2004 [2005] OJ C325/07

Commission Notice 97/C 23/03 on the internal rules of procedure for processing requests for access to the file pursuant to Articles 85 and 86 of the EC Treaty and Articles 65 and 66 of the ECSC Treaty and Council Regulation 4064/89 [1997] OJ C23/3

Communication from the Commission to the European Parliament and the Council, *Ten Years of Antitrust Enforcement under Regulation 1/2003: Achievements and Future Perspectives*, COM(2014) 453

Directorate-General for Competition, *Cooperation Between Competition Agencies in Cartel Investigations*, Report prepared by DG COMP to ICN Annual Conference 2007

Directorate-General for Internal Policies, 'Openness, Transparency and Access to Documents in the EU', European Parliament Policy Note, 2013

Impact Assessment Report: Damages Actions for Breach of the EU Antitrust Rules, Accompanying the Proposal for a Directive of the European Parliament and of the Council, COM(2013) 404 final

Labayle, H, 'Openness, Transparency and Access to Documents and Information in the EU', Note from the European Parliament, Policy Department C: Citizens' Rights and Constitutional Affairs, 2013

OECD, *Fighting Hard Core Cartels: Harm, Effective Sanctions and Leniency Programmes*, (2001)

OECD, *Challenges of International Co-operation in Competition Law Enforcement* (2014)

Panizza, R, 'Transparency, integrity and accountability in the EU institutions', Briefing for the PETI Committee, European Parliament, March 2019

Proposal for Establishing the ICN Framework for Promotion of Sharing Non-Confidential Information for Cartel Enforcement, available at www.internationalcompetitionnetwork.org/wp-content/uploads/2018/05/CWG_nonConfidentialInfoFramework.pdf

United States Federal Sentencing Guidelines Manual (2011), ch 2, pt R, available at www.ussc.gov/guidelines-manual/2011/2011-2r11

INDEX

www.ingramcontent.com/pod-product-compliance
Ingram Content Group UK Ltd.
Pitfield, Milton Keynes, MK11 3LW, UK
UKHW020241290926
15470UKWH00002B/675

9 781509 942480